THE RADICALIZATION OF IRISH DRAMA 1600–1900

The Rise and Fall of Ascendancy Theatre

DESMOND SLOWEY

Foreword by Christopher Murray

IRISH ACADEMIC PRESS
DUBLIN • PORTLAND, OR

First published in 2008 by Irish Academic Press

44 Northumberland Road,
Ballsbridge,
Dublin 4, Ireland

920 NE 58th Avenue, Suite 300
Portland, Oregon,
97213-3786 USA

www.iap.ie

British Library Cataloguing in Publication Data
An entry can be found on request

ISBN 978 0 7165 2957 6 (cloth)

Library of Congress Cataloging-in-Publication Data
An entry can be found on request

Printed by Biddles Ltd, King's Lynn, Norfolk

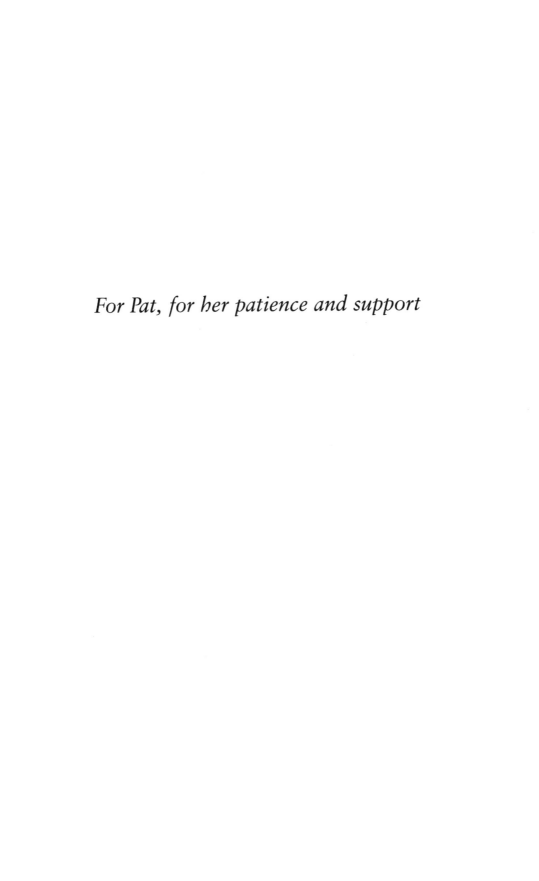

For Pat, for her patience and support

Contents

Acknowledgements

I owe a great debt of gratitude to Dr Pat Burke, Head of Drama at the English Department of St Patrick's College, Drumcondra, for his patience, expertise and encouragement as my thesis supervisor. His kindly but eagle eye missed nothing; under his gaze ambiguities disintegrated and flocks of redundant semi-colons scattered and fled. My thanks also to Dr Brenna Clarke, of St Patrick's College and Professor Christopher Murray of UCD for their invaluable suggestions and continued support, and to Dr Noreen Doody for her work on correcting the work in progress. I am grateful also to Ms Molly Sheehan, of the Cregan Library at St Patrick's College, for sourcing obscure and elusive texts.

Foreword

From time to time in the Irish theatre we can experience by means of a forgotten play what it must have been like to live in another age. In recent times, I daresay, Lennox Robinson's *The Big House* (1926) was such a revelation in its 2007 revival at the Abbey, focusing on the War of Independence but bringing us inside the Anglo-Irish Alcock family, mired in Irish history for centuries and now struggling for their very existence. Behind the Alcocks in that play stretches a great landscape of Anglo-Irish life and its relation to the vexed questions of ownership, identity, colonialism, justice and power. When we consider the lives of both sides of this long divide, this 'gulf', as Robinson termed it, it is like watching, in palpable frustration, an old silent film – not at all as approachable as the (over-accessible) *The Wind that Shakes the Barley* – as it flickers away.

But, going back further, what must it really have been like to live in the seventeenth or eighteenth century? To be sure, we can turn to the books on social history, to Constantia Maxwell, Maurice Craig, Edward McLysaght and others, and create in our minds something of the way of life, the culture, the dress, the card-games, the duels, the liquorish landlords, the rack and the ruin in one class alongside the deprivation in another, creating 'the short and simple annals of the poor'. But we do not hear the people speak, whether Anglo or Irish or a compound of both. For that we need to turn to the drama. Brian Friel's 1990 adaptation, under the title *The London Vertigo*, of the eighteenth-century comedy by Charles Macklin, *The True-Born Irishman* (1761), gave us the dialogue, the raw energy, the colourful characters of Macklin's time with far more immediacy – especially when seen in 1992 on the Dublin stage, at the now lamented Andrews Lane, with the acting talents of John Hurt, John Kavanagh and the incomparable Gemma Craven – than a dozen books of social history could muster between them. The play's the thing wherein we catch the conscience of a nation. One of the distinguishing aspects of Irish drama, wherever we find its point of origin, is its metaphorical power, its ability to transfer 'then' and 'now' with imaginative interchange.

Within its solid and scholarly analysis, this is one of the major achievements of Desmond Slowey's book. It presents to us, in summary and in vivid cameos, the social life and ideology of three centuries in colonized Ireland, as coded and recorded by sometimes forgotten early playwrights such as George Farquhar, William Philips, Charles Shadwell, whose plays – *Love in a Bottle, St. Stephen's Green, Irish Hospitality*, among others – can still bring the 'felt life' of a vigorous past before us. And in the nineteenth century such fascinating figures as Sheridan Knowles, Dion Boucicault and the melodramatists who wrote for the Queen's in its heyday: J.W. Whitbread and P.J. Bourke.

It is not, however, only comedies and melodramas that are persuaded to disclose a continuing narrative and debate. Bearing in mind the tragic core of Robinson's *The Big House*, we find in this book a similar dynamic. We begin to appreciate the Irish theatre's abiding concern with history itself, its processes as much as its conditions. Plays about the anxieties of the Anglo-Irish garrison in the seventeenth and eighteenth centuries in the face of a hostile Irish population can be received ironically today but we can also appreciate the unease while we comfortably transpose the terms of reference. In the same way we may be amused by the victory of our national saint over those benighted Druids in Shirley's *St Patrick for Ireland*, recognizing that the enlightenment Patrick brings is coolly co-opted as British colonization and knowing too that Yeats would reverse matters in favour of the Druids and Celts and so put all to rights. But in between we are encouraged to enter the mind-set of a people creating its own version of colonial nationalism, and the serious history plays which seek to construct this enabling dream of liberty can and do challenge conventional notions of such images. These plays, on the Danish invasion, for example, can seem to us wrong-headed, unhistorical, upside-down, perhaps a kind of unacceptable mirror-writing, but on examination they reflect the views, hopes and fears of a pre-revolutionary era. Were they, in Yeats's phrase, 'no petty people'? They deserve to be heard. So, too, the quite different voices of the liberal Sheridan Knowles in the nineteenth century (whose version of *William Tell* is still a rousing read, whatever the parallels), and even the mushy quasi-republicanism of Boucicault's Irish melodramas. Indeed, mediating popular culture, even the romantic stuff of the Queen's patriotic melodramas in the 1890s, provided audiences with fresh questions on the construction of heroes and the moulding of nationalism after the Act of Union.

Desmond Slowey interrogates the Anglo-Irish project with great skill in a seamless narrative that reinstates a lost tradition. There is much here that is welcome in its intelligent revisionism: principally, a challenge to the point of view that for a long time held sway (and is classically articulated in Andrew E. Malone's influential 1929 book, *The Irish Drama*) that the Irish theatre before the arrival of W .B. Yeats was merely an extension of the London theatre and therefore to be ignored. Since Malone's day, to be sure, others have addressed this point before Slowey – among them Peter Kavanagh, Christopher Wheatley, Christopher Fitz-Simon and Christopher Morash – but to date no one has so sure-footedly and in such detail, covered the tracts of Irish history, Irish theatre and their interactions as Anglo-Irish discourse. No one has been so succinct in his judgements and interpretations of so many early comedies, tragedies and history plays which engage fruitfully with expanded and expanding notions of tradition and change.

In the era of the Belfast Agreement, one may claim that this is a timely book, encouraging a fresh look at the whole body of Irish drama before 1899 – not all of it good but all in search of an audience – which is rooted in colonialism but moves on in the nineteenth century to interrogate its own position in the light of new nationalism threatening to change everthing. Clearly, discontinuity followed upon this final stage of the Anglo-Irish project. The new chapter in Irish theatre history, to be written by Yeats, Lady Gregory and Synge after 1899, sought to erase the earlier scenario. But that narrative did not go away, remains as a stubborn reminder of Ireland's long and tangled story, and is here re-investigated and revised with great conviction, rhyming hope and theatre history.

Christopher Murray
Dublin, October 2007

THE RADICALIZATION OF IRISH DRAMA
(1600–1900)

Introduction:
The Role and Image of the
Ascendancy in the Irish Theatre

Role has a double meaning. Firstly, it denotes the physical and active participation of the Anglo-Irish Ascendancy in creating, promoting, writing, presenting and receiving the Irish theatre. Secondly, it signals the way in which the Ascendants portray themselves and are depicted in that theatre. This second meaning elides into the idea of 'image' – how they copied their lives to the stage and copied the stage in their lives, how they portrayed themselves as loyal Englishmen or equivocal patriots, for example. It also covers how they played out in their lives the examples that the stage had given them. A persistent motif of 'play-acting' runs through Anglo-Irish drama; from the seventeenth century down to the plays of Lennox Robinson the theme recurs of Anglo-Irish civilization as a theatrical performance. To Daniel Corkery, an outsider, it was 'a tragi-comic side-show'.[1] Maria Edgeworth, on the inside, also saw her characters in theatrical terms: 'After we have beheld splendid characters playing their parts on the great theatre of the world, with all the advantages of stage effect and decoration, we anxiously beg to be admitted behind the scenes, that we may take a nearer view of the actors and actresses.'

THE IRISH THEATRE

While the date of 1601 is usually given as the beginning of theatre in Ireland, with the production at Dublin Castle of *Gorboduc*, there was certainly drama in the country before then. The European cultural matrix imported by the Normans in 1169 included the medieval morality and nativity plays known from Kilkenny and Dublin, as well as Church plays in Latin. The theatrical activities of the Dublin guilds are well documented.[2] The idea that there was no drama in Gaelic

Ireland has also been overturned. Alan Fletcher's *Drama, Performance, and Polity in Pre-Cromwellian Ireland* (2000) considers 'Drama [...] as a continuum in which theatricality and performance is subsumed',[3] and excavates a formidable range of performers – poets, story-tellers, harpers, jesters, clowns, jugglers, and farters[4] – and public performances. Some of these activities were covered by the word *cluichí*, which may be translated as 'plays'. The idea that Gaelic culture favoured the individual performer exclusively was supported, if not created, by Derricke's illustration of an Irish bard performing for a chief, accompanied by a harper.[5] But this was not a solo: at least two performers were involved. The Bardic schools that produced the class of professional poets were inflexibly conservative institutions, but most of the familiar texts that have survived are trial pieces by the students, called *óglachas*, and often break into dialogue;[6] *Agallamh na Seanórach*, a dialogue between Oisín and St Patrick, is a prime example.

The memoirs of the first Marquis of Clanricarde, published in 1722, give an intriguing account of the workings of the Bardic schools. Clanricarde describes how the *filí* (elite poets) were given a theme, then lay in the darkness of their room and worked on it for a day before emerging with a completed poem. The last part of the process was the presentation of the poem to its patron, not by its composer but by a troupe of bards under his direction: 'With a great deal of Ceremony in a Consort of Vocal and Instrumental Musick. [...] The poet himself said nothing, but directed and took care that everybody else did his Part right. The Bards having first had the Composition from him, got it well by Heart, and now pronounc'd it orderly, keeping even pace with a Harp.'[7]

This suggests that the introduction of secular, vernacular drama into Ireland had fertile soil to fall on, even though it was centred in the seventeenth century on Dublin Castle, and used by the colonial authorities to reflect their own society and to create and forge an identity for themselves.

THE ASCENDANCY

Not all the Anglo-Irish belonged to the upper classes. In Dublin there were tradesmen, place-seekers, and hangers-on. Richard Head's play, *Hic et Ubique* (1663) showed this lower stratum in action, and James Shirley, in *The Doubtful Heir* (1637), dealt with the tension between the military men who ruled from the Castle and the tradespeople who lived off them. The Plantations attracted a number of riff-raff into the country, according to Stewart, a contemporary divine:

From Scotland came many, and from England not a few, yet all of them generally the scum of both nations, who from debt, or breaking or flee-ing from justice, or seeking shelter, came hither, hoping to be without fear of man's justice, in a land where there was little as yet, of the fear of God [...] Going to Ireland was looked on as a miserable mark of a deplorable person; yea, it was turned into a proverb, and one of the worst expressions of disdain that could be invented was to tell a man that 'Ireland would be his hinder end'.[9]

A lot of those who took land in the hope of rapidly amassing a fortune soon became disillusioned and moved out, but those who stayed and consolidated their holdings evolved into the Anglo-Irish Ascendancy. But other strands persisted – squireens, tradesmen, shopkeepers, sol-diers, adventurers, writers, clergymen and layabouts. The image that was portrayed in the plays of the period was seldom of these lower ech-elons, but almost always showed the upper crust of this society. Others may have been used as foils, to throw them into relief, and many of the playwrights may have been looking up at them from below – Farquhar in *Love and a Bottle*, Philips in *St Stephen's Green* – but there is no doubt that this theatre existed for and about the Ascendancy; this was their stage to strut and fret an hour. They comprised, according to Mark Bence-Jones, 'the lords and landowners of Ireland, known, together with their relations, as the Ascendancy long after they had ceased to be in the ascendant'.[10] The landed Gentry formed the back-bone of the Ascendancy, but along with them we have to include 'their relations' – the Anglo-Irish military, clerical, professional and adminis-trative strata, many of whom stemmed from the landed families and partook prominently in the running of the country.

I use the term 'Ascendancy' to refer to the mostly Protestant rulers of Ireland in the eighteenth and nineteenth centuries. This was the ruling class that achieved total control after the triumph of William of Orange in 1690. Lecky, in his *History of Ireland in the Eighteenth Century*, looked at the state of the country at the end of the seventeenth century and concluded: 'When the eighteenth century dawned, the great major-ity of the former leaders of the people were either sunk in abject poverty or scattered as exiles over Europe; the last spasm of resistance ceased, and the long period of unbroken Protestant ascendancy had begun.'[11] It was only during the nineteenth century that the term 'Ascendancy' grad-ually became the Irish rough equivalent of 'aristocracy'.[12] Though I use the term in speaking of the eighteenth, and even of the seventeenth, century as a synonym for 'nobility and gentry', I do so retrospectively. 'Protestant Ascendancy' emerged as a popular shibboleth in the late eighteenth century in response to Catholic demands for the removal of the Penal Laws. Initially, it referred to the principle and apparatus of Anglo-Irish domination over the Irish Catholic majority, but it was a new name for an old reality – 'New *ascendancy* is the old mastership', Edmund Burke declared.[13] Gradually, however, personnel replaced principle, the religious adjective became more implied than declared, and the term came to refer to the elite of the Anglo-Irish, wilfully alienated from the majority in their own country.[14]

Anglo-Irish Ascendancy civilization glittered considerably on the surface, but the sectarian flaw at its heart was to prove fatal. Sean O'Faoláin observes:

> They were to bring to Ireland a greater concentration of civil gifts than any previous, or later, colonisers: one may, indeed, be done with it in one sentence by saying that culturally speaking the Anglo-Irish created modern Ireland. [...] All about the country they built gracious houses [...] which are the epitome of the classical spirit of that cultured and callous century. They were, however, a separate enclave. They resided in Ireland. It was their country, never their nation. [...] One of the most cultivated and creative societies in western Europe during the eighteenth century was also politically barbarous.[15]

The overt decline of Anglo-Ireland began with the Act of Union, and social and fiscal undermining led to its apparently precipitous collapse when Gladstone and his successors stripped the Ascendancy of its land in the late nineteenth and early twentieth centuries. It was land that set them up; it was the land they depended on, and it was the loss of that land that pulled them down. Without their estates, the Ascendancy withered and died. That 'noisy side-show, so bizarre in its lineaments, and so tragi-comic in its fate', ground to a sad and pathetic curtain.[16]

IRISH OR ANGLO-IRISH?

'Anglo-Irish' is the usual term of description, but the Irish is by far the more potent part of the duality; from the early eighteenth century, the colonists never considered they needed a hyphen to be Irish. The term Anglo-Irish arose from the antipathies within the Gaelic revival of the nineteenth century. The democratic tendency redefined the idea of Irishness as Gaelic, in order to diminish the claims of the aristocratic strain. One of the Beresfords noted ruefully: 'When I was a boy, "the Irish people" meant the Protestants; now it means the Roman Catholics.'[17]

Irish writers in England were always aware of a distance between themselves and the sphere in which they moved; the Irish drama charts the opening of that gap. The physical distance and separation of the two islands was its basis, but the mental separation that resulted was painful for the colonial mind. 'There is no distinction which we are or indeed ought to be fonder of than that of Englishmen,'[18]   Thomas Prior declared in 1771, and yet he was conscious of himself 'as a native of Ireland, and have my whole fortune settled here'.[19] Location did not decide nationality; the main signifier was birth or blood; the literature is full of people who are well-born, who are proud of their blood. To be well-born was not to be well-bred, as Maria Edgeworth demonstrated in her novel, *Ennui.* Breeding has changed its meaning since the eighteenth century, where it referred to rearing and education, not to birth.

The Anglo-Irish soon came to regard Ireland as their country; they were 'the English of Ireland', 'the English nation of this land'.[20] The colonists may have considered themselves impeccably English and part of the old country, but the old country did not hold the same view. The experience of the colonists in both America and Ireland was almost identical. The country in which they lived was not *their* country. They were expected to put the good of the mother country before their own good, especially in material matters, relating to trade and manufacturing, while at the same time they were considered to be less than the citizens in the homeland, their accents laughed at, their pretensions mocked. Prior lamented:

> And yet, it cannot but seem hard to be used and considered as aliens by those who [...] persuaded numbers of our people [...] to come over hither and spend their blood in their service to extend their Empire, Commerce and Power, and may not the children of those Englishmen who have planted in our colonies in America be as justly reckoned Indians and savages as such families who are settled here be considered and treated as mere Irishmen and aliens?[21]

Protestant Patriots saw no part for the native Irish in any political activity; that was carried on between themselves and London. Swift could see clearly enough the terrible conditions of the indigenous inhabitants but no involvement for them in the solution of their own problems. In the late nineteenth century, Standish James O'Grady, the father of the Literary Revival, berated the Ascendancy at large for their apathy and failure to take their rightful place at the head of the entire nation:

> The weakness of a ruling class [...] is neglect of duties and responsibilities, love of pleasure, sport, and ease, lack of union and public spirit, selfishness, stupidity, and poltroonery. These weaknesses, you see, are

moral. [...] But as an aristocracy, as a class of men owning the soil of Ireland, and gathering the rents of Ireland, strict Justice, weighing your merits in the scales against your demerits, sees the last go down like lead and the former, starting up like a rocket, kick the beam.[22]

O'Grady was not content simply to castigate; he had a vision for the rejuvenation of the Ascendancy. He urged their leaders to 'reshape themselves in a heroic mould',[23] so that they might at last become the real leaders of Ireland. Unless this happened, he prophesied anarchy and civil war 'which might end in a shabby, sordid Irish Republic', ruled by corrupt politicians and the ignoble rich.[24]

The Literary Revival was such an attempt by Ascendancy Ireland to direct the course of the emerging nation, but the rising Catholic middle class had no intention of allowing any Ascendancy counter-revolution, and took over the Literary Movement, the Abbey Theatre, and, eventually, the State, finalizing the undermining process they had been engaged in for over a century.

NOTES AND REFERENCES

1. Daniel Corkery, *The Hidden Ireland* (Dublin: Gill and Son, 1925), p. 30.
2. Maria Edgeworth, *Castle Rackrent* (London: Penguin Books, 1992), p. 3.
3. Alan J. Fletcher, *Drama, Polity and Performance in Pre-Cromwellian Ireland* (Cork: University Press, 2000), ch. II, pp. 61–125.
4. *Ibid.*, p. 5.
5. *Ibid.*, pp. 12–27: *Fochloc, senchaid, cruittire, fuirseoir, druth, cleasamnach, braigetóir.*
6. John Derricke's 'Image of Irlande' in Christopher Fitz-Simon, *The Irish Theatre* (London: Thames and Hudson, 1983), p. 8.
7. An Seabhac, 'Réamhrá', in *Filíocht Fiannaíochta*, ed. by An Seabhac, (Áth Cliath: Comhlucht Oideachais na hÉireann, 1954), p. 12.
8. Corkery, *Hidden Ireland*, p. 67.
9. James Seaton Reid, *History of the Presbyterian Church in Ireland: comprising the civil history of the province of Ulster, from the accession of James the First: with a preliminary sketch of the progress of the reformed religion in Ireland during the sixteenth century and an appendix, consisting of original papers.* (London: Whittaker, 1853), I, p. 97.
10. Mark Bence-Jones, *The Twilight of the Ascendancy* (London: Constable, 1987), p. xv.
11. W.E.H. Lecky, *A History of Ireland in the Eighteenth Century*, 3 vols (London: Longmans, Green and Co., 1892), I, p. 134.
12. W.J. McCormack, *Ascendancy and Tradition in Anglo-Irish Literary History from 1789 to 1939* (Oxford: Clarendon Press, 1985), p. 60.
13. *Ibid.*, p. 78.
14. *Ibid.*, p. 92
15. Sean O'Faoláin, *The Irish* (West Drayton, Middlesex: Penguin Books, 1947), p. 87.
16. Corkery, *Hidden Ireland*, p. x.
17. J.C. Beckett, *The Anglo-Irish Tradition* (London: Faber and Faber, 1976), p. 10.
18. Terence de Vere White, *The Anglo-Irish* (London: Victor Gollancz, 1972), p. 63.
19. *Ibid.*, p. 63.
20. J.C. Beckett, *Anglo-Irish Tradition*
21. deVere White, *The Anglo-Irish*, p. 63.
22. Standish James O'Grady, 'Toryism and Irish Democracy', *Selected Essays and Passages*, ed. by Emmet A. Boyd (Dublin: The Talbot Press, n.d.), pp. 202 & 203.
23. Bence-Jones, *Twilight of Ascendancy*, p. 83.
24. *Ibid.*, p. 83.

1

Enter the 'Nobility and Gentry'

The English colonists of the sixteenth century regarded the Irish as an inferior race, hardly more than animals, and to be treated no better. In 1585, Andrew Trollope wrote to Walsingham that the Irish were 'not thrifty or civil and human creatures, but heathen or rather savage and brute beasts'.[1] The best course would be to exterminate them: 'Thou shalt smite them and utterly destroy them; thou shalt make no covenant with them, nor show mercy unto them,' was the admonition of George Andrews, bishop of Ferns and Loughlin.[2] This attitude towards the natives was supported in the colonists' minds by their emblematic image of Ireland as a wilderness ferociously resisting the imposition of order and discipline; what should have been a decorous garden was an anarchic wasteland, infested by savages. In *As You Like It* Shakespeare refers to Irish rats and wolves,[3] and in *Richard II* he likens the natives to snakes, 'which live like venom where no venom else but only they have privilege to live'.[4] They wilfully stamp on the gift of civilization that the English had unselfishly proffered. Henry VI deplores 'rebels up', 'the civil indiscipline', when 'the incivil kerns of Ireland are in arms and temper clay with blood of Englishmen'.[5] The Earl of Clarendon, as late as 1719, was still berating the Irish because 'they wantonly and disdainfully flung those blessings from them'.[6]

The chaos of Ireland was of deep concern to the English: they regarded anarchy as contagious, inclined to creep like a pernicious weed that must be extirpated: 'The Government believed [...] that the one effectual policy for making Ireland useful to England was, in the words of Sir John Davis, "to root out the Irish" from the soil, to confiscate the property of the septs and clans and plant the country systematically with English tenants.'[7] If *The Tempest* expresses something of the English idea of Utopia, an island where man's will and art tames and keeps in control the elemental forces, then Ireland was a Dystopia, and the Irish were all Calibans.

Through the reign of Elizabeth, the English fought a war of extermination against the Irish. Like all such wars, it produced waves of refugees, who fled rather than face certain death. Ironically, they fled to England, one place that was not full of rampaging English soldiers. And so, numbers of Irish characters began to appear on the English stage, as menials and the butt of jokes about their inability to speak properly. So well-known had the Irish become as a recognizable minority that three plays from the first half of the seventeenth century have characters disguising themselves as Irish. In Thomas Dekker's *Old Fortunatus* (1600), the young hero masquerades as an Irish costermonger; *The Welsh Embassador,* of unknown authorship, has a runaway brother of the king pretend to be an Irish footman; in Beaumont and Fletcher's *The Coxcomb* (before 1625) the lover disguises himself as an Irish servant to gain access to his mistress; Ben Jonson's Lady Frampul, in *The New Inn* (1629), pretends to be an Irish beggarwoman.[8] These 'low' characters indicate the attitude of the English to the Irish diaspora, but there were other stories being told too. The first stage Irishman is reckoned to be Captain Macmorrice, in Shakespeare's *Henry V,* a type of the *miles gloriosus,* and a template for the rattling, cursing, boasting Irishman. A closer look however, reveals a somewhat subtler portrait. Macmorrice is, in fact, the first Irish aristocrat to appear on stage.

THE FIRST STAGE—IRISH ARISTOCRAT

Commentators have been very severe with Macmorrice and his successors: 'The braggart-warrior as Stage Irishman made one of his earliest if brief appearances as Captain Macmorrice in Shakespeare's *Henry V,* and thereafter he became a stock figure of ridicule, the roaring and blundering Celt with his standard equipment of bulls, blarney, and brogue.'[9] This evaluation is too simple and political a reading of the part. It misses the crucial point that Macmorrice is not a stage-Irishman; he is a stage-soldier, who happens to be an Irishman.

In *Henry V*, Act II, Macmorrice is the director of the siege of Harfleur. The Duke of Gloucester is nominally in command but 'the order of the siege is given' to Macmorrice.[10] He is the sapper, the siege expert; he is also a Gentleman: the attack 'is altogether directed by an Irishman, a very valiant gentleman'.[11] He is not overseeing the siege from a distance, but is taking an active part, leading the engineers, digging under the walls to blow them up and make a breach. He needed another hour to complete his delicate, dangerous work, and is furious when a retreat is called at such a critical juncture. He was, after all, supposed to be in charge of the siege. 'Ish ill done,' he repeats angrily.[12]

Shakespeare's portrayal of The Soldier is not unsympathetic: his blood is up in the presence of danger, and he is spoiling for a fight. Holding a conference at this critical stage of the siege is, to him, a complete waste of time: 'It is no time to discourse [...] it is shame on us all [...] and there is throats to be cut.'[13] He is in a foul humour at being called back when he had almost dug through, and is in no mood to bandy arguments with the garrulous Fluellen about the relative merits of gunpowder and ancient Roman methods. The two are at opposite ends of the military spectrum: Fluellen is a man of words, Macmorrice a man of action. But even with his attention elsewhere, he can sense an insult from the Welshman, who privately thinks 'he is an ass as is in the world' because he had departed from classical tactics in the conduct of the siege.[14] When Fluellen mentions his 'nation', Macmorrice takes instant offence. It is interesting to note that, in Fluellen's mind, Macmorrice is of a different nation from him and from the English, that there is a distinct Irish nation, and Macmorrice belongs to it. Macmorrice takes umbrage at Fluellen's remark because of its connotations of alienation and inferiority; like Thomas Prior two hundred years later he does not consider himself a member of a separate nation but one of the 'English of Ireland'. We can see in him the personal re-imagining that is so prevalent in early Irish drama: he is remaking himself in the English army to blend in and become acceptable. As a consequence, he seems to deny his Irishness. 'What ish my nation?' he cries. 'Who speaks of my nation? Ish a bastard, and a knave, and a rascal.'[15] There are two ways of taking this remark, however. One is that this is catchpenny stuff to massage the groundlings by denigrating the Irish. This was 1599, at the height of the Nine Years' War; Essex was currently floundering around in Ireland. But Macmorrice is also refusing to allow any distinction or distance between himself and his English peers, a familiar refrain among the English of Ireland. He correctly evaluates the remark as a veiled insult, and reacts accordingly with a volley of personal abuse directed at the prosy, obtuse Welshman.

Having taken being excluded severely amiss, he becomes even more irate when Fluellen attempts to equate himself with him in professional skill and in birth. Macmorrice snarls like a true aristocrat:

FLUELLEN   Being as good a man as yourself, both in disciplines of war, and in the derivation of my birth.

MACMORRICE   I do not know you as good a man as myself: so

Chrish save me, I will cut off your head.[16]

But a parley sounds and Macmorrice has to go and attend to the siege – his professionalism claims him and he instantly forgoes the row for more important things.

Apart from his odd language and his quick temper, Macmorrice comes across as an, active, expert soldier, a leader of men and impatient of talkative fools. The language that Shakespeare gives him rings authentically of someone using English but thinking in Irish and using Irish idioms. 'Give over' is still used as a past-participle in English by native Irish speakers – 'the siege is give over' could have been said today by someone from Donegal. But Macmorrice is not a Donegal name; it is a concoction by Shakespeare. The name is obviously Fitzmaurice, which only becomes MacMuiris in Irish, a language Macmorrice would decline to use. This makes him Norman-Irish, or Old English, puts him firmly among the aristocrats, and accounts for his being a captain and a person of importance, holding the premier authority at the siege. Perhaps Shakespeare did not use the name Fitzmaurice because such an obvious Norman patrimony would give him too much caste and overbalance the scene.

He is not a braggart or a *miles gloriosus*, as the commentaries have decided, nor is he a 'pugnacious braggart with a mouth-full of oaths',[17] just because he repeats 'so Chrish save me', a sort of soldier's mantra, four times. He is one of the bilingual Anglo-Norman gentry, owing a feudal allegiance to the king of England, and trying to be accepted by the English aristocracy by excelling at 'the disciplines of the war'.[18] With the rise of English power in Ireland, a number of the old Norman families were sloughing off their Irish ways and reverting to English manners.[19] What we have in Macmorrice is the rare spectacle, in drama, of one of the Old English on his way to becoming one of the New English, denying his separateness, insisting on the status of his birth and blood, and pursuing his goals in the time-honoured fashion of his Norman forbears – on the field of battle.

People take offence at Shakespeare's attempt to render his speech, but Shakespeare does no more than aspirate his 's' sound, to produce, not the clean 's' of English speech but the sibilant 's' of Hiberno-English. At the same time he gives Macmorrice a distinguishing verbal tic – 'so Chrish save me' – just as he gives Fluellen a Welsh 'look you', and a Scots 'gud' to Jamie. To call him a stage Irishman rather than an Irish character on the stage is a pejorative and political assessment, not a dramatic criticism.

A character on stage, who begins with all the appearance of stereotype, can, with sympathetic acting, develop into a rounded character. Captain Molineux in Boucicault's *The Shaughraun* is another case in point. What starts as a sort of cartoon Englishman should grow and develop in the course of the performance into a credible personage. The part of Molineux is written economically and in the hands of a poor actor can degenerate into caricature. With this English role in front of an Irish audience, it would be tempting for an actor to create a lazy characterization from ready-made tics and hand-me-down business. This is what happened to Irish parts before English audiences. What impresses an audience is the actor's performance, not the writer's; a good actor can make a convincing character out of a stereotype. We cannot blame Boucicault and Shakespeare for the stage-Irishman – they simply wrote the part; the actor then either fleshed it out to a felt reality or lazily presented it with a bag of tricks that was already familiar to the audience. The theatrical voltage is the text transmitted by the actors to the theatregoers. The charge may be created behind the proscenium arch, but it is the audience that induces the political wattage, that determines the amount of heat and light. The crucial factor in the equation is the resistance level of the spectators. Victor Turner declares: 'Cultures are most fully expressed in and made conscious of themselves in their ritual and theatrical performances,'[20] and the stage-Irishman was a sort of underhand convention, surreptitiously agreed between actors and audience. George Bernard Shaw recognized this in *John Bull's Other Island*:

> Is it possible that you don't know that all this top-o-the-morning and broth-of-a-boy and more-power-to-your-elbow business is as peculiar to England as the Albert Hall concerts of Irish music are? No Irishman ever talks like that in Ireland, or ever did, or ever will. But when a thoroughly worthless Irishman comes to England, and finds the whole place full of romantic duffers like you, who will let him loaf and drink and sponge and bray as long as he flatters your sense of moral superiority, by playing the fool and degrading himself and his country, he soon learns the antics that take you in. He picks them up at the theatre and the music hall.[21]

The stage Irishman, then, could be considered as an illusion produced by mixing national sensitivity with bad acting.

THE FIRST PLAY: SACKVILLE AND NORTON'S 'GORBODUC', DUBLIN CASTLE, 7 SEPTEMBER 1601

The Dublin city guilds staged dramatic productions in English on high-days and holidays all through the sixteenth century, and probably much earlier.[22] The students and bachelors of Trinity College and the law students at the King's Inns also performed plays towards the end of the century, but it was the interest and enthusiasm of the Dublin Castle set that created the theatre and it was their patronage that kept it going. High society, centred on the Lord Deputy and the Castle, had taken up dramatics as a modish recreation during Lord Mountjoy's regime, which covered the last three years of Elizabeth's reign. Amateur performances took place in the dining hall or the audience chamber.[23]

The earliest record of a surviving text being performed in Ireland is emblematic of the place the theatre acquired in the country's culture and politics, and of the way that drama and politics were to intertwine over the centuries. Gilbert writes in his *History of Dublin* (1854):

> Mr Ogilby, the Master of the Revels in this kingdom (who had it from proper authority), informed Mr. Ashbury that plays had often been per-formed in the Castle of Dublin, when Blount, Lord Mountjoy, was Lord Lieutenant here at the latter end of the reign of Queen Elizabeth. And Mr. Ashbury saw a bill for wax-tapers, dated the 7th day of September, 1601 (Queen Elizabeth's birthday), for the play of *Gorboduc* done at the Castle, one and twenty shillings and two groats.[24]

That this was an elaborate and important production is shown by the amount of money spent by the authorities on wax tapers to light the show, not tallow but the best-quality candles. The cost was huge, con-sidering that The King's Company, London's leading group of actors, who visited Youghal during 1625, were only paid 5 shillings, all told.[25]

The occasion was used to make a political statement: the birthday of the queen was marked by a play mounted with expensive display. The lavish celebration of her birthday was a conspicuous declaration of loyalty but at the same time an acknowledgement of the great age she had achieved. She was 68 on that day and there was no heir to the throne. The kingdom was insecure, and it is to this uncertainty that the choice of *Gorboduc* spoke.

Thomas Sackville, one of the authors of the play, had risen in the world to become High Treasurer of England. Sackville was, as publicly as was politic, an adherent of the claims of James VI of Scotland to the throne of England. Mountjoy was of the like opinion, and that is what the subtext of the performance was communicating, while demon-strating an unswerving allegiance to the existing power.

The occasion was used to pour some judicious birthday praise on the existing ruler:

> Your majesty doth know
> How under you, in justice and in peace,
> Great wealth and honour long we have enjoy'd:
> So as we cannot seem with greedy minds
> To wish for change of prince or governance.[26]

But there are other issues to be addressed; it was politically imperative to give some consideration to an eventual 'change of prince or governance'. The play repeatedly expresses the necessity for a clear line of succession, and demonstrates the dangers of not passing the monarchy cleanly and without mistakes or equivocation to the next generation:

> And this doth grow, when lo, unto the prince,
> Whom death or sudden hap of life bereaves,
> No certain heir remains, such certain heir,
> As not all only is the rightful heir,
> But to the realm is so made known to be;
> And troth thereby vested in subjects' hearts,
> To owe faith there where right is known to rest.[27]

'Certain', 'rightful', 'faith' and 'right' strike like hammer-blows along the verse, ringing out the importance of clarity and agreement in the line of descent.

Elizabeth's lack of an heir had led to interest from various foreign powers who felt they had some claim by inheritance on the throne, but the preference for a native heir is clearly stated over the importation of some foreigner:

> Right mean I his or hers, upon whose name
> The people rest by mean of native line,
> Or by the virtue of some former law,
> Already made their title to advance.
> Such one, my lords, let be your chosen king,
> Such one, so born within your native land;
> Such one prefer, and in no wise admit
> The heavy yoke of foreign governance.
> [...]   Keep out also
> Unnatural thraldom of stranger's reign;
> Ne suffer you, against the rules of kind,
> Your mother land to serve a foreign prince.[28]

James VI of Scotland was being put firmly in the frame. He would bring the old line of Henry VII back onto the throne; James was his great-great-grandson. The line of Henry VIII would die out with

Elizabeth. James, although a Protestant, was unassailable by Catholics as he was the legitimate heir in the direct line.

A powerful signal was being sent to all who chose to see it. Mountjoy was taking advantage of his position in Ireland to present a play which might not have got past the Master of the Revels in England, where, due to the volatile political situation, there was a general ban on all works dealing with English history. He used it to make a complex and subtle statement of loyalty to the queen, to express concern about her age and the absence of an heir to the throne, to indicate his support for the most likely successor, and at the same time to flatter the author of the play, who was a powerful and rising man.

This first known play in the Anglo-Irish theatre already shows the main tendency of that dramatic tradition: it was an activity for Englishmen of the Irish court whose interest and advancement lay across the water, and whose eyes were fastened there. It was for the government and functionaries clustered around Dublin Castle and the gentry in town for the occasion. It took no account at all of the country in which it occurred, or of its natives. The participants saw themselves as Englishmen who were physically separated from events at the centre by distance, just like those in far-flung corners of England, but who mentally still inhabited the same space as anyone in London. The distance, however, and the status as a separate kingdom, was to prove crucial in the long run.

THE FIRST THEATRE IN IRELAND: WERBURGH STREET, 1634

At the death of Elizabeth, James of Scotland did succeed to the English throne, but tension between the Parliament and the Stuart monarchs intensified as the seventeenth century progressed. Shifting allegiances were common, and one of the most notable turncoats was Thomas Wentworth, who went over to King Charles the First's side in 1628 and became one of his most rabid supporters.[29] Wentworth, ruthless and ambitious, was made, at his own request, Lord Deputy of Ireland in 1633, and set about turning the country into the king's private fief, where, as he said himself, the king was to be 'as absolute here as any Prince in the whole world can be'. Wentworth came to Ireland with a three-fold aim – to increase the king's revenues, to augment the king's prestige in defiance of Parliament, and to make Ireland a test case in absolute monarchy, before implementing it at home. 'The object of this great and wicked man', according to Lecky, 'was to establish a despotism in Ireland as a step towards despotism in England.' [30]

But for all his power in Ireland, the enemies of 'Black Tom Tyrant' used his absence from court to conspire against him. To combat this it was necessary for him not just to be a bountiful provider of land and money for the king, but to attract as much favourable notice as possible. As with Mountjoy thirty years before, Whitehall was his centre of attention, and everything he did was to keep his name and abilities in the forefront of the royal mind.

Wentworth did all he could to boost the prestige of his own position: he enlarged and extended Dublin Castle, and introduced the pomp of a court. His project was to build a city that reflected his importance as the king's regent and its own importance as the capital of the Kingdom of Ireland. His court at the Castle became the focus for the top echelons of Dublin and Anglo-Irish society. Receptions and entertainments were frequent. Sir Adam Loftus wrote that in January 1633/4 he saw 'a play acted by his lordship's gentle [men]',[31] and, in January of the following year: 'We saw a tragedie in the parliament house, and which was tragicall, for we had no suppers.'[32]

John Ogilby arrived from England around this time, either as tutor to Wentworth's children, or as a secretary to the Lord Deputy,[33] and he erected the only pre-Restoration theatre outside of London in Werburgh Street, near the Castle. The date is uncertain, but 1634 seems most likely. Wentworth himself may have instigated the project because he 'considered the establishment of a theatre an effective provocative of wit and grandeur'.[34] But at any rate he was soon its enthusiastic supporter and patron, and in February 1638 he created Ogilby Master of the Revels in Ireland on his own authority.

This patent tied the new theatre firmly into the establishment around the Castle. It left no doubt that the new theatre was for them, and, by implication, about them. In the royal simulation that was the viceregal court, the warrant from the viceroy 'stamped Ireland's first theatre as the official godchild of the English Ascendancy'.[35]

Wentworth, like Mountjoy, was exploiting, and demonstrating to his coterie, the political power of the theatre to create and bolster an image of a powerful individual or of a society. The strategy worked: news of the new theatre reached London, and managed to lure the leading playwright of the day, James Shirley, to Dublin, to supply it with plays between 1636 and 1640. The plague closed the London theatres in 1636 and 1637,[36] but Shirley tells us himself that he was attracted by the success of Wentworth's propaganda:

> When he did live in England, he heard say
> That here were men lov'd wit and a good play;

> That here were gentlemen, and lords, a few
> We're bold to say; there were some ladies too.[37]

Therein he defined his prospective audience: gentlemen, lords and ladies: – an aristocratic theatre.

At first Shirley produced work to the same template that had succeeded in London, but there developed an air of increasing exasperation in his addresses to the audience. He encountered unexpected difficulties; he did not realize how restricted his potential audience was, for example. The theatre was small and the audience was tiny; it was confined to the court circle, the administration and the military officers. They could probably all fit in the theatre on one night: in the Prologue to *The Sisters* Shirley speaks of a play 'though ne'er so new, will starve the second day'.[38] Shirley came with a set of expectations, but found that they were not being fulfilled. We can follow, through his plays, prologues and epilogues, his attempts to understand his audience, and his increasing frustration at his lack of success.

His play *The Royal Master* got his Dublin career off to a flying start. It was performed in the theatre with such success that the printed edition has no fewer than nine laudatory prologues attached, one of which runs:

> This play o' th' public stage,
> Hath gained such fair applause, as't did engage
> A nation to thy Muse; where thou shalt reign
> Viceregent to Apollo.[39]

The play was obviously a great success, and the playwright is flattered by being compared to the viceroy, whose invocation ties him to the endeavour. Also note that mention of 'nation', in opposition to Macmorrice's disclaimer in *Henry V*, and which already bears, even in the 1630s, a connotation of separateness, and identifies the 'nation' as the English colonists. The published play of 1638 was dedicated to George Fitzgerald, Earl of Kildare, the premier nobleman of the Kingdom of Ireland, 'her first native ornament and top branch of honour',[40] which seems to align Shirley with the Old English, whom he appears to regard as the indigenous inhabitants, but he was also keeping well in with the authorities that were presently in the ascendant. As well as its performance in the theatre, the play was presented by command on New Year's Day 1637, 'before the Right Honourable the Lord Deputy of Ireland, in the Castle'.[41] Shirley topped his achievement with a gracious Epilogue to mark the New Year, addressed directly to Wentworth, using the occasion to burnish the regent's reputation, and flattering his magnificence in the presence of his coterie:

                    The day,
having looked on you, hath hid his face,
and changed his robe with stars to grace
and light you, going to bed, to wait
with trembling lustre on your state.
All honour with your fame increase,
In your bosom dwell soft peace,
And justice, the true root of these!
        Wealth be the worst, and outside of your fate;
        And may not heaven your life translate,
        Till for your ROYAL MASTER and this isle,
        Your deeds have filled a chronicle![42]

The Royal Master, which he probably brought with him, has no local colour, but in his next play, *The Doubtful Heir*, Shirley began to glance at the Irish scene. The main plot has to do with the adventures of a lost heir and the constancy of his love for his betrothed through a series of vicissitudes, giving the play its two alternative titles: *Rosania; or, Love's Victory*. But he included a subplot which is a lot more interesting in that it examined the relationship between the Castle garrison and the tradesmen and shopkeepers of the town, and satirized the adventurers and place-seekers clinging to the viceregal court. The play was designed to secure the goodwill of the military officers. It is openly partisan on their behalf; the Prologue – love is a battle or a war – is couched in a military metaphor. The viewpoint throughout is that of the Captain, who, as well as assisting the two principal lovers, is beset by his creditors, stupid and greedy city merchants. The Captain makes fools of them, first by selling them false patents to raise money, and then by impressing them into the army when they seek redress. Since the lower classes were lampooned in this fashion, they cannot have been part of the audience. The Captain is by far the most attractive character in the play, and the piece praises the military's role in securing the comfort and safety of the citizens, at the expense of its own. The war-footing of the country is discernible behind the drama: the military are held up as the saviours and guardians of this society, living a difficult and dangerous life, while the middle classes enjoy the fruits of their hardships:

> 'Tis we that keep your worships warm and living
> By marching, fasting, fighting, and a thousand
> Dangers; you o'ergrown moths! You that love gold
> And will not take an angel sent from heaven,

> Unless you weigh him.
> [...]
> These are walking sicknesses, not citizens.[43]

Shirley was beginning to feel his way into his adopted society, trying to separate his audience into different strands, and in *The Doubtful Heir* he was looking to win the approval of the military class, who were hedonistic, well-bred, fond of the theatre, and fond of spending money, even if they did not have it.

This was a factionalized society, and there were other strands of this social tapestry that Shirley did not greatly care for. He was a committed Catholic Royalist, who later fought on the king's side in the Civil War. The administration under Wentworth was made up of Protestant Royalists, but the country as a whole was dominated by the Old English. Most of them clung to Catholicism, and saw unswerving loyalty to Charles I as their best hope of retaining their estates. But the Protestant New English were incensed at Charles' softness in restoring to the older colonists land that had been taken from them in the Plantations. The Puritan tendency was confined largely to the middle-class citizens, who did not attend the theatre, and spent their time making money. But they were gaining ground, and in the light of Charles' loosening grip, a number of the Ascendancy royalists were getting ready to change sides, if it should prove necessary.

From its inception, part of Werburgh Street's problem was the narrowness of its clientèle, and this was further aggravated by Wentworth's failure to call any Parliament together between 1636 and 1639, depriving Dublin of the regular presence of the lords and leading commoners who had no imperative need to come to town, and so leaving the city without its leaders of fashion and *ton*. 'Oh do not bury all your brain in glebes,' Shirley pleads in one of his Prologues,[44] because the fashionable coterie was shrunk to the administrators, the military and the legal profession. Sessions of the law courts went some way to boost the attendance, but he still finds fault, whacking his audience with a legal metaphor:

> Are there no more? ...
> We did expect a session, and a train
> So large, to make the benches crack again.
> There was no summons, sure; yet, I did see
> The writs abroad, and men with half an eye
> Might read on every post – this day would sit
> Phoebus himself and the whole court of wit.[45]

In the Prologue he wrote to Fletcher's *No Wit to a Woman's* Shirley was forced to admit that his audience had a personality of its own, and to see that it would not do simply to reiterate his method of writing for the London theatre. The audience looked to London as the centre of the universe, but they also wanted to see something of their own experience on the Dublin stage. He twigs them with their insularity, invoking yet again the metaphor of Ireland as a garden stubbornly resisting cultivation:

> It is our wonder that this fair island, where,
> The air is held so temperate,
> [...]
> That to the noble seeds of art and wit,
> Honour'd elsewhere, it is not natural yet.
> [...].
> While others are repaired and grow refined
> By arts, shall this only to weeds be kind?[46]

This was probably a mistake: no audience likes being talked down to. Shirley then went on to compound the error, implicitly calling the theatregoers Irish by evoking the image of the snakes:

> Let it not prove a story of your time
> And told abroad to stain this promising clime,
> That wit and soul-enriching poesy,
> Transported hither, must like serpents die.[47]

He threatened to leave town with his Players: 'Awhile to the country, leave the town to blush / Not in ten days to see one coat of plush.'[48] This was an empty threat, given his well-known aversion to the country and preference for the town. He became increasingly annoyed by the failure of his audience to fully appreciate him: 'Were there a pageant now on foot, or some / Strange monster from Peru or Afric come / Men would throng to it,' he spits.[49]

Shirley set his plays in foreign countries, usually Italy, but the incidents and the social intercourse were those of the contemporary scene, either London or Dublin. He had previously been in trouble in London for putting unflattering portraits of recognizable characters into his play *The Ball*. An entry in the office book of the Master of the Revels, dated 18 November 1632, concerning that play, complains:

> There were divers persons personated so naturally, both of lords and others of the court, I took it ill, and would have forbidden the play, but that Biston promised many things which I found fault withal should be

left out, and that he would not suffer it to be done by any poet any more, who deserves to be punished. And the first that offends in this kind, of poets or players, shall be sure of public punishment.[50]

Shirley was willing to take the Irish Ascendancy's patronage, but he insisted on his independence; he was prepared to state what he saw. He was finding that the audience wanted, and expected, to see themselves imaged on the stage, but did not identify with his creations. – The humours, in Jonsonian terms, did not ring true; what he observed around him was not what they wanted to see. Shirley seems, from his own remarks, to have offended some sectors. His relationship with the lawyers was, at best, ambiguous:

> We are sorry gentlemen, that with all the pains
> To invite you hither, the wide house contains
> No more. Call you this term? If the courts were
> So thin, I think, 'twould make your lawyers swear,
> And curse men's charity, in whose want they thrive.[51]

He was fond of referring to himself as 'The Poet', and he reserved the poet's prerogatives. He was the outsider in this society and saw it as his duty, not just to entertain them, but to point out their shortcomings, criticize their taste, and even attack the corruption of the highest among them. There is a barbed passage in *Saint Patrick for Ireland* that seems to point straight at Wentworth himself and his legal banditry: 'Great men in office that desire execution of the laws; not so much to correct offenses, and reform the commonwealth, as to thrive by their punishment, and grow rich and fat with a lean conscience.'[52]

Shirley's tendency to plain speaking did not endear him to the courtiers either. He wrote of himself in 1639: 'I never affected the ways of flattery: some say I have lost my preferment by not practising that court sin.' In a poem dedicated 'to the excellent pattern of beauty and virtue L(ady) E(lizabeth) C(ountess) of O(rmond)' he asserts his inability to flatter and prostitute his poetry:

> I never learn'd that trick of court to wear
> Silk at the art of flattery; or made dear
> My pride, by painting a great lady's face
> When she had don't before, and swear the grace
> Was Nature's.[54]

It is obvious enough that he was no courtier, and there is no doubt that he gave offence; in the Prologue to *Saint Patrick for Ireland* he accused some of the audience: 'They come not with a purpose to be pleas'd.'[55]

We may suppose then that they came to be displeased, and the likelihood is that his bluntness had outraged the ladies of the court, because he went on to add: 'Nor confine we censures; would that each soul were masculine.'[56] He had a grating habit of reminding the great and the good that their glory will come to an end, and that we will all die and mingle in the grave. His best-known poem expresses it succinctly:

> Sceptre and Crown,
> Must tumble down,
> And in the dust be equal made
> With the poor crooked scythe and spade.[57]

He had done his best to create a dramatic genre for this audience, which had turned out to be less sophisticated, more factional than London, and unsure of what it wanted. They expected to see themselves mirrored on the stage, but did not like what he had to show them. Their taste was poor, Shirley told them bluntly, their 'palates are sick'.[58] They had a taste for spectacle rather than poetry. In a Prologue to a lost play called *The Toy*, he stated that, if their preference is for rubbish, that's their own fault, there's better stuff available:

> So sickly are the palates now-a-days
> Of men that come to see and taste our plays,
> That when a poet hath, to please some few,
> Spent his most precious sweat, Minerva's dew,
> And after many throes, a piece brought forth,
> Legitimate in art, in nature, birth,
> 'Tis not received, but most unhappy dies,
> Almost as soon as born, wit's sacrifice.
> When children of the brain, not half so fair
> And form'd, are welcome to the nurse and air.[59]
> [...]
> But please yourselves, and buy what you like best.
> Some cheap commodities mingle with the rest:
> If you affect the rich ones, use your will,
> Or if *The Toy* take, you're all welcome still.

He seems to have come to his wits' end when he hit on his boldest stroke, the idea of creating a myth for the colony in *Saint Patrick for Ireland*, by colonizing Irish legend. In the Prologue, he plaintively asked the audience for some sort of consistency in their likes and dislikes:

> We should be very happy if at last
> We could find out the humour of your taste,

> You were constant to yourself and kept
> That true.[60]

He was doing this in an attempt to gratify the tastes of his audience, but it was their choice, not his. They were dictating what was being written, an open acknowledgement that this theatre belonged, body and soul, to its clientèle. He may have hoped to create in Ireland a theatre of poetry, in which the word would reign supreme. In his first Dublin play, *The Royal Master*, he had declared his intention of abandoning the masque: 'Pretty impossibilities', he wrote contemptuously, 'Some of the gods, that are good fellows, dancing, / Or goddesses; and now and then a song / To fill a gap.'[61] But he acknowledged defeat with *Saint Patrick for Ireland*. He chose a subject with a local resonance, and used the full panoply of theatrical effect – song, dance, masque, spectacular scenery and special effects, including two snake scenes and a trap with fire for Hell's mouth. Shirley had been forced to slant the subject from the point of view of the colonial masters, the embryo Ascendancy, and in his play the lineaments of their bigotry, intolerance, and conviction of superiority can be traced.[62] In *Saint Patrick for Ireland* the native Irish aristocracy are shown as dissolute buffoons, their priests as panders and charlatans, the Bard a drunken ballad-singer. Saint Patrick is an incoming English aristocratic figure spreading reason and light, banishing the snakes of superstition and ignorance: 'at whose approach the serpents all unchained themselves, / and leaving our prisoned necks, crept into the earth'.[63] Irish culture, as represented by Archimagus and other Irish nobles, is immoral and decadent, needing to be replaced by the benignity and moderation of English observances.

Saint Patrick's banishing of the snakes is a metaphor for victory over the Irish. Patrick bestows the benison of English civilization on these decadent savages: 'Like wolves, you undertake / A quarrel with the moon.'[64] His introduction of himself and his followers is, 'We are of Britain.'[65] They are under divine protection: 'In vain is all your malice, art and power / Against their lives, whom the great hand of heaven / Deigns to protect.'[66] He is even accompanied by a guardian angel called Victor. In this play, Shirley claims Patrick for the English colonial effort. Patrick, he is saying, brought enlightenment from Britain in the fifth century, and the present colonists are repeating the process in the seventeenth. The political and the religious modes merge in the High King's invitation to Patrick, which is a feudal submission to an overlord:

> We give thee now our palace, use it freely;
> Myself, our queen and children, will be all
> Thy guests and owe our dwellings to thy favour.[67]

And Patrick's reminiscence of his Call to return to the country takes on a distinctly imperialist tinge:

> This supreme King's command I have obey'd,
> Who sent me hither to bring you to him,
> And this still wand'ring nation.[68]

God is definitely on the English side: the Irish god is a devil: 'a fury, the master fiend of darkness; and as hot as hell could make him',[69] who holds the Irish in subjection. But the struggle to bring the Irish to the light will not be easy; sacrifice and 'the blood of many martyrs'[70] will be demanded before the final victory. Thus Shirley turned the subduing of the country into a crusade. The Irish, contrary to the known facts, swear to kill all the Christians, and drench the land with their blood, falling into the bloodthirsty rhetoric of barbarous rebels:

> Were there no red in heaven, from the torn heart
> Of Christians we that colour could impart
> And with their blood supply the crimson streaks
> That dress the sky, when the fair morning breaks.[71]

Those who embrace the new dispensation will thrive and their children prosper. Conallus, the king's son, convinced by the power that Patrick demonstrates, swears fealty to him: 'To him that can dispense such blessings, I must owe duty, / And thus kneeling pay it.'[72] He is rewarded by a grant of the kingdom and a prophecy of his descendants' success: 'Your crown shall flourish, and your blood possess / The throne you shall leave glorious.'[73]

Those who oppose the new regime will suffer the fate of Archimagus, who is punished by the agents of the new power who 'shall catch my falling flesh upon / their burning pikes'.[74] The Irish, even those who expressed loyalty, were not to be trusted. The king, Leogarius, embraces Patrick and swears friendship, but promptly goes off to plot another rebellion; Patrick remarks once he is gone, 'I suspect him still.'[75] Only when all the snakes/Irish are banished, dead, or subdued, he says, will the island at last be safe for civilized people:

> Hence, you frightful monsters,
> Go hide, and bury your deformed heads
> For ever in the sea! From this time be
> This island free from beasts of venomous nature.[76]

Shirley was very clever in rifling Irish history to create a myth for the colonists. This intervention, he says, has happened before, and with fruitful results, but decadence set in and the scheme now has to be rescued; you are following in this proud tradition; your mission is to civilize these savages once again. He was stoking their prejudices and at the same time creating for them an image to live up to, that of a civilizing crusade among all these benighted pagans. Saint Patrick's religious mission is hardly mentioned; we are shown two rival magical systems in conflict. The superior one is that with the more powerful magic, therefore that is the right one. Power equals truth. The power of the magus, Patrick or Archimagus, demonstrates the power of his god. The English conquest of Ireland reflects the will of the almighty English god. If Power equals truth, then the winners are always right, so the English conquest of the country reflects the will of the more powerful English god. Saint Patrick represents the New English incursion; religion is just a smokescreen.

Shirley was confident that with this play he had got it right for this audience; he had massaged the sensibilities of the courtiers and hangers-on at the viceroy's court, and created for them a legend of belonging and of high moral purpose. He had made a showcase for his own talents and exploited all the theatrical tricks, techniques and possibilities of his day. His play mirrored the character and attitudes of the theatregoers, reflected their conviction of their own rectitude, and showed that God was on their side and that they were the inheritors of an ancient civilizing endeavour. He was clearly pleased with the work, so much so that he mentions in both the Prologue and the Epilogue that he is ready to start Part Two. The present play was published as Part One but there is no record of his ever producing the second part; the imminent rebellion of 1641 probably made it impossible.

Criticism is levelled at the Old English in *Saint Patrick for Ireland*. The question is implicit: what has happened to the civilization that Patrick and his followers brought with them, in the light of present conditions? The Irish were decadent idolaters, but a great number of the previous English colonists, instead of cleansing and enlightening the country, had actually embraced the wicked ways of the Irish. They may be considered worse decadents because they had further to fall. The subtext of the play is that Ireland is in sore need of a new cleansing, a fresh shaking by the scruff of the neck to bring it up to scratch. The native Irish were in no position to respond to this charge, but the Old English, descendants of the Norman invasion and the earlier Plantations, were, and they also had their say in the new theatre at Werburgh Street.

The only other Irish play that survives from the period could be taken as a riposte to *Saint Patrick for Ireland* from the other side of the political divide. Henry Burnell's *Landgartha* was 'first acted St Patrick's Day, 1639, printed Dublin 1641, as it was presented in the new Theatre in *Dublin*, with good applause'.[77] Henry Burnell, of Castleknock Castle, was a well-established member of the Old English aristocracy, who had never even been to England.[78] He was married to a daughter of the Earl of Roscommon, and was to be a founder member of the Confederation of Kilkenny during the rebellion of 1641.[79] He is the first Irish-born dramatist that we know of, and his play speaks of his dissatisfaction with the state of the country at the date of its first performance. There is a strong hint that the play is an answer to Shirley, who was known as the heir to Ben Jonson: 'that discipleship to Ben Jonson which he was ever ready to acknowledge'.[80] In a dedicatory poem to *Landgartha* Burnell is eulogized:

> Let others boast of their own faculties,
> of being Son to *Jonson*. I dare say,
> Thou art far more like to *Ben* than they
> That lay claim as heirs to him, wrongfully:
> For he survives now only but in thee
> And his own lines; the rest degenerate.[81]

The plot of the play concerns the quarrel between Landgartha, a warrior queen of Norway, married to Reyner, king of Denmark. Landgartha is the blameless wife, who is wronged by her husband, but when she leaves him, he finds himself hapless and regretful. Landgartha represents the Old English, whose contest with the New English over control of the country was about to boil over. The two groups should be natural partners, but the treatment of Landgartha by her husband is such that she cannot support him any longer.

The play reflects the uneasy balance in the power structure. From the start of the seventeenth century the New English Protestant colonists controlled the central administration in Dublin, but the Catholic Old English controlled the local administrations and the towns. The native Irish were broken as a military and political power for the moment, but, however demoralized, they could be held down by the limited numbers of the New English only with the support of the Old English. These descendants of the Norman incursion still controlled most of the wealth of the country, but they were not trusted, in spite of their proclaimed loyalty to the Crown.[82] They were being kept out of the central corridors of power on account of their religion, and both sides were easy game for Wentworth and his policy of divide and rule: whereas if they could have co-operated they might have resisted him.

Burnell would have approved of such co-operation, but he was too pessimistic, or too much a realist, for any such happy ending; he has Landgartha rescue her husband from his difficulties, but then leave him again because of his conduct. Burnell casts the blame on the New English, but gives approval to the idea of a permanent power-sharing: not pleasing to either side, but broadly tolerable to both. The idea, says Burnell, is that a 'Tragi-Comedy should neither end Comically or Tragically, but betwixt both.'[83]

In the play, the Old English are represented by the female charac-ters, the New English by males. The play opens with a Prologue spo-ken by 'an Amazon with a Battle-Axe in her hand',[84] and the first two acts show Landgartha and her warrior women performing feats of val-our and winning battles. Burnell endows the Old English with the fem-inine virtues of chastity, fidelity and forgiveness, but shows them also as strong and martial. The New English have the male vices of licen-tiousness, inconstancy and self-indulgence. It was the Old English who won and preserved the country, he is saying, but, in everybody's best interests, they were willing to share it with the new colonists, enacted in the solemn marriage of Landgartha and Reyner:

> Wisdom bids be silent, this poor kingdom
> Being already torn too much by tyranny and troubles.
> Things past our help with patience must be borne,
> Until a fit time.[85]

But the New English were unfaithful to the bargain, and now wanted to get rid of the old colonists, in the belief that they did not need them any more.

Burnell now prophetically imagines a rebellion in the country. The rebel leader looks for assistance from Landgartha, against her husband, in revenge 'for her repudiation and disgrace'.[86] But she comes instead to the aid of her estranged husband, and puts down the rebellion. She forgives her husband, and allows the marriage to stand, but refuses any intimate contact with him. In his dedication to the published play, Burnell states that she 'took not then, what she was persuaded to by so many, the King's kind night-embraces'.[87]

Landgartha gives us a glimpse of the simmering discontent and grievances of the older colonists as the country balanced on the brink of civil war; it shows us the older Ascendancy's humiliation and sense of outraged virtue. The play is, simultaneously, an assertion of loyalty, a reminder of past favours and accomplishments, a complaint about maltreatment, and a warning to the dominant strain in the Anglo-Irish colony that their policies will lead to disaster. As indeed they did, but in the long run it was disaster for the Old English, and left the New Protestant nobility even more firmly in control.

Landgartha is not a good play, and the main characters have nothing particularly definitive about them; they embody arguments without bringing them to life. But, apart from its exposé of Old English and New English attitudes, the play is significant for the character of Marfissa, the first appearance of a particular type of Anglo-Irish Ascendancy female, the 'character of the witty, volatile, fox-hunting Irishwoman',[88] a figure with a long future ahead of her. She is described as 'a humorous gentlewoman of Norway';[89] she speaks with an Irish turn-of-phrase: 'Herself dare not deny it, sir';[90] she is also Irish in her dress:

> *An Irish Gown, tuck'd up to mid-leg, with a broad basket-hilt Sword on, hanging in a great Belt, Brogues on her feet, her hair dishevell'd, and a pair of long-neck'd Spurs on her heels.*[91]

What Burnell is describing here is a member of the Old English who has gone native. Her absorption extends beyond dress, to embracing Irish ways, in defiance of the main tenet of any colonial outpost, the preservation of distance and identity. In the course of the masque to celebrate the marriage of Reyner and Landgartha, the harmony achieved is expressed in two dances. The royal couple tread a stately measure, while Marfissa and her companion *'dance the whip of Dunboyne merrily'.*[92]

It is an image of harmony and compromise between two sides of the same culture that was about to come spectacularly apart due to relentless aggression and legal banditry by the powerful newcomers. Burnell's play was published in Dublin in April 1641. In October of that year the Irish in Ulster rebelled, and before long the entire country was engulfed. Wentworth had been recalled in 1640, and Shirley returned too, probably on the same ship. The Lords Justices who now ran the country ordered the theatre at Werburgh Street to close, and its owner, Ogilby, went back to England to join the Royalist army in the approaching Civil War.

NOTES

1. Hugh Kearney, *Strafford in Ireland, 1633-1641: A Study in Absolutism* (Cambridge: Cambridge University Press, 1959, revised 1989), p. xxv.
2. *Ibid.,* p. xxvi.
3. *As You Like It,* ed. by Albert Gilman, Signet Classics (New York: New American Library, 1963), III. 2. 173 & V. 2. 108.
4. *Richard II,* ed. by Peter Ure, Arden Shakespeare (London: Methuen, 1956), II. 1. 157.
5. *Henry VI, Part 2,* ed. by Andrew S. Cairncross, Arden Shakespeare (London: Methuen, 1957), III. 1. 310.
6. Kearney, *Strafford in Ireland,* p. xxxv.
7. Lecky, *History of Ireland,* I, p. 14.
8. G.C. Duggan, *The Stage Irishman: a history of the Irish play and stage characters from the earliest times* (Dublin: The Talbot Press, 1937), p. 184.
9. David Krause, 'The Theatre of Dion Boucicault', in *The Dolmen Boucicault,* ed. by David Krause (Dublin: The Dolmen Press, 1964), p. 39.
10. *Henry V,* ed. by J.H. Walter, Arden Shakespeare (London: Methuen, 1954, reprinted 1960), III. 2. 69.
11. *Ibid.,* III. 2. 70.
12. *Ibid.,* III. 2. 91.
13. *Ibid.,* III. 2. 110.
14. *Ibid.,* III. 2. 74.
15. *Ibid.,* III. 2. 125.
16. *Ibid.,* III. 2. 132.
17. Hugh Hunt, *The Abbey: Ireland's National Theatre, 1904–1979* (New York: Columbia University Press, 1979), p. 3.
18. *Henry V,* II. 2. 197.
19. J.C. Beckett, *The Anglo-Irish Tradition,* p. 28.
20. Richard Schechner, *Performance Studies: An Introduction* (London: Routledge, 2002) p. 13.
21. George Bernard Shaw, *John Bull's Other Island* and *Major Barbara: also How He Lied to Her Husband* (London: Constable, 1930), I. p. 5.
22. Walter Harris, *The History and Antiquities of the City of Dublin,* Cch. VII: 'Of the interludes and plays antiently represented on the stage by the several corporations of the city of Dublin' (Dublin: printed for Laurence Flynn in Castle-Street & James Williams in Skinner-Row, 1763–) http://indigo.ie/~kfinlay/Harris/chapter7.htm [accessed 12/12/2002] (pp. 1–3).
23. Sir John Gilbert, *Gilbert's History of Dublin,* (Dublin: McGlashan and Gill, 1854–59) http://indigo.ie~kfinlay/Gilbert/gilbert1.htm[accessed 12/12/2002] (p. 17 of 21).
24. *Ibid.,* (p. 17).
25. William Smith Clark, *The Early Irish Stage: The beginnings to 1720* (Oxford: The Clarendon Press, 1955), p. 19.
26. Sackville and Norton, *Gorboduc,* in *Medieval and Tudor Drama,* ed. by John Gassner (New York: Bantam Books, 1963), I. 2. 148.
27. *Ibid.,* V. 2. 408.
28. *Ibid.,* V. 2. 327.
29. Kearney, *Strafford in Ireland,* p. 7.
30. Lecky, *History of Ireland,* I, 31.
31. Clark, *Early Irish Stage,* p. 27.
32. *Ibid.,* p. 27.
33. 'John Ogilby, who came over in 1633 in the train of the Lord Deputy Wentworth, by whom he was occasionally employed as an amanuensis': Gilbert, *History of Dublin,* p.17.
34. La Tourette Stockwell, *Dublin Theatres and Theatre Customs (1637–1820)* (New York: Benjamin Blom, 1938, reprinted 1968), p. 2.
35. Clark, *Early Irish Stage,* p. 32.
36. Gilbert, *History of Dublin,* p. 17.
37. *Ibid.,* p. 18.

38. A.H. Nason, *James Shirley, Dramatist* (New York City: Arthur H Nason, 1915), p. 134.
39. Stockwell, *Dublin Theatres and Customs*, p. 10.
40. James Shirley, *The Dramatic Works and Poems of James Shirley*, ed. by W. Gifford and A. Dyce, 6 vols. (New York: Russell & Russell, 1833; reprinted 1966), IV, p. 103.
41. *Ibid.*, Shirley's dedication to the 1638 edition of *The Royal Master*, IV, p.102.
42. *Ibid.*, Shirley's epilogue to *The Royal Master*, IV, p. 187.
43. *Ibid.*, *The Doubtful Heir*, I. 1. IV, p. 285.
44. *Ibid.*, 'A Prologue to the Irish Gent', VI, p. 492.
45. Prologue to *The General*, in Gilbert, *History of Dublin*, p. 19.
46. Shirley, *Dramatic Works*; Prologue to *The Irish Gent*, VI, p. 491.
47. *Ibid.*, p. 491.
48. *Ibid.*, Prologue to *The General*, IV, p. 496.
49. *Ibid.*, 'A Prologue to Another of Master Fletcher's plays', VI, p. 493.
50. Nason, *James Shirley, Dramatist*, p. 231.
51. Shirley, *Dramatic Works*, Prologue, *No Wit to a Woman's*, VI, p. 492.
52. *Ibid.*, *St Patrick for Ireland*, V. 1. , IV, p. 427.
53. Dedication to *The Maid's Revenge*, Nason, *James Shirley, Dramatist*, p. 120.
54. Shirley, *Dramatic Works*, VI, p. 432.
55. *Ibid.*, IV, p. 365.
56. *Ibid.*, IV, p. 365.
57. 'Song from *The Contention of Ajax and Ulysses*', in *The Penguin Book of English Verse*, ed. by John Hayward (Harmondsworth Middlesex, 1956, repr.inted 1966), p. 101.
58. Shirley, *Dramatic Works*, Prologue to *Saint Patrick for Ireland*, IV, p. 365.
59. *Ibid.*, VI, p. 494.
60. *Ibid.*, IV, p. 365.
61. Christopher Morash, *A History of the Irish Theatre (1601–2000)* (Cambridge: University Press, 2002) p. 7.
62. 'the particular prejudice of a provincial outpost', Stockwell, *Dublin Theatres and Customs*, p. 12.
63. Shirley, *Saint Patrick for Ireland*, I. 1. in *Dramatic Works*, IV, p. 371.
64. *Ibid.*, V. 2. p. 441.
65. *Ibid.*, I. 1. p. 373.
66. *Ibid.*, V. 2. p. 441.
67. *Ibid.*, III. 1. p. 395.
68. *Ibid.*, I. 1. p. 374.
69. *Ibid.*, IV. 1. p. 414.
70. *Ibid.*, IV. 1. p. 421.
71. *Ibid.*, IV. 2. p. 421.
72. *Ibid.*, V. 1. p. 434.
73. *Ibid.*, V. 1. p. 438.
74. *Ibid.*, V. 1. p. 442.
75. *Ibid.*, V. 2. p. 442.
76. *Ibid.*, V. 3. p. 441.
77. Stockwell, *Dublin Theatres and Customs*, p. 18. According to the old calendar, 1640 did not begin until April 1st; St Patrick's day of 1639 would, using the modern calendar, actually be St Patrick's Day of 1640.
78. 'Thou England never saw'st': Prologue to *Landgartha*; Catherine M. Shaw, '*Landgartha* and the Irish Dilemma', in *Eire-Ireland*, Spring 1978, 26–39 (p. 27).
79. 'Henry Burnell' http://www.pgil-eirdata.org/html/pgil_datasets/authors/b/Burnell,Henry/ life. htm [accessed 08/01/2003] (p. 1 of 1).
80. *Cambridge History of English and American Literature*, VI, Part 2 [accessed 23/12/2002] (page 1 of 2).
81. Catherine M. Shaw, 'Landgartha and the Irish Dilemma', p. 29.
82. J.C. Beckett, *The Anglo-Irish Tradition*, p. 28.
83. Burnell 'Afterword', *Landgartha*, in *Irish Plays of the Seventeenth and Eighteenth Centuries*, ed. by Christopher Wheatley and Kevin Donovan, 2 vols (Bristol: Thoemmes Press, 2003) I, p. 68.
84. Gilbert, History of Dublin [accessed12/12/2002] (p. 19 of 21).

85. ELSINORA, *Landgartha*, II. 3. 165. in Wheatley and Donovan, Irish Plays, I.
86. Ibid., IV. 4. 11.
87. Ibid., 'Afterword', *Landgartha*.
88. Stockwell, *Dublin Theatres and Customs*, p. 21.
89. Clark, *Early Irish Stage*, p. 38.
90. *Landgartha*, III. 1. 106. in Wheatley and Donovan, *Irish Plays*, I.
91. *Ibid.*, III. 1.
92. *Ibid.*, III. 1.

2

Politics and Pageantry:
Restoration Theatre in Ireland

When the theatre was undammed after the Restoration of Charles II in 1660, two distinct streams of drama emerged – the Heroic Tragedy and the Comedy of Manners. They diverted into separate channels, comedy attempting to demonstrate the reality of life, tragedy to show the ideal.

The English court, immersed in European aristocratic culture for eleven years, had returned to an England that lacked style or sophistication, and immediately set about raising the country to a Continental level. Dryden laid down literary standards; Robert Boyle founded the Royal Society to promote Science and reinvent the English language; Wren re-imagined the city of London; Locke and Hobbes rejected Plato and embraced Empiricism.

In drama, the Restoration court was intent on creating a gilded image of itself and its king. They had endured tragedy and dispossession in the downfall and execution of Charles I. Now they had re-established their heroic, aristocratic superiority: order was restored and the reign of Saturn come again. The splendour that Richelieu had created for the young Louis XIV was their envy and their ideal. Restoration plays glorify Restoration society: the comedies show its denizens as glittering wits, the tragedies as creatures of noble, exalted virtues.

This court was a corrupt and devious place, however, and the problem of right or ethical action was skewed by the convention of Dissimulation, by the necessity of concealing the reality of one's personal thoughts and feelings behind a mask of proper manners. The end result of this ethos was the impossibility of knowing what anyone else was thinking or feeling, or of knowing what anyone was really like. If Dissimulation was a passive concealment strategy, its active twin was Affectation – actively living a lie, a vice scourged repeatedly by the Restoration playwrights. Wycherley, in *The Country Wife*, has Horner say: 'A pox on 'em, and on all that force nature and would be still what she forbids 'em. Affectation is her greatest monster.' [1]

Dissimulation and Affectation posed huge problems in relation-ships, and were the fertile ground for Restoration comedy, which explored this distance between the mask and the face, and proposed ways across it in the interests of comic dramatic resolution. In this, comedy embraced the Empirical theory, but tragedy clung to the Platonic. Restoration tragedy pushed Dissimulation and Affectation to their limits and created an entirely artificial world, of superhumanly ethical heroes and impossibly moral heroines – a world of ideals. They took this model from Corneille, but expanded it further. This is how we should be, their tragedy says, this is how the best people should behave: we see ourselves raised on a plateau above the rest of human-ity, creatures to be astonished at, to enkindle *admiration* in the com-mon herd.

After the Restoration, Irish and English dramatic tastes ran comfort-ably together, but then a rift opened, a gap which reflected the politi-cal and legal climate. Ireland was dwindling from a kingdom to a colony; the mainland English were treating the English in Ireland as colonials, not metropolitans, a shift that outraged the first Earl of Orrery. When the English Parliament passed laws forbidding the importation of Irish cattle and corn, he protested: 'Since the export of cattle was forbidden, the land was put in tillage [...] and if now our corn were forbidden, and by the name of foreign corn, we should not only lose much, but lose it by being called foreigners, which was a name more grievous to us than the prohibition itself.' [2]

The tentative attempts at dialogue, assimilation and accommodation among the different factions of the Irish gentry that Burnell had sug-gested were blown away by the rebellion of 1641, the Civil War and the Cromwellian invasion and Plantation. The Irish theatre after the Restoration belonged to the winners. It showed no differentiation from that of London: what was successful there was quickly put on in Dublin. Katherine Philips tells us that Ogilby snatched from her the text of *The Adventures of the Five Hours*, which was the London success of that sea-son, eager to present it with the minimum delay. [3] It is also worth remem-bering that at Ogilby's new theatre at Smock Alley, with Philips' *Pompey* and Orrery's *The Generall*, Dublin was for a brief period ahead of the London theatrical fashions. This affinity of the two cities and the two the-atres eventually led to the exodus of Irish actors and playwrights to London, where the population was ten times larger and the rewards of success correspondingly so. But the popularity of the Heroic Drama waned in England long before it did in Ireland. 'Between the years sixty and seventy, the taste of *England* was for Rhyming Heroic Fustian,' John Dennis wrote in 1696.[4] The reason for its much longer survival in Ireland was the partiality of 'the little circle of *grands seigneurs* at Dublin for it'.[5] When we look at the plays known to have been performed in Dublin during the Restoration period (1660–1685), what is striking is the almost complete absence of comedy. The works of which we have a record, apart from those of Shakespeare, were almost all 'Rhyming Heroic Fustian'.[6] This was the type of play that satisfied the leaders of fashion and taste in Dublin and continued to do so after the trend had waned elsewhere.

The zeitgeist in England shifted to the Empirical and the comedies began examining real life and showing it on the stage, while the Heroic Tragedies stayed with the Platonic, and presented an ideal world. We may conclude then that the English court's tastes developed in such a way that they wanted to see their own lives, with their problems and ramifications, on the stage, but the Irish court did not. These '*grands seigneurs*' did not desire to see themselves as they were, but as noble heroes in a superstition-ridden wilderness, a bridgehead of civilization in a savage country. This idea of a heroic self-image was the sort of representation Shirley had been aiming for in *Saint Patrick for Ireland*. Such characters and plays were not meant to depict real life, but one lived on an exalted, superhuman plane where Honour, Glory, Justice and Destiny ruled, and debate took the place of action – not on a small island bedevilled by violence where too many claimants were jostling in a grubby, sectarian scrum for land and advancement.

The noble, heroic, love and honour tragedy was not just an aesthetic style. The splendour of Ormond's regency, starting in 1661, had a political rationale, attempting to impress the population with its pomp and to plant firmly in its mind the notions of supremacy, worth and strength – aesthetics as an arm of Government. The Dublin theatre was part of this environment of pageantry. Restoration comedies were subversive of established authority, but the tragedies affirmed the aristocracy in their exalted ideas of their own worth. Just as in the work of Corneille and Racine, nobody except aristocrats appeared in the Heroic Tragedies. In the ten years after the Restoration this affirmation was needed, but by 1670 the English aristocracy had nestled snugly into their old positions of authority, and comedy began to sprout tentatively. The relative insecurity and instability of the Irish situation caused the prolongation of the Heroic Tragedy and a corresponding suppression of comedy. The Irish theatre was not driven by playwrights but by the patronage of the Castle and the inclinations of its aristocratic audience. Farquhar, Southerne and Congreve went to London with their comedies, not just because the rewards were greater, but because new comedy was not wanted in Dublin. Shakespeare, Beaumont and the like were allowed – they were safe – but subversive comedy was not encouraged. Farquhar alludes to this in *Love and a Bottle*:

> LUCINDA   But why no Poets in *Ireland*, Sir!
> ROEBUCK   Faith, Madam, I know not, unless Saint Patrick sent them a packing with other venomous Creatures out of *Ireland*. Nothing that carries a Sting in its Tongue can live there.[7]

Love and a Bottle was not a play that was likely to succeed in Dublin in 1699. The conservative, puritan tendency of the Irish gentry left them, paradoxically, ahead of the times: the neo-puritanism demanded by the rising mercantile classes in England, and articulated by Jeremy Collier in his pamphlet *A Short View of the Immorality and Profaneness of the English Stage* (1698), was exactly what had always been demanded and delivered to the theatre of the Anglo-Irish nobility. Farquhar's first play was not one to satisfy such an audience: it looked back to the indecent comedies so popular in London after 1670. It was this certainty of rejection, as well as the possibility of a greater audience and profit, that drove Farquhar to London with it. Nor was it very popular in London; the day for such a play was over, and Farquhar quickly realized that, changed his material to suit his audience and soon achieved a brilliant success.

Charles II was restored to the throne of England in May 1660, and almost immediately he gave orders to re-open the theatres. William Davenant and Thomas Killigrew were mounting productions by November of that year. Davenant, in a fast move that shows the importance of Dublin as the second city of the three kingdoms, obtained permission on the 26 November 1660 to open one theatre in Dublin, and at the same time got himself appointed Master of the Revels for Ireland, thereby reifying the position that Wentworth had unofficially created for Ogilby in 1638. The warrant that granted the patent to Davenant rejected the Puritan attitude to the theatre and insisted on its harmlessness and usefulness. It authorized 'such public presentations of tragedies and comedies for the harmless recreation and *divertisement* of our own subjects',[8] but then sounds a note of appeasement: 'with a strict injunction that all such tragedies and comedies shall be purged and freed from all obsceneness and profaneness and so become instructive to morality in our people'.[9]

Ogilby's theatre in Werburgh Street 'fell to utter ruin by the Calamities of those times' after its closure in 1641;[10] but Ogilby promptly appealed Davenant's warrant, on the grounds that he had been appointed Master of the Revels for Ireland by the Earl of Strafford and had expended 'great preparations and disbursements in building a new Theatre, stocking and bringing over a Company of Actors and Musicians and settling them in Dublin'.[11] Davenant's grant was revoked and the office of Master of the Revels in Ireland royally bestowed on Ogilby, to erect 'such Theatre or Theatres as to him shall seem most fit'.[12]

He built his theatre at Orange Street or Smoke Alley, which soon waggishly became known as 'Smock' (meaning 'chemise') Alley because of the secondary industry the playhouse generated.[13] This was the first purpose-built Restoration theatre in the three kingdoms, with sliding scenery, music gallery above the stage and, crucially, a proscenium arch. This was an innovation brought from the royal theatres of France, especially that of Richelieu at the Palais-Royal in Paris. The theatre in Smock Alley was paid for and owned by the nobility and gentry. Ogilby and Sir Thomas Stanley, the knight of Grangegorman – 'a Cambridge man who had translated *The Clouds of Aristophanes*'[14] – raised the money to build it by subscription, and even the bishops subscribed, according to Patrick Adair, a Presbyterian commentator, 'though they refused at the time to give countenance or assistance for building a church at Dame Street, where there was a great need'.[15]

The old theatre at Werburgh Street had had one box, for the vicere-gal party; the new one had a whole tier of boxes encircling the auditorium for the attending gentry, who could also sit in the pit on padded benches or, at a later date, on the stage. For discreet clergymen, or ladies who did not wish to sit openly in a box, nor trust in the disguise of a 'vizard mask', there were screened boxes, called 'lattices', built into the sides of the proscenium arch, available for hire when not needed for balcony scenes. In line with the improving and educational tone of the original warrant, two upper galleries were provided for seating the less well-off, although inflation over the period of the Commonwealth had caused the cheapest price of admission to rise from a penny to a shilling, making attendance quite expensive.

We may conclude from the seating arrangements that the nobility and gentry were attending in great numbers and anxious to make an impact with their private boxes, that the ladies were out in force and that the lower classes were catered for by the provision of two galleries but discouraged by the high price of admission. The upper galleries were mostly occupied by servants, footmen and students from Trinity College, and fights between the different factions were a regular occurrence. The Castle ascendancy still controlled the theatre, but they were sharing their playground with the lower classes for financial as well as social reasons.

So popular was the upper gallery that it collapsed due to overcrowding. On St Stephen's Day of 1670 it fell, bringing the lower gallery down with it, on top of the viceroy's box; four people were killed:

> His Excellency the Lord Lieutenant, with his Lady, happened to be there, but thanks be to God escaped the danger without any harm; part of the Box where they were remaining firm, and so resisting the fall of what was above; only his two Sons were found quite buried under the Timber; the younger had received but little hurt, but the eldest was taken up dead to all appearance, but having presently been let blood, and other remedies being timely applied to him, he is at present past all danger.[16]

There was great rejoicing among the Puritans at the fall of the gallery, and their joy was compounded by the fact that it had collapsed during the scene where a Puritan clergyman was being mocked and put in the stocks. 'Such providences', thundered Patrick Adair, 'so circumstantial in divers respects, will not pass without the observation of impartial and prudent persons, for surely they have a language if men would hear.'[17]

The three tiers of Dublin society are displayed here: the commoners crowding in to gaze from a distance at the glittering Ascendancy frolicking in their theatre, and the Puritans, their teeth now drawn, watching with intent disapproval from outside.

The balance of power had permanently shifted. The Old Irish were finished as a political or military force, and the Catholic Old English were terminally damaged; the future belonged to the New Protestant Ascendancy that consisted of the New English colonists and such of the Old English and native Irish who had converted. This new aristocracy was defined by its membership of the official Reformed Church, which was at that time the badge of a modern, enlightened attitude. Sir Audley Mervyn, the speaker of the new Irish Parliament, summoned in 1664, congratulated the members in his inaugural address on their success in finally turning the Irish Catholic wilderness into an English Protestant garden: 'I may warrantably say, since Ireland was happy under an English Government, there was never so choice a collection of Protestant fruit that ever grew within the walls of the Commons House.'[18]

The people who attended the Parliament dominated the Theatre; their social and political life merged seamlessly, and it is no surprise to find their political concerns expressed on the Dublin stage. The tradition of political theatre in Dublin, promulgated by Mountjoy, Shirley and Burnell, continued unabated at the new theatre in Smock Alley. The Dublin theatre was not just a place of entertainment, but a stage on which the consciousness of the English colonists in Ireland was created and debated. The opening of a theatre was in itself a political declaration of support for the Royalist cause, and the warrant allowed the theatre to be styled 'Royal'. John Dunton, in his letter from Dublin, observed: 'The theatre is applauded by a modern gentleman for the representation of those things which so mightily promote virtue, religion, and monarchical government.'[19] The segregation by boxes overturned the egalitarianism of the Commonwealth and re-instituted the manifest superiority of aristocracy, while the use of a proscenium arch expressed architecturally its links to the Royal Theatres of France, and the Whitehall masques designed by Inigo Jones. However, in spite of the extended seating for the lower classes, and their increasing attendance, the absence of a solid audience of middle-class citizens left the Smock Alley Theatre in the grip of the Castle set.

This was made manifest in the production of *Pompey* in February 1663. This translation of Corneille's *La Mort de Pompeé* was by Katherine Philips, who had arrived in Ireland after the Restoration trailing a reputation as a poet and ardent Royalist. Mrs Philips introduced to the viceregal court the 'Society of Friendship', a sort of game or cult, which drew for its inspiration on the Platonic craze that had spread from Paris and infected the court of Charles I. It had, by this time, died off in both those places but Katherine Philips introduced the Society to Dublin, where it was all the rage for a while. Many of the Castle courtiers were already familiar with it from their time in exile, and it fitted perfectly into their artistic preference for the ideal rather than the real, which also informed their taste for Heroic Tragedy.

The members of the Society wrote to and addressed each other by assumed classical names drawn from the French Romantic novels of the mid-seventeenth century, and aimed at developing and maintaining an intense but purely spiritual relationship between its members. Katherine Philips herself was always referred to as 'the matchless Orinda', Sir Edward Dering as 'the noble Silvander', Lady Dungannon as 'the excellent Lucasia', and so on. One of those to come under the influence of the Society of Friendship was Roger Boyle, Baron Broghill and later first Earl of Orrery. While he and his brother had been attending the University of Paris, his brother had written to their father, the Earl of Cork, denying the charge of time-wasting: 'As concerning my reading of Romances and Playbooks, I never (thanks be to God) have been much inclined unto them before your Lordships commands to ye contrary.'[20] Orrery was definitely 'inclined unto them': he produced a huge Romantic novel himself, *Parthenissa*, in six volumes, first published at Waterford in 1654, which had a remarkable success, perhaps as a novelty; such things were rare in English.[21]

The plays of Corneille, which also exhibited to a lesser degree the Platonic influence, were popular in London. Their insistence on noble idealism, the exalted virtue of their heroes and heroines, and the excellence of the self-conscious aristocratic code in meeting every challenge and overcoming every obstacle, was designed to evoke peer approbation and create an example for posterity. All the restored aristocrats, from the king down, wanted to see this fashionable theatre of the French court transposed into English.

Katherine Philips' Society of Friendship was a further development of the cult of affectation and the ideal world of the French plays. It was also an attempt to civilize the goatish men of the Restoration, as the women and troubadours had tried to do in medieval Provence – to create an ideal mannered world of civilized social intercourse and discourse which was mapped out in the mental rather than sensual faculties, a space in which men and women could socialize without the constant interference of sexual impulses.

Orinda's asexual Platonics dovetailed perfectly into the world of the Heroic Tragedies; they both create an artistic space where ideas and emotions could move and mingle independently of any physical expression, any 'carnal fruition'.[22] Friendship was seen as the purest relationship; all the virtues were subservient to it, and pressed into its service. Orrery wrote in *The Generall*: 'Know Friendship is a greater tie than blood.'[23] Since love was removed from sex, the object of the emotion could be of any gender. Verbal expression did not entail any physical involvement. Argument became the meeting ground of civilized human beings, and verbal actions – the duel of wit and teasing out of moral conundrums – replaced plot.

The Smock Alley production of *Pompey* grew in the making. Katherine Philips had already started work when Orrery got to hear of it. She wrote in a letter of August 1662: 'By some Accident or another, my Scene of *Pompey* fell into his Hands, and he was so pleas'd to like it so well, that he sent me the *French* Original.'[24] From this we may conclude that she had been writing her own play of that name, perhaps based on Corneille, but Orrery prevailed on her to translate the original. Orrery had already finished his first play, *The Generall* – also called *Altemera* – by the command of the king, if Orrery's account is to be believed. Morrice, who was Orrery's chaplain and biographer, recounts a discussion between Charles and his courtiers as to whether the French fashion of rhymed couplets would work in English, and Orrery being decidedly of the opinion that it would. 'And his majesty being willing a trial should be made, commanded his lordship to employ some of his leisure that way, which my lord readily did.'[25] At the beginning of 1661 Orrery had completed *The Generall* and had sent it for approval both to the king and the new lord lieutenant, the Duke of Ormond, but it had not been published or produced.

Orrery was following Mountjoy and Wentworth in using the drama to attract attention to himself in Whitehall and to curry favour with the king. He was greatly in favour of Orinda also producing a translation from the French, 'in ten feet of verse and rhyme',[26] and his interest and enthusiasm for the project turned it into something of an Ascendancy circus. He personally donated £100 for the elaborate costumes, a huge sum that transformed the occasion into a gala event. The Society of Friendship became involved: the Earl of Roscommon wrote a Prologue, Sir Edward Dering an Epilogue; the dances were choreographed by Ogilby himself, including a military dance for stage-struck soldiers; Mrs Philips added masques and musical intervals to the play at several points. Some of the gentlemen and ladies may also have appeared in these: they were much given to appearing in private theatricals and masques. Queen Anne used to appear drunk, in a short skirt, in masques at court, and Orrery's wife, Margaret Howard, had 'played an important role in the last Caroline masque at Whitehall, Davenant's *Salmacida Spolia*'.[27] The Smock Alley *Pompey* had taken on the colouring of a parish concert: if 'Orinda' Philips herself appeared on the stage that afternoon, there is a good chance she persuaded some of her followers and friends to accompany her.[28]

The production had drifted a long way from the austerity of Corneille, but the translation itself is still full of interest. It is easy to see why it appealed to Orrery, a notorious apostate himself, with its dissection of divided loyalty, its consideration of how a soldier can behave honourably in the event of a split at the very summit of the command structure. Orrery's official account of his treachery was that he had been apprehended by Cromwell in London while on his way to visit Charles II in France and given the choice of spending the rest of his life in the Tower of London or serving Parliament by commanding its army in Ireland. He had injudiciously chosen the latter course, and the play gives form to the view that a subordinate can never know which is the right way to jump until after the event, and when the dust has settled success justifies and failure condemns his actions.

At the end of the play, in one of the departures from Corneille's original, Mrs Philips inserted a masque in which the Egyptian priests summarized the lessons of the play for the contemporary audience:

> Then after all the Blood that's shed,
> Let's right the living and the dead:
>   Temples to Pompey raise;
> Set Cleopatra on the Throne;
>   Let Caesar keep the World h'has won;
> And sing Cornelia's praise.[29]

In Corneille's play, this final speech is given by the victorious Julius Caesar, not by a normalizing chorus, and it is he who majestically closes the action by raising Cleopatra to the throne and deifying Pompey.[30] He imposes his will on the survivors and on the dead. There is no question of anyone allowing him to keep 'the world h'has won'; he holds it by right of victory. In Philips' version, the use of a chorus articulated a communal voice, and it was not the voice of the winners. It acknowledged the undoubted victory of Caesar, but also evoked the possibility of dissension by advising against it. This is no part of Corneille's text, but an addition by Philips in order to appeal to her immediate audience. The burden of this chorus is a loser's apologia: let's forget the old quarrels, they sing, and humanely implement the new arrangements – a message that was intensely relevant and political in 1662 Dublin, a garrison town full of equivocally loyal soldiers. It was the position that Orrery himself articulated in *The Generall*: 'For nought is virtue which success does want.'[31]

Of the aristocratic audience watching *Pompey* on its opening night, the Duke of Ormond and the Earl of Orrery stood at two opposing poles. Ormond, the newly re-appointed lord lieutenant, was the leading member of the Old English aristocracy, whose pedigree and roots in the country stretched back to the middle ages. He was an instinctive royalist who had behaved honourably throughout the traumatic years of Civil War and Commonwealth. He had commanded the Royalist forces in Ireland and, after their defeat, had gone, at colossal expense to himself, into exile in France with Charles II. His loyalty to the Stuarts was never shaken or questioned. Orrery's title, in contrast, had been bought for him by his father, the newly created Earl of Cork. Orrery stood at the opposite end of the Irish aristocracy from Ormond on the great question of loyalty. For Ormond it was absolute; for Orrery, conditional. Orrery had changed sides when Parliament had gained the upper hand and had become one of its leading supporters, a member of its Cabinet Council, and a friend of Oliver Cromwell, until he switched back again in order to ingratiate himself with the restored regime. To Orrery, expediency and personal advancement, hidden under the cloak of patriotism, were the extent of his ethical system. The proposition to forget the past and accept present loyalties at face value, which 'Orinda' Philips invoked, was also needed by Orrery if he was to put his indiscretions behind him and achieve success in the new order. The subtext of the additions which Philips added to Corneille contradicted the main theme of the play, asserting that politics cannot be conducted along Corneillean lines. Honour, it maintained, must yield to pragmatism in the real political world. This is a variation that vanished completely in the development of the Heroic Tragedy. At this early stage, though, the Heroic Drama still had some slight grip on reality, and the theme of the necessity of obliterating the past in order to manage the present was one that Orrery also addressed in his first play, *The Generall*, the first original Heroic Drama in English to find its way on to the stage.

Orrery invented the genre of the English Heroic Tragedy with this play. Its main theme was the irreconcilable demands of Love and Honour, but more interesting is the fact that Orrery set this and his other plays against a background of constant war. This enabled him to consider more political matters, and this extra dimension was accepted in his own time as an important part of his work. John Crowne, a contemporary and admirer of his, saluted 'the soldier and statesman in you [...] that of your poetry is so large a theme'.[32] In *The Generall* this military backdrop gave Orrery space to lament the loss of the clarity and cleansing effect that action brings, to bemoan the quagmire of political choice, to expose and examine the quandaries and compromises that a political soldier is faced with and also to plead to the betrayed monarch and his viceroy for understanding and forgiveness.

Orrery had argued, during the Commonwealth, that Cromwell should be crowned king; he set out his argument in a pamphlet published opportunely, just in time for the Restoration in 1660: *Monarchy asserted to be the best, most ancient and legal form of government, in a conference held at Whitehall with Oliver Lord Cromwell and a Committee of Parliament.*[33] But this argument was not bolstered by any loyalty to a particular king. After encouraging Cromwell to crown himself, he then turned around and in *The Generall* damned the usurper and exalted the rightful monarch:

THRASOLIN: That man who rules us now
                Is both a tyrant and usurper too.
                For when Evandor with the fight did fall
                That monster was the Army's Generall.[34]
MELIZER: His guilty sword I slight.
                A tyrant never a true king could fight.[35]
THRASOLIN: A true king's virtue does dispense such light
                That 'twas too glittering for a Tyrant's sight.[36]

He was perfectly prepared to befriend Cromwell at the time and damn him afterwards. He exalted friendship as the highest virtue in his plays and in his correspondence, but ruthlessly pursued his own interests behind his supposed friends' backs. He protested the enormity of his regard for Ormond while at the same time plotting against him, until Ormond remarked ironically: 'He will conclude with deep protestations of sincerity and friendship, wherein my confidence is somewhat abated.'[37]

Orrery sent *The Generall* to Charles II, who passed it on to Killigrew, the manager of The King's Men in London, who, although he was Orrery's brother-in-law, did nothing about it for three years. Orrery also sent it to Ormond, the incoming lord lieutenant, with a covering letter claiming distinction as a royal favourite, and implying that the play should be treated, therefore, as a document of importance. It was typical of Orrery's pushiness and lack of background that he thought Ormond might be impressed by his access to the king. The play itself directly addresses the issue of allegiance by the General, Clorimun, to a nameless usurper, and the proper attitude the restored rightful monarch should take to those who had betrayed him by reneging on their sworn loyalty. Orrery argues that expediency and the necessity of saving the country from the rebels had to take precedence over a principled withdrawal from public affairs:

THRASOLIN: Then your assistance bring
              And save your sinking Country and your King.
CLORIMUN: He's an usurper whom for King you own.
THRASOLIN: I call him king because he fills the Throne
[...]

              But if for him you will not undertake
              this war, yet do it for your country's sake.

> Your sinking country which on you does call,
> Who we are certain can prevent our fall. [38]

Orrery was the most notable of the Irish turncoats, but he was not the only one. He spoke for a large section of the New English Ascendancy when he advised leniency and amnesia, and dramatically pledged their allegiance to the restored rightful king:

> Since in a Tyrant's cause we prospered so,
> In a true King's our swords should wonders do.
> On the wrong side we know how we can fight.
> Let's prove now we can do it on the right. [39]

And Melizer, the restored rightful king, in Orrery's wishful scenario, forgives his erring subjects for their treason, without even being asked:

> MELIZER: You that such news have brought
> Deserve a pardon sure for any fault.
> My mercies still shall be to those more great
> Which to it trust, and for it do not treat.
> Past faults I'll never to remembrance bring,
> For which the word I give you of your king. [40]

Orrery expected that he and the others in his position would be forgiven without the humiliation of having to beg for it, because of the services they had rendered in bringing about the Restoration. He had miscalculated in throwing in his lot with Cromwell and Parliament; he never expected the Stuarts to return. He knew now that he had jumped too soon, pursuing his own advantage. Charles II, Ormond and the other loyal Royalists knew it too. Orrery spent the rest of his life paying for this mistake: they were willing to make use of him, just as the Cromwellians did, but they never trusted him. Orrery was quite open in the play about his position and his apologia. *The Generall* justifies his apostasy during the Civil War, claiming that he had saved the kingdom of Ireland for the king by his disloyal actions. At the same time it displays an undercurrent of resentment against an ungrateful monarch, who did not honour his obligations and recognize the General's worth, after what he had done for him, and who passed over him for preferment, just as Charles had by appointing Ormond over Orrery:

> CLORIMUN: He's an ungrateful man, and well you know
> [...]

THRASOLIN   Denying you your due,
         He wrong'd himself more than he injured you.[41]

Orrery did not attend Ormond's triumphal return to Dublin as lord lieutenant. He had been relieved of his lord justiceship, returned to Munster, and there been detained by a politic fit of the gout.

He was so anxious to get his point of view into public discourse that, in response to Killigrew's tardiness, he organized a private production of *The Generall* at his home at Thomas Court in Dublin on 18 October 1662 for 'the Lord Lieutenant and most of the persons of Honour in these parts'.[42] In February of the following year he disseminated his ideas to a wider audience by a public performance at Smock Alley, two weeks after *Pompey* had spelled out the same message.[43] And finally he had the play produced at the Theatre Royal in London in September 1664, under its alternative title, *Altemera*.[44]

His objective was to impress his aristocratic audience, not to create a work of art. He wanted to be admired and in the public eye, especially the king's. His other dramas continued to mine the vein, introduced in *The Generall*, of Love versus Honour, until his audience became very tired of it, and of the Heroic Tragedy in general, with its interminable debates and lack of action. Pepys remarked in his diary on the opening of Orrery's fifth tragedy, *Tryphon*, on 8 December 1668: 'For the very same design, and words, and sense and plot, as any one of his plays have, anyone of which alone would be held admirable, whereas so many of the same design and fancy do but dull one another.'[45]

Pompey and *The Generall* show the importance of the role the theatre played in the formation of Anglo-Ascendancy consciousness and attitudes, and its contribution to public debate in post-Restoration Ireland. The Duke of Ormond's contribution to the development of the Irish theatre was in a different area. His efforts were bent on infusing the theatre with the pageantry of the court to create a public and dramatic spectacle; to him, the theatre was a branch of government and an instrument of policy.

James Butler, the first Duke of Ormond, re-invested as lord lieutenant of Ireland in 1661, was the grandest of the Irish *grands seigneurs* and remained, whether in or out of office, the most influential Irishman of his day until his death in 1688. He was by nature conservative and clung to the older ideas of aristocratic privilege, ideals and responsibilities. His objective was to build up the splendour and nobility of the Irish viceregal court; he disliked London and was appalled by the licence of the Restoration era.[46] His own life was heroic and selflessly dedicated to the royal cause; his single-minded espousal of the Stuarts cost him about a million pounds, in seventeenth-century money.[47] His conduct and character were exemplary. His loyalty and sense of duty were unwavering even in the face of Charles' capitulation to Buckingham's Cabal and Orrery's intrigue to have him removed from the position of lord lieutenant in 1669. In 1675, Charles re-appointed him with the words: 'I have done all I can to disoblige that man, and to make him as discontented as others; but he will not be out of humour with me; he will be loyal in spite of my teeth; I must even take him in again, and he is the fittest person to govern Ireland.'[48]

Ormond insisted on the importance of monumental grandeur, and conducted his court with regal pomp and theatrical splendour. His entries and exits from Dublin Castle were filled with drums and fanfares, flags and the firing of great guns. The Calendar of State Papers for Ireland shows how carefully his first entry to Dublin after his re-appointment was choreographed. Different scenarios were planned depending on which side of the river he disembarked; the order of precedence, the nature and armaments of the troops, the drawing up of the regiments in the Castle Yard, the choice, number and timing of the ordnance to be fired, were all carefully laid out in advance, as well as who could approach his exalted personage on that day, and who was to be kept away from Dublin Castle.[49] Dunton wrote of the daily Dublin Castle ceremonies: 'Whenever the government go out or come in they are received with colours flying and drums beating as the King is at Whitehall, and indeed the grandeur they live in here is not much inferior to what you see in London.'[50]

Ormond fully appreciated the power of pageantry in bolstering the royal authority in Ireland, and he treated the theatre as part of that pageantry. He was aware that 'it was necessary not only to reconstruct, but also to reimagine Ireland. One of the ways in which this expressed itself was in the development of state ritual.'[51]

He saw the country organically and holistically: he believed his role was to bring all sectors of the population into harmony with each other and into their proper and traditional allegiance to the Crown. This goal was complicated, however, by the absence from the country of the king, so Ormond had to burnish his own persona and his court to mimic as closely as possible the royal court and to dazzle with as much reflected brilliance as possible. As a protégée of Thomas Wentworth, Earl of Strafford, Ormond was acutely aware of the importance of image in politics and in him we meet one of the most persistent Anglo-Irish themes in its full-blown form: that of the Ascendancy as a performance. Judging it necessary, with the king elsewhere, to create and maintain a regal role, he expended great efforts, in the pomp of his court, his development of the cityscape and his patronage of the theatre, to forge the bond between the people and their king, with the lord lieutenant as the crucial link – the visible manifestation of the royal authority, the image of the absent king.

Like Wentworth and Mountjoy before him, Ormond arrogated the theatre as part of his own magnificence, and allowed it to shine with some of his prestige. So embedded had the theatre become in the political display that Robert Ware wrote in 1678, towards the close of Ormond's reign, that the authorities had foolishly allowed the public pomp of government to diminish and would need to compensate by further boosting the occasional pageantry of the theatre:

> The Mayor and Aldermen ought to compensate so great a neglect of duty by resorting on [holy] days and festivals to the *King's Theatre* in their own Persons, and the causing a general resort of Freemen on these times to that place, besides an allowance to every of their Apprentices of twelve pence a piece to recreate themselves at these times at the *Theatre*, in lieu of these sports this City was bound to entertain them with.[52]

Ormond's influence as a patron of the theatre at Smock Alley was enormous. It sheltered under his prestige; his regular attendance, and that of his family, drew a fashionable crowd, but his influence extended beyond that. He tended to regard the Smock Alley players as his own company, just as Charles II did with The King's Company in London. Ormond took the opportunity of bringing the Dublin company over to Oxford for a successful season, while he was chancellor of the university in 1677 – The King's Company was barred for breaking windows the previous year. He also sent them to Edinburgh in 1681 to present plays at Holyrood Castle before the future James II and Queen Anne. When Ormond went to Kilkenny each summer, the players followed.[53]

The playwright John Dancer held a position in the household of Ormond's son, the Earl of Ossory, and was, therefore, under the patronage of the lord lieutenant. When Ormond was removed from the lord-lieutenancy in 1669 by the factions and intrigues around Charles II, he returned to Dublin to a reception more tumultuous than that given to his incoming replacement as viceroy. He may have been out of favour at Whitehall, but he continued to exercise influence in Ireland as first peer of the realm. He also continued his interest and patronage of the theatre. Ormond's successor, Lord John Roberts, was of a puritan outlook, and on his appointment in 1669 he closed down Smock Alley Theatre. 'He stopped the public players, as well as other vicious persons,' as Gilbert puts it.[54] In 1670, when Roberts was recalled and the theatre re-opened, Dancer translated and presented Corneille's *Nicomede*, a dangerously political play, at Smock Alley.[55] *Nicomede* had been premiered at Paris nineteen years previously, and the audience had seen parallels between it and the current situation in the country – the imprisonment and eventual release of the Prince de Condé, the most prominent exponent of the consciously Heroic style of the '*noblesse d'epeé*' in the teeth of Mazarin's drive to centralize all political authority. The character of Nicomede was seen to echo Condé, in his virtue, *générosité,* and ability to understand and forgive his imprisonment.

In the Dublin of 1670 the political implications in the play were equally apparent. The noble, virtuous Ormond had been deposed by the intriguing of a wretched Cabal led by Buckingham and Orrery, who 'buzz it in your father's ears', as the play says of their constant rumour-mongering to the king.[56] He was still loved by the people, who were outraged at his treatment, but he had steadfastly refused to complain or manoeuvre against his enemies in return:

> They may perhaps ensnare
> Themselves, in those traps they for us prepare.
> The People love you, and abhor their Arts,
> And he Reigns safest who does Reign o'er Hearts.[57]

He trusted to the king for justice, but was disappointed: 'I know he'll to the King for Justice call, but from that Justice he shall find his Fall,' sneers his main opponent.[58] Throughout, Nicomede retains his equilibrium, shows himself a man of virtue and nobility, and 'against such virtue there is no defence'.[59] Nicomede eventually triumphs over his enemies and reconciles them to himself and to each other:

> You should believe him worthy of my Faith,
> I should disown him had he not a mind
> Revenge can't animate nor passion blind,
> Did not in him all that is generous dwell.[60]

So far all is fairly innocuous but, in dealing with the treatment of Nicomede by the king, Dancer, like Corneille before him, was on dangerous ground. The play contains too much that can be construed as criticism of Charles' actions, and too accurate an evaluation of his weakness for yielding to whomever could apply the most pressure. It could also be seen as an uncomfortably accurate assessment of the standing of Ormond in Ireland: the king in the play complains: 'for you're indeed king here, I'm but the shadow'[61] – an interesting reversal of the 'reflection' image usually invoked to describe the viceroy's position. The argument given by Dancer against powerful subordinates was perhaps, not entirely to the taste of the Butlers:

> That Subject must be false who's grown too high,
> Although he never thought a Treachery.
> Power, Sir, in Subjects is a Crime of State,
> Which prudent Princes, ere it be too late,
> By wisely clipping of their Wings, prevent
> From meriting severer Punishment.[62]

But this argument is more than balanced in the play by the repeated declaration of Nicomede's *vertu,* and *générosité*:

> Prince Nicomede's thoughts are all so just,
> 'Twere injury to virtue to mistrust.[63]
> I fear that virtue which to Rome he owes
> Has taught him, there's no Glory so sublime,
> Can recompense the hazard of a Crime.[64]

The play was published in London in 1671, not in Dublin as one would expect, and it lacked any dedication by Dancer. The short Preface was inserted by the printer, 'in the absence of the author', and directed at Ormond's son, the Earl of Ossory.[65] So it would seem that, while Dancer balanced the arguments for and against the cutting down of great men to prevent them falling on the State, such frankness was seen as a little too pushy. The simultaneity of Ormond's temporary fall and the play appearing at Dublin is too close to be accidental, but Ormond is nowhere associated with the published play, except in the half-hearted effort of the printer, who plainly felt that this play should be of interest to the Butlers. Ormond, however, did not choose to be tied to the sentiments or charges which the play expresses, whether in his favour or not. Even while in disfavour with the king for six years, his loyalty and constancy did not waver.

The spectacular aspect of the theatre was significant, but the political was crucial, and its reach was greatly enhanced by the publication of the texts of plays. There are plays that survive only in manuscript or even by report. Those which were printed were considered important enough in the context of public debate and education to be given to a wider audience: *Pompey* was hurried into print, for example, as was *Landgartha*. They took their place alongside pamphlets, tracts and broadsides in informing and shaping public opinion. Some plays were not written for production at all, but directly for publication. At this time Irish culture was in transition from oral to written culture, evidenced by the fact that many of the polemic pamphlets are couched in dialogue form.[64]

There is also a genre of military memoirs cast in dramatic form dating from this period. Some of these, such as *A Royal Voyage,* or *The Royal Visit,* are mere propaganda. Others are efforts at using drama to bring a personal narrative to the public notice. The best examples of this are John Michelburne's and Henry Burkhead's plays. Burkhead used the interval of peace in 1644 to publish his play *Cola's Furie; or, Lirenda's Miserie*, a savage attack on the activities of Sir Charles Coote during the war, and a defence of the Irish Confederate position. The play was never acted[67] but was written primarily to be circulated and discussed. Michelburne's *Ireland Preserved,* a two-part work consisting of *The Troubles of the North* and *The Siege of Derry*, appeared in 1692,[68] and is a good illustration of the power of play-publishing. Michelburne was the commander at the Siege of Derry, but fell on hard times afterwards, due, he thought, to inadequate appreciation of the importance and worth of his leadership. He first published his apologia as a prose pamphlet to draw attention to the injustice he felt had been done to him, but it was not until he cast his memoirs into dramatic form that he made any impact. He makes himself the hero of the plays, and claims a decisive role in the siege and in the overall victory of William of Orange. This play was never meant for production, but for private publication and circulation. It is a document on the lines of Caesar's *Gallic Wars*, part propaganda, part news, part political tract and part local colour. It is full of maps and detailed descriptions of military actions, meant to be appreciated by other veterans and by influential members of the ruling elite. Michelburne probably wrote it to attract attention to his plight while in prison for debt but, once in dramatic form, his justification lasted for centuries. The play had a very long life, being used as a school textbook in Ulster right up to the early twentieth century, and as a venerable playscript (published regularly in one volume with Ashton's *The Battle of Aughrim*) for Protestant children to re-enact the glories of their ancestors in preserving their freedom, religion and laws.

The publication and circulation of plays, which had become popular while the theatres were closed during the period of Puritan rule, was an important factor in the formation of public opinion among the

English of Ireland; the coffee houses of Dublin were known as places where publications were read and debated. Plays formed a crucial segment of the business of publication in the days before the rise of the novel. The Earl of Cork warned his sons off reading playbooks; Polly Peachum's father, in *The Beggar's Opera*, believes his daughter's head has been turned by reading their romantic nonsense; John Ogilby eagerly snatched the play she was reading from 'Orinda' Philips and, in William Philips' *St Stephen's Green*, Bellmine recommends himself to the young ladies by claiming to have the latest from London: 'New Fashions, New Tunes, and New Plays'.[69] The Duke of Ormond had in his library in 1685, in addition to the works of Shakespeare and Jonson, forty-two volumes of plays. By 1715, the library had grown to sixty-one such volumes, and seven of those listed in 1685 had been lent or given away, to circulate and spread their ideas among the Irish Ascendancy.[70]

NOTES

1. William Wycherley, *The Country Wife*, ed. by Thomas H. Fujimura (London: Edward Arnold, 1965), I. 1. 148.
2. *The Calendar of State Papers for Ireland, 1666–1669*, ed. by R.P. Mahaffy (HM Stationery Office, 1905), p. 762.
3. Clark, *The Early Irish Stage*, p. 65.
4. W.S. Clark, 'Preface', in *Dramatic Works of Roger Boyle, Earl of Orrery*, ed. by William Smith Clark II (Cambridge Mass.: Harvard University Press, 1937), p. xi.
5. As cited by Stockwell, *Dublin Theatres and Customs*, p. 33.
6. Clark, *Early Irish Stage*, Appendix C, pp. 204–206.
7. George Farquhar, *Love and a Bottle*, in *The Complete Works of George Farquhar*, ed. by Charles Stonehill (New York: Gordian Press, 1967), I. 1, p. 14.
8. 'Manual Warrant to the Lords Justices', 26, Nov. 1660, in *Calendar of the State Papers for Ireland, 1660–1662*, ed. by R. P. Mahaffy (HM Stationery Office, 1905), p. 99.
9. *Ibid.*, p. 99.
10. 'Petition by John Ogilby for the grant of Office', Stockwell, *Dublin Theatres and Customs*, p. 23.
11. *Ibid.*, p. 23.
12. 'Warrant for the issue to John Ogilby of a patent to the Office', *Signet Docquet Books*, Index 6813 (London: Public Record Office, March 1660/1), p. 4; in Clark, *Early Irish Stage*, Appendix A, p. 180.
13. John Dunton, letter no. 6 from Dublin: 'Stands in a dirty street called Smock Alley, which I think is no unfit name for a place where such great opportunities are given for making smock bargains'; in Edward McLysaght, *Irish Life in the Seventeenth Century* (Cork: University Press, 1939; reprinted Shannon: Irish University Press, 1969), p. 384.
14. S.C. Hughes, *The Pre-Victorian Drama in Dublin* (Dublin: Hodges Figgis, 1904), p. 3.
15. Richard Bagwell, *Ireland under the Stuarts and during the Interregnum*, 3 vols (London: The Holland Press, 1909–1916; reprinted 1963), I, p. 104.
16. Clark, *Early Irish Stage*, p. 70. Lord Berkeley was viceroy at the time.
17. Bagwell, *Ireland under the Stuarts*, p. 104.
18. Gilbert, *History of Dublin*, III, p. 60.
19. McLysaght, *Irish Life in the Seventeenth Century*, p. 384.
20. Lismore Papers, 2nd ser. III, 278; Clark, 'Historical Preface', in *Dramatic Works of Roger Boyle*, p. 7.

21. The tiresome length of *Parthenissa* is caustically commented on by the *Dictionary of National Biography*, II, p. 1033: 'The writer of the notice of Orrery in *Biographia Britannica* attributes the neglect of the romance to its remaining unfinished, but finished it certainly was, and if it had not been, its tediousness would not have been relieved by adding to its length.'
22. Clark, Introduction to *The Dramatic Works of Roger Boyle, Earl of Orrery*, p. 12.
23. Orrery, *The Generall*, I. 3. 297, in *Dramatic Works of Roger Boyle*.
24. Morash, *History of the Irish Theatre*, p. 23.
25. Clark, 'Historical Preface', in *Dramatic Works of Roger Boyle*, p. 23.
26. Orrery to Ormond, in *CSPI*, 1660–1662; Morash, p. 14.
27. Clark, *Dramatic Works of Roger Boyle*, p. 10.
28. Chetwood tells us that the first performance after the Treaty of Limerick, 1691, when the theatre had been closed for three years, was a free performance of *Othello*, in which the minor male roles were taken by officers from the Castle, and that the young people of the Dublin *beau monde* presented a comedy in the Bishop's Palace near St Patrick's Cathedral; Clark, *Early Irish Stage*, p. 99.
29. Morash, *History of the Irish Theatre*, p. 29.
30. Corneille, *Pompeé*, ed. by Pierre Lièvre, Théâtre Complet, 2 vols (Paris: Bibliothèque NRF de les Pléiade, 1950), I, p. 1054:
    Couranne Cléopâtre et m'apaise Pompeé,
    Élève a l'une un trône, a l'autre des autels,
    Et jure a tous les deux des respects immortels.
31. Orrery, *The Generall*, I. 1. 179, in *Dramatic Works of Roger Boyle*.
32. John Crowne, Preface to his play *Juliana*; in *Dramatic Works of Roger Boyle*, p. 46.
33. DNB, II, p. 1033.
34. Orrery, *The Generall*, I. 1. 34, in *Dramatic Works of Roger Boyle*.
35. *Ibid.*, IV. 6. 462.
36. *Ibid.*, IV. 6. 481.
37. Clark, *Dramatic Works of Roger Boyle*, p. 45.
38. Orrery, *The Generall*, IV. 2. 330, in *Dramatic Works of Roger Boyle*.
39. *Ibid.*, IV. 2. 92.
40. *Ibid.*, V. 1. 407.
41. Orrery, *The Generall*, IV. 2. 334, in *Dramatic Works of Roger Boyle*.
42. Clark, *Early Irish Stage*, p. 58.
43. Morash, *History of the Irish Theatre*, p. 14.
44. Clark, *Early Irish Stage*, p. 59.
45. Samuel Pepys, *The Diary of Samuel Pepys*, ed. by Robert Latham and William Matthews, 11 vols (London: Bell & Hyman, 1976) III, 1668–9, p. 389.
46. *DNB*, II, p. 510.
47. *Ibid.*, II. p. 510.
48. DNB, II, p. 511.
49. *CSPI*: 1660-62, p. 563.
50. John Dunton, letter no. 6; in McLysaght, *Irish Life in Seventeenth Century*, p. 386.
51. Raymond Gillespie, 'Political Ideas and their Social Contexts', in *Political Thought in Seventeenth-Century Ireland – Kingdom or Colony?* ed. by Jane H. Ohlmeyer (Cambridge: University Press, 2000) p. 123.
52. MS. De Rebus Eblanae, 74, f. 175, in Clark, *Early Irish Stage*, p. 83.
53. 'Since his grace the duke of Ormond went to Kilkenny the players with all their appurtenances strolled thither, to entertain the company there as they gave out, though everyone knows where the carrion is the crows will follow, for Dublin was then without much of the people that are usually in it, many of them in the summer retiring into the country.' Dunton, letter no. 6, McLysaght, *Irish Life in the Seventeenth Century*, p. 385.
54. Gilbert, *History of Dublin*, II, p. 68.
55. Title page, *Nicomede*, A Tragi-Comedy, translated out of the French of Monsieur Corneille, by *John Dancer*. As it was Acted at the Theatre-Royal, Dublin...Licensed Dec. 16. 1670. Early English Books Online: http://wwwlib.umi.com/eebo/ [3/11/2003]
56. *Nicomede*, I. 1. p. 3.
57. LAODICE, *Nicomede*, I. 2. p. 4.
58. *Nicomede*, I. 5. p. 11.
59. ARSINOE, *Nicomede*, V. Last, p. 55.

60. LAODICE, *Nicomede*, V. 7, p. 54.
61. PRUISIAS, *Nicomede*, II. 2, p. 16.
62. ARASPES, *Nicomede*, II. 2, p. 14.
63. ARASPES, *Nicomede*, II. 1, p. 12.
64. ARSINOE, *Nicomede*, I. 5, p. 10.
65. Title page, *Nicomede*, 'printed for Francis Kirkman, and [...] to be sold at his Shop in *Thames-Street*, over against the *Custom-House*, 1671.'
66. Gillespie, 'Political Ideas and their Social Contexts', p. 112.
67. La Tourette Stockwell, '*Lirenda's Miserie*', in *Dublin Magazine* (July–Sept. 1930), 19–26 (p. 20).
68. Published under this title in 1705, but appeared anonymously under the title *Piety and Valour; or, Derry Defended in 1692*.
69. William Philips, *St Stephen's Green; or, The Generous Lovers*, ed. Christopher Murray (Dublin: The Cadenus Press, 1979), I. 1. 75.
70. Gillespie, 'Political Ideas and their Social Contexts', p. 118.

3

The Generous and the Mercenary; or, the Qualities of the Quality

‘Many of those in the ascendant in early eighteenth-century Ireland had risen suddenly to that position. The new landed aristocracy, according to McLysaght, 'as a result of the territorial upheaval following the advent of Cromwell, consisted of people whose origin was by no means aristocratic'; they had little idea of the conduct expected of them.[1]

The native Irish, for the most part, had revered the old gentry, Irish and Old English, but they inclined to despise the New English. They had been quite prepared to take the new overlords to their hearts, given a little encouragement, but the mentality of most of the New English was one of ruthless class and racial superiority over primitive aboriginals. The new landowners were not secure in their holdings until after the Treaty of Limerick, and few had any sense of aristocratic largesse. They were mostly ex-soldiers or speculators who had advanced money to the government during the war and were paid off with confiscated land. They had no roots in the country, no sense of place and no idea of tradition. They were strangers in a strange land, with a different language, religion and culture, who despised the original inhabitants, and were detested in return.

The main complaint from Gaelic Ireland about this new Ascendancy was their lack of open-handed hospitality. The older gentry had been generous to the point of profligacy but, to begin with, the newcomers were parsimonious. Gaelic poetry of the period constantly inveighs against the meanness and lack of nobility of the new lords of the country. Geoffrey Keating called them: 'foreign filth', 'brood of every foreign sow', 'worthless rabble',[2] and sneered at their lowly birth and the notion that nobility could be conferred by the Patent Rolls that granted them title to the confiscated estates: 'There are gangs on the rise in these plains of Lugh the lithe / A base-born breed, though they flaunt their Rolls on high.'[3]

The new masters, for the most part, were intent on establishing a society firmly based on race, class and religion. In the years following Ormond's death, his vision was overturned and the racial and social superiority of the Protestant interest was built into a rigid caste system, in which religion and language were the prime signifiers. Daniel Corkery puts it bluntly: 'The first article in an Ascendancy's creed is, and always has been, that the natives are a lesser breed, and that anything that is theirs (except their land and their gold!) is therefore of little value.'[4] By extension, neither are the natives of much value. As the Protestant nation of Ireland came into being, the native population was relegated to the status of the other flora and fauna on the island, and had no part to play in the political or theatrical activities of the next fifty years. William Molyneux, the father of 'colonial nationalism', published in 1698 the clearest statement of the political claims of the English of Ireland, *The Case of Ireland's being bound by acts of parliament in England, stated*, in which the indigenous Irish have become invisible: 'The great body of the present people of Ireland are the progeny of the English and Britons that from time to time have come over into this kingdom, and there remain but a mere handful of the ancient Irish at this day, I may say not one in a thousand.'[5]

With the old Irish nobility broken, their land confiscated and the Brehon Laws overturned, the political energy of the Anglo-Irish was concentrated, not on the harmonious development of all the strands within the island, which had been Ormond's ideal, but on working out the relationship between the English of Ireland and the English authorities in London. Molyneux's tract was the statement of the position held by 'this nation', by which he meant the New English Protestant nation (though he did broaden his argument, crucially, to include the descendants of the Norman incursion). Molyneux denied the right of the English Parliament to legislate for Ireland. Like James Shirley's *Saint Patrick for Ireland* in 1640, he rooted the claims of the seventeenth-century colonists in the soil of Irish history in order to establish their legitimacy. He argued that, as the submission of the Irish lords to Henry II in 1171 was voluntary, it granted to the Irish the same freedoms and rights as those enjoyed by the subjects of the king living in England, in particular the right to trade freely and to have a free parliament. He stated 'that those who joined the conqueror in war were free of any subjection to him',[6] and from this he deduced that the Norman settlers and their descendants could by no means be treated as a conquered race. 'England may be said more properly to be conquered by William I than Ireland by Henry II,' he wrote.[7] Molyneux insisted that the restrictions imposed on the country by the decrees of the aggressive English Parliament over the previous fifty years had been an attack on the rights and liberties which the Anglo-Irish had enjoyed for half a millennium. 'I have no other notion of slavery', he adds, 'but being bound by a law to which I do not give consent. If one law may be imposed without consent, any other law whatever may be imposed upon us without our consent. [...] To tax me without consent is little better, if at all, than downright robbing me.'[8]

The English Parliament and court were scandalized by Molyneux's book. Isaac Newton protested: 'Ireland is one of the English plantations [...] and is, and ought to be, inferior to this kingdom and subservient to its interests.'[9] A committee appointed to investigate the matter concluded that Molyneux's work was part of an attempt 'by the king's subjects of Ireland to shake off their subjection to and dependence on this kingdom [...] by denying the authority of the king and parliament of England to bind the kingdom and people of Ireland, and by denying the subordination and dependence that Ireland hath, and ought to have, upon England'.[10]

It was this controversy that underpinned two Irish plays of the late 1690s – William Philips' *St Stephen's Green* and George Farquhar's first play, *Love and a Bottle*. The relative merits of Irish and English society is the theme underlying both plays, but the emphasis is different, in consideration of their different audiences. Farquhar's play was put on at Drury Lane in 1698, and published in London, and he was at pains to subvert the English audience's preconception of Irish character and society. *St Stephen's Green* (1699) was targeted at an Irish audience and ridiculed the Irish tendency to copy slavishly English fashions and ideas. But at the root of each play lay a Molyneuxesque assertion of the equal worth of English and Irish aristocratic society, and a demand for parity of esteem.

St Stephen's Green had a strong political base: the Irish setting and characters followed Molyneux's lead. In the teeth of a determined effort by the English authorities to reduce Ireland from a kingdom to a colony, the play denied that Ireland is a lesser country or Dublin society inferior to London's; it strove to validate this on the stage, and perhaps as importantly, by publication.[11] The play was Molyneux's work transposed into another key – that of culture rather than politics. Philips gave an implied critique of English society itself and an overt demolition of English attitudes to Ireland, in particular; he assailed their arrogant assumption of Ireland's subservient colonial status, rather than accepting it as an equal nation and society. He further tried to raise the level of Irish consciousness by lampooning those who look to England for their lead in fashion or morality, insisting on at least an equal footing for Ireland, and possibly a superior moral and ethical sense. The play went out of its way to berate those Irish who demeaned and ridiculed their own country at home or abroad. The 'generous' union of equals it enacted between the English Freelove and the Irish Aemilia was the one it implied as the ideal political solution as well – neither party looking for material or economic dominance, but a union of noble minds that brought a train of material benefits as its own reward.

William Philips, like Farquhar, was a member of a prominent family from County Derry. He was intimately acquainted with the Irish aristocracy, and dedicated his first play, *The Revengeful Queen,* staged at Drury Lane in 1698, to the theatre-loving second Duke of Ormond, because 'your family have vouchsafed to be Patrons of mine for several Generations'. The play was a Heroic Tragedy set in Italy, and was not a success, partly because of a charge of plagiarism by Davenant, who had adapted the same story from Machiavelli.[12]

For his next effort, Philips changed course completely, and wrote *St Stephen's Green*, a modern comedy set, presented and published in Dublin – the first contemporary portrait of Irish Ascendancy society to reach the stage. He retained the close contact with the aristocracy, this time in the form of William O'Brien, third Earl of Inchiquin, a privy councillor to Queen Anne and to George I. Philips, in his dedicatory epistle to *St Stephen's Green* left no doubt about the earl's attachment to the theatre and, in spite of neo-puritan hostility, his interest in dramatic fashions: 'This Play has a double Reason for seeking Shelter under Your Lordship; I writ it, and for our *Irish* Stage, and You are the chief Friend which either has.'[13] He went on to justify the theatre in general by invoking the earl's approbation as a defence: 'I am confident the greatest zealot would slacken his fury against the stage, and join you in supporting it, did he know how earnestly you wish it reform'd from the corruption of Manners, to the encouraging Virtue and exposing Vice; and with what Decency, Modesty and Good Breeding, you wou'd have it regulated.'[14]

Philips was aligning himself here with the neo-puritan backlash against theatrical permissiveness that had culminated in Jeremy Collier's pamphlet, *A Short View of the Immorality and Profaneness of the English Stage*, in the previous year, 1698. It now seems that Collier's publication was following fashion rather than setting it. In England, the rising middle class was demanding a new style of drama:

softer, more humane, more sentimental, that conformed to outside moral standards rather than to its own internal balancing system. Ironically, this was the sort of ethic that Dublin had never abandoned; in fact, in the previous year, Joseph Ashbury, the director of Smock Alley, had been fined for swearing on stage.[15] The intrinsic conservatism of the first Duke of Ormond and of the Irish gentry had kept the Dublin theatrical fashions so far behind London that now they found themselves ahead of it again.

The influence of the Earl of Inchiquin in this play went beyond a generalized interest. Philips tells us: 'You may remember you Caution'd me to observe these Things, when I first acquaint'd you that I had a Design to Write this Comedy and I have attempted to Obey you.'[16]

The playwright and the patron had a discussion as to what this new Irish type of play was going to be, and agreed a set of guidelines which would conform to the most exacting moral standards. This was to be a play set among Dublin's high society; there was to be no indecency and no immorality; Virtue would be encouraged and Vice exposed; the Corruption of Mannered Comedy would be excluded from the stage, and all would be done with Decency, Modesty and Good Breeding. This would satisfy the demands of Lord Inchiquin and the conservative Irish aristocracy and put the Irish theatre on an equal footing with the latest trends in London. In fact, Philips went further: within the play he contrasted the two societies, and found that in all matters of morality and behaviour Irish society equalled or surpassed the English. By invoking this contrast, he followed Molyneux's doctrine of a discrete but equal nation, and encouraged the further development of playwrighting that was distinctly Irish. He finished his 'Epistle Dedicatory' with a call for other writers to follow his lead in setting plays in Ireland and dealing with Irish situations and concerns: 'I should be extremely pleased, if my Success would move any other who has a happier Genius, to divert this Town with some Performance of this kind.'[17]

What both *Love and a Bottle* and *St Stephen's Green* asserted was the equality of the two societies. Farquhar did it in passing, but it was central to Philips' play. The mere fact of setting it in St Stephen's Green subverted accepted standards: it was saying that Dublin had places, characters and materials as good as there were in the squares and parks of London. Stephen's Green became an active symbol for this society.[18]

The view of Dublin expressed in the play is exactly observed, designed to evoke a positive response to the city and its society. The impression given is one of ease and gossip, of fresh air and high jinks around Stephen's Green. Bellmine introduces his English friend,

Freelove, to the intimate size of Dublin by telling him: 'I'll undertake you shall not be three days in town, but every Body in town will know you; nay, and know whence you came, how long you stay, what's your Business, and if you have none, they will feign enough for you.'[19] Vainly assures the newcomers: 'I'll make you acquainted with the whole Town this Afternoon.'[20] This is only a difficulty for someone like Bellmine, who wants to 'be thought a very Lewd Fellow', and who thinks 'such a Character do[es] a Man effectual Service with Women',[21] but who needs a large population to do it with anonymity: 'In *London*, 'tis difficult to be known; here, impossible to be conceal'd. […] There you may make a thousand Cuckolds, yet they will never hear of your Name. Here, you cannot make one without being Intimate with him.'[22]

The attractiveness of strangers and visitors from London is acknowledged, but not approved, and it is the visitors who are satirized for their glib superiority and condescension. Marina, the local woman, refuses to be impressed by Bellmine's metropolitanism. Two strands of social criticism join here; the first is directed at London society: the general impression given in the following scene is that it is not a pleasant place, for all its frenetic activity and self-importance. London is overtly evoked and rejected, as it is implicitly criticized throughout the play. The other strand alludes to the qualities inculcated by the education of a gentleman. Travel and knowledge of the world, which Bellmine displays here, were giving way to the perceived primacy of morality or Virtue in the formation of the ruling class, and this is a quality markedly absent in Bellmine for the present:

> MARINA   That supposition shews you are Strangers, or you would know that to be so is a recommendation here.
>
> BELLMINE Does that humour reign here? I hope it does in you too; then I may succeed; for I assure you I am but this moment arriv'd; and to make me still the more acceptable to thee, my Pretty Dear Creature; know that I have brought over some New Fashions, New Tunes, and New Plays; I can tell you which house has the best Audience, which Player is most Applauded; who the Celebrated Beauty of the Town, who keeps the best Equipage; I can tell you who Loves who, and who does worse; what Duels have been lately Fought; who Kill'd, who Hang'd, who Jilted, who Married, who ——
>
> MARINA   And so Convince me you go abroad for the same wise Intent most of our Young Sparks do. But you may as soon Borrow Money of a grave Citizen by this Character of your self as expect any Favour from me by it.

> BELLMINE Will this not please you? Why then I can give you an account of the Court; I can tell you which Lord has the greaest Levy; I can tell you of great Favourites who scarce could Breathe for Crowds of servile Sycophants, and in a day's time as lonely as if it had been Writ over their Doors, *'This House is infected with the Plague'*. I can tell you of the Advancement of Fools and Knaves, and the Disgrace of Men of Sense and Worth, I can —
>
> MARINA Hold, hold, you will only persuade me you have met with some Disappointment there, for few rail at the Court for any other Reason.
>
> BELLMINE Let me have one Stroke at Rogues in Power —
>
> MARINA Not a Syllable, or I shall believe you are vext, because you cannot be one in your turn.
>
> BELLMINE Will not this do? why then have at the Parliament —
>
> MARINA Worse and worse.[23]

Bellmine has made his advances to Marina, metropolitan to provincial, typical of the Comedy of Manners, but has been comprehensively rebuffed.

The unsympathetic characters are villainous or ridiculous in direct proportion to their London fixation. The libidinous Sir Francis Feignyouth enters in a rush and demands from the new arrivals: 'Well, and what price bear Wine and Women in London now? hah! does the *Mall* swarm with Masks, and is *French* Wine admitted yet?'[24] The biggest idiot in the play, Vainly, is besotted with England and its fashions:

> VAINLY I am glad we have Gentlemen come to us now that understand Breeding and Conversation; 'Tis not to be had here. I protest, Sir, I am forced to go to England once a year, to refine my understanding.
>
> BELLMINE What need you put yourself to that Trouble? Cannot you keep a Correspondence with your Tailor?
>
> VAINLY: With my Tailor, Sir?
>
> BELLMINE Yes; for all you learn by your Journey is a new Fashion; and all you understand is whither your Clothes be well made.[25]

Philips provides an antidote to this provincial myopia when the two English stewards, Trickwell and Timothy, meet. The point is made that the enlightened English do not take kindly to those Irish who belittle Ireland in order to ingratiate themselves with London society:

TIMOTHY   Ease and Plenty have made this Alteration. Eating well and Lying soft. Thank my Stars, I thrive very well in this Country.

TRICKWELL   Then I suppose you Despise it.

TIMOTHY   That's but an odd Reason.

TRICKWELL   A very common one; for I have observ'd that none Despise *Ireland* so much as those who thrive best in it. And none are so severe in their Reflections upon it as those who owe their Birth and Fortune to it; I have known many of 'em, when they first come to *London*, think there is no way so ready to purchase the Title of a Wit as to Ridicule their own Country.[26]

This informed attitude to Ireland, by those who know it, contrasts tellingly with Farquhar's satirical tilt in *Love and a Bottle* at the ignorant, credulous opinions of the English at large in their own country:

LUCINDA   Are you then one of the Wise Men of the East?

ROEBUCK   No, Madam; but one of the Fools of the West.

LUCINDA.   Pray what do you mean by that?

ROEBUCK   An Irish-man, Madam, at your Service.

LUCINDA   Oh horrible! an Irish-man! a mere Wolf-Dog, I protest.

ROEBUCK   Ben't surpriz'd Child; the Wolf-Dog is as well natur'd an Animal as any of your Country Bull-Dogs; and a much more fawning Creature, let me tell ye.
            [Lays hold on her.]

LUCINDA   Pray, good *Cesar,* keep off your Paws; no scraping acquaintance, for Heaven's sake. Tell us some news of your Country; I have heard the strangest Stories, that the people wear Horns and Hoofs.

ROEBUCK   Yes, faith, a great many wear Horns; but we had that among other laudable fashions, from London......

LUCINDA   Then you have Ladies among you?

ROEBUCK   Yes, yes, we have Ladies, and Whores; Colleges and Playhouses; Churches, and Taverns; fine Houses, and Bawdy-Houses; in short, everything that you can boast of, but Fops, Poets, Toads and Adders.

LUCINDA   But have you no Beaux's at all?

ROEBUCK   Yes, they come over, like the Woodcocks, once a year.

LUCINDA   And have your Ladies no Springes to catch 'em in?

ROEBUCK   No, Madam; our own Country affords us much better Wildfowl. But they are generally stripp'd of their feathers by the

> Playhouse and Taverns; in both of which they pretend to be Criticks; and our ignorant Nation imagines a full Wig as infallible a token of a Wit as a Laurel.
>
> LUCINDA   Oh Lard! and here 'tis the certain sign of a Blockhead.[27]

Beneath the farce, the duel of wit and banter, lies a truth about the naked ignorance and prejudice of English society, and the equality – or even superiority – of Irish society. Roebuck, while commenting ironically on his own country, is in fact comparing it favourably to the decadent foppish society of London, and sneering openly at the idea of the superiority of English fashions and ideas. His tirade describes Ireland as a place well able to combat and belittle any such imported ideas. England may show a powerful example, but Irish society, as Marina also displayed, refuses to be gulled or impressed by those who would treat it with condescension.

All of these strands come together in the most remarkable passage in *St Stephen's Green* (III. 1), which enacts the dismissal of English fashionable and moral authority in favour of an Irish independence of mind:

> VAINLY   You are so obliging, Sir. Truly I think this Coat is very well Cut, fits with a Good Air. I had it sent me by and Express from *London*; for I cannot bear any thing but what comes from thence. Oh, 'tis a happy Place! and in a blessed Country, where there are all things necessary, where there are such pleasures, and such Conveniences to enjoy them!
>
> FREELOVE   I have been told you have all those here.
>
> VAINLY   Oh not one, Sir, not one.
>
> FREELOVE   You have good Wine?
>
> VAINLY   Yes, yes, that's true, I had forgot that.
>
> FREELOVE   Plenty of all sorts of Fish and Flesh.
>
> VAINLY   Phoo, they are perfect Drugs. Plenty of Meat and Drink; but nothing else.
>
> FREELOVE   The people are Civil and Obliging.
>
> VAINLY   Especially to Strangers.
>
> FREELOVE   And Hospitable.
>
> VAINLY   To a Fault, Sir.
>
> FREELOVE   The Air is Good, a temperate Climate.
>
> VAINLY   Much the same as in *England*.
>
> FREELOVE   The Soil is Rich.
>
> VAINLY   Oh, 'tis too Rank.
>
> FREELOVE   What necessaries then, or what pleasures do you want?

> You have fine Women.
>
> VAINLY   They are kind, I am sure.
>
> FREELOVE   To you chiefly, I suppose.
>
> VAINLY   Shall I make a Confession then among my Friends? I do not believe ever any Man has been so successful. I do not know that ever I ask'd in vain.
>
> SIR FRANCIS   I can hold no longer. Why dost thou little worthless Contemptible Wretch! Do you entertain Strangers with your aversion for your Country, without being able to give one Reason for it; and can you give but one Reason for liking it, which if it were true, would make all others abhor it? The Women fond of thee! Why the Common Hackneys who live by thee, Contemn thee. But such as he think if he is not affronted, he is belov'd.[28]

All the significant attitudes are represented in this scene. Vainly's English obsession is exposed in its invincible stupidity by the returned Irishman, Bellmine, and he is quietly ridiculed about his attitudes to his own country by the enlightened Englishman, Freelove, until the most significant representative of the Irish Ascendancy in the play, Sir Francis, is forced to acknowledge how ridiculous such attitudes, of which he himself is not free either, really are.

There is no argument for separate identity here;[29] it was the *equality* of the two societies that Philips was asserting: he was using their resemblance to boost the idea of Ireland as an equal partner in the relationship between the two countries; he was not claiming Dublin society as unique and different, but as equal and similar. The idea of a distinctly Anglo-Irish identity would only emerge in the next twenty years in the face of a continual downgrading and belittling of the Anglo-Irish by the English authorities. By the time Philips came to write his next play, in 1722, his outlook had hardened into a distinct sense of separate identity.

Vainly is the main carrier of the theme of the absurdity in elevating all things English and despising all things Irish. The problem with him is that his Anglophilia represents a sizeable chunk of Irish Ascendancy opinion. He may be a fool but he is still a gentleman, and moves in the best society in town, whose attitude to him is summed up by Bellmine:

> BELLMINE   Nay, it often happens that a Man is admired by some for that very Quality for which other despise him. And *Vainly* has one Qualification will make many Men, and most Women, value him.
>
> FREELOVE   And what is that?

BELLMINE   A Good Estate.

FREELOVE   Those who want one imagine it to be a much greater
Blessing than it is found to be by you, or any who possess it.

WORMWOOD   For my Part, I cannot help fretting that such dull
Rogues as that should have one. 'Tis a gift of Fortune as much
misapply'd as to confer swiftness on the Blind; for he can make
no use of it; and that is all my Comfort. He squanders it all
away in Sword, Perriwigs, Essence, Powder, and such material
Things.[30]

Here is sounded a main theme of the play: is Vainly a gentleman? and if
so what makes him one? What is a gentleman, what does society consider to be a gentleman, and what, if any, are the discrepancies between
the two? English plays of the latter half of the seventeenth century dealt
with this from an English perspective, but only Farquhar and Philips
added to the mix the question, what constitutes an *Irish* gentleman? The
above quotation provides evidence that Irish and English society were
of one mind on this subject. The dominant trope in the play is that one
cannot be a gentleman in Ireland without an estate – landed gentry are
the only gentry; only land produces genteel income, and an estate
bestows moral worth. Vainly is considered a gentleman by virtue of his
land, regardless of good sense or behaviour, and though he is ridiculed,
his social position is not called into question. Sir Francis is a libidinous
old rogue, and Bellmine a licentious young one, yet society at large has
no doubts of their position. It is Freelove who upsets the apple-cart: he
has all the appearance and manner of a gentleman, but has no estate.
How can this be? And since he clearly is a gentleman, what makes him
so?

This was a question much aired at the time. I have already noted the
contemptuous attitude of Gaelic Ireland to the new colonists; even
after the weaker spirits sold up and left, a lot of those remaining were
landed but hardly gentry. The dispossessed Irish were not alone in
despising them: the English upper classes were perfectly aware of the
way in which the Irish aristocracy had been diluted and corrupted.
From this time, in parallel with the political diminution of Irish sover-
eignty, the English Establishment began to find its Irish equivalents
lacking in the manners, poise and style of English gentlemen. While
Philips defends the standards of the Irish, he also laments, in the person of Vainly, the mercenary and mannerless style of some of the rising
gentry. Marina harpoons him and his like with her remark on the
means of acquiring an estate: 'Tis as Difficult to be thought so here,
without an Estate; as it is to be thought Honest and Get one.'[31] This is

one of the few overt flings in the play at the 'knaves and fools' who have risen to positions of prominence, even though one of the main concerns of *St Stephen's Green* is defining the idea of a proper gentleman. The play prefers instead to take a positive approach and plots a blueprint for the behaviour of a society whose standing is threatened by the rise of knaves, fools and those mannerless upstarts, such as Vainly, or Mockmode in *Love and a Bottle*, whose idea of gentility extends no further than their clothes or their money – a caricature of the real thing. Philips recommends a code of action that regulates itself according to noble instincts and the finer feelings, a way of life that is noble and generous rather than calculating and mercenary.

Language is considered a better indicator than clothes or money: you can recognize a gentleman or lady by the way they talk and by what they say. But that assumption also carries dangers. Farquhar, in *The Beaux' Stratagem*, a play also much concerned with real and imagined gentility, has one of the characters observe that she had 'known several footmen come down from London set up here for dancing masters, and carry off the best fortunes in the country'.[32] The outer accidentals of gentility can be learned by close acquaintance and study, so what differentiates a real gentleman or lady from a false one?

The answer given in *St Stephen's Green* to the conundrum that Freelove exemplifies is the quality of his mind – his 'generosity'. This is another weasel word that has shifted its meaning over the last three hundred years. In 1699 'generous' was understood as a translation of the French *généreux*, meaning 'of noble birth' or 'behaving in a noble manner', and was the adjective from *générosité*. This was a key concept in the work of the French dramatists, particularly Corneille, who dealt with the behaviour of aristocrats conforming to a lofty set of ethical and moral principles, regardless of the consequences to themselves. With Corneille, it is tied to another quality, *vertu*, which was the natural judgement and correct ethical action of the 'generous' mind. The open-handedness that went with nobility has nowadays overtaken the primary meaning. The key to the question, and to Philips' play, lies in its subtitle, *The Generous Lovers*. Freelove and Aemilia are 'generous', that is, noble in mind and spirit, even though they do not have a shilling between them. That particular handicap, in everybody's opinion but their own, disqualifies them from the marriage stakes completely. Sir Francis regards it as positively indecent for an openly penniless suitor to be paying court to his niece – it flies in the face of the collective wisdom of upper-class society. His regard for Freelove waxes and wanes at the same rate as his knowledge of his fortune:

SIR FRANCIS   What say you Sir, have you no Estate?

FREELOVE   Not an Acre, Sir.

SIR FRANCIS   Nor Money?

FREELOVE   Not a Penny.

SIR FRANCIS   *(Aside)* A strange dull Fellow this! *(To him)* And have you really now the Conscience to make Love to my Niece? Can you imagine she will throw herself away upon you in the Bloom of her Youth; one of her Wit and Beauty? But perhaps you think she has an Equal Stock of Money, and so hope to make your Fortune by her. But I can assure you, she is in the same Circumstances as you are, not worth a Penny.

FREELOVE   I knew it when first I saw her, yet my Love receiv'd not the least Check by that; I hope she will prove as Generous.

SIR FRANCIS   Generous do you call it? Death! you make me mad. What a pox is there no way to be thought Generous but by becoming Mad and Begging? And pray Sir, if I may ask you a Civil Question, if she were Generous enough, as you call it, and mad enough, as I call it, to Marry you, how would you Maintain her, Sir?

FREELOVE   Oh, trust to our Stars for that.

SIR FRANCIS   I hope she will have more Grace. Trust to your stars for that! I would as soon trust you for ten Thousand Pounds. *(Aside)* I have not heard a fellow talk so Sillily in all my life. [...] A Perfect Fool! Methinks too a very ugly ungentile Man, as ever I saw![33]

St Stephen's Green keeps bringing up the idea of 'fortune' – the absolute necessity in upper-class society of money for matrimony. This idea diametrically opposes generosity, that is, following the emotions, and acting instinctively without too much calculation. The older generation think a man without a fortune has no business getting married at all unless he marries a woman with money, and vice versa; or two fortunes can marry. What they find really reprehensible is two people in society without money marrying each other. In fact Sir Francis finds it opprobrious that Freelove has not even the decency to pursue his niece clandestinely:

SIR FRANCIS   Look here, Niece, here is a Gentleman has given him self the trouble to come hither to make Love to you, without having Money enough to pay for a License, or the Wedding Dinner.

FREELOVE   Madam, I own —

SIR FRANCIS   *(Interrupting)* Ay, ay, he owns it, what wou'd you have more; a very honest undesigning Gentleman as ever I saw.

FREELOVE   I have no hopes you shou'd ever have a favourable thought
for me, if it is to be purchas'd with Wealth. But if the sincerest
Passion, the humblest Adoration, a Heart immov'd by any thing but
you, can atone for the want of Wealth —

SIR FRANCIS   Satisfy yourself Sir, they will not. Nor your fine person, nor
your Wit, nor your Courage, nor your Stars, nor a thousand things
more.[34]

The moral of Philips' play is that Sir Francis is wrong, and that
Generosity *is* more important than Fortune. But at the end, he has the
pleasure of believing that he was right all along. On hearing that
Freelove, far from being destitute, has an English estate of £3,000 a
year, he exclaims: 'Admirable! Excellent! Nay, I always thought he
deserv'd one. A most compleat Gentleman!'[35]   He has all the other
attributes of a gentleman, why not an estate as well, if the world is
properly ordered?

The attitude of all the characters to Freelove and his ambitions is the
same; we have to accept that the overriding view of Irish, and English,
society is being articulated. Aemilia discusses his merits with her cousin
Marina, and highlights the split that separates their thinking. Aemilia
displays a 'generous' soul, while Marina shows herself 'mercenary':

MARINA   But what Reputation has he in the World? For I regard that
more than his Person or his Wit.

AEMILIA   As I, so he, was to most a Stranger. All agreed he had no
Estate, but a fine Gentleman.

MARINA   How's that! No Estate, and a Fine Gentleman! Advise him
to keep where he is, if he would preserve that Character.

[...]

AEMILIA   All are not of that Opinion; for if *Bellmine* had no Fortune,
I suppose you'd think him a Fine Gentleman.

MARINA   I thank Heaven he has a very good one, and really Cousin, I
find it much for his Interest in my Heart, that I never Considered
him without One.

AEMILIA   You are mercenary.

MARINA   Not wholly so; perhaps I should not esteem an acquain
tance the worst; but I think a Good Estate is one of the prettiest
Qualifications a Husband can have; my Love may decay, but an
Estate is a certain Good.[36]

Mercenary – acting in hope of reward, or behaving like a bourgeois
merchant – is the opposite of generous, and it is of that quality that

Aemilia is accusing Marina. The two ideas are openly class-conscious, and both primary and secondary meanings are played with by Philips in the play, even though no mercantile characters appear. But since money is an absolute necessity for living in society, Philips balances these two opposing attitudes by introducing a third idea as a compromise between them: he plots a middle course by invoking the quality of 'sense'. Too much calculation is bloodless, too little is foolish; but sense will steer a course between the two.

Farquhar used these two polar opposites in *Love and a Bottle* to create two types of Irish gentry. Lovewell is sober and calculating, and Roebuck a spontaneous rakehell. Farquhar was expressing the same duality, and asking the same questions: which of these attitudes is more genteel, and – which in the new dispensation comes to the same thing – which is superior morally? Farquhar was playing with English preconceptions of the Anglo-Irish character: he gave his audience Roebuck as the wild, untamed Irishman, of just the type that the English upper-classes were finding wanting in gentility, but he slipped Lovewell past them almost unnoticed, sober, calculating, and just as Irish as Roebuck. Farquhar is equivocal as to which of these characters is morally superior: his solution is to have them exchange some of their characteristics, so that each will be the more complete for it. To Philips, however, it is the generous lovers who hold the moral high ground. The first act of *St Stephen's Green* lacks a moral centre. Who, we ask ourselves, is the moral touchstone here? Not the English Lady Volant, whose pretensions are dismissed long before she is exposed as a fraud; not Sir Francis, who should be the natural figure of authority, but his behaviour is flawed; not Vainly, who is silly, snobbish and easily led, nor Wormwood, because he is so bitter and cynical he can be disregarded as a Cassandra. Bellmine could be a contender, as a returned local with worldly experience, but he has been corrupted by his time in London. The moral authority eventually comes to rest in Freelove and Aemilia, the generous couple who are free from mercenary corruption. Age has to learn from youth, and the generous union of Irish woman and English man is not only morally and sentimentally superior, but ultimately economically advantageous to both. Their generosity enables them to accept each other, based on personal attraction and estimation of each other's spiritual worth, without any intrusion by the demands of economics. Freelove says of Aemilia:

FREELOVE And is not she a Fortune without Money?
WORMWOOD Ha! ha! ha! the Man's mad. Why, what the Devil is Fortune but Money, or What is Woman or Honour or any thing else without it.

FREELOVE   Has she not Virtue, Sense and Beauty?

WORMWOOD   The Woman is not ugly, that's the Truth on't. But
where has thou been Educated? where hast thou spent thy time? who
hast thou converst with? Nothing but old Fables and Romances. [...]
In this Age talk of Virtue and Sense![37]

Wormwood is unaware that the temper of the age has changed and
these 'old Fables and Romances' are once again in fashion. The play
promotes the recognition of the paramount value of virtue and sense,
and their necessary reward by a fortune. With proper management,
and a balance of sense and generosity, the lovers can have the best of
both worlds; the play becomes a moral drama for a virtuous society, a
pattern for the best people to follow. The agreement between patron
and playwright has been honoured. To modern eyes this arbitrary settlement of a fortune on the protagonists seems like cheating, a clumsy
grafting on to the trunk of the play, but virtue must be rewarded and
vice exposed. Virtue can be seen to be rewarded through a long and
happy life, but that is not possible within the conventions of the seventeenth-century stage, so the best, if not the only way, to show this is
to give the lovers the means towards a long and happy life, and have a
convenient fortune fall into their laps. The two generous lovers,
English man and Irish woman, are rewarded for their equal and
unmercenary attraction and union; the desirability of a similar political arrangement is implied. The Dublin gentry of the late seventeenth
century are shown to be, for the most part, 'Decent', 'Modest', and of
'Good Breeding', as Philips promised his patron in his 'Epistle
Dedicatory'. Irish society, in spite of the tendency in some of its more
feeble members to allow themselves to be dominated by England, is
seen to be well able to stand on its own moral ground, and exercise its
independent judgement.

Philips goes further by insinuating that Dublin's morality is superior
to that of London. Freelove is an English rake who is instantly
reformed by stepping on Irish soil and catching sight of Aemilia.
Bellmine has been corrupted by his sojourn in London, but his attempts
to spread that corruption in Dublin are rejected and thwarted by
Marina, who goes on to engineer his reformation too. The other
English characters, Lady Volant and Timothy, are exposed as
imposters, and Vainly, who loves England and despises Ireland, is a
complete fool. The only local character whose morality is ambiguous
is Sir Francis Feignyouth, and he is saved ultimately because his innate
gentility overrules his foolish, Anglophile behaviour.

Sir Francis is the most interesting of the Anglo-Irish characters. At one level he is a foolish, amorous old man in the *Commedia* tradition who must be chastened but, when he duly is, he breaks into a lamentation that would not have disgraced Synge – an early indication of the linguistic riches that Irish drama would come to offer: 'What had I to do with a wife, what had I to do with a wife! Had I not Ease enough, had I not Freedom enough, had I not Wealth enough! I had everything but Wit enough – Oh, I am a Jest to the World, a Scandal to my Name, a Curse to my Family, and a Hell to my self.'[38]

At another level he shows signs of evolving into a Molyneuxesque state of political awareness, when he berates Vainly for 'entertain[ing] Strangers with your aversion for your Country'.[39] This aspect of him remains largely undeveloped, as Philips steers him towards learning his lesson in how to behave with the dignity and gravitas called for by his age and position. Philips is careful not to pander to English society's prejudices in any of his characters, and none of them display any characteristics that can be pointed to as overtly Irish (if we except Sir Francis' outburst presented above).

Previous to Philips' play the Irish on stage were mostly servants, soldiers or priests, but Philips shows us Irish high society for the first time. Generally speaking, the characters are derivative rather than original: their prototypes in Restoration drama are recognizable. Bellmine is a rake on the point of reformation, pretending to be virtuous in public, in order to get the opportunity of being vicious in private: 'You'd be thought Virtuous, that you may be the more Conveniently Wicked.'[40] Restoration comedy always had a moral base, in spite of the surface indelicacy, and Philips' play has a secondary hero who reforms in the last act, but his main hero is reformed from the beginning. Christopher Murray remarks that 'it can be said that by Philips' time the implicit moral theme of Restoration comedy had become explicit'.[41] Vainly is in the tradition of Sir Fopling Flutter, but with the Irish twist that he looks to London for his fads rather than Paris. He has the same thick skin, complete lack of self-awareness and a mind stuffed with fashion and gossip. The two young ladies, Aemelia and Marina, are typically smart, independent, opinionated and lively heroines, who express the two sides of the question: one is generous, the other mercenary.

Philips drew all these characters in fairly broad strokes, with little sense of local colour, taking care not to give comfort to the prejudices of those who disagreed with him. Farquhar, on the other hand, in a typically bravura move, took those prejudices and built dramatically on them. In *Love and a Bottle*, he gave us, in Roebuck and Lovewell, two contrasted portraits of Irish gentlemen. Lovewell is hardly nationalized at all, but this was one of the means by which Farquhar undermined his audience's preconceptions: he is sober, careful and modest. Roebuck is by far the more arresting figure of the two. He is the Irish type the English expect – penniless, wild, reckless and lecherous – and Farquhar gave them exactly that, but then proceeded to explore the character and overturn those preconceptions. Roebuck is an Irish version of an Ascendancy rake. His name marks his aggressive masculinity, but his emblem in the play is not the buck but the Irish wolfhound: 'a mere Wolf-Dog, I protest', says Lucinda.[42] His behaviour throughout is like that of a dog – galloping gleefully after a scent, but veering off when another supervenes. He is a big playful mutt; he might hurt you, but he means no harm: 'The Wolf-Dog is as well-natur'd an animal as any of your Country Bull-Dogs.'[43] His conduct, however outrageous, is an expression of his nature, and his behaviour towards women follows his own strange code of honour – he sees nothing wrong in seducing them, but thinks it heinous to tell about it: 'The tongue is the only Member that can hurt a Lady's Honour. [...] It must be private as Devotion – No blabbing.'[44] He is much addicted to his two vices that form the play's title: 'Drinking and Whoring',[45] as they are less elegantly categorized by Lovewell. But Roebuck is steadfast in what he sees as honourable action, and has the seeds of redemption in him; his generosity is innate. Leanthe claims he is 'Wild as Winds, and unconfin'd as Air. – Yet I may reclaim him. His follies are weakly founded, upon the Principles of Honour, where the very Foundation helps to undermine the Structure.'[46] Farquhar was using the audience's expectations against them; the vivid Irishness of Roebuck blinds one to the subdued Irishness of Lovewell. It's a classic conjuror's trick: it only dawns gradually that the virtuous, sober one is as Irish as the wild one.

In the play, Lucinda is courted by three suitors, who are three very different aspects of The Gentleman. The third point of this triangle is Mockmode, who throws Roebuck and Lovewell into relief. He is an English country squire, and in this character Farquhar was taking a satirical swipe at the university system. Learning ranked very low as a genteel accomplishment at the end of the seventeenth century; moral training, travel, worldly experience and involvement in public affairs were considered of much greater importance.[47] Nor was attendance at university any guarantee that anything was learned there. Mockmode has a country estate and a university education, but that doesn't make him much of a gentleman. We can see here a difference between the attitudes of the two countries. In Philips' play, Vainly is accepted by Dublin society because he has the primary requirement – a substantial estate; in England, Farquhar finds, something more is needed. Mockmode rolls into town like a country bumpkin – 'He's newly come to Town from the University, where his Education could reach no farther than to guzzle fat Ale, smoke Tobacco and chop Logick'[48] – while Roebuck and Lovewell slide easily into society, high or low. The grafting on of the attributes of fencing, dancing and playing the flute do not improve Mockmode. His mistake is in wanting to be a beau, in taking the caricature of a gentleman for the real thing. In a beau, the obvious externals are exaggerated, the inner essence is ignored or absent. Farquhar slyly makes the point that the Irish Roebuck – penniless, dishevelled, disowned by his father and with no education but 'the world' – is more of a gentleman than an English estate owner with a university education: 'His Mien and Air shew him a Gentleman,' says Lucinda.[49] He is gentry in demeanour, behaviour and excess: a Restoration gentleman, before neo-puritanism equated nobility with virtue and created a new type of Sentimental gentleman of whom Lovewell is already an example.

The question being asked by Farquhar was, which of these is the right, or acceptable, model of a gentleman? His answer was, none of them. Mockmode has the estate, Lovewell has the sobriety and Roebuck has the 'Mien and Air'. All are incomplete, yet each is convinced that his is the right model. Squire Mockmode, as his name tells us, thinks that by aping the activities and manners of the extravagant beaux, he will rise from the lowest class of gentleman into the nobility; to him, as to Vainly in *St Stephen's Green,* only an estate and outer image count for anything. Appearance is all:

> MOCKMODE   I have a great Estate, and want only to be a great Beau, to qualify me either for a Knight or a Lord. By the Universe, I have a great mind to bind myself 'Prentice to a Beau. – Could I but dance well, play upon the Flute, and swear the most modish Oaths, I would set up for Quality with e're a young Nobleman of 'em all.[50]

Roebuck and Lovewell care not a whit for appearance, and an estate, while convenient, is only the means of their maintenance. Lovewell does not hesitate to share the fruits of his estate with Roebuck, yet he disagrees diametrically with him as to the correct behaviour of a gentleman:

> LOVEWELL   Yes, you are my friend. All my thoughts were employ'd about you. In short, I have one request to make. That you would renounce your loose wild Courses, and lead a sober life, as I do.
> ROEBUCK   That I will, if you'll grant me a Boon.

LOVEWELL You shall have it, be't what it will.

ROEBUCK   That you wou'd relinquish your precise sober behaviour,
and live like a Gentleman as I do.

LOVEWELL That I can't grant.

ROEBUCK   Then we're off. [51]

Farquhar is at pains in Act 1 to establish Roebuck in the minds of his
audience as a wild Irishman – penniless, lecherous and pugnacious – and
then proceeds during the course of the play to question and undermine
this perception, by showing his underlying code of honour and inherent
genteel qualities. He allows Roebuck's Irishness to fade into the background while he concentrates on his 'wildness', a trait that identifies
him with the other rakish heroes and heroines of Restoration comedy. [52]
Lovewell's Irishness is invisible at first under his sober demeanour; his
openly acknowledged nationality at the play's end comes as something
of a shock. Farquhar shows that neither the sober gent nor the wild
buck is the perfection of gentility, merely different aspects of it.
Roebuck is too wild, Lovewell too sober. During the course of the play,
they exchange characteristics, as Farquhar has prefigured in the piece of
dialogue quoted above. Roebuck gains some gravitas, and Lovewell
becomes reckless under the stimulus of love. Both of the Irish gentlemen
are tamed by the power of a woman: Lovewell is loosened by his passion
for Lucinda, Roebuck is calmed and seduced by Leanthe's constancy.
Neither takes anything from Mockmode (except his money for
Roebuck's paramour). They have no interest in him or in what he wants
to become. The Englishman's idea of gentility, Farquhar is saying, is far
too concerned with the outer shell; in the Irishmen, gentility is inherent, it is not to be learned. It can be recognized, but not taught. Its true
nature does not lie in fashionable accomplishment, or the latest clothes,
but in the superior qualities of the generous mind. A commoner disguised as a gentleman will always be exposed, and a gentleman, or lady,
disguised as a commoner will shine through the disguise. Cherry in *The
Beaux' Stratagem* tells Archer: 'Your discourse and your habit are con-
tradictions, and it would be nonsense in me to believe you a footman
any longer,' [53] and Roebuck's dishevelment at the start of *Love and a
Bottle* does not conceal the mien and air of an aristocrat.

Mockmode, for all his new accomplishments, remains a 'Squire.
Being born in that stratum of society at the lower edge of what may be
considered a gentleman, he cannot escape it:

MOCKMODE   Mr. Lyrick, is this your Poetical Friendship?

LYRICK   I had only a mind to convince you of your 'Squireship.

English high society at that period was starting to open up to the bourgeoisie, but only to those with money and manners enough to make the transition, and Mockmode has a long way to go. In Ireland, as Philips has shown us, there was no sign of that social change as yet. In his later plays, Farquhar observed this rising phenomenon. By the time he came to write *The Beaux' Stratagem* (1707), he was firmly of the view that English society was one that respected wealth more than virtue. Philips had remarked in *St Stephen's Green* on the unlikelihood of being honest and acquiring an estate; Aimwell and Archer, in *The Beaux' Stratagem*, coolly observe London society, where the noble Jack Generous is shunned for his poverty, while Jack Handicraft – 'a handsome, well-dressed, mannerly sharping rogue'[54] – and Nick Marrowbone – 'a professed pickpocket and a good bowler'[55] – move in the best company in town because of the status awarded by their ill-gotten gains. Our two heroes have had to leave town before their poverty turned them from eligible bachelors into social pariahs. At the start of the play, the two are indignant at this injustice: 'We are men of intrinsic value, who can strike our fortunes out of ourselves, whose worth is independent of accidents in life, or revolutions in government.'[56] But at the end they have changed their tune. Aimwell says of his accidental good fortune: 'Thanks to the pregnant stars that framed this accident.'[57] They have come to acknowledge that this is a world and a society in which a man's value owes a lot more to his extrinsic than to his intrinsic qualities. As the case of Jack Generous has already shown, 'There is no scandal like rags, nor any crime so shameful as poverty.'[58]

Farquhar, in his later plays, acknowledged growing middle-class dominance in society and the theatre. He used *The Recruiting Officer* and *The Beaux' Stratagem* both to depict bourgeois society and to look sideways at genteel society. Philips, in *St Stephen's Green*, proved the superiority of the generous over the mercenary; Farquhar, in the two plays mentioned, acknowledged the triumph of the mercenary over the generous, and showed that genteel society considered a person's financial worth to be equal to his worth morally. His heroes and heroines have to learn to act against this set conviction, and to behave generously. They are then rewarded materially for their superior morality. He was acknowledging a tendency in late seventeenth-century comedy to see economics as the primary reality, itself an offshoot of the development of empiricism. When we look at human activity and motivation, the basic reality is economic; politics, law, philosophy, religion, the arts, patriotism and all the finer feelings follow in the wake of economic survival. This reality was obscured while the drama only dealt with the rich and powerful; then honour and heroism could thrive. But once the drama moved to consider the lives of ordinary people, the primacy of economics became glaringly obvious. The jostling on the dramatic social ladder was a ruthless business; the rise or fall could be sudden or brutal, like that of Jack Generous in *The Beaux' Stratagem*, or the fallen favourites to whom Bellmine refers in *St Stephen's Green*. Since one could not live without money in the upper reaches of society, Farquhar asked how far is one prepared to go to obtain it, in order to preserve or elevate one's social standing.

In this matter Farquhar showed us the lower gentry and the upper-middle classes aping the mercenary actions and attitudes of those above them, and made his disapproval quite clear. In *The Recruiting Officer* and *The Beaux' Stratagem* it is the characters who reject the mercenary and embrace the generous who are rewarded. In *The Recruiting Officer* Plume scorns to pursue Silvia when she is rich, preferring 'the generous, good-natured Silvia in her smock';[59] she, in turn, refuses to exploit her fortune to raise her social standing, and pursues and wins Plume. Aimwell in *The Beaux' Stratagem*, out of love and decency, acts decisively against his own economic interests by confessing to Dorinda, and she finds this an expression of his innate gentility: he is 'generous' and has a 'gentleman's honour',[60] and she accepts him anyway.

Farquhar's work was revolutionary in shifting the epicentre of drama towards the middle classes without losing the sparkle and lightness that was associated with genteel comedy. What he did was broaden the range of genteel comedy to include the rising middle classes as equal partners in the plays, sharing the limelight with their upper-class betters. This enabled him to use his comedy to evaluate genteel society, and genteel comedy itself. *The Beaux' Stratagem* keeps asking the audience what, in their opinion, within a rapidly changing society, constituted true gentility. Characters are always ready to assert their right to be considered gentlefolk.[61] Cherry sees herself as entitled to marry 'nothing under a gentleman'.[62] Scrub is a servant but swears without irony, 'upon my honour, as I'm a gentleman'; Gibbet the highwayman considers that style is of the utmost importance in the conduct of a robbery: 'There's a great deal of address and good manners in robbing a lady; I am the most a gentleman that way that ever travelled the road.'[63] Boniface, the landlord of the inn, who sees all sorts, thinks that Aimwell 'is so much a gentleman every manner of way, that he must be a highwayman'.[64] The linking of the beaux and the highwaymen points out that both were scouting the country to relieve some lady of her wealth.

Farquhar's later plays can be seen, in this context, as a sort of pendant to Philips' inquisition of the relative moral worth of English and Irish high society. Philips implied that English high society was corrupted by the pursuit of materialism and position; Farquhar demonstrated its shameless pursuit of worldly gain, its fervid embrace of economics as the prime motivator of all its activities, its trampling on those who did not have money enough to satisfy its demands, and its dismissal of those who could not meet its mercenary standards. In *The Beaux' Stratagem*, Farquhar questioned and undermined his audience's automatic assumptions about what constituted true gentility, as he had done in *Love and a Bottle*. In the earlier play Farquhar also undercut the audience's casual evaluation of the Irish gentry and nation. At the end of that play, he brought the audience full circle; he had not alluded to the nationality of Roebuck since the first act, and not at all to Lovewell's but, at the end, he reminds the audience that our heroes are Irish gentlemen, when Lucinda recommends that Lovewell make over an Irish estate to his sister and Roebuck. Farquhar then drives the lesson home by using an Irish entertainment to finish the comedy: 'An Irish *Entertainment of three Men and three Women, dress'd after the* Fingallion *fashion*'.[65] The Irish gentlemen have shown themselves possessed of the generous virtues: Lovewell's jealousy has broken open his sober carapace and allowed him to trust Lucinda; Roebuck adopts virtue as the proper course. The dramatic action that Roebuck embodies is the growth from Restoration rake to Sentimental gentleman; he has added Virtue to the list of his accomplishments, subdued his wildness, and gained an estate. From being the exemplar of a wild Restoration character, he has grown into an upright example of the Anglo-Irish gentleman of the eighteenth century.

NOTES AND REFERENCES

1. McLysaght, p. 233.
2. Seathrún Cheitinn, *Om Sceol ar Ardmhagh Fáil*, 'brioscar bíobha', verse 1, line 2; 'ál gach cránach coigríche', verse 2, line 8; 'treod gan tásc,' verse 3, line 9. http://www.pgil_library/classics/Keating,G/htm. [accessed 12/12/2003]
3. *Ibid.*, verse 4. Atáid foirne ag fás san gclarsa Logha liofa dar chóir bheith táir gé hard a rolla-scaoileadh.
4. Daniel Corkery, *The Hidden Ireland*, p. x.
5. J.G. Simms, *Colonial Nationalism 1698–1776: Molyneux's The Case of Ireland...Stated* (Cork: The Mercier Press, 1976), p. 31.
6. *Ibid.*, p. 31.
7. *Ibid.*, p. 30.
8. *Ibid.*, p. 35.
9. *Ibid.*, p. 39.
10. *Ibid.*, p. 39.

11. Raymond Gillespie, 'Political Ideas and their Social Contexts', p. 118.
12. Christopher Murray, ed., Introduction to William Philips, *St Stephen's Green*, p. 11.
13. William Philips, 'Epistle Dedicatory', in *St Stephen's Green*, p. 57.
14. *Ibid.*, p. 57.
15. Stockwell, *Dublin Theatres and Customs*, p. 40.
16. Philips, 'Epistle Dedicatory', in *St Stephen's Green*, p. 58.
17. *Ibid.*, p. 58.
18. Murray, Introduction to *St Stephen's Green*, p. 45.
19. Philips, *St Stephen's Green*, I. 1. 351.
20. *Ibid.*, II. 1. 117.
21. *Ibid.*, I. 1. 321.
22. *Ibid.*, I. 1. 345.
23. *Ibid.*, I. 1. 225.
24. *Ibid.*, II. 1. 256.
25. *Ibid.*, III. 1. 235.
26. *Ibid.*, IV. 1. 12.2.
27. George Farquhar, *Love and a Bottle, in The Complete Works of George Farquhar*, ed. by Charles Stonehill (New York: Gordian Press, 1967), I. 1. p. 14.
28. Philips, *St Stephen's Green*, III. 1. 235.
29. See Morash, *History of Irish Theatre*, p. 41.
30. Philips, *St Stephen's Green*, II. 1. 195.
31. *Ibid.*, I. 1. 44.
32. George Farquhar, *The Beaux' Stratagem*, ed. by Michael Cordner, New Mermaids Study Drama (London: Ernest Benn, 1976), III. 3. 113.
33. Philips, *St Stephen's Green*, III. 1. 373.
34. *Ibid.*, III. 1. 109.
35. *Ibid.*, V. 2. 280.
36. *Ibid.*, I. 1. 37.
37. *Ibid.*, II. 1, 220.
38. *Ibid.*, V. 2. 169.
39. *Ibid.*, III. 1. 273.
40. *Ibid*, I. 1. 310.
41. Murray, *Introduction to St Stephen's Green*, p. 33, footnote 54.
42. Farquhar, *Love and a Bottle*, I. p. 14.
43. *Ibid.*, I. 1. p. 14.
44. *Ibid.*, II. 1. p. 24.
45. *Ibid.*, II. 1. p. 22.
46. *Ibid.*, II. 1. p. 39.
47. See George C. Brauer: *The Education of a Gentleman: Theories of Gentlemanly Education in England*, 1660–1775 (New York: Bookman Associates, 1959).
48. Farquhar, *Love and a Bottle*, I. 1. p. 13.
49. *Ibid.*, I. 1. p. 14.
50. *Ibid.*, II. 2. p. 25.
51. *Ibid.*, II. 1. p. 24.
52. A characteristic described also by Etherege, *The Man of Mode*, I. 1. 100 & 129.
53. Farquhar, *The Beaux' Stratagem*, II. 2. 185.
54. *Ibid.*, I. 1. 132.
55. *Ibid.*, I. 1. 137.
56. *Ibid.*, I. 1. 156.
57. *Ibid.*, V. 4. 106.
58. *Ibid.*, I. 1. 128.
59. *Ibid.*, V. 3. 21.
60. Farquhar, *The Beaux' Stratagem*, V. 4. 89.
61. *Ibid.*, II. 2. 8.
62. *Ibid.*, III. 3. 5.
63. *Ibid.*, IV. 2. 137.
64. *Ibid.*, II. 2. 58.
65. Farquhar, *Love and a Bottle*, V. 3. 72.

4

'The Ruling Follies of this Spacious Town': Charles Shadwell's Irish Comedies

Up to the beginning of the eighteenth century, Smock Alley was very much under the influence of Dublin Castle and the viceregal court, but after 1700 the hold of the Castle on the theatre gradually weakened, as the grip of the newly risen 'bourgeois gentry' began to take hold. A large part of the wealth that stayed in the country was finding its way to Dublin, where the landed gentry spent the rents from their estates, the executive and its officials spent their incomes, the military spent their pay and the merchant class fattened on them all.[1] This society and audience was, according to Stockwell, 'a psychological unit. [...] Its country was England, its civilization was English, and it looked towards London as Mohammedans look to Mecca.'[2] But it was not as unified as she suggests: the shoots of disaffection could already be seen sprouting in Molyneux's *Case of Ireland ... Stated*. All Catholics were barred from office or advancement as a matter of course, but even the Castle Protestants were excluded from the highest offices. The English executive did not trust any Irishman to run the country in the way that maximized English advantage.[3]

Dublin Castle had, by the first decade of the eighteenth century, fallen into disrepair, and the social hub had shifted to Trinity College, the Dublin Philosophical Society and the theatre at Smock Alley, which had become 'the indoor equivalent of St Stephen's Green'.[4] The patronage of the nobility was still important to the theatre: the second Duke of Ormond, when he returned to Ireland in 1697, became the chief patron of the Smock Alley Theatre and brought the company to perform in Kilkenny during the off-season.[5] When Ormond became lord lieutenant in 1703, he was given a lavish civic reception for his arrival in Dublin, at which the poem of welcome was delivered by Richard Estcourt, one of the Smock Alley actors and, in the following year, Ormond's attendance at Farquhar's benefit contributed to a crowded house, from which Farquhar derived £100 profit, twice the usual amount.[6]

About 1715, Charles Shadwell praised the lord lieutenant, Lord Bolton, because 'plays and players are by him approved',[7] and he was 'the great supporter of the Stage'.[8] The lord lieutenant's semi-royal persona was acknowledged in the splendour of his box at the theatre. On grand occasions, the viceroy was received in the vestibule by the patentee of the theatre, dressed in regulation court attire and bearing lights in two silver candlesticks.[9] In 1745, when Lord Chesterfield was lord deputy, he was met by Thomas Sheridan, the manager of the theatre, and David Garrick, who was appearing on his second visit to Dublin, and led to his box with two lighted candles. 'It is related', writes Constantia Maxwell, 'that [...] he spoke kindly to Sheridan, but did not even return Garrick's salute.'[10] Thomas Sheridan, to Chesterfield, was an important man, but Garrick was just an English actor.

The subsidizing of plays or certain nights at the theatre became an important part of the revenues of whichever theatre was holding the title 'Royal' at the time. Such affairs were known as 'government plays', and the Theatre Royal received 'a certain sum annually from the government for performing of plays on particular nights, such as the King and Queen's birth-day, his Majesty's accession, &c.'[11] On those occasions, in order to promote the most fashionable audience, the ladies were admitted free, a device which, however, attracted the low with the high. In Shadwell's *The Hasty Wedding* a lady of the *demi-monde* tells us that: 'My Lord talked a great deal to me in the Lettice last Play night, I know he likes my colour, and he praised my hand and neck.'[12] In *The Sham Prince*, also by Shadwell, Lady Homebred, who is a thrifty manager, tells us that government nights are among the free entertainments that she and her daughters frequent: 'I give 'em diversions enough, for when the Government invites, they always see the play; and when the Corporations ride the Fringes, I carry 'em to a relation's of mine in Castle Street, where they take their bellies full of the show.'[13] Government nights were agreed to be the most glittering occasions in the theatrical calendar. In 1722, the grant assigned to the playhouse was £56, and appropriated, curiously, under 'Account of Secret Service Money', perhaps indicating a perception of the theatre as an instrument of clandestine government policy. By 1776 Spranger Barry at Crow Street was given £120, 'payable by government for four plays within the year'.[14] By 1800 it had grown to 'one hundred and fifty pounds sterling [...] payable by Government for the five Government

Plays to be performed in each and every year'.[15] Dublin theatres were receiving a government subsidy almost two hundred years before the Abbey Theatre was established.

The nobility and gentry financed the building of the theatres. They funded and held the shares in Smock Alley and, when the new theatre was opened in Crow Street in 1758, the finance was raised by subscription 'by many noblemen and persons of quality'.[16] They also took a part in deciding the repertoire of plays produced: *The Dublin Evening Post,* in 1740, reports that: 'A great number of the Nobility and Gentry [...] have subscribed for six plays to be acted in the theatre in Smock Alley, the first of which is to be *The Provoked Wife* and will be performed on Thursday next.'[17]

'Waiting on the gentry' became an established custom, whereby the leading actors, actresses and managers visited the ladies and gentlemen of the town in order to advertise or sell tickets for their performances. Such patronage, and the coteries that grew from it, became acrimonious with the establishment of theatres in competition with Smock Alley. The ladies were inclined to become partisans of one of them, and exercise their influence on behalf of their favourites. From 1715 to 1720 the ladies were constantly appealed to in the prologues and epilogues of Shadwell to use their charms on behalf of the playwright and the theatre:

> Unless bright nymphs, who in the Circle sit,
> Command some mercy from th'adoring Pit;
> [...]
> To you bright charmers of the blooming age,
> [...]
> To you we humbly sue and thus complain:
> Be you our friends, the Pit we're sure to gain.[18]

The influence and importance of the society ladies is further indicated by Shadwell's dedication of his *Collected Works* to Lady Newton, to express his gratitude for her support: 'The success I have met with was in great part owing to Your Ladyship. The countenance you have shown and the persons of Quality you have brought with you are convincing demonstrations how much the spirit of gaiety of *Dublin* centre in Your Ladyship.'[19]

Favourite actors were much cherished; the Duke of Ormond, prior to his departure from Dublin in 1705, 'appealed to the Lords Justices and the nobility of the Irish Kingdom to undertake a subscription for the support of the Smock Alley Players'.[20] The military command contributed too: about 1708, Hitchcock tells us, 'Mr. Thurmond did for his better Encouragement to continue in the Kingdom receive a Day's Pay from each officer of Coll. Munden's and another Regiment then in Dublin'.[21] But Thurmond took the money and absconded. This, and other drains from his acting pool, led the theatre manager, Richard Ashbury, to turn the theatre into a company in which the players were shareholders, but in return were bound by a contract not to bolt to London, but 'did mutually enter into articles and Bonds to continue in the Kingdom for the Diversion of the Nobility and Gentry'.[22] Five years later, Thurmond returned, armed with a letter from Ormond, now exiled, and demanded to become one of the shareholders. Ashbury refused and appealed to Ormond, saying he would reinstate Thurmond at a salary of £60 a year instead. Ormond favoured Ashbury's argument, and Thurmond accepted his verdict.[23] The hold the Butlers had over the country and the stage was still strong in spite of the duke's absence.

As the century advanced, the highest offices in Ireland, rather than being a reward for the merits and talents of the local population, became a dumping-ground where English politicians in difficulties could recoup their fortunes, a sinecure for partisans or a place of exile for out-of-favour statesmen.[24] Few, if any, of the lords lieutenant were committed to the welfare of the country; many actively opposed it.[25] The theatre became a forum where dissatisfaction with the current regime could be aired, on the stage and in the auditorium, as English policy concentrated on blocking the flow of Irish commerce and diminishing self-regulation in Irish affairs.

The mercantile and landed middle classes rose to positions of power during the eighteenth century, and also expanded to fill the social roles previously occupied by the nobility. Sackville Street, extending now from Rutland Square to the new Carlisle Bridge, was reputed to be the broadest and finest in Europe,[26] and was lined with the houses of rich merchants. As the city and country grew more prosperous over the century, the increasing wealth and confidence of the middle classes led them to assume the pursuits of the gentry and nobility. Political developments had infiltrated and changed the character of the theatre, making it, with the rise of bourgeois Protestant Ireland, a sounding board for the concerns and divisions of that class, which, as in France and America, was taking most of the positions of power.

In Ireland, the comedies of Charles Shadwell provide us with a diorama of the early stage of this bourgeois ascension to the summit of Irish society.

Charles Shadwell and the Rise of the 'Bourgeois Ascendancy'

Farquhar had alluded, in his plays, to the triumph of the mercenary over the generous, and it was the triumphant mercenary society of Dublin that was the milieu of Charles Shadwell's Irish comedies, a mercantile class that had risen to near-aristocratic status. The 'nobility and gentry' was a frequently used mantra in the theatrical documents of the early eighteenth century, before the later coinage of 'Ascendancy' took over but, while the phrase remained intact, the nature of what was signified underwent radical alteration. Charles Shadwell shows us the extent of the changes, both current and already completed.

In the plays of the late seventeenth century the merchant classes tended to be treated with contempt, but towards the end of the century there was a shift in attitude. The success of Farquhar and others moved the theatre's centre of gravity away from the aristocracy and towards the rising middle class and, in the second decade of the eighteenth century, Dublin had, in Charles Shadwell, its own resident playwright to articulate the concerns of that up-and-coming class and interrogate the claims of the upper class on its behalf. Shadwell was writing for and about a new audience of the *haute bourgeoisie* that had advanced with astonishing speed, a new Commonwealth flowing from the Glorious Revolution and the 1689 Bill of Rights, a new gentry of merchants and smaller landowners, of bankers and baronets, of people whose status was determined by their income. The older aristocracy are, in Shadwell's plays, a sort of distant myth; he wrote about the upper middle class and their satellites, and wrote for them too. In the epilogue to *Irish Hospitality* (1717/18) he outlined their tastes and preferences:

> Ladies will smile if scenes are modest writ
> Whilst your double entenders please the pit.
> There's not a vizard sweating in the gallery
> But like a smart intrigue, a rake, and raillery.
> And were we to consult our friends above,
> A pert and witty footman 'tis they love.
> And now and then such language as their own,
> As 'Damn you dog, you Lie!' and knock him down.
> Consider then how hard it is to show,
> Things that will do above, and please below.[27]

To please those above in the galleries and below in the pit, he drew on 'the reigning Follies of this spacious Town' to create his plays[28] and, as one would expect, there was considerable effort made to identify the originals of his characters. In his Prologue to *The Hasty Wedding*, Shadwell coyly denied that this was possible:

> The plot and scenes are laid within this town
> The people are inventions of his own.
> For none of you can have so little wit
> As e'er to think your characters are hit.[29]

But in the Prologue to *The Sham Prince* (1718/19), which was based on actual events,[30] he tells us that the originals of his characters came to see themselves represented on the stage. He was at pains, however, not to alienate any sector of his audience, especially the merchant classes that now formed its backbone:

> As the design was to expose a public cheat, and to show the folly of some tradesmen, who were drawn in upon that occasion, I took care to do it so, that even the people from whom I stole my characters could not take it ill, and came to see themselves represented. The play indeed might have been much better, had I but made use of the hints given me; but there were too many people of good sense and reputation concerned to be exposed: so I turned that into a comedy, which was a tragedy to many.[31]

The society and sensibility demonstrated by Shadwell are a long way from the plays of William Philips; Philips lauded the superiority of the generous mind; Shadwell acknowledged that superiority, but what interested him more were the successes and dangers of the mercenary society.

The main character in *The Hasty Wedding* (1716/17),[32] Sir Ambrose Wealthy, is a banker, the ultimate mercenary – an 'honest trader' of money.[33] Sir Ambrose's character and language are formed by money; it is his religion. His material value is to him the same as his intrinsic moral worth. Instead of prayer, Sir Ambrose begins each day with an invocation of his own value: 'Every morning, let me have a specimen of my accounts, an abstract of debtor and creditor; I love to be satisfied about my intrinsic value.' The language of business infuses the play, whose overriding imagery is taken from commerce. Cash, Sir Ambrose's accountant, has all his lines couched in economic metaphor; he equates the disguised Squire Daudle to coinage illegally reduced in value: 'Good now, he was disguised; he looked very much defaced; he was clipt of his gentility; nobody would take him for current coin, in ditto dress.'[34]

It's not just in metaphor that commerce appears in the play; business is discussed with obsessive fascination. We are left in no doubt as to the overwhelming commercial ethic of the characters and of the interest of the audience. In one scene, Shadwell compares the industry and thrift of a Huguenot with the indolence of the Irish. The Frenchman lives frugally, 'in hopes of gathering together as much money here, as he left behind him in France'.[35] Sir Ambrose approves heartily of such industry and attention to business: 'A good intelligible fellow this. I warrant you people of the country here grumble at these foreigners.'[36] He displays scant sympathy for his less industrious countrymen: 'If our own countrymen were but as industrious, they would not want business; but they never care to work, till they begin to grow hungry.'[37]

The only persons in the play to rise above this commercial outlook are Sir Ambrose's daughter, Aurelia, and her young man, Townley. Aurelia is the moral centre of the work, and the model of correct behaviour and attitudes. Sir Ambrose considers himself, and is considered by the other characters, as a member of the top echelon, but his behaviour and attitudes are a far cry from the *générosité* proposed by William Philips. Sir Ambrose's daughter, however, is unambiguously generous. She outclasses all the other women in the play, and is, in tone, manner, language and character, the pattern of gentility. When her father arbitrarily and whimsically marries the Widow Friendless and brings her and her daughter, Herriot, into his house over Aurelia's head, Shadwell compares the three women and their friend Lady Daudle in a scene which gives us different versions of female gentility. He uses the occasion to contrast proper manners, breeding and etiquette with the *arriviste* idea of them. The new Lady Worthy insists on being called 'Your Ladyship', because neither she nor her daughter knows any better, but Aurelia does: 'I thought it had been the height of good manners to have said Madam to the Queen herself,' she observes.[38] Aurelia has managed her household in a proper, distant, aristocratic manner, with her father's approval: 'she manages her expenses frugally, supplies my Family decently, and governs my servants prudently.'[39] The new Lady Worthy takes the suspicious bourgeois attitude: 'A housewife! and trust the keys to her maid, pretty management indeed.'[40]

The way in which the upper classes can spot a class intruder is by what Shadwell calls 'a solecism in breeding'[41] – an involuntary lowering in language or behaviour. The Widow Friendless and her daughter make themselves ridiculous by accusing Aurelia, whereas it is their own conduct that is rife with solecisms. The new Lady Worthy carries the narrow middle-class attitudes up the social ladder with her: independence in young women, for example, a notably aristocratic trait, is not to be encouraged: 'She has been a great while left to herself; and when young women are left to themselves, they make but awkward creatures.'[42] But Shadwell also uses such characters to show how they have experienced the behaviour of those above them by having them copy it when they believe they have risen in society.

The Sham Prince (1718/19) is a burlesque of nobility: a sort of twelfth-night inversion of authority, where the lower classes take on the behaviour and attitudes of their betters, and demonstrate to us by this device their resentment of the world of nepotism and corruption in which the upper classes coast along. Dublin and Irish society is viewed in the play through a complex arrangement of ironic lenses. Shadwell presents to us the social layers: the nobility 'appear very fine and very gallant, but they never pay their debts, and they will pawn their honour for a quid of tobacco';[43] the private gentlemen 'are a very good sort of people, only they are always drunk';[44] merchants and tradesmen are 'very idle, very prodigal: imitating the gentlemen, and their wives put on Quality airs, wear gold watches, drink tea out of silver tea-pots, and visit one another with as much ceremony and formality as if they kept assemblies'. This group portrait is painted in an inverted, satirical way, as Shadwell pretends he is describing German society, which is mean-spirited, corrupt and grasping; Irish society is drily invoked as the pattern of virtue called for by Philips:

> CHEATLY   Our men of Quality here are known, not by fine clothes and equipages, but by strict Virtue, Honour, and Integrity. [...] Here sobriety is the distinguishing quality of a gentleman. [...] Our tradesmen are sober, painstaking, laborious men, and their wives, most of them, assist their husbands in the way of trade, and are no gadders abroad.[46]

The argument is conducted, however, as a competition of frauds: a footman pretending to be the ambassador of the Princess of Passau attempting to deceive an even bigger fraud, Cheatly, who is simultaneously deceiving society and being deceived himself. The audience's viewpoint overrides all of these in an ironic appreciation of the sarcastic, equivocal praise that is being heaped on Irish society.

Deceit is endemic, and paranoia universal. The rising mercantile class that is central to Shadwell's comedies is threatened by imposters and fortune hunters; its capital is not yet safely locked away in land and its social antennae not fully tuned. *The Sham Prince* is the most notable in a line of plays dealing with the fragile gentility of Dublin, the ease of fooling provincial opinion and the unease felt by the Anglo-Irish about their provincial status and perceptions. How could they be sure that the outward show of gentility does not conceal a different underlying reality? The problem was made acute by Dublin's distance from the hub of fashion and culture and becoming, therefore, the target for all kinds of chancers on the prowl. It is no accident that the imposters in the plays are almost always English; as late as 1790, Irish newspapers were carefully pointing out that many of the criminals and con artists in the city dressed well and spoke with English accents. The *Hibernian Magazine* reported that:

> Dublin at this moment swarms with a flight of English sharpers – adepts in the mysteries of their profession in the arts of shop-lifting, pocket-picking, ring-dropping, swindling and coming. They assume all shapes and appearances – clergymen – farmers – horse-jockies – agents – riders – and are straight or deformed, young or old, lame or otherwise just as occasion suits.[47]

Sir Ambrose Wealthy, in *The Hasty Wedding*, is acutely paranoid; in his mind, his daughter and his ducats are welded together: who steals the one steals the other. The fear of cheaters and sharpers is a very bourgeois one; Shadwell shows us, in Sir Ambrose, the hard-working merchants who are terrified by the idea that the wealth they laboured to accumulate will be squandered by some plausible scoundrel, and everyone will laugh at them in their graves, their lives' work wasted. Their faulty sensors for imposters were a great cause of concern for them, whereas the settled gentry, like Trueman in *The Sham Prince*, could spot them a mile off. A father with a nubile daughter and money in easily realizable assets was in the most vulnerable position. Sir Ambrose is the embodiment of mercantile uneasiness: every morning he says the Banker's Creed, while at the same time agonizing over the vulnerable spot in his defences, his unmarried daughter: 'I know the true value of half-a-crown, but yet am not niggardly of a pound, but what would vex me in my grave, to have my fortune fall into the hands of a rake-hell, one that would throw away my money first, and my daughter afterwards.'[48]

The irony is that his daughter is quite well able to exercise her own judgement. In plays, young girls with money need to keep their wits about them, and are usually immunized by being emotionally attached already to someone who is suitable personally and emotionally, but not financially; the plays' action is to bring him into line financially as well. It is Sir Ambrose himself who falls for the confidence trickster. His distrust of Aurelia, and of all women, distracts him from his own vulnerability: 'But Aurelia is a woman – and a woman's a fool – and a fool dotes on a coxcomb – and a coxcomb will spend my estate like a puppy – and everybody will say I was a blockhead for taking pains to get it for him.'[49]

In *The Hasty Wedding* Sir Ambrose's money has an almost physical presence: it oppresses some and attracts others. While Aurelia is the heiress she is watched and defended, as if she were the Estate incarnate; but once she is disinherited, she feels that a load has been lifted off her: 'And what is the greatest pleasure of all to me: I that was tired out of my life about marriage, and the fear of being stole, may now be trusted out alone; I shall be brought down to a moderate Fortune for a private gentleman, and never will be forced to marry the man I don't like.'[50]

When Herriot Friendless' mother marries Sir Ambrose, and Herriot becomes the heiress, she has now to be kept under surveillance; she has risen from being a girl to being a fortune: 'Now she is become a Fortune, there will be spies about her, and it will be hard to get opportunities of being alone with her', mourns Dareall.[51] But nobody is so oppressed by his money as Sir Ambrose himself: it leads him into all sorts of suspicions and foolishness, and into the bizarre hasty wedding of the title.

But the point is made repeatedly that his suspicions are legitimate and well-founded: scoundrels abound. 'Stealing' heiresses was a growing problem, and plausible imposters were a constant nightmare for a family with a marriageable one. In 1668 the kidnapping and rape of the heiress Mary Ware in an attempt to force her into marriage caused a major scandal.[52] In *The Sham Prince* there is a disturbing suggestion that the whole process of deceiving and 'stealing' an heiress has become reified as a financial speculation: Trueman is distressed by the attention paid by Cheatly to his Araminta: 'I am well assured, 'tis all designed to gain my Araminta, some usurer has advanced money on the intended project.'[53] In *The Hasty Wedding* a letter found in the basket of the procuress, Mrs Go-between, proposes a financial deal which depends on the success of the deception:

> *I am certain she has two thousand pound. Give her the letter, but don't let her know I am turned out of the army; you may call me Major, or Colonel which you will; what's done must be done quick, for my tailor swears he will arrest me before Saturday night. You know I am not worth a groat, and if I am sent to jail, there I must lie. If I succeed you shall certainly have a hundred pound.*[54]

It wasn't just the men who were plying the trade. Another letter in Mrs Go-between's basket gives the female side:

> *Dear Gobetween, wait upon my Lord; I hear he is very flush of money. Persuade him I have eloped from my husband somewhere in the* North. *The Counsellor before he turned me off equipped me with very handsome clothes, and my lodgings are genteel. Upon my honour I am sound: for I have lain with no one but the Brig. this two months; manage this matter well, and Poz you shall go halves.*[55]

The language of adultery and intrigue is laced with the metaphor of commerce: the investment is 'sound' and taking a hand in it will gain a half of the yield, while 'sound' also indicates freedom from venereal disease.

Deception and imposture occur at every turn in Shadwell's plays; plausible scoundrels attempt to exploit the unwary in order to snap up an easy fortune. The penalties were severe: Shirley, the guilty party in the Mary Ware affair, absconded to escape hanging, and his estates were confiscated. Sir Ambrose, in *The Hasty Wedding*, threatens the disguised Squire Daudle: 'Doest thou know, Sirrah, that I can hang thee, my daughter is an heiress; now that dismal dog the *Squire*, has laid a scheme for stealing her, thou, being an accessory to the fact, shall be hanged as well as he.'[56]

The possible penalties apparently did nothing to discourage the fortune-hunters. Church-going was particularly popular with them. Sir Ambrose fulminates against their activities: 'What shoals of fortune-hunters frequent our Church! Fellows who, because Nature has made 'em six foot high, set themselves up to auction, not to be sold by inch of candle, but by dint of impudence, moulded into the shape of a woman's fine gentleman, at the charge of a tailor and a seamstress.'[56]

The imposter and fortune-hunter in *The Hasty Wedding* is Jack Ombre, an English sharper, lurking behind the disguise of Sir John Dareall, 'of the race of cheats, that scorn to get their living any way but by imposing upon other peoples' understandings'.[58] Idle fellows are prowling Tories, unwilling to buckle down to honest endeavour; such chancers are anathema to hard-working Whig merchants. So much so that when Sir John Dareall is found out, and he pleads *noblesse oblige* – 'I beg you would not expose me, for I am a gentleman, tho' an unfortunate younger brother'[59] he gets short shrift from these gentlemen-merchants, who are the primary target of such schemes, and feel no class solidarity with him:

SIR AMBROSE.   So much the worse for that; when gentlemen turn rogues, they always prove the greatest, and ought to be made the greatest examples. Therefore away with him to Justice Quibus.[60]

Sir John's genteel, English manner had seduced Sir Ambrose, but he also wormed into his affections because he spoke fluent Business, especially the Business of Matrimony. He told Sir Ambrose he broke off his match in Somersetshire, not for any sentimental, moral or social reason, but because it would have been a bad bargain: his prospective father-in-law would only give £6,000 with his daughter, yet wanted £1,500 a year settled on her out of her future husband's estate, which only brought in £2,000 a year. So that, after four years, she would become a net drain on her husband's finances:

> I was to have parted with the six thousand pound, to have paid my sisters' Portions, and I have but two thousand pound a year in all, so that in case of my mortality, I might have left half a dozen children starving upon the five hundred a year, whilst my young gay widow, would have been flaunting it about, upon the fifteen hundred.[61]

Aurelia complains mildly about her father's financial and matrimonial mistrust: 'I beg, Sir, you will not be uneasy about my conduct. 'Tis time enough to complain when I have done a foolish action.'[62] Shadwell did not share the profound suspicion of the judgement and virtue of women expressed by the men in his plays. The status of women and the negotiation of their inferior economic position was a common theme of his. He presents a range of unmarried young women, from the free Araminta, to the servile Miss Sevelle, both in *The Sham Prince*, and a range of variations in between. We are also shown different views of a widow's position, but very few married women; in fact, Lady Daudle is the only one of any significance. In *The Sham Prince* there are allusions to merry widows and wives who are kept on a short leash, because they would embarrass their husbands if they had too much money and freedom: 'I know my own income to a shilling,' boasts Welldon, 'and will supply her with just money enough to appear in the Quality which becomes my wife.'[63] Marriage may be the goal of the women, as Lady Homebred's daughters demonstrate, in that they see it as setting them free, but the delights of marriage are surpassed by the freedom of a young widow with a decent jointure. Shadwell did not care for wives. In the Prologue to *The Hasty Wedding*, he remarks:

> If for two nights we can your persons see,
> 'Tis well, a play becomes a wife in three.
> So cold, so careless you to us appear.[64]

At the end of the play Sir Ambrose has cause to 'rejoice abominably'[65] when he is freed from his hasty marriage to Mrs Friendless: 'I tremble when I think of the Danger I have escaped; a termagant wife is the nearest resemblance to the Devil, that ever I met with.'[66] The shortage of wives in Shadwell's plays is balanced by an abundance of unmarried women and widows. It is taken for granted that the women will pass from the one stage to the other, without much in between, and that it is vital to ensure that the correct settlement is put into place before the marriage to accommodate the widow after it is over. Shadwell was using his plays to plant a little subliminal advertising for his other business of Widows' and Orphans' Assurance.

The Hasty Wedding and his other plays mark a perception by Shadwell, and on the part of his characters, of a disillusionment at marriage by women, which we may also presume to reflect an interrogation of the institution among members of the audience. This is tied to the question of the value placed on women.

Sir Ambrose harries his daughter constantly with her economic helplessness: 'I would have you do nothing against your inclinations; but if your inclinations run contrary to mine, you will be turned out of doors, and you may go starve, my dear.'[67] She is an asset, who could turn into a liability if not closely guarded. His distrust of his daughter is founded on his distrust of women in general:

> 'Tis well resolved, were there such a thing as prudence belonging to your sex; but when gentlewomen marry footmen, ladies fall in love with coachmen, and widows ruin their first brood to make way for a second, who can depend upon a woman's resolutions? I know you all have a natural tendency to virtue, and many of you with pains and care are so, but there is pride and vanity, flesh and blood, hat and feather, the world and the devil, to encounter with, and nothing but a virtue, and a weak woman, to stand against 'em all.[68]

This attitude, that women are not to be trusted with their own interests, is adopted by the male characters to a large extent, but the action of the plays negates it. It is Sir Ambrose himself who is the fool that dotes on the coxcomb, Sir John Dareall, and who is totally infatuated with his apparent financial charms: 'He's a jewel of a man – such an estate – and if you prove but a little coming, he will make such a jointure, that thou hast happiness thrown into the very mouth of thee.'[69]

What Sir Ambrose sees is the perfect match, not of two persons, but of two fortunes.

Aurelia, however, has her rights, and states her position openly to Dareall: 'My father may, when he pleases, command me not to marry; but it is never in his power to command me to marry.'[70] Her father can only apply pressure indirectly, by using his economic weapons against her, but she has the invincible shield of refusal. There is a sense here of a negotiation, within the audience and the society, about the rights and position of women in the family and in matrimony. Aurelia is certainly offended by overhearing the men bargaining for her; the female part of the audience, of which Shadwell was acutely conscious, must have shared her outrage when she protests to her father at such treatment: 'What Sir, am I to be bargained and sold to a stranger, without ever being consulted in the matter?'[71]

> SIR AMBROSE   I will lay down ten thousand pound, with some trinkets and jewels that shall be nameless; I will settle all that I have at my death on you, and the heirs of her body, and I will not be unkind in my lifetime.
>
> AURELIA   *(aside)*   Poor miserable creature, 'tis dismal to hear the bargain made.
>
> SIR JOHN   Most generously offered, Sir Ambrose, and not to be behind-hand with you, I will jointure her in a thousand pound a year, settle Hartwell Hall on her, with all the plate, and jewels for her life; and allow her three hundred pound a year pin money.
>
> SIR AMBROSE   Fairly closed, Sir John, it is a match.[72]

The contrast between the impression Sir Ambrose has of Sir John, and Aurelia's opinion of him, is acute. To her, this stranger that her father dotes on is ridiculous. In Shadwell's plays, as in Philips', a 'man of sense' is the ideal marriage partner, often invoked, but in very short supply. Mostly it is the women who show the greatest understanding and sensibility, while their suitors, having left the bargaining table, approach them on some elevated plane of ludicrous sentimentality. Aurelia, like the other young women, find the expressions of the gallants to be so exaggerated and formal as to be meaningless: she condemns Dareall's declaration to be 'Romantick', 'Heroick', and 'Comical'.[73] Araminta, in *The Sham Prince*, repeatedly berates her suitor Trueman for his elevated theatricality: 'Prithee, none of your Fustian to me.'[74] Penelope in *Irish Hospitality* cannot take her suitor seriously on account of his high-toned, foreign style of wooing: 'To make a goddess of a poor country girl, I have no Patience, I cannot bear it.'[75] In the eyes of the women the suitors that are economically attractive are ridiculous on a personal level, and it is clear that Shadwell sympathizes and shares this view. Aurelia speaks for, and to, the female part of the audience; when threatened by her father she states the sentimental ideal: ''Tis better living in a cottage with the man we love, then in a coach-and-six with him we hate.'[76] She stands on her own value as a person and a woman, and resists, on the one hand, the commodification forced on her by a mercenary society and, on the other, the equally false sentimental hyperbole addressed to her by her notably un-heroic suitors.

****

Charles Shadwell had his early plays presented at Drury Lane,[77] and came under the patronage of the Butlers of Ormond while serving in Portugal under Major-General Newton, to whom he dedicated his play *The Humours of the Army*, and to whose wife he dedicated his collected works. In 1713 Shadwell set up in business in Dublin, as an insurance broker in William Street,[78] and from 1715 to 1720 produced five plays set in Ireland for Smock Alley. Three were set in Dublin: *The Hasty Wedding*, (1716/17), *The Sham Prince* (1718/19) and *The Plotting Lovers* (1719/20); *Irish Hospitality* (1717/18) was set in Fingall, and the fifth was the historical play *Rotherick O'Connor* (1719/20). All of these, with his earlier works and poems, were published in Dublin in 1720, with the dedication to Lady Newton. The plays were published by subscription, with 160 subscribers listed. The list is a Who's Who of Irish society, headed by Lady Newton and a few representatives of the peerage: the Earl of Antrim, for example. It includes some of the gentry – knights and baronets, some Honourables and Rt Honourables, and a sprinkling of colonels and captains. But by far the largest number come from the nexus where gentry and bourgeoisie intertwine, the sphere of Mister and Esquire, and there is also a small number of merchants openly listed by the title 'Mer'.

This egalitarianism also manifested itself in Shadwell's plays' main focus: the upper bourgeoisie and the lower gentry. This shift is surprising given the popularity of the Heroic Drama in Ireland, and it indicates the waning of the influence of the *grands seigneurs* of the viceregal court, and the rise of the Whigs, the party of the Glorious Revolution.

John Locke's teachings became the gospel of William of Orange's supporters, who mutated into the Whigs, the proponents of change and conditional monarchy. Throughout the eighteenth century Locke's influence held sway over the Protestants of Ireland, most of whom took the Whig side in the political war of attrition between the Whigs, who considered themselves the vanguard of the Enlightenment, and the Tories, who clung to a more rigid, hierarchical ideal. Throughout the century, this conflict caused uproar in the theatres, in Parliament and on the streets.

The archetypal Whig play was *Tamerlane* (1701) by Nicholas Rowe; its eponymous hero is the ideal constitutional monarch, who is opposed by the unrestrained tyrant Bajazet. In 1714, after the death of Queen Anne and the overthrow of a Tory ministry, 'about 400 gentlemen, the Lord Mayor and 20 Aldermen marched through the city and replaced King William's truncheon in his statue at College Green [see below]. Afterwards they attended the performance of *Tamerlane* complete with Garth's prologue, "without interruption" and "to the great satisfaction of all the company."'[79]

Tamerlane had been banned during the Tory administration that controlled the last four years of Queen Anne's reign but, from 1714, it staged a triumphant return in London and in Dublin.[80] The performance of Garth's Prologue, 'without interruption', was an infallible sign of Whig supremacy. That 'Prologue for the 4 of November 1711' had been written by a fanatical Whig called Samuel Garth. When Ashbury, the Smock Alley manager, had applied to the Lords Justices for permission to present it, they, being Tories, had refused. On William of Orange's birthday the following year Ashbury applied again and was again refused, and this time it provoked the first known riot in the Dublin theatre. Dublin was a Whig town but there was a substantial Tory minority that was reluctant to accept the legitimacy of the House of Orange. Healths were openly drunk to the Stuart Pretender, and the stealing of King William's truncheon was a recurring and potent symbol of dissent.[81] On the night of the *Tamerlane* riot, some of the ladies wore red roses 'in Honour of the English Nation',[82] while the opposition sported orange ornaments – the 'great Whig and Tory' badges referred to by Shadwell[83] A leading Dublin Whig climbed on to the stage and delivered the Prologue himself, in which he berated the 'red rose' brigade, who 'ask his protection, but yet grudge his Power',[84] at which the Tory contingent took umbrage, and disturbances broke out in the audience until the soldiers stationed expectantly on the stage came down and restored order. Some of the leading Whigs were charged with rioting; Ashbury testified against them, but the case was thrown out by a sympathetic jury.

In spite of the inroads the English Parliament was making in the matter of their independence, and the indifference or hostility of successive constitutional monarchs, the Whig state of mind suited the Protestant Irish best, as implying their ultimate right to make their own decisions and regulate their own affairs. The Whigs were also unashamedly the party that supported the expansion of commerce and business, without being too scrupulous ethically, and Dublin was, as Shadwell shows us, a mercantile society.[85] *The Sham Prince* was an openly Whig play for a Whig audience, presented in 1718 or 1719. In it Shadwell lampooned the nature of absolute authority and asseverated the superiority of rule based on the rights of the citizens and the common good. The dominant note is sounded at the Prologue, which invokes the image of King James fleeing from the Boyne about twenty-five years previously, and strongly states the case against the absolutism of the Stuarts and other despots:

> The night before that ever glorious day,
> His Highness, very fairly ran away.
> [...]
> Despotic princes will do what they please,
> And ne'er consult the harmless subjects' ease.
> They come, they go, and never tell the cause,
> Their arbitrary will is still their laws.[86]

The play develops as a fable of trust and deception, carried along on an undercurrent of Whig ideology that frequently bubbles to the surface. The main action of the play is that the pretender, Cheatly, seems to be a prince, and is accepted as such as long as he furthers the interests of his followers; if the deception had continued to serve their purposes, they would have been quite happy to prolong their allegiance, but once he is perceived to put his own interests before that of his subjects, their trust in him fails and his authority collapses; he no longer serves their purpose and they remove him.

The Sham Prince is filled with Whiggish metaphors and allusions. Cheatly, on becoming Prince of Passau, begins to take on the negative attributes of a Tory despot: 'The princes of Germany are all arbitrary, their will is their law.'[87] This is contrasted with the robust Whiggery of the bailiffs who come to arrest him, to whom nobody is above the law, not even a king: 'We an't afraid of a prince; we have arrested your kings and princes too before now.'[88]

The play is bracketed with examples of Whig propaganda. The Prologue called up the image of James II running from the Boyne, and when, at the end of the play, the Sham Prince also runs away, he sends back a letter whose comic insolence is an open declaration of Tory doctrine. In it, he equates himself with the Stuart Pretender, and sees nothing amiss in having his actions governed by a whim. In a truly regal stroke, he signs himself as 'William' and, in a grand Ubu-like finale, claims to be lodging at the Court of St James in London, before taking over as King of Sicily:

> Sovereign Powers often do things out of the way, which appear whimsical to their subjects, but I charge you all upon your allegiance, not to censure my sudden departure, as an act of folly, indiscretion, or trick; for I had received certain information that the Government would seize me, some people having told them I was the Pretender; had I been catched I should have been beheaded immediately. I shall stay a few days at St James's, to concert measures, and I think you will hear no more from me, till I am settled in the Kingdom of Sicily, which I now tell you, I am declared king of.
>
> Yours,
> William.[89]

The Sham Prince implies, as do all of Shadwell's plays, that the nobility have been superseded now that the Glorious Revolution has succeeded, and that the risen bourgeoisie, in the form of private gentlemen, merchants and landed gentry up to the rank of baronet, are the new Ascendancy. The five plays Shadwell left us were the first extended portrayal of the Anglo-Irish, but Shadwell dealt only with the gentry and the higher bourgeoisie. The mantra of 'nobility and gentry' that was frequently invoked throughout the eighteenth century is deceptive; the list of subscribers to Shadwell's works indicates that those who had sufficient interest in the theatre to subscribe to his publication were for the most part the middle and merchant classes. This is the evidence that his plays evince too: the bourgeoisie are the new gentry.[90] Shadwell's patrons may have been the Butlers, but he never sets his dramatic sights that high, preferring to draw on the strands of society he was well acquainted with.

The Sham Prince is built from an elaborate interweaving of trust and deception permeating that society. What we are presented with in the play is an imposture reflected back on itself and intensified. The Cheatlys, father and son, are pretending to be gentlemen who have newly come into a title and estate. The son has taken to calling himself

Sir William, but this does not fool the real gentlemen in the play. Sir Bullet Airy and his friends Welldon and Trueman know that Cheatly is no gentleman. They resolve to make Cheatly look ridiculous by exploiting his greed for social position and fooling him into thinking that his imposture falls short, that he is in reality even grander, not just genteel but royal, and on the point of becoming Prince of Passau. Cheatly falls completely for the deception. In attempting to fool the town, he is deceived by his own magnified reflection and demonstrates his lack of gentility and breeding by being tricked by Trip's false gentleman. The elaborate ruse succeeds beyond the expectation of the perpetrators and a number of other characters are sucked into it. Society is a web and every part affects and supports every other one; the creation of a nobleman, even a false one, has an effect on all of those connected to him. This gives Shadwell the opportunity to show Cheatly's interpretation of royal behaviour, and the conduct of the lower classes when raised by his proximity

What we are given is mostly an elaborate structure of aspiration and pretence – everybody putting themselves up a class or two, giving Shadwell the opportunity to comment on those classes by their imitative behaviour. He doesn't put royalty and nobility on the stage and lampoon them; he presents their imitations and performs a double analysis – of the imposters and of the real thing. Cheatly tries to act like a prince, Sevelle like a courtier, others as lord this or that. As in *The Hasty Wedding*, the gentry and nobility are being satirized without ever making an appearance.

The Whig philosophy of trust and self-reliance, articulated in the main theme of the play, is recapitulated in other keys: the political theme has a minor variation in the private relations between Lady Homebred and her daughters. In contrast to their cousin Araminta, who is free to decide her own actions, and decides well, Lady Homebred keeps her daughters on a very tight leash, and they defy her by going behind her back and asserting their own freedom of action: 'As for my part, I have but a few days to be under her tyranny; [...] Severity makes more hypocrites than any sort of discipline,' says one of them.[91] In *Irish Hospitality*, Shadwell goes even further in showing that the Whig way is not just a political theory, but a template for right action and a philosophy capable of guiding one through life's moral dilemmas. This is the emergence of what Canfield calls the emergent 'master trope of the bourgeois era, self-reliance'.[92] In plays of the era he sees a pattern of success for 'those who stand fixed on the firm centre of self-control as opposed to those who yield to lawless passion',[93] a convergence of public and private morality. Shadwell gives exact expression to this trope in *Irish Hospitality*. Goodlove, who is one of the touchstones of right action in the play, evokes the Whig ideal as the great good, in his attempts to make Charles Worthy act properly, thereby implying that Whiggery is synonymous with Enlightenment, that it is the proper guiding light even in non-political life – the social or the mercantile. Reason, moderation and self-discipline, the refusal to be governed by arbitrary monarchs or passions, the ability to stand by one's own moral standards, are the highest pinnacle of human achievement:

> GOODLOVE   But as our politic notions of the world teach us to hate tyranny and slavery, and to make noble stands for the preserving of our liberty, so we should subdue the arbitrary power of the flesh – there, self preservation should exert itself; 'tis then indeed the first principle of nature, which we ought to make use of, to depose the corrupt monarchy of sin.[94]

This Whig moral utopia is invoked, though, not in mercantile Dublin, but in rural Fingall. For *Irish Hospitality; or, Virtue Rewarded,* Shadwell moved out of the city, and for the first time we have Irish country life among the gentry portrayed on the stage.

Fingall occupied a symbolic space in the Anglo-Irish imagination during the seventeenth and early eighteenth centuries. It was a place removed from the centre, where normal standards and activities were skewed, and the usual boundaries became more elastic. Sir Jowler Kennel marked its uniqueness when he claimed to have 'the best pack of hounds in Ireland, Fingall, or the County of Wicklow'.[95] Farquhar's *Love and a Bottle* ends in a Fingallion dance, an indication that it was a place where Irish and English cultures intermingled. It also provided an aperture through which native Irish culture broke into the consciousness of the English of Ireland by way of music and dancing. In *The Hasty Wedding,* Irish musicians gather under Sir Ambrose's window with their 'drums, trumpets, fiddlers and bagpipes, all come to wish you joy of your wedding, [...] an impertinent custom, but they have pleaded it time out of mind'.[96] In *Irish Hospitality,* Fingall is a melting-pot where different patterns of Ascendancy attitudes and models of character and behaviour are explored and tested. Shadwell portrayed it as a Whig Commonwealth, in which the boundaries of class and race melt and dissolve, and status and advancement are determined by merit, not birth or breeding. Of the series of marriages that end the play, two are inter-class matches, and one is inter-racial.

Many of Shadwell's preoccupations remained intact in this play but he added some new ones. In particular he used the play to explore the place and character of the Ascendancy landlord in the country at large, his influence and responsibilities, the different types of character that were emerging, and different models for the landed gentry.

The ideal is Sir Patrick Worthy, the proprietor of Mount Worthy: 'A generous tempered Gentleman, who having a plentiful estate, keeps open house to all comers and goers.'[97] His favourite pastimes, when not ministering to the needs of his family and tenants, are 'the bliss of contemplation, the conversation of a friend, and that delightful attribute of man, the will and power of doing good'.[98] He has had the benefit of a liberal education, and has embraced the civilized, enlightened balance of the Augustan age, unlike his younger brother, appropriately called Clumsey, a rude countryman who resists all Sir Patrick's attempts to raise him to a gentle standard of behaviour. 'I was in hopes', says Sir Patrick, 'gentleman-like example, and good company, in time might make him hate his sordid ways.'[99] But Clumsey is incorrigible and resists all enticements to refinement:

> CLUMSEY   He's so whimsical as to find fault with my laying my elbows on a table when I'm weary; nay, if I have ever so much meat sticking between my teeth, he will frown on me only for picking 'em with a fork.[100]

Clumsey is a type of rough squire, who only knows country ways and is proud of his bucolic ignorance; to him, the town and its allurements are ridiculous, and Sir Patrick's attempts to gentrify him nothing but a confounded nuisance. He is happy in his hedonistic squalor:

> CLUMSEY   Thank my honest country education [...] Oh, that I could but sit in an elbow-chair after dinner, smoke in the parlour, and sleep there, what a heavenly life I should live. [...] I think everybody's business in this world is to please themselves; and life is short, and generally so troublesome, that there's no study like that of studying to be easy. I would sleep when I'm weary, rise when I'm hungry, smoke for my digestion, drink to raise my spirits, hunt for my health, and never do anything that should give me trouble.[101]

Their neighbour, Sir Jowler Kennel, is the earliest instance in Irish theatre of the rattling, hunting Irish squire, who thinks of nothing but his dogs and horses, whose delight is chasing a fox, and whose every thought and utterance is couched in the language and metaphor of the hunting field: 'a gay pert country baronet, a true sports man, setting a greater value upon his horses and dogs, than those of his own species'.[102]   In his attempts to woo the two disdainful daughters of Sir Patrick Worthy, he displays a vein of good-natured ignorance, which disgusts the girls and allows the narrowness of his mind and his life to be satirized:

> SIR JOWLER   You are a couple of very pretty pusses, and I don't set any value upon my person. Not but I have been taken for a proper lusty man, and have two thousand pounds a year, [...] and I love a true-bred dog, as I love my life, and that's a great sign of good nature, and a good natur'd man will always dote upon a woman. You must know I am in winter a very little trouble in a house, for I am all weathers, wet and dry, upon the back of Primrose. Then as to my eating and drinking, if you put hops enough in my March-beer, and malt in my October, I shall never find fault with your cookery. I hope you're not apt to be jealous, for I must own I love my huntsman mainly. Now if you can't sleep with a good many dogs upon the bed, why none but Beauty, Ranger, Cesar and Sweetlips shall lie of my side; and if you have an aversion to smoking, as I know some ladies have, why I'll chaw, 'tis all one to me.
>
> PENELOPE   Pray, Sir Jowler, are these your good qualities, or your bad ones?[103]

This array of landlords is more than just a gallery of portraits: it has a wider dimension socially and politically. Sir Patrick is most definitely an active and present landlord; everything else flows from that. He is not far removed from the moral and economic paternalism recommended by Maria Edgeworth.[104] Absenteeism is frowned upon from several angles. Looming in the background is the failure of the neighbouring estate of Sir Run-away Spendthrift, whose failure to attend to his estates resulted in ruin:

> SIR JOWLER   'Twas my old friend's Sir Run-away Spendthrift's, poor soul; he was nobody's foe but his own. He would spend his time in Dublin when he should be running his dogs, and before the hunting season was half over, he was fool enough to go to Bath for his health, and he no sooner got it, but he went to London and there lost that and his estate too.[105]

Sir Patrick, at the end of the play, marries his son to an Irish peasant girl, uniting him with the ancient inhabitants of the land, in order to root him there and keep him to his work and obligations. But even though they have been landlords in Fingall 'above these hundred years', what is lacking in the play is any sense of characters embedded in the landscape, of the sort that Boucicault displayed a hundred years later.[106]   The consciousness displayed by them is still colonial and exploitative, predicated on what the country can yield rather than any spiritual consideration. They talk of the hunting, rents, lifestyle or charity, all of which are products of the land, but show no feeling for the country itself.

Such sentimental attachment to a place would not be part of Sir Patrick Worthy's philosophy. He is an enlightened gentleman, the quintessence of Philips' generous man, and he is also the epitome of what Canfield sees as the upright bourgeois standing on his own moral judgement. In him bourgeois self-reliance meets aristocratic generosity. In *The Hasty Wedding*, we saw, in the shape of Sir Ambrose Wealthy, the urban bourgeois characters taking the next step up the social ladder: Sir Ambrose was intent on marrying his daughter into the landed gentry. In *Irish Hospitality* we see the process actually taking place. The estate of Sir Run-away Spendthrift has been bought by Sir Would-be Generous. Sir Would-be tries to imitate the generosity and hospitality of Sir Patrick, but he hasn't got the manner and ease of the proper Irish gentleman. His heart rebels from such profligacy, and he does it 'with an awkward grace, and for want of a cheerful countenance, his generosity hardly seems favours'.[107]   The climax of the play turns on the two meanings of generosity. Sir Would-be thinks that generosity is the physical act of giving away money; Sir Patrick has to show him that it is a much wider and more elusive interweaving of virtue, morals, manners and good taste. Sir Would-be, in their duel of *générosité*, is completely overthrown:

> SIR WOULD-BE   This act of generosity has indeed disarmed me, and you have given me convincing proofs that you are the good man I ought to be. [...] By your wondrous generosity [you] show me such a heap of vices hovering around my soul that it shocks my very nature.[108]

In *Irish Hospitality* Shadwell was beginning to explore the ways in which the Anglo-Irish Ascendancy was filling the metaphorical, imaginative and spiritual space left by the fall of the Irish Chieftains. Sir Patrick appears as the perfect spiritual and physical embodiment of a landed gentleman. Sir Would-be may have the money to buy the estate but he doesn't have the style – he inhabits the physical space but not the metaphysical. That is still occupied by the former owner, poor Spendthrift, who had the style, and is fondly remembered while Sir

Would-be is despised; money, by itself, is not enough. Sir Patrick is rich, landed, open-handed, liberally educated and perfectly fitted to his habitat; he has assumed the easy, graceful *flaithiúileacht* of the old Gaelic lords, as the play's title indicates. He occupies the metaphysical space, which Sir Would-be cannot, though he still lacks historical and spiritual continuity. The wedding of his son Charles and the peasant girl Winnifred Dermott will provide that spiritual union of the island races, and in the play *Rotherick O'Connor*, Shadwell will reach for the historical justification as well.

Sir Patrick's paternalistic authority is another Whig metaphor for constitutional monarchy: it is latent rather than intrusive. He does not force his convictions on his subjects, but when needed he swings into action and solves all problems; otherwise he allows his daughters, his brother, his sister, his son, and his tenants, to choose their own ways. When a crisis occurs, however, he intervenes and imposes his own will, for their greater good, and they all willingly comply, like obedient Lockean subjects. Otherwise, he contents himself with setting the best example of attitude and behaviour. The political implications are clear enough: he runs his estate for the benefit of his people, not for himself, as England should do for Ireland, or a constitutional monarch for his subjects. The liberty of the citizens is limited only by the common good.

The awareness of Ireland that Shadwell exhibited is remarkably inclusive and meritocratic: anything is possible to those who work for and deserve it. The vision of Sir Patrick Worthy includes not just his immediate but also his extended 'Family'. In *Irish Hospitality*, the notion of family extends to include all servants and tenants on Sir Patrick's, or Sir Jowler's, estates, even the virtuous Irish – those who have embraced civilization and English ways. Sir Patrick displays very strongly the paternalistic colonial outlook: that proper example and regulation will socialize the indigenous inhabitants and once they have abandoned their old ways and embraced the new, they can and should be assimilated into enlightened society, and even, as in the case of Winnifred Dermott, raised to the position of Lady of the Manor. Virtue and Worth, he holds, can be found anywhere, in cabin or mansion, and, as the subtitle, *Virtue Rewarded*, asserts, must be encouraged and rewarded wherever it is found. The raising of Winnifred Dermott by marriage to the son of the Baronet is the most startling example of this rising in society, but it extends also to the female servants, who ultimately marry into a higher stratum. Another inter-class marriage takes place between Lucy, the maid, and Sir Patrick's brother, Clumsey; who protests to her: 'What should you be ashamed of marriage for?'[109] Although he is her superior socially, Lucy is wary of marrying him, because of his uncouthness. Sir Patrick instantly gives the match his blessing and gives them his hunting lodge to live in. He agrees with Lucy that she is superior to Clumsey in everything but birth: 'Rise, Lucy, perhaps thou may'st polish him a little.'[110] She has taken advantage of the example given by the Big House, Clumsey has not, and, as a result, she is more civilized than he is. This is contrasted with the men-servants, who are berated for shamming gentility rather than displaying intrinsic merit; they have acquired the manner but not the essence. Trusty is physically attacked by Clumsey for aping polite manners:

> CLUMSEY   Here's a dog! Why, Sirrah, this is worse than calling
> me names. Thou art an incendiary, a complimental rascal; thou
> art enough to debauch a whole Family with thy formalities. I'll
> teach you to be a coxcomb, and pull off your hat and bow, I
> will, Sirrah.
> *Follows him out and beats him.*[111]

Clumsey is objecting to the gentrification of the lower class, who, as they become richer, can assume the customs and manners of the upper classes; he beats Trusty and complains about 'wenches impertinently full of manners'.[112] He sees manners as the prerogative of the higher classes, even though he has none himself. Clumsey is deploring the inevitable progress of civilization, the spreading of enlightenment out from Dublin into Fingall, which was the great hope and aim of the English colonists, but anathema to Sir Patrick's 'stupid brother'.[113] It is a sign of his failure to stop this trend that he himself ends up married to the maid, whose 'breeding' exceeds his own.

The social pattern in Shadwell's plays shows a society constantly re-forming itself. His view of society and education is fraternal rather than hierarchical; education and example are the tools which fashion society. Birth, in this analysis, is relatively unimportant:

> SIR PATRICK   Besides Charles, you are young, the temptations of the
> world are great, and virtue is not born with us.
> CHARLES   I hope I shall never do anything that will be contrary to
> that honour you have imprinted in me.[114]

Both agree that virtue and honour are not inborn but are learned by education, in this case by the example of Sir Patrick. Charles' failure to live up to this standard elevates Winnifred over him. Virtue, attainable by everyone, is valued over birth, estate or education. Sir Patrick even offers to marry Winnifred himself, if Charles proves unworthy:

> SIR PATRICK   I love thee well, thy parentage might be indeed an obstacle to my designs, but thou hast a world of virtue, and of goodness too; my title will make thee a lady, and in return all our children shall inherit thy virtues.[115]

Society and persons within it develop by taking advantage of the education and example available, but not without virtue as an underlying requisite. Virtue is an idea that harks back to ancient Rome, and is a slippery enough concept; it is not simple goodness, as Sir Patrick showed when he said to Winnifred: 'Thou hast a world of virtue, and of goodness too.'[116] It rather combines the idea of correct judgement leading to right action and the strength (*virtus*) to see it through in the face of opposition. It holds the meaning of bourgeois self-reliance and individual action based on personal conviction. Education and example can also corrupt, if virtue is not present in the learner, as in the cases of Charles and Trusty.

The play shows the worthy Irish native being raised to equal status socially and economically. The only thing against Winnifred is her birth as an Irish peasant, but her education has been as a companion to Sir Patrick's daughters, a further instance of Sir Patrick's belief in education by example, this time a successful one. This democracy or meritocracy that Shadwell espouses is very marked, and he implies that the role of the gentry is to educate and raise the native Irish by the best example, which they experience in this play only from Sir Patrick and Ned Generous; the rest set very bad examples indeed. Shadwell's attitudes are critical of the performance of large sections of the Ascendancy.

Charles is 'notwithstanding his liberal education and his father's good example, a vicious young fellow'.[117] Sir Patrick is convinced that the best example at home is a more potent educator than Oxford, and it is vital for the Ascendancy to set the proper standards. He moves to counteract the pernicious foreign influences Charles imbibed while away and elects to keep him at home where he will have him under his watchful eye, and married to a woman who is a pattern of virtue, which is the currency of worth, takes advantage of the opportunities offered and leads to the right people rising in society. In Shadwell's plays, these are always the women.

The young women in Shadwell's plays are penned in economic cages, but there are strong indications of a change in their readiness to tolerate the situation, as shown by Aurelia in *The Hasty Wedding*, the young Homebreds and, especially, Araminta in *The Sham Prince*. It is in these that we see the rebellion most obviously taking place, but it stretches across all classes, down to the servants. The men and the older women want them to stay in their subservient place, but the mobility of society is invested in the young women. They refuse to conform to the expectations of the men. Sir Patrick Worthy's daughters are determined not to be matched with the sporting Sir Jowler Kennel, who evaluates them as if they were two horses: 'Let me see *(looking at Myra)*, there's about fifteen hands high, *(looking at Penelope)* and there's about fourteen and a half; they are both full chested, close ribbed, and carry their heads well.'[118] The girls, however, have no intention of settling for the bucolic squalor so beloved by Clumsey and Sir Jowler: 'Oh, the happy state of living in a sty,' Penelope observes sarcastically, 'where one may grunt and wallow out one's days, eat one's swill without ceremony, and live the life of that charming creature, a hog.'[119] The Homebred girls, in *The Sham Prince,* have been brought up to housewifery, and Araminta castigates their mother for so narrow an attitude: 'You breed 'em as if they were decayed gentlewomen, and that you had hopes of recommending 'em to be housekeepers in a great family, where they are to keep an unruly set of servants in awe.'[120] The heroine, Celia, in *The Plotting Lovers*, will be a nun before she marries the booby her father has chosen for her: 'I will go beyond the sea, change my religion, and throw myself into a nunnery,' she threatens.[121] Aurelia, in *The Hasty Wedding,* refuses to bow to her father's will, even though she will lose everything by it. All these are exemplars of an independence of mind, and a refusal to accede to the commodification of women in the marriage market that Shadwell constantly questions. The culmination is the character of Araminta in *The Sham Prince* who speaks and acts as freely as any man, because of her economic independence. The world of men seems static by comparison. The rising generation of women was clearly different from what went before, all to some degree, and some to an extreme degree. It was they who carried the changes upward into the stagnant male world. The motif of the independent-minded Irish female aristocrat runs through Irish plays, already emerging here as 'your fine, gay, sprightly Irish Women'.[122] They are more practical than the men, who frequently behave idiotically, and they are the engines of social change. They do not suffer fools gladly, and it is the females, influencing their men to fortitude or flexibility, as necessary, who are moving into position to control Anglo-Irish society from the background.

They have a surprising amount of personal freedom. The Homebred girls have no intention of accepting their mother's standards and reach out for aristocratic liberty. Araminta, all through, shows a truly aristocratic contempt for others' opinions, but Lady Homebred says it's because her fortune sets her above the attitudes of the town – a mercenary but shrewd enough observation, and one that Farquhar would endorse. Araminta's economic independence gives her the freedom to behave and talk like a man in public. She reserves her softer side for her private life: 'Prithee, none of your Fustian for me; if we are to play the Fool, let it be in private; keep your soft things to say to me then,' she instructs her suitor.[124] Shadwell predated Marxist theory that all social activity is based on economics, and all economic activity, he showed, following Hobbes, was based on trust. His plays explore the uses and abuses of trust, and how it spiralled up and down the social and business network. The Sham Prince was abusing the trust that was the basis of society, so Trueman and Welldon turned his abuse back on him; Lady Homebred did not trust her daughters, so they paid her back by deceiving her; Sir Ambrose Wealthy's refusal to trust his daughter led him into all sorts of foolishness and grief. Winnifred Dermott and her family, on the other hand, honoured the social contract they had entered into with Sir Patrick Worthy, and were rewarded with an estate and a high position for their daughter.

Shadwell, in *Irish Hospitality*, recommended the best practice for managing the country, based on Lockean ideas of inclusion and meritocracy, reaching out to, and including, the native Irish. This play has a Utopian agenda, and can be seen as a pattern for an enlightened Ascendancy that might attempt to bind the different strands and races together under a benign and moderate authority. In this, Shadwell went well beyond the creed of Protestant or colonial nationalism, whose concern was for the maintenance of its own supremacy. Sir Patrick, in his role as enlightened moral authority, imposes this union for the common good, and unites the two strands of the Irish race. Sir Patrick's son, Charles, has tried to force Winnifred into submission, but has been prevented by his father's intervention and, instead of being a 'wronged maid', she becomes a virtuous wife. The metaphorical and physical spaces merge, and a new ruling class is forged, to which the entire population can give allegiance, and which controls the present and the future.

The past, however, is trickier to command. Legitimacy was a growing concern of the Anglo-Irish and, as they drifted away from England, it was becoming increasingly necessary for them to recreate Irish history in their own image. In *Rotherick O'Connor*, Shadwell continued the work of Shirley in appropriating Irish history, in treating the Irish past as a metaphorical and imaginative space that could be colonized like a physical one.

NOTES AND REFERENCES

1. Cullen calculates that the outflow of absentee rents was not as great as is commonly supposed, but accounted for between one-sixth and one-quarter of the total rent-rolls of the country. In 1698, this amounted to £100,000, and in 1720 had risen to £300,000. L.M Cullen, *An Economic History of Ireland since 1660* (London: B.T. Batsford, 1972), p. 46.
2. Stockwell, *Dublin Theatres and Customs*, p. 174.
3. *Ibid.*, p. 177.
4. Clark, *Early Irish Stage*, p. 145.
5. *Ibid.*, p. 109.
6. W.R. Chetwood, *A General History of the Stage* (Dublin: Printed for the Author, 1750), p. 130.
7. Prologue to *Irish Hospitality; or, Virtue Rewarded,* in Charles Shadwell, *Works of Charles Shadwell*, 2 vols (Dublin: printed for GEORGE RISK and JOSEPH LEATHLEY in Dame's-Street and PATRICK DUGAN on Cork-Hill, Booksellers, 1720), II, p. 202 [The two volumes are published in one cover, but with separate pagination. There is a mistake in the pagination of the second volume in the 1720 edition in the National Library of Ireland, where the numbers of the pages skip suddenly from page 104 to page 141, but I have followed the pagination used in that text.]
8. 'Epilogue to be Spoken in Mourning the last time the Duchess of Bolton comes to the Playhouse before she leaves Ireland', in Shadwell, *Works of Shadwell*, II, p. 341.
9. *Ibid.*, p. 183.
10. Constantia Maxwell, *Dublin under the Georges* (London: Harrap, 1936; reprinted Portrane Co. Dublin: Lambay Books, 1997), p. 232.
11. Stockwell, *Dublin Theatres and Customs*, p. 183, citing Hitchcock.
12. Shadwell, *The Hasty Wedding*, IV. in *Works of Shadwell*, p. 61.
13. Shadwell, *The Sham Prince*, I, in *Works of Shadwell*, p. 174.
14. Stockwell, *Dublin Theatres and Customs*, p. 184
15. *Ibid.*, p. 184.
16. *Ibid.*, p. 186.
17. *Ibid.*, p. 185.
18. Shadwell, Epilogue 2 to Shadwell's *Rotherick O'Connor*, in *Works of Shadwell*, p. 270.
19. Shadwell, Dedication to *Works of Shadwell*, p. VI.
20. Stockwell, *Dublin Theatres and Customs*, p. 121.
21. *Ibid.*, p. 186.
22. Clark, *Early Irish* Stage, p. 126.
23. *Ibid.*, p. 135.
24. Stephen Gwynn, cited by Stockwell, in *Dublin Theatres and Customs*, p. 177.
25. Swift, *Drapier Letters*, IV: 'I have known upon occasion some of these absent officers as keen against the interest of Ireland as if they had never been indebted to her for a single groat,' in *The Portable Swift*, ed. by Carl Van Doren, Viking Portable Library (New York: The Viking Press, 1948), p. 189.
26. Constantia Maxwell, *Dublin under the Georges*, p. 58.
27. Shadwell, Epilogue to *Irish Hospitality*, in *Shadwell's Works*, I, p. 203.

28. *Ibid.*, Epilogue to *The Hasty Wedding*, in *Shadwell's Works*, I, p. 5.
29. *Ibid.*, Prologue, in *Shadwell's Works*, I, p. 3.
30. Clark, *Early Irish Stage*, p. 166.
31. Shadwell, Preface to *The Sham Prince*, in *Shadwell's Works*, II, p. 157.
32. Date given at http://www. pgil-eirdata.org/html/pgil_datasets/authors/Shadwell,C/life. htm [accessed 10/04/02] (p. 1 of 4).
33. Shadwell, *The Hasty Wedding*, I, in *Shadwell's Works*, I, p. 9.
34. *Ibid.*, p. 48.
35. *Ibid.*, p. 40.
36. *Ibid.*, p. 40.
37. *Ibid.*, II, p. 41.
38. *Ibid.*, IV, p. 83.
39. *Ibid.*, I, p. 26.
40. *Ibid.*, IV, p. 83.
41. *Ibid.*, IV, p. 89
42. *Ibid.*, IV, p. 89.
43. Shadwell, *The Sham Prince*, IV, p. 224.
44. *Ibid.*, p. 224.
45. *Ibid.*, p. 225.
46. *Ibid.*, p. 224.
47. Maxwell, *Dublin under the Georges*, p. 15.
48. Shadwell, *The Hasty Wedding*, I, p.10.
49. *Ibid.*, p. 25.
50. *Ibid.*, IV, p. 76.
51. *Ibid.*, V, p. 143.
52. *CSPI*, 1666–69, p. 566. This was a notorious case of abduction and rape carried out in an attempt to force the heiress Mary Ware to marry a certain Shirley, for which she had him charged in the courts. Shirley fled when arraigned and his estates were confiscated and sold; he fled to England and succeeded sufficiently in ingratiating himself at Whitehall as to lobby for the return of his estates. His last mention in the State Papers is in a letter by the sheriff claiming that he has returned, and requesting instructions as to whether or not he is to be apprehended. The answer has not survived.
53. Shadwell, *The Sham Prince*, I, p. 168.
54. Shadwell, *The Hasty Wedding*, II, p. 61.
55. *Ibid.*, p. 62.
56. *Ibid.*, p. 45.
57. *Ibid.*, I, p.10.
58. *Ibid.*, V, p. 149.
59. *Ibid.*, p. 149.
60. *Ibid.*, V, p. 150.
61. *Ibid.*, I, p. 20.
62. *Ibid.*, II, p. 48.
63. Shadwell, *The Sham Prince*, I, p. 165.
64. Prologue to Shadwell, *The Hasty Wedding*, p. 3.
65. *Ibid.*, V, p. 152.
66. *Ibid.*, p. 153.
67. *Ibid.*, II, p. 50.
68. *Ibid.*, I, p. 12.
69. *Ibid.*, II, p. 30.
70. *Ibid.*, p. 28.
71. *Ibid.*, III, p. 50.
72. *Ibid.*, II, p. 49.
73. *Ibid.*, p. 28.
74. Shadwell, *The Sham Prince*, V, p. 259.
75. Shadwell, *Irish Hospitality*, III, p. 254.
76. Shadwell, *The Hasty Wedding*, III, p. 66.

77. *The Fair Quaker of Deal* in 1710, and *The Merry Wives of Broad Street* in 1713.

78. 'Office of Assurance for the Support of Widows and Orphans', advertisement in *The Dublin Intelligencer*, Dec 19, 1713; cited in Helen M. Burke, *Riotous Performances, The Struggle for Hegemony in the Irish Theatre, 1712–1784* (Notre Dame Indiana: University of Notre Dame Press, 2003), p. 68.

79. Stockwell, *Dublin Theatres and Customs*, p. 153.

80. Lindsay, David W. and Hampden, John, eds., *The Beggar's Opera and other Eighteenth Century Plays* (London: J.M. Dent, 1974) (first pub. Everyman's Library, 1928), p. vi: 'The three main phases of political influence can be defined by reference to the theatrical career of an archetypal Whig play, Rowe's *Tamerlane*: having been performed intermittently until 1710, this work was excluded from the repertoire during the last four years of Queen Anne's reign, but performed several times each season from 1715 onwards.'

81. Maxwell, *Dublin under the* Georges, p. 182.

82. Clark, *Early Irish Stage*, p. 129.

83. Shadwell, *The Hasty Wedding*, II, p. 50.

84. Clark, *Early Irish Stage*, p. 130.

85. Swift, as a committed Tory, detested the Whigs: Van Doren, 'Editor's Introduction', in *The Portable Swift*, p. 15:' They were for him, only a brawling faction, hungry for profits, and not more than a tenth of England. [...] Having made their fortunes at the expense of the majority, [they] meant to go on making other fortunes, and would stop at no lying, no plotting no uprising, no overthrowing which might serve their factious ends.'

86. Shadwell, Prologue, *The Sham Prince*, p. 159.

87. *Ibid.*, II, p. 197.

88. *Ibid.*, III. 2, p. 214.

89. *Ibid.*, V, p. 257.

90. The nobility consists of the five ranks of the Peerage: duke, marquis, earl, viscount and baron. Baronets are the highest rank of Private Gentlemen, or Gentry; they do not belong to the Nobility.

91. Shadwell, *The Sham Prince*, III, p. 214.

92. Canfield, 'Shifting Tropes of Ideology', p. 199.

93. *Ibid.*, p. 200.

94. Shadwell, *Irish Hospitality,* V, p. 286.

95. *Ibid.*, II, p. 234.

96. Shadwell, *The Hasty Wedding*, IV, p. 79.

97. Dramatis Personae, Shadwell, *Irish Hospitality*, I, p. 204.

98. *Ibid.*, I, p. 215.

99. *Ibid.,* p. 222.

100. *Ibid.*, I, p. 209.

101. *Ibid.*, I, p. 213.

102. Dramatis Personae, *Ibid.*, p. 204.

103. *Ibid.*, II, p. 234.

104. Maria Edgeworth, *Ennui*, in *Castle Rackrent, & Ennui,* ed. by Marilyn Butler (London: Penguin Books, 1992): 'When I saw on Lord Y's estate and on those of several other gentlemen [...] the neat cottages, the well-cultivated farms, the air of comfort, industry, and prosperity, diffused through the lower classes of the people, I was convinced that much may be done by the judicious care and assistance of landlords for their tenantry.'

105. Shadwell, *Irish Hospitality II, p.* 236.

106. *Ibid.*, I, p. 223.

107. *Ibid.*, I, p. 217.

108. *Ibid.*, V, p. 293.

109. *Ibid.*, V, p. 302.

110. *Ibid.*, V, p. 303.

111. *Ibid.*, II, p. 231.

112. *Ibid.*, IV, p. 257.

113. *Ibid.,* V, p. 299.
114. *Ibid.,* V, p. 299.
115. *Ibid.,* V, p. 300.
116. *Ibid.,* V, p. 300.
117. Dramatis Personae, *Ibid.,* p. 204.
118. *Ibid,* I, p. 233.
119. *Ibid.,* II, p. 256.
120. Shadwell, *The Sham Prince,* I, p. 174.
121. Shadwell, *The Plotting Lovers, in Shadwell's Works,* II, p. 311.
122. Shadwell, *The Sham Prince,* IV, p. 235.
123. *Ibid.,* V, p. 259.

5

Cultural Colonization: Summoning 'Hibernia'

The balance of the Irish ruling class in the early decades of the eighteenth century had shifted decisively towards the gentry and away from the nobility. An emerging strain during the period was the native Irish aristocracy, which seemed to have almost died out after Aughrim, but re-asserted itself as the eighteenth century progressed. The Penal Laws were designed as a form of social engineering, a means of excluding Catholics, considered to be under the command of their clergy and the Popes of Rome, from the levers of land, power and the constitution, where they could not be trusted to protect the liberty that the Glorious Revolution of 1689 had bestowed on them. Even the first Earl of Charlemont, in the late eighteenth century, while abhorring the Penal Laws, still held the view that 'he did not think it safe to grant liberty to those who did not believe in liberty themselves'.[1] Daniel Corkery's *The Hidden Ireland* asserts that the surviving Gaelic aristocracy that clung to Catholicism cultivated invisibility during the eighteenth century, but he is inclined to exaggerate the rupture between the English and the Irish, and to imagine a vigorous underground Gaelic culture that continued to thrive beyond the ignorant ken of the Protestant English Ascendancy. There was, however, a minority of the Irish aristocracy that held on to some or all of its holdings without hiding or embracing the Established Church. The Earls of Antrim (McDonnells) and the Viscounts Kenmare (Brownes), for example, bestrode both cultures. Irish Ireland had not become, as Corkery asserts, purely a peasant nation.[2] Apart from the McDonnells or the Brownes, the activities of the exiled Irish nobility on the Continent – 'an Irish Catholic nation in waiting, with its colleges, its army, its wealthy diaspora'[3] – was followed with avid interest in their place of origin. The influence of the newly risen bourgeoisie was also becoming manifest. Many of them were Catholics and belonged to the remnants of the dispossessed families – middlemen like O'Dogherty in Macklin's

The True-born Irishman. More importantly, those who converted to the Established Church still retained the loyalty and regard of the buried majority of Catholics.

Those who did convert did not automatically abandon their former aristocratic positions within Irish culture; the conversion was often viewed as a necessary ruse by the family followers, though arousing deep suspicion among the more recently arrived English of Ireland. The established aristocracy, however, tended to look benignly on such dynastic manoeuvres. The last Earl of Thomond, for example, was given permission by George I to ask his Catholic cousin, Viscount Clare, then serving in the French army, to convert to Protestantism and inherit the title.[4] The aristocracy understood the urge to preserve and consolidate family property and prestige, regardless of religious or political rifts. The lower strata of the Protestant Anglo-Irish regarded the practice of timely conversion with a more jaundiced eye. *The Conduct of the Purse in Ireland*, a pamphlet of 1714, complains:

> They frequently after their Conversion retain their former intimacy with the Papists, and are as well and as cordially received by them as ever. They never make or endeavour to make any new Acquaintance or Alliance with the old Protestants; [...] excepting that they sometimes go to Church, they remain in all respects to all appearances the very same men they were before their conversion.[5]

Such sniping continued all through the eighteenth century, as the Catholic majority found ways around and through the Penal Laws, and proceeded to question and undermine the rule and legitimacy of their colonial masters.

The concern for legal and spiritual legitimacy that the rulers of Protestant Ireland felt was explored, bolstered or questioned in a series of historical plays during the eighteenth century. At the root of all these works lay Molyneux's triple argument: that Ireland was never conquered because the Norman-English arrived by invitation and were paid for their assistance by grants of land, that the voluntary submission of the Irish chieftains to Henry II gave them equal rights to their counterparts in England, and that the willing assistance given by the colonists to the authorities in subjugating the rebellious Irish, all gave the English of Ireland a legitimacy and a right to constitutional freedom under the Crown as good as that enjoyed by any English citizen. The plays, however, betrayed the depth and range of their uncertainty about the nature, status and legitimacy of their tenure. The playwrights went well beyond the position expressed by Molyneux and Swift, and questioned the dismissal of the native Irish as nonentities, suggesting a *rapprochement* between the two races. In hindsight, the playwrights can be seen to be wiser than the established authorities, who pursued Protestant hegemony rather than the inclusiveness recommended by the plays, and who remained suspicious even of the converted Irish. The majority of them chose to live the illusion of the Protestant Nation, sealed off from the underclass, untouched and untouchable.

Several Irish plays of the early eighteenth century examined the legitimacy question in a historical context. In doing so, they created a story and fashioned a myth for the English of Ireland, if they would choose to believe it. Every society needs a founding myth, the story it tells to itself, the illusion that sustains it. The founding myth of the Anglo-Irish was the taming of a savage country and bringing to it civility and laws, but this myth was crumbling visibly, and what we have in these historical plays was the creation of a new story to feed and nourish the colonists' imagination – the Story of Hibernia.

The distance and tension between the story and the event has always exercised writers – how do facts become story? A story achieves a more potent actuality than a mere list of occurrences; art and language give it shape and meaning. In these plays, events are moulded into a new shape and meaning for the Anglo-Irish ruling class. From James Shirley onwards, Irish playwrights have been creating myths; events are transformed by language into story, which then assumes its own transformational reality. But belief is essential: only those who can embrace the fullness and reality of the story, as opposed to the reality of the event, can experience the renovative magic that it dispenses. This probably finds its finest expression in Synge's *The Playboy of the Western World*, where 'there's a great gap between a gallous story and a dirty deed',[6] and only those who believe the Word are saved – Pegeen Mike can't, Old Mahon can. Pegeen Mike pulls back from the story and demands that raw, bald reality be ultimate; Old Mahon cheerfully accepts the reality of the poetic creation that is the new Christy, and together father and son escape from the stultifying diurnality of the shebeen. The Anglo-Irish in the eighteenth century also failed to respond to the imaginative leap that the playwrights made in the creation of an inclusive society, and clung to what seemed to them the reality of the Irish Protestant Nation, one of racial and religious superiority and their God-given right to civilize and rule the country. This was in fact just a different, exclusive story. The speech that Lord Clare made to the Irish Parliament on the Union in 1800 reminded them of what they chose to ignore or forget: that their position was based on force and confiscation:

The whole power and property of the country has been conferred by successive monarchs of England upon an English colony, composed of three sets of English adventurers, who poured into this country at the termination of three successive rebellions. Confiscation is their common title, and from their first settlement they have been hemmed in on every side by the old inhabitants of the island, brooding over their discontents in sullen indignation.[7]

This speech Elizabeth Bowen described as 'a speech of superb detestable realism. On the Anglo-Irish illusion, each phrase of Fitzgibbon fell like a hammer.'[8] It also indicated how far the aspirations of the playwrights were out of step with the accepted orthodoxy of Ascendancy society.

Shadwell's *Rotherick O'Connor* (1720) was the first attempt since Shirley's 1640 *Saint Patrick for Ireland* at fashioning a new Story for the Anglo-Irish by mining Irish history as a source. Like the latter, it was more concerned with contemporary resonance than historical accuracy. It was the past selected and interpreted to justify the present – the present encoded in a historical metaphor.

Rotherick O'Connor was Shadwell's *Tamerlane*; the Whig-Tory opposition of tyranny versus freedom is made perfectly explicit in the Prologue and the play itself:

> He brings to view, five hundred years ago
> [...]
> Kings that governed with an Arbitrary Sway,
> and slavish Subjects, born but to obey.
> [...]
> Learn then from those unhappy days of yore
> to scorn and hate an Arbitrary Power,
> To praise and love those laws that make you Free,
> And are the great Bullworks of your Liberty.[9]

In an interesting reversal of nationalist history, MacMorough, the man who brought over the Normans, is the hero, and Rotherick O'Connor, who fought to keep them out, is a villain, an absolute monarch who acts on impulse, indulges all his whims, and treats his subjects as slaves. The character is written with the crudity of a pantomime villain, without light or shade, unscrupulous and immoral in both private and public spheres:

> ROTHERICK A monarch's made to rule each petty slave,
>   To bid him live,

or send him to his grave.
[...]
No human passions should a king control.
[...]
And all is just and good that monarch's say.[10]

Contrasted with him are Dermond[11] MacMorough and Strongbow, who are the champions of liberty and law. MacMorough is shown as weak and elderly, the wronged and rightful king, querulous and conciliatory, fretting about his son and daughter. He is an insubstantial figure beside the vigour and passion of Strongbow, but also a necessary brake on Strongbow's bloodthirsty nature; between the two of them they form the Whig ideal of consensus backed by power. The portrayal of Strongbow, the seminal figure for the English colonists, is by no means idealized: he needs the restraint and statesmanship of MacMorough and his council, and he is kept as a supplicant, in spite of his martial success, by the steadfast refusal of Dermond's daughter, Eva, to legitimize his claim to the throne by becoming his wife.

In *Irish Hospitality* the character of Winnifred, the peasant girl, extends by implication to represent the subservient majority of the Irish people; the *Aisling* poetry had found its way into Shadwell's consciousness. In the character of Eva in *Rotherick O'Connor* he took a further step in creating a female representation of the country. Eva gives expression to the Irish point of view at all times, invoking Irish virtues, and rebuking any intimations of inferiority:

> EVA   You have forgot you were in Ireland born,
>   Where pure religion, by Saint Patrick taught,
>   Is still kept up, with a becoming zeal;
>   [...]
>   Perhaps with artful engines made for war,
>   These strangers may strike terror through the field,
>   [...]
>   But when the Hibernian spirit's roused,
>   These strangers will not be such mighty men.[12]

As the daughter of MacMorough, she is equated with his kingdom, and is the repayment to Strongbow for his services; she is the reward, the kingdom is her dowry:

> DERMOND   Take her my faithful friend and ally,
>   And with her, take my crown, and take my kingdom.[13]

As the play progresses so does this identification of Eva with Ireland,

and further elements from the *Aisling* creep in – she is the sorrowing female who cannot think of love or marriage while the country is in a state of unrest, whose grief is both personal and political:

> EVA   But, horror to my soul, what grief is that,
> To wed the creature whom my country hates.[14]

Throughout the play the military success of the Normans is balanced against Eva's attitude to them. She begins in outright opposition and disgust at her father's actions in inviting them, and outrage at being gifted in marriage to Strongbow.

> STRONGBOW Suppose it were tonight, what hinders it?
> EVA   What may hinder it an age, my consent;
> Know you not that it is necessary?[15]

She moves then from firm refusal to grudging acceptance of him as regent in her father's place:

> EVA   The Earl of Chepstow comes to set me free,
> And he is now the only friend I've left.[16]

Although O'Connor has been overthrown and the Normans triumphant, she still withholds her consent to uniting herself in marriage to Strongbow. The resonance with the contemporary scene in 1720 is obvious: the country may have been subjugated, but it did not willingly accept it, and still withheld its consent.

The central founding myth of the Anglo-Irish was no longer tenable; the image of civilizing the Irish barbarians had been shattered. A knowledge and understanding of Irish history and culture had spread among the colonists, and Shadwell, in this play, began the appropriation of this legacy. He showed the Irish displaying admirable qualities. They possess courage and loyalty: 'We act what men dare do,' declares Regan, 'and always justify what we think right.'[17] They are fiercely loyal to their country, but not to any particular monarch or authority. They are spontaneous rather than calculating: 'We are governed by Nature's dictates/ Not by dissembling Art which teaches men/ To act quite opposite to what they think.'[18]

For his main argument, Shadwell revisited Molyneux and, as we might expect from Shadwell, he interpreted the events of the Norman incursion from a commercial perspective: the exchange between MacMorough and Strongbow is portrayed as a contract in the business sense. As ever in Shadwell, the play is loaded with commercial metaphors of 'interest', 'credit', 'obligation', but especially the principal conceit of 'contract', overriding even familial loyalty and affection:

> STRONGBOW   But why this mighty care to save your son?
> Is it consistent with the agreement made?
> How can you fulfil your sacred contract?
> [...]
> Perhaps
> you do repent you of the bargain made?[19]

The counter to this insistence on contractual rigour in the play is Strongbow's invocation of conquest, but this is effectively negated by its context. Strongbow suggests it to Catholicus, the bishop of Tuam, in private, as the way the Norman incursion is to be sold to the native Irish, the spin it is to be given:

> CATHOLICUS   The clergy in their pulpits shall declare
> That you have all the right you would have;
> We'll found it on what principle you please.
> STRONGBOW   The right of conquest is the right I own.
> CATHOLICUS   Then they shall preach up that, and in such terms
> That were you beaten, they should say you conquered.[20]

Strongbow's statement is devalued by Catholicus's enthusiastic embrace of it; he transforms it into propaganda. Catholicus is a Machiavellian churchman, continuously manoeuvring to achieve the best possible position for himself and his Church. He blows in the wind like a weathercock, and is willing to confer legitimacy on anyone who has power. He moves without a scruple from being a lackey of Rotherick O'Connor to being a vassal of Strongbow. His embracing of Strongbow's statement annihilates it, while everything else in the play acts to contradict it. Any conquering Strongbow does is as an employee of Dermond's:

> REGAN   My royal master, willing to recover
> Rebellious subjects to their true allegiance,
> Hired this noisy lord, and all his knights,
> To serve him in the war, and they assume
> A power, a command, as if they conquered,
> And we and all the country were their slaves.[21]

Note Regan's 'as if they conquered', saying quite clearly that they did not. The Irish characters refer to the bargain between Strongbow and Dermond with dismay, but have no doubt as to its nature or validity – a transaction in which Strongbow will be rewarded for services rendered. If conquest is the accepted story, it confers no legitimacy, as it is obvious that a stronger military force has as good a right to overthrow it. So it has become necessary to put in place a legal and historical justification for the English takeover. This is why Shadwell cast the Norman incursion as a commercial transaction, to be executed and paid for, and legitimate because, to the risen bourgeoisie of the new Ascendancy, such a contract, as Strongbow observed, was 'sacred'.

But both parties need to be satisfied as to the validity and fairness of the bargain; Strongbow has overcome Dermond's enemies, but he cannot rule without the consent of Eva/Ireland, which, by the play's end, has not yet materialized. After MacMorough's death, Strongbow acknowledges the primacy of Eva, as queen of Leinster, not of his own claims to rule:

> Guards, secure the princess, and if I should die,
> Proclaim her Queen of Leinster, and obey her:
> It is with joy, my fairest, I proceed,
> to vindicate your right.[22]

With Dermond's death, she inherits both the kingdom and the contract. Strongbow then fights to restore Dermond's line to the throne of Leinster, to establish Eva's right to be queen, not his to be king. The role he seeks will be as her consort, and she, bowing to the inevitable, appoints him, in the interim, as regent:

> EVA   I beg you would command my father's army,
>   Rule and govern well his kingdom, curb his foes,
>   And give his poor and wretched subjects ease.[23]

The play is consistent with Shadwell's Whig philosophy, and echoes Shirley's *Saint Patrick for Ireland*. Shirley showed the Irish as worshippers of false gods, from which the English and Saint Patrick rescued them; Shadwell depicted them as worshippers of false politics, having despotic, tyrannous kings and priests from whom the Normans delivered them to liberty and justice. Strongbow summarizes his gifts to the Irish:

> STRONGBOW   I come not to destroy but give you liberty
>   And bring this barbarous nation to such laws
>   As will draw peace and plenty to your country.[24]

But, by 1720, such sentiments were becoming unsustainable. Medieval Irish civilization could no longer be characterized as barbarous. Sarah Butler had published her collection of *Irish Tales* in 1716, the first example of Anglo-Irish fiction.[25] She called her Preface to that work 'On the Learning and Politeness of the Ancient Irish', and, instead of praising the role of the colonists in civilizing the Irish, she openly blamed them for the present barbarous state of the native inhabitants: 'Although they may seem (so Rude and Illiterate a People), in the Circumstances they lie under (having borne the heavy yoke of Bondage for so many Years, and have been Cow'd down in their Spirits) yet that once Ireland was esteem'd one of the Principle Nations in Europe for Piety and Learning.'[26]

Strongbow's assertion of 'liberty and laws' gives the opposite side of that argument – the colonial creed of the English of Ireland. *Rotherick O'Connor* embraces both points of view and suggests a joint venture between the two races that share the island, and Shadwell's plot and characterization pursue this outcome. Rotherick O'Connor is a reprehensible tyrant, but Strongbow is not much better, being fierce and bloodthirsty. The play shows his force and power being tamed, harnessed, and directed, first by Dermond MacMorough and his council, and later by his need to win the support and esteem of Dermond's daughter, which he achieves by becoming her personal champion. *Rotherick O'Connor* rewrites history from the Anglo-Irish point of view to emphasize the legitimacy of their claims and titles. It follows then that all the Old English are valid and legitimate stakeholders in the country. Historical plays are never about the past; they are historical metaphors for the present. *Rotherick O'Connor* ends with all the Irish chieftains dead and Eva reluctant. Strongbow alone stands as the institutor of the new dispensation – the father of Hibernia, but Eva still has to be convinced to be its mother. The message is that the Normans/English will rule, bringing peace and prosperity; the native Irish need to acquiesce for their own good, but the Norman/English cannot succeed without winning their consent.

Shadwell's use of bourgeois values and his insistence on the Anglo-Irish right of tenure and the pre-eminence of Whig values were perfectly consistent with his other plays. It would be reasonable to expect that his portrayal of a bourgeois gentry and his appropriation of history on their behalf would be greeted with enthusiasm by his audience, but the secondary theme of native Irish consent and the need to find a form of productive sharing of the island must have cancelled that out. The play was not well-received.

Shadwell's earlier comedies, while no masterpieces, were competent dramas and had been reasonably successful. They were solidly constructed and written, with some flashes of clever plotting and verbal felicity. The characters were conventional humour-based types, but displayed some excellent comic quirks; the bucolic spleen of Sir Patrick's brother Clumsey in *Irish Hospitality*, for example, or the gleeful berating of his betters by the disguised servant, Trip, in *The Sham Prince*, were well written and structured, and dramatically apposite. Shadwell also used those plays to draw some startling conclusions and to air some controversial ideas in public, about the position of women, for instance, or the necessity of absorbing the native Irish into the social and political fabric of the country.

So, while successful, he did not shy from controversy, and, with *Rotherick O'Connor*, he showed that he was prepared to go well beyond what his audience wanted or expected. The indications are that this time he went too far. This appears to have been his last play, and the prologues and epilogues to the published work show us that Shadwell was aware that it was not popular with its audience. The first prologue, '*by Colonel Allen. Designed to have been spoke, but came too late*',[27] ironically insists that the Colonel tried to persuade Shadwell out of writing the play, but that he was not to be deflected:

> I told him what he enterprised was hard,
> Presumptious in a Greek or Irish bard.
> [...]
> These friendly hints I gave, but 'twould not do,
> Full of himself, he would his own pursue. [28]

In the first epilogue, Shadwell apologized for the play and promised to confine himself to comedy from now on, because of the audience's reception:

> Our poet swears by all that's great and good,
> No more he'll dip his hands in human blood,
> It is his first effort in tragic strains,
> And knows not how it came into his brains.
> [...]
> But do say something in the man's behalf,
> And faith, when next he writes, he'll make you laugh.[29]

The play is no better or worse than his others, but is more ambitious, being a tragedy and written in blank verse. The verse is competent, and the tragedy is engineered rather than organic; and, though it suffers from excessive exposition, and has characters given to declaration rather than dialogue, it is not that bad a play. It is full of interest to the modern reader, and should have been more so to its contemporary audience. Part of the problem, Shadwell tells us, was the upper gallery's insistence on treating everything as comedy, and the inattentiveness of the fashionable world in the middle gallery:

> Now 'tis observed, our friends two story high
> Do always laugh when other people cry,
> And murdering scenes to them are comedy.
> The middle regions seldom mind the plot
> But with a Vizard chat of you know what,
> And are not bettered by the play one jot.[30]

That mention of 'bettered' indicates the didactic role that Shadwell intended. The play itself, while broadly supporting the political and patriotic position of Protestant nationalism, presented some very challenging ideas to its Anglo-Irish audience about their relationship with Ireland and the native Irish. In this it followed in a direct line from *Irish Hospitality*, a play that culminated in a symbolic mixing of races, cultures and classes. This is a good example of the artist being so far ahead of his audience that he loses them. Shadwell's plays placed the early eighteenth-century Dublin bourgeoisie as a potent force in the forging of the Irish Protestant Ascendancy, but, as a playwright, and a foreigner, he spoke to and about his Dublin audience; he did not speak for them.

Another voice crying in the wilderness was William Philips, author of *St Stephen's Green*, who returned to playwrighting after more than twenty years, to pursue, as before, a definite agenda. His objective this time was to position the revived Irish aristocracy at the head of the emerging Ascendancy.

Philips' *Hibernia Freed* (1722) has the appearance of a reaction to Shadwell, but uses history to create a different metaphor. In Philips' play, the Danish invader is defeated by a combination of his own folly, the stoicism of the Irish, and the craft and sagacity of the Irish nobility. Shadwell had acknowledged Irish virtues in his play, but Philips' drama imagined an ancient Irish society displaying both the neo-stoic virtues of the Enlightenment and a civilization equal to ancient Greece and Rome. He surpassed Shadwell in embodying Ireland as a woman, equating conquest with rape, and asserting the refinement, culture and superior morality of the embattled Irish. Philips was declaring the surviving Irish nobility as the natural aristocracy of the country. He could hardly have gone further to overturn the civilizing foundation myth of the Anglo-Irish, as expressed by Shirley and repeated by Shadwell.

There can be no doubt that it was quite deliberate. Philips has never been given his due as the first Irish patriotic writer, his work flickering behind the ferocious blaze of Swift. In *St Stephen's Green* Philips outlined the superiority of Dublin's generous society, and in *Hibernia Freed* he re-invented the ancient Irish nobility as a gift to contemporary Ireland. From this play, we can date the revival of the native aristocracy, in ruins after Aughrim, as it bid to take its place at the head of the Protestant ruling class.

Philips' strategy was to use classical names – Sabina, Eugenius, Herimon – and Latin forms of place names – Ultonia, Connacia and, especially, Hibernia. The old Latin name was the one preferred by the Anglo-Irish writers at this period for Protestant Ireland. Hibernia was the Irish Protestant Nation called into being by the eighteenth-century playwrights – a free state of Protestant aristocrats, growing naturally and legally out of ancient Ireland, a free parliament and people, a Utopia without a resentful Catholic sub-class or English interference. It was an artefact of refinement, culture, free-trade and neo-stoic bourgeois independence, a literary creation that elides several centuries and unites a glorious past with a bright future through a determined refusal to accept the contentious present. Illusion was a large factor in Anglo-Irish civilization: their houses, their relationship with the dispossessed, their extravagant, profligate lifestyle were all facets of their play-acting, but Hibernia was the greatest illusion of all. According to Ibsen or Arthur Miller, such reiteration creates, not a sustaining Story but a lie large enough to live in. The difference is that, in Ibsen or Miller, structures of belief are founded on suppression or falsehood, not on a communal embracing of an interpretation, not on the enrapturing power of language but on the corroding protection of concealment. The two conflicting stories of Anglo-Ireland epitomized both of these approaches; Hibernia achieved two Janus-like faces: the inclusive story of the playwrights utilizing language and interpretation, and the exclusive vision of the rulers, based on ignoring the realities that were glaringly obvious to the Earl of Clare.

In both *Hibernia Freed* and *Rotherick O'Connor*, Hibernia was established by a wedding, or proposed wedding, between the different traditions in the country. This gave the Anglo-Ascendancy some anchorage in the older traditions of the island. In this Augustan age, the regaining of classical poise and civilization was always a goal, and in order to gain access to the ancient Gaelic traditions, Philips created the illusion of a classical civilization on an island that never knew the Romans.

Hibernia Freed fabricates a classical state of Hibernia, sings its virtues, and sets it free, thereby fusing the tenth and eighteenth centuries. The play rejects the idea of conquest and shows that superior force or guile can and should overthrow it. Turgesius and the Danes are despots whom their Irish subjects have to endure as a punishment for disunity and immorality. The Norman incursion, however, is legitimized as 'invited to our aid', and will succeed because it will voluntarily blend the two 'bloods' into the new nation.[31]

There is no record of the play being presented in Dublin,[32] though it was reprinted and published there immediately after its staging and publication in London.[33] However, the records of Dublin productions from this period are patchy, consisting mainly of handbills for charity or author's nights. *Hibernia Freed* was singularly successful in London, opening in Lincoln's Inn Fields' Theatre (capacity about fourteen hundred) on 13 February 1722, and was performed seven times, allowing the author to have two benefit nights – one every third night. The second benefit night was very profitable. The takings were '£86 2s. 6d. in cash, and another £52 10s. in ticket sales; after house charges of forty pounds, Philips took home nearly £100'.[34] It would seem likely that such a play would have been produced successfully in Dublin, but, if this had happened, some mention of it should have survived, and, in the absence of such evidence, it is more likely that it was not. Perhaps the management of the theatre did not care for its sentiments, or were fearful of inciting upheaval in the theatre and in the streets at a volatile time. A contemporary account described the enthusiasm that greeted the play at its London production: 'I never knew a play so clapped [...] till a Friend put me in Mind that half the Audience were *Wild Irish*.'[35] Dublin in 1722 was in a ferment of excitement. Trade restrictions were a constantly perceived injustice, and the Declaratory Act, popularly known as the Sixth of George I, had infuriated the country by giving the English Parliament the right to enact legislation directly for Ireland. George I, the first Hanoverian king, was far from universally popular. Dublin was a Whig stronghold, but many of the Irish still favoured the Jacobite cause; the Duke of Ormond was in disgrace and in exile, and, in this very year of 1722, Charles Boyle, the fourth Earl of Orrery, was incarcerated in the Tower of London because of his Jacobite sympathies. A cautious, conservative management may have deemed it prudent not to antagonize the authorities, or risk the fittings of their theatre, by exciting people further with a play so subversive in its implications. An enterprising publisher, though, had no qualms about disseminating it in print.

Hibernia Freed is strongly opposed to tyranny, which is personified in Turgesius the Dane, a rampant despot almost comical in his intensity. Turgesius too equates conquest with rape; his creed is the opposite of the Enlightened ideal of self-control and moderation:

> Why have I fought, to what has conquest served,
> But for unlimited despotic power?
> And what is pow'r, but to indulge the will?
> To love, to have, to leave, and love anew.
> He that controls his passion is the slave,
> Slave to the pow'r which he himself creates.
> That man is free who gratifies desire,
> And whatsoe'er he wills, unchecked, performs.[36]

The Irish king, O'Brien, shows the essential bourgeois characteristics of neo-stoic resolution and constancy under the duress of superior force, while he works to overthrow it. He points out that the right of conquest has no permanence, that anyone who can exert sufficient force has the right to overthrow the existing conqueror. The conqueror has no rights, only strength:

> Faith, justice, laws, obedience, gratitude,
> Are cobweb bonds when empire is in view.
> [...]
> And by the ills which he himself has wrought,
> Others are taught to overthrow the state.[37]

The subtext here needs scrutiny: Philips almost certainly had Jacobite leanings, and here he covertly questioned the validity of the current regime. The overthrowing of the Stuarts by force, he is saying, in an echo of Shakespeare, opens the way to anarchy, as now anyone who can summon sufficient force can overthrow the House of Orange or Hanover, and they have been taught to do so by the very success of the present incumbents. He sailed even closer to the wind in the next act by implicitly questioning the method by which the House of Orange came to rule. There is an exact parallel between the deal that Turgesius offers Sabina and that offered to William and Mary by the English Parliament: if she will accept the crown in her father's place and marry the Dane, the two of them will ignore her father's and brother's right to the throne and rule the country together:

> TURGESIUS   Reign in thy father's stead, receive his crown,
>   And be thyself the mistress of this isle.
> SABINA   What! snatch the crown from him who gave me life,

> Deprive my brother of his native right,
> And gall my country with tyrannic power!
> Shall I do this, shall I incur such guilt?
> So as to posterity transmit my shame.[38]

The play, then, while deploring tyranny, slyly questioned whether the current regime, for all its trumpeting about freedom, was based on anything but superior force – a message that may have been too incendiary for early Georgian Dublin.

When he speaks directly of Ireland's condition in *Hibernia Freed*, Philips' anger becomes palpable:

> O'Brien lives to see his people slaves'
> Compelled to rob and strip the lab'ring hinds
> To feed the Dane and to support his riot.[39]

These were Ireland's present complaints in the guise of historical comment. Philips and his audience knew that the Danes never conquered the country, yet that is the context he set for his play; he chose to show a situation analogous to the English supremacy, in which Hibernia was under Danish/English rule that had to be resisted and overthrown by the righteous Hibernians. This is an angry play, but, in contrast to Swift's writings, the anger is diffused, not narrowly targeted, and Philips' language is inadequate for the task he undertakes. His phrasing and imagery are largely conventional; he does not succeed in matching his anger with a poetic language that would cause the verse to spark and burn. In *St Stephen's Green*, the prose format demonstrated his ear for spoken dialogue, but in *Hibernia Freed* his sparkle is dimmed: the verse and the exalted rhythms of tragedy restrain his exuberance, blunt his language, and confine him to the formulaic and declaratory.[40]

The parallels with *Rotherick O'Connor* are striking, and indicate that the play may have been written in response to it: the invitation to settle, the overrunning of the country, the refusal of the heroine to entertain the advances of the conqueror, the symbolization of the country as a female, the attempted rape of the heroine and the equating of the conquest to the rape of the country, all occur in Shadwell's play. Where Philips differed was in his invocation of the nobility and refinement of the pre-invasion culture. He went out of his way to celebrate the pedigree of the Irish kings, as he outlined in the Dedication to Right Honourable Henry O'Brien, Earl of Thomond:

An O'Brien is my hero, the head of that illustrious family will vouchsafe to be my patron. [...] None are ignorant that your lordship is lineally descended from the monarchs of it. [...] As love of my country induced me to lay the scene of a play there; so the particular honour I bear to, and ought to have for, your lordship's family, obliged me to search for a story in which one of your lordship's ancestors made so noble a figure; for what is so noble as to free one's country from tyranny and invasion.[41]

In the play itself, the scope is broadened to include the pedigrees of all the Old Irish nobility:

> O'CONNOR   Or is he aided by his noble blood?
>   I without boasting can allege the same.
>   From the renowned Milesius we descend,
>   From that illustrious source our monarch springs.
>   [...]
>   Recording bards
>   Sing to their harps the mighty deeds of Ir,
>   The hundred battles by Milesius gained,
>   And paint Gadelus' fame, and show us sprung
>   from them. [42]

When the victorious O'Neill arrives to claim Sabina's hand, she para-phrases the dedication of the play in praise of him 'who frees his coun-try from a foreign yoke', and at the same time evokes for Irish culture a correspondence with the grandeur and dignity of the classical world in contrast to the barbarism of the Danes, an important piece of appro-priation in contrast to the received idea among the English of the uncouthness and savagery of the Irish:

> SABINA   Bring garlands hither; strew with flow'rs his way;
>   Statues erect, triumphal arches build,
>   Fame stretch thy wings, thy trumpet sound aloud,
>   Employ thy hundred tongues in his renown
>   Who frees his country from a foreign yoke.[43]

O'Neill compares himself with Achilles, both in love and war:

> O'NEILL   Thus Thetis' son forsook the sanguine plain,
>   And war and glory courted him in vain.
>   At Deidamia's feet supine he lay,
>   Resigned himself to love's more gentle sway.
>   Till called by fate, the hero flew to arms,
>   And glory pleased, and war again had charms.[44]

Champions are needed because the country is in a sorry state, and Ireland of the ninth century is linked with Hibernia of the eighteenth, smarting under English injustice:

> O'BRIEN   Fertile Hibernia! Hospitable land!
> Is not allowed to feed her native sons,
> In vain they toil, and amid plenty starve.
> The lazy Dane grows wanton with our stores,
> Urges our labour, and derides our wants.
> Hibernia! Seat of learning! School of science!
> How waste! How wild dost thou already seem!
> Thy houses, schools, thy cities ransacked, burnt![45]

The dedicatee O'Brien, who was a member of the Irish Privy Council, is being summoned to head the opposition, not, perhaps, to action, but to leadership, with Ormond in exile and Orrery in jail. The idea is bruited, that it was the sins of the people that caused the calamity:

> EUGENIUS   The people's crimes have drawn this vengeance down
> Which the king's virtue only can remove.[46]

O'Brien is given a messianic role in lifting the curse. The idea that he will relieve the plight of his people sanctifies him, and he must do it by enduring, by being a signal example of neo-stoic forbearance:

> O'BRIEN   Teach me to bear, and give me grounds to hope.[47]
> [...]
> My mind is armed to bear impending ills.[48]

Shadwell was concerned to provide a story for the new bourgeois Ascendancy, but Philips aimed to place the story of the Irish, now Protestant, Ascendants centre stage. His play was not advocating breaking the link with England, as the United Irishmen were. In the 1720s, the movement for reform was barely on the horizon, and he and Shadwell were advocating a movement towards unity among the people of Ireland. They were in spirit closer to Wolfe Tone than to Jonathan Swift, who saw himself only as a spokesman for the English who lived in Ireland. Philips and Shadwell were building a different story, calling into being an Ireland in which the two strands of native and colonist unite to form the nation of Hibernia.

O'Brien illustrates this in the play by invoking the native ancestor, Milesius, and the English St Patrick as equal protectors of the Irish race. This speech unites the two traditions on the island against the invading enemy:

O'BRIEN   And thou, great sire! from whom we boast descent,
    Implore success to thy Milesian race!
    And thou, blest saint! the patron of our isle,
    Who first didst plant among us faith divine,
    Join in the prayer and strengthen his request.
    And as envenomed insects fled the land,
    Forced by the virtue of thy sacred wand,
    A greater blessing may thy prayers obtain,
    Drive tyrants hence, and break the Danish chain.[49]

Substitute 'English' for 'Danish' and 'break the chain' has an eighteenth-century ring: the chain of safety connecting the Hibernians to
England had became a symbol of servitude and powerlessness. The
imagery and action of the play are not finally pessimistic, though.
Denying the justification of conquest, it ends with a prophecy of co-
operation in which another nation is 'invited to our aid', and the two
races mix to their mutual advantage:

Another nation, famous through the world,
    For martial deeds, for strength and skill in arms,
    Belov'd and blest for their humanity.
    Where wealth abounds, and liberty resides,
    [...]
    The happy parents of a happy race,
    They shall succeed, invited to our aid,
    And mix their blood with ours; one people grow,
    Polish our manners, and improve our minds.[50]

O'Brien continues to accept whatever will happen as the will of fate or
heaven, and that the English annexation will all be ultimately for the
best, and justice will prevail:

O'BRIEN   Whatever changes are decreed by fate,
    Bear we with patience, with a will resigned.
    Honour and truth pursue, and firmly trust,
    Heav'n may at last prove kind, it will be just.[51]

The second-to-last line is an instruction to the contemporary audience
to work patiently for the Irish cause, which is just, honourable and
truthful, and will succeed in the end, led by O'Brien, O'Neill, whom
'all Ultonia owns her native lord',[52] and O'Connor, who leads 'a faithful band from Connacia'.[53] It was not just O'Brien that was being rehabilitated, but the generality of the Old Irish aristocracy that was being
summoned to take command of the new Hibernia.

Fifty years later, two rather turgid plays – Francis Dobbs' *The Irish Chief; or, The Patriot King* (Smock Alley 1773), and Gorges Edmund Howard's *The Siege of Tamor* (Smock Alley 1774) – also delved into Irish history and legend in order to find a parallel for their contemporary situation. In them we can see the complete identification of the Protestant Nation with Ireland. Their heroes are the ancient Irish nobility; their villains are the Danish oppressors, who approximate the despotic and unjust actions of the English.

In the characters of their plays, Howard and Dobbs created a template for a ruling class of Hibernia by blending the perceived virtues of the Anglo-Irish with the acceptable traits of the ancient Irish nobility to manufacture a metaphoric unity of the two races – a middle ground which rooted them in the country and freed them from the necessity of English husbandry. The process of annexation, begun by Shadwell, continuing throughout the eighteenth century, climaxed in Dobbs and Howard. The barbarous savages of the fifteenth century have metamorphosed into a refined and cultured civilization. Howard in his Address to the Reader claims: 'Ireland was at the time, the island of saints, the seat of the muses, and the nursery of heroes.'[54]

The symbols of Irishness have been annexed, some accepted, some rejected, some re-evaluated; the Hibernian Ascendancy has been recast in a mould that combined the best of Anglo-Irish Protestant virtues – stoicism, endurance, steadiness – with the desirable traits of the Irish – valour, learning, resourcefulness – to create a hybrid ancestry that was echoed in the inclusive views that the plays displayed. Dobbs and Howard were reformers, not revolutionaries, and both ended their plays with a rapprochement between the antagonists, once the injustices experienced by the Irish have been rectified. They repeated Philips also in that the method they recommended was not revolution but endurance, on insisting on the right thing until it became fact by reason of its self-evident rightness: God would favour the right cause and the Irish cause was just.

Both Dobbs and Howard were, like Philips, members of the Irish Parliament and adherents of the Patriot party; they had no desire to break with England. Theirs was a bourgeois dream: to achieve control over their own affairs, insofar as it affected their commerce, free of the meddling of the English parliament and vested commercial interests. Unlike Shadwell or Philips, they had no agenda for furthering any particular section of the Irish Protestant Nation. Howard, in *The Siege of Tamor*, was concerned to combat the factionalism that bedevilled the country, the parliament, and, eventually, the Volunteers themselves.

Dobbs, who was a protégée of the first Earl of Charlemont, preached against the dangers of democracy or the mob, and the necessity of an enlightened ruler's ignoring democratic pressure and following his own judgement. Both plays dipped into Irish history to find a mirror for the tangled web of Patriot politics: Ceallachan, in *The Irish Chief; or, The Patriot King* is a good example of a Hibernian Ascendancy figure, an annexed ancestor and a part of its story. The symbolization is no longer of brogue and cabin, but of kingship and noble rhetoric: the Anglo-Irish have selected their symbols and planted their roots.

These were essentially plays, like *Hibernia Freed* and *Rotherick O'Connor*, of the enlightened, liberal Ascendancy – the inclusive strand of the Irish Protestant Nation of Hibernia. But this strand did not carry the day; the forces of reaction and entrenched sectarianism were too strong. We must accept that the playwrights from the Anglo-Irish tradition in the eighteenth century were not typical: they did not express the views of the majority of their class and race. The writers indicated one set of attitudes and convictions, events tell of another, and the events spoke for the majority. The Irish Lords Justices, their henchmen, churchmen and other Protestant Ascendancy figures blocked every attempt at reform in Ireland that was not to their own advantage – particularly pertaining to the majority Catholic population. They were not moved by art or the theatre. Plays of the eighteenth century are a poor relation to its architecture: Charlemont House, Leinster House, Parliament House or the Four Courts are triumphal and declaratory. Hibernia was dotted with their Big Houses, classical structures that imposed their exclusive vision on the landscape in which they stood. Most of the ruling class preferred to spend their time in gambling and drinking at 'private routs, cards, and hazard', that 'blunts all the finer feelings and precludes that intellectual pleasure which the stage affords in other nations'.[55] Anglo-Irish society in the eighteenth century, in spite of its surface sheen, was 'philistine, snobbish, limited, and on the whole, pretty graceless'.[56]

In Henry Brooke's epilogue to *The Siege of Tamor* (1782) we can hear the author's sigh of frustration and disillusion:

> Her country! Yes, her country – we are told;
> A country was a precious thing of old;
> Though now –
> Of no use in the world – but to be sold. [57]

This disillusion was openly articulated in Mary O'Brien's slight comedy, *The Fallen Patriot*, at the end of the eighteenth century and in

Macklin's plays it was loud and clear. These were the realists, who described what they saw, not what they wanted to see. Shadwell and Philips displayed a Utopian view, in which reconciliation and co-oper-ation prevailed, rather than aggression, bigotry and racism. Unfortunately, the latter was more common within the country, and was aptly expressed by Frederick Ashton's *The Battle of Aughrim*, first published in 1728.

This play has a peculiar history: there is no evidence of it ever getting a professional production, but it was probably the most popular play written in Ireland before the twentieth century.[58] It is a good example of the reach of the printed play: after its second publication in 1756 it ran to twenty-five more editions between then and 1840, and was com-monly used as a schoolbook in Ulster.[59]

It is an extraordinary piece. The work of a twenty-year-old student, it tells the story of the battle in rollicking verse; it's easy to see how its crude energy and rhyming couplets appealed to those who like things painted in broad strokes and primary colours, but its appeal was endur-ing. Its impact is immediate; its action is vigorous; it is intensely, some-times overly, vivid. While its derivation seems to be from the rhyming tragedies of Orrery and his contemporaries, a form that had been extinct for decades, its actual style is closer to that of a folk play. In fact, its continued popularity was due to its achieving the status of folk-lore, especially in Ulster.[60] The printed play was so widely disseminated that it became absorbed in the folk tradition, and re-emerged as a per-formance piece to mark communal occasions, like an Orange celebra-tion, or a Christmas mumming.[61] Ashton would have been familiar with the mumming tradition, given his Derry background, and in Donegal a mumming play that survived into the mid-twentieth century contained Patrick Sarsfield as well as St George and the Grand Turk. William Carleton recollects this process of assimilation:

> In the town of Augher, this stupid play was acted by Catholics and Protestants, each party of course sustaining their own principles. The consequence was, that when they came to the conflict with which the play is made to close, armed as they were on both sides with real swords, political and religious resentment could not be restrained, and they would have hacked each other's souls out had not the audience inter-fered and prevented them. As it was, some of them were severely if not dangerously wounded.[62]

The play's crudity would militate against it ever being taken seri-ously by professionals, but it gripped the popular imagination in the late eighteenth century and retained its hold for decades. It was popular because it precisely reflected the deep divide in Irish society: Ashton showed accurately the schism that split the country on racial and religious lines. The account of the Battle of Aughrim given by Ashton did not reflect the reality of 1691, but the perceptions of 1728 and, even more, the religious and racial polarization that occurred from the mid-eighteenth century on, when the play was reprinted and successfully caught the prevailing zeitgeist. The period from the English Civil War, through the rebellion of 1641, the Cromwell years, the Restoration and the War of the Two Kings, with its constant shifting of allegiance, is so confused as to defy understanding;[63] this perhaps accounts for *The Battle of Aughrim*'s ambiguity, and its final settling on the religious division of Catholic against Protestant as the main conflict in the play. The British/Irish opposition, the William/James conflict, the English/French dimension, are all completely overwhelmed by the religious war.

The play does not balance evenly; it devotes twice as much time to the Catholic and Irish side. As in Philips, the Irish protagonists are loaded with images of republican Rome and the heroes of antiquity; the opposition has a few such allusions, but nothing like the same number. The characters in the play are polarized between those who want to impose Roman Catholic rule on the country, and those who hate Rome and the Catholic Church, which is a historical absurdity, since the Popes were more likely to support William of Orange and oppose the expansionism of Louis XIV. This is the familiar pattern of appropriating and twisting Irish history to serve a propaganda purpose and to justify the present alignment of forces within the island. This play's enormous reach and influence may have been an agent for rewriting the Williamite wars as a sectarian conflict, or a war between the Irish and the English, without any pausing to wonder why the main protagonists are a German and a Frenchman.

The play is deeply divisive. It presents the two opposing arguments strongly, to the point of caricature, without any interaction or discussion between them. This was the source of its attraction to the two factions, and the reason it often begot violence. It makes no effort to balance the arguments, or to tease out where the truth lies, or to conduct a debate between the two positions; it simply states them as forcibly as possible, and lets them collide. Hence the fight that Carleton describes. Ashton's writing is curiously ambivalent — he gilds the Irish/Catholic side with copious classical allusions, yet, in his introduction, he equates Catholicism and despotism, and says Aughrim finished both. He conflates the English and Anglo-Irish, and implicitly excludes the Irish as a hostile race – racially, politically and in religion:

> This memorable battle, on which the fate of Ireland then depended, was fought on Sunday, July the 12th 1691. The effect of which, was the entire subversion of popery and arbitrary power, and surely an action which acquired so much glory to the English nation ought not to be forgot.[64]

The Catholic commanders, though, have the best part of the lines, scenes, characters and imagery. Although they lose the battle, the Irish leaders are educated, cultured aristocrats. The prologue, by Charles Usher, gives the wrong impression, and it is openly racist, dismissing the Irish Catholic forces with the contemptuous appellation 'Teague'. Here again Hibernia is invoked as the Protestant Nation of Ireland, and Usher holds to the exclusive vision:

> Here may we view how in a crimson field,
> Britain's dread sons taught France and Teague to yield,
> Withstood their fury in Hibernia's cause.[65]

But Ashton and his play are not so dismissive: in his own prologue he overturns the demeaning and belittling associations of 'Teague', and clothes the battle in Epic and Heroic colours:

> Not Pompey's triumphs nor great Scipio's fame,
> Could once compare with glorious William's name:
> 'Tis true, the Irish found it to their cost,
> They fought that battle bravely which they lost,
> Even like Hectors for a time they stood,
> And ere they run, they dyed the field in blood.[66]

These are not ignorant 'Teagues', but aristocrats misguided by their religion and allegiance to Rome. Sarsfield, Talbot and O'Neill, the leaders on the Irish, Catholic, Jacobite side, were the Gaelic and Norman aristocracy, and Ashton knew that, though defeated and their society and way of life more or less broken, they had not by any means disappeared. Some had made their mark on the Continent, but others had stayed, and, through judicious conversions and other manoeuvres, their sons and grandsons were already stepping back as figures of authority into the corridors of Hibernian power, ready, as Philips put it: to 'mix their blood with ours; one people grow'.[67] By 1730 it had become clear that the Irish nobility, through its converts, was becoming once again a force in the country.

NOTES

1. Maurice James Craig, *The Volunteer Earl: Being the Life and Times of James Caulfeild First Earl of Charlemont* (London: The Cresset Press, 1948), p. 188.
2. Daniel Corkery, *The Hidden Ireland* (Dublin: Gill and Son, 1925), p. 8.
3. Kevin Whelan, 'An Underground Gentry? Catholic Middlemen in Eighteenth-Century Ireland', in *Eighteenth-Century Ireland*, 10, (1995), 7–23 (p. 8).
4. Christopher Wheatley, *Beneath Ierne's Banners: Irish Protestant Drama of the Restoration and Eighteenth Century* (Notre Dame Indiana: University of Notre Dame Press, 1999), p. 52.
5. Helen M. Burke, *Riotous Performances*, p. 131.
6. J.M. Synge, *The Playboy of the Western World* in *Plays*, ed. by Ann Saddlemyer (Oxford: University Press, 1968), p. 75.
7. Elliot Fitzgibbon, *Earl of Clare: Mainspring of the Union* (London: The Research Publishing Company, 1960), p. 78.
8. Elizabeth Bowen, *Bowen's Court*, 2nd edn. (London: Longmans, 1964), p. 220.
9. 'Prologue written by Mr. Shadwell', 11 & 21, in Christopher Wheatley & Kevin Donovan, eds., *Irish Plays of the Seventeenth and Eighteenth Centuries*, ed. by Christopher Wheatley and Kevin Donovan, 2 vols (Bristol: Thoemmes Press, 2003), I, p. 169.
10. Shadwell, *Rotherick O'Connor*, II., in *Shadwell's Works*, I, p. 283 .
11. Instead of Dermot, Dermod or Diarmaid, Shadwell opts to call him Dermond, which appears to be a conflation of Ormond and Desmond, but is topographically meaningless.
12. Shadwell, *Rotherick O'Connor*, I. 1. 70.
13. *Ibid.*, V. 1. 20.
14. *Ibid.*, III. 1. 18.
15. *Ibid.*, V. 1. 103.
16. *Ibid.*, V. 1. 396.
17. *Ibid.*, I. 1. 105.
18. *Ibid.*, I.1. 74.
19. *Ibid.*, II. 1. 17 & 23.
20. *Ibid.*, V. 1. 207.
21. *Ibid.*, V. 1. 307.
22. *Ibid.*, V. 1. 412.
23. *Ibid.*, V. 1. 440.
24. *Ibid.*, V. 1. 200.
25. 'Sarah Butler', http://www.pgil-eirdata.org/html/pgil_datasets/authors/b/Butler,Sarah/life. htm [accessed 9 August 2004] (p. 1 of 2).
26. *Ibid.*, (p. 1 of 2).
27. Wheatley and Donovan, *Irish Plays*, I, p. 168.
28. '[First] Prologue to *Rotherick O'Connor*', line 5, in Wheatley and Donovan, *Irish Plays*, I, p. 168.
29. Ibid., 6, p. 219.
30. 'Epilogue written by Mr. Shadwell', 1720 edition of *Shadwell's Works*, I, p. 268.
31. William Philips, *Hibernia Freed*, V. 317.
32. There is an uncorroborated date of March 31st 1722 suggested by Clark, (probably after Lawrence), given in Helen M. Burke, *Riotous Assemblies*, p. 301, n. 3.
33. Title page: '*Hibernia Freed* [...] Dublin reprinted by Patt. Duggan, 1722.'
34. *The London Stage, 1660–1800: a calendar of plays, entertainments & afterpieces together with casts, box-receipts and contemporary comment: compiled from the playbills, newspapers and theatrical diaries of the period.* Part 2, 1700–1729, ed. by Emmett L. Avery (Carbondale Ill.: Southern University of Illinois Press, 1960); cited by Wheatley and Donovan, *Irish Plays*, I, p. 301.
35. *Ibid.*, I, p. 301.
36. Philips, *Hibernia Freed*, III. p.127.
37. *Ibid.*, III. 386.
38. *Ibid.*, IV. 89.
39. *Ibid.*, I. 43.
40. 'The sentiments [are] hackneyed with the phrasing of the later Augustan poets.' Duggan, *The Stage Irishman*, p. 27.
41. Dedication of *Hibernia Freed*, 'To the Right Honourable Henry O'Brien, Earl of Thomond', in Wheatley and Donovan, *Irish Plays*, I, p. 305.

42. Philips, *Hibernia Freed*, I. 295.
43. *Ibid.*, II. 270.
44. *Ibid.*, III. 83.
45. *Ibid.*, I. 1. 62.
46. *Ibid.*, I. 1. 54.
47. *Ibid.*, I. 1. 91.
48. *Ibid.*, I. 1. 197.
49. *Ibid.*, II. 300.
50. *Ibid.*, V. 295.
51. *Ibid.*, V. 304.
52. *Ibid.*, I. 1. 241.
53. *Ibid.*, I. 1. 116.
54. Gorges Edmund Howard, '[First Address] to the Reader (1773)', *The Siege of Tamor*, in Wheatley and Donovan, *Irish Plays*, I, p. 145.
55. Stockwell, *Dublin Theatres and Customs* , p. 190.
56. Bowen, *Bowen's Court*, p. 125.
57. Henry Brooke, Esq. '*Epilogue to The Siege of Tamor*', in Wheatley and Donovan, *Irish Plays*, I, p. 229.
58. Wheatley and Donovan, *Irish Plays*, I, p. 361.
59. Duggan, *The Stage Irishman*, p. 31. The play was usually published in its later editions with Michelburne's *Ireland Preserved*, the two functioning as a history as well as an English text-book.
60. Wheatley and Donovan, *Irish Plays*, I, p. 364: 'The drama of the battle was in the hands of every intelligent schoolboy in Ulster, who strode an imaginary stage as Sarsfield or Ginkel according to his sympathies.'
61. Thackeray testifies to its ubiquity: he spent a rainy night in Galway reading it after discovering it in an old bookshop in the town in 1842. He paraphrases and quotes extensively from it in his Irish Sketchbook (Dublin: Gill & Macmillan, 1990), pp. 181–189.
62. Wheatley and Donovan, *Irish Plays*, I, p. 365.
63. Maurice James Craig, *The Volunteer Earl*, p. 12.
64. Ashton's dedication to *The Battle of Aughrim*, in Wheatley and Donovan, *Irish Plays*, I, p. 366.
65. 'Commendatory Verses' to *The Battle of Aughrim*, in Wheatley and Donovan, *Irish Plays*, I, p. 367.
66. Ashton's Prologue, in Wheatley and Donovan, *Irish Plays*, I, p. 367.
67. Philips, *Hibernia Freed*, V. 317.

6

The Humours of Hibernia

The historical plays in the previous chapter indicated two contending paradigms within the citadel of Hibernia – an inclusive against an exclusive strand. Any colonial society is predicated on a caste system, with colonists at the top, supported and serviced by the indigenous inhabitants; the Penal Laws were an attempt to engineer such a society. But the native Irish spotted their weak point: the laws were based on religious affiliation, and offered Catholics the path to self-betterment in the expectation that they would not take it. The framers of the Penal Laws belonged to the English tradition and were intrinsically respectful of law and order; the Irish treated the law, and especially the Penal Laws, with contempt, and soon found ways around and through them. In 1752, a commentator noted that 'the acts relating to purchases made or leases taken by papists are so eluded by perjuries, trusts in protestant names and other contrivances that they are of little significance'. Ignatius Gahagan, a convert from Catholicism in 1757, dismissed any moral squeamishness: 'I would rather at any time entrust God with my soul than the laws of Ireland with my lands.'[1]

The result was that, by 1745, Hibernia found itself with a powerful and, in many cases, wealthy underclass, led by an insolent, contemptuous gentry that had vaulted easily over its defences by observing the letter of the law in converting to the Established Church, while retaining its atavistic hold on the indigenous population. The tensions and oppositions between these two tendencies in Hibernia, as well as the increasing strain between the Hibernians and England, can be followed in the plays of the period and in the events that effected the theatres and those who worked in them.

In 1747 the Theatre Royal at Smock Alley, under the management of Thomas Sheridan, provided an unwelcoming platform for the clash of these two ideologies, by provoking an explosive debate on the ongoing obsession about the nature and image of a gentleman in Ireland. The ensuing dispute served to highlight the tensions between the two alternative versions of Hibernian society – the infiltrators and the defenders.

The rebellion of Scotland in 1745 had set Britain in an uproar before the final elimination of the Jacobite threat at the Battle of Culloden, but for the duration of that war Ireland remained quiet; all the rhetoric of the Gaelic poets came to nothing as the leaders of the Catholic interest hastened to assure the authorities of their unswerving loyalty to the Hanoverian dynasty. Protestant churchmen were foremost in encouraging their congregations to avoid any intimidation or annoyance of their Catholic neighbours, and the crafty, prudent machinations of the viceroy, Lord Chesterfield, convinced Catholics that the English authorities were the best guarantors of their safety against any Protestant outrages. The quiescence of the country emphasized the placidity and Augustan self-control of Hibernia, but the flurry of activity indicated a deeper instability that had to be managed, that was too important to be ignored but too widespread to be repressed.

The resurgence of the native Irish gentry, partly as an aristocracy, partly as a plutocratic Catholic or convert middle class, instead of furthering an inclusive Hibernian society, as envisaged by William Philips in *Hibernia Freed*, provoked a hostile response from the Protestant Establishment, who were, in their turn, despised as 'mushrooms' by the scions of the old Irish families. After the Plantations, many of the older families had become middlemen on their former lands, becoming again the *de facto* owners and forming a semi-underground gentry, while prominent converted families allowed their Catholic branches to flourish in the shadow of their protection – the Butlers of Kilkenny and the MacMurrough Kavanaghs of Wicklow, for example. The true-blue Protestants protested against the rising prosperity and insouciance of the Irish Catholics or converts (they lumped them together) and, as the Catholic Committee was formed in 1756 to demand the reform of the Penal Laws and the end of discrimination, the country was set to split on the sectarian lines that gave rise to the popularity of *The Battle of Aughrim*, which had its second of many publications in that same year.

Thomas Sheridan, the manager of Smock Alley from 1745, compared his theatre to the state – 'wherein the Lives and Properties of all Subjects are equally under the protection of the laws', he wrote, 'wherein no man shall be restrained from saying or doing anything that is consistent with Reason and Truth',[2] and the theatre enacted in microcosm the dissensions within the state. The first convulsion came with the Kelly riots of 1747, which spread to become the controversy known as the Gentlemen's Quarrel.

Edmund Burke was a student of Trinity at the time, and gives an account of the 'grand Theatrical squabble between Mr Kelly, gentle-man, and Sheridan the Player':[3]

> Sometime ago there was a play performed here which greatly pleased the town called Aesop. During the performance Mr Kelly comes in flushed with Liquor and going into the Green Room where the players dress began to entertain the actresses with the most nauseous bawdy and ill language, called them bitches and whores, put his hands under their petticoats and would have forced some of them (if his ability answered his inclination). This was represented to Sheridan who is manager of the theatre, upon which he ordered Kelly out of the house. Enraged at this he goes into the pit and as soon as Sheridan came on the stage pelted him with oranges [...] and called him a thousand ill names, bidding him go off the stage and quite interrupting the performance. At length Sheridan advances to the front of the stage and tells him that unless some gentleman takes care of him he would be obliged to turn him out of the house. Ten times more enraged at this, he goes after the act to Sheridan's room and insults him again. Sheridan represented calmly to him his abuse of the female players and of himself – and he persisting in his ill language, Sheridan gave him a good flogging, which he bore with Christian patience, not however without vowing revenge – which he effected the next night by bringing such a party as hindered Sheridan from playing, broke open all the doors, and would probably have killed him if he had not escaped, (by the usage they gave the playhouse tailor). These doings made him shut up the playhouse and indict Kelly, who also indicted him. During this time thousands of States of Cases, answers, replies &c flew about from both parties, and a great deal of dispute concerning the word Gentleman; for it seems Sheridan had said he was as good a gentleman as Kelly or (as others would have it) as any in the house. This gained Kelly a great party who called their cause the Gentleman's quarrel, taking it extremely ill that a Gentleman should be struck by a Player, and insisted that Sheridan should never play till he had publicly asked Kelly's pardon.[4]

Kelly's behaviour seems outrageous to the modern sensibility, but his conduct was not unprecedented for its time, nor for Smock Alley. Garrick had the same problems in London, and the young gentlemen of the town were no worse in Dublin than elsewhere. Sheridan's assistant deplored their conduct: 'I have often exclaimed loudly and publicly against the indecency of the scenes, by the admission of every idler that had a laced coat, the youth of the College were in the custom of crowding to every morning rehearsal. I have seen actors and actresses rehearsing within a circle of forty or fifty of those young gentlemen.'[5] Common though the problem was, the Kelly incident was a stone that dislodged an avalanche, because it polarized the two factions in the country and set them at loggerheads – two ideas of a Gentleman, and two visions of Hibernia.

On the one side was Sheridan, who was inching the theatre and the acting profession towards respectability, who was a friend of the viceroy and caressed by the Castle. He came of a family embedded in the Establishment, and chose plays and commissioned prologues and epilogues, during the unsettled days of 1745, that were designed to appeal to the Anglophile, Whig, Protestant bourgeoisie of Dublin. On the other side, from the Establishment's perspective, were ranged the old forces of disorder and discord, in the theatre and the state, many of whom were native Irish, many converts, many secret Jacobites, newly assertive of their ancient lineage, who despised the New Protestant hegemony, and who seized on the opportunity to pick on Sheridan as a weak link in the Establishment chain. The Establishment reacted angrily to this rowdy jostling into its defining, reflective, theatrical mirror by attempting to subdue or expel it. The theatre became the cockpit for a broader ideological struggle between alternative versions of Hibernia.

To the resurgent Irish gentry, obsessed with pedigree and genealogy, the idea of a player being a gentleman was ridiculous, but within the metropolitan experience of Sheridan, the aspiration was not abnormal: Ogilby, Ashbury and Elrington, previous managers of the theatre, had mingled easily with the social and political powers of Dublin, and Sheridan always saw himself as a manager rather than a player, drawing his income from the profits of the theatre but taking no payment for his acting. He loved the trappings of respectability and revelled in the title of Esq., by which the gallery delighted in calling sarcastically for him.[6] His protestations, however, betrayed the weakness of his case: he was clearly only too aware of the stigma attached to the profession of actor, even though great efforts were being made at the time to raise its status. The playwright Charles Macklin sardonically observed that previously:

> The players all resided in the vicinity of the theatres, so that they could attend rehearsal without inconvenience, or expense of coach-hire. But I do not know how the change has been effected; we, the actors, are all now looking out for high ground, squares, and genteel neighbourhoods, no matter how far distant from the theatres, as if local selection could

give rhythm to the profession, or genteel neighbourhoods instanta-
neously produce good-manners.‾

The Beefsteak Club that Sheridan formed to bind himself closer to the
authorities in the Castle was presided over by Peg Woffington, because
of her beauty, intelligence and wit, but as Sheridan's daughter, Alicia Le
Fanu, points out : 'her moral character was such as to exclude her from
the society of her own sex. Mr. Sheridan found it impossible, therefore,
to introduce her to his wife.'[8] Mrs Bellamy or Garrick could enjoy a
huge success in Dublin, grace the Castle balls, be guests of honour at
the viceroy's levees, but still be barred from the drawing rooms of
respectable women. Actors could be gentlemen by birth, but they lost
caste by going on the stage. The Sheridan family had estates in Cavan,
so Thomas Sheridan's standing by birth was not in doubt, but his enemies held that by becoming a player he had forfeited the title of gentleman. In the trial that followed the Gentlemen's Quarrel, the lawyer
defending Kelly ridiculed Sheridan's pretensions:

> Mr Daly stood up, and said, my Lord, I am employed as counshill for –
> Kelly, Esquire; but I don't understand who this Th—— S———n,
> Gentleman, is. Sh———n's council answered, it was Mr Sh———n pat-
> entee of the Theatre Royal in Smock Alley. Oh! says he, I understand tish
> Mr Sheridan the actor: well, I have heard of gentleman shaylors and
> gentlemen tailors, but it is the firsht I heard of gentlemen actors and gen-
> tlemen merry andrews. [9]

The crux of the matter was that Sheridan, a 'Player', even in Edmund
Burke's sympathetic account, had thrashed a gentleman as if he were a
servant or a peasant, and the gentleman he had beaten was of the faction of prickly Irish converts; it was an action begging for trouble. The
Kelly faction, because they did not consider Sheridan a gentleman,
would not challenge him to a duel, so their only course of action was
to punish him personally or through his theatre, which they proceeded
to attack. The Gentlemen's Quarrel split Hibernian society: the
Establishment, in the form of the Courts, the Protestant Patriots and
the scholars of Trinity College, all took Sheridan's part. They saw
themselves threatened by a riff-raff of Catholics and dubiously converted Irish gentlemen, who flaunted on the one hand the supremacy
and age of their claims to gentility, and on the other the equality of
their attachment to the present regime. The Establishment's response
was to isolate and humiliate this troublesome upstart element of
Hibernia.

Edmund Burke's account continues:

The Scholars, who had till now stood neuter, [...] took the affair on themselves and encouraged Sheridan to open the Theatre again, which he did and acted Richard III, where a numerous body of the Scholars appear'd to keep peace. At the beginning the party began to be riotous but by proper menaces they were kept quiet and one or two of the principal turned out. Thus the play went on regularly to the satisfaction of the audience. Next night was to be acted *The Fair Pentitent* for the benefit of the Hospital for Incurables; the Scholars were persuaded that common humanity on account of the charitable design of the play would keep the faction quiet, so not above seven or eight were there that night – but they were mistaken, for no ties of Honour or Religion could bind 'em. They raised another tumult, called for Sheridan to wreak their Vengeance on him and drove the actors off the stage. Not content with this, some of them abused the few Scholars that were there, pelted them with oranges, declared there were no Gentlemen among them, but that they were all a pack of scoundrels. The Scholars being informed of this, early next morning searched the whole town for Mr Martin, the principal offender, [...] They made him rise and brought him to the College where after making him sensible of his crime, he kneeled down in a large circle of us and owned his fault and begged pardon. Then we agreed to seize Captain Fitzgerald and went to the number of about a hundred well armed to Castle Street where he lived, and as they opened not the door, went in at a window and brought out Mr Fitzgerald whom they put in a coach with John Browne Esq. of the Neale,[10] and two Scholars well armed and conveyed the coach under a strong guard of us to the College where he was obliged to make his submission. Kelly then to avoid ill usage came of himself and did the same. [...] Those above mentioned Gentlemen notwithstanding their promise of better behaviour, threatened the lives of the Scholars when they met any of 'em alone and hired ruffians to assault them at night. The Scholars incensed at this once more were resolved to punish 'em, but the Provost, to avoid bloodshed, ordered that none of the Scholars should be suffered out, and in the meantime sent those whose lives were threatened to my Lord Chief Justice, who sent a tipstaff for Martin, so that affair ended. Kelly and Sheridan's trials came on a Thursday, in which Sheridan was honourably acquitted and Kelly found guilty and fined this day £500 – a month's close imprisonment, and to give security for his behaviour for seven years. So ended this affair in which justice took place.[11]

After the Gentlemen's Quarrel, Smock Alley became a more orderly place, and Sheridan was able to clear the stage of its spectators, and impose other reforms on the auditorium, but it came to reflect its manager, as Edmund Burke pointed out in his paper *The Reformer*, in its orderly dullness, its championship of English plays and English ways, and its dangerous unwillingness to reflect any other strand in Irish society.[12] Burke ridiculed Sheridan's title of 'Reformer': taming the audience does not make for better theatre; all it does is produce the same quotient of dullness in the auditorium as is already to be found on the stage – a safe theatre, well-tried plays, an unadventurous repertoire, a dull theatre for dull burghers.[13] Sheridan was dedicated to giving them what they wanted, and what the bourgeois gentry wanted was established works, indicative of their equal level of culture with London. The only thing that excited them was the prospect of trouble in the theatre, or a perceived racial insult displayed in practically any Irish character created for the stage.

With rare exceptions, the Irish characters in eighteenth-century plays are sympathetically drawn gentry: none of the nobility, and few enough of the lower classes appear. Even though the villainous Irishman was very rare, playwrights had to take pains in their published work to justify their Irish creations, and to insist on their good faith, lack of malice and Hibernian Correctness. George Colman the Elder's portrait of an Irish adventurer in *The Oxonian in Town* (1769) so offended the Irishmen in the London audience that they rioted and closed it down, but Colman insisted in his Preface to the Irish edition that he had been misunderstood: 'So far from intending to cast an illiberal reflection on the Irish nation, it was evidently the author's main design to vindicate the gentlemen of that country from the reproach deservedly incurred by worthless adventurers and outcasts. The gentlemen of Ireland appeared the foremost in his defence.'[14]

The Rivals (1775) by Richard Brinsley Sheridan (son of Thomas) was badly received at first. 'A Briton' wrote to the London *Morning Post* complaining of Sir Lucius O'Trigger: 'It is the first time I ever remember to have seen so villainous a portrait of an Irish Gentleman, permitted so openly to insult the country upon the boards of an English theatre.'[15] Sheridan promptly recast the part, giving it to Lawrence Clinch, whose playing transformed it. The main problem, however, was not Sir Lucius but the play's excessive length, and Sheridan reduced it by cutting down the parts of Julia and Faulkland. He was aware that offence had been taken to Sir Lucius, but in the Preface to the published play, while he regretted its earlier faults, he did not apologize for him. He implied that those who were offended were too sensitive, and were objecting (as happened later to Synge) not to the character, but to the author's perceived intention of offending, which he totally denied. He did not recant on the accuracy of Sir Lucius:

> It is not without pleasure that I catch at an opportunity of justifying myself from the charge of intending any national reflection in the character of Sir Lucius O'Trigger. If any gentleman opposed the piece from that idea, I thank them sincerely for their opposition; and if the condemnation of this comedy (however misconceived the provocation) could have added one spark to the decaying flame of national attachment to the country supposed to be reflected on, I should have been happy in its fate, and might with truth have boasted that it had done more service in its failure than the successful morality of a thousand stage-novels will ever effect.[16]

Richard Cumberland's *The West Indian* (1771) summed up in Major O'Flaherty many of these Irish characters: their natural virtues are manifold, their occasional linguistic idiosyncrasies may be comic but were not intended by the author to be disparaging:

> A brave, unthinking, animated rogue,
> With here and there a touch upon the brogue;
> Laugh, but despise him not, for on his lip
> His errors lie: his heart can never trip.[17]

But Francis Dobbs' Prologue to *The Irish Chief: or, The Patriot King*, two years later, took the opposite tack, and insisted that the depiction of the Irish on stage had been racially inaccurate and linguistically demeaning:

> Full oft hath honest Teague been here displayed;
> And many a roar have Irish blunders made;
> The bull, the brogue, are now so common grown,
> That one would almost swear they were – your own.[18]

This refers to unflattering portraits of the Irish that have built up a false impression, but since so many of the playwrights and actors were Irish, it is reasonable to expect truth in the Irish characters created, and the characteristics they display are benevolence, spontaneity, wit and natural goodness. There is nothing to object to, except, perhaps, the way they speak – with 'an Irish howl…*by Jasus* or *upon my shoul*', as Dobbs has it.[19] But the playwrights did not write brogue; as a rule, they wrote standard English, with Irish interjections – what Cumberland called 'here and there a touch upon the brogue'. The actors may have been responsible, as this was the age in which the actors' prestige rose to great heights while the literary value of the plays declined, but the evidence indicates that the actors did not emphasize the brogue either. There is a deal of difference between an Irish accent, which is natural, and an Irish brogue, which is essentially artificial; the brogue would only interpose a layer of obfuscation between the actor and the audience. Irish actors, like Joseph Millar, 'had a great success with their spirited renditions of Irish characters, and they did it without resorting to a brogue'.[20]

The archetypal popular Irish stage character, referred to above by Dobbs, was Teague in *The Committee; or, The Faithful Irishman* (1690), by Robert Howard, one of the most popular plays of the eighteenth century: it was republished nine times between 1710 and 1797, and anthologized at least four times.[21] 'Honest' Teague, who was so popular he became generic, was a crafty servant in the tradition of Plautus, and a prototypical resourceful Irish menial. He was, however, native Irish and a servant; the Hibernians did not care how their servants were portrayed on stage, nor did they care about any distorted representations of the native Irish. Servants speaking with brogue and blunder did not reflect any discredit on Hibernia. Nor did the picture of Teig O'Divilly, the lecherous Irish priest, created by Thomas Shadwell (the father of Charles), bother them in the least; the two plays in which he appears, *The Lancashire Witches* and *The Amorous Bigotte*, were popular in Dublin and constantly revived.[22]

What they were objecting to was the portrayal of the Irish gentry, yet such characters were almost invariably drawn with a sympathetic touch. If they were rogues, they were lovable rogues; if they were adventurers, they were honourable after their own fashion, like Roebuck in *Love and a Bottle*, Major O'Flaherty or Lieutenant O'Connor in Richard Brinsley Sheridan's *St Patrick's Day*. Their virtues easily outweighed any vices they may have had, and the vices were not really vicious, but a prickly sense of their own, and their country's, worth and honour, a weakness for drink and women, and a penchant for swearing and bending the English language. But though the Irish gentry were shown in a flattering light, what the Hibernians disliked were the external signifiers of Irishness that they carried; above all it was the brogue that they objected to most strongly, as Dobbs indicated, with its connotations of linguistic inferiority that spread to encompass a general cultural dismissal. The citizens of Hibernia found the mere act of differentiation offensive; insecure in their provincialism, they were quick to take offence and challenge anyone who dared to diminish them. Shadwell's merchant, Tradewell, in *The Plotting Lovers* is a typically prickly bourgeois: 'And does your Squireship take us Merchants of Dublin to be such Cods-heads,' he snarls at the English Trelooby.[23] But through the century there was a trend that is marked very clearly in the plays under discussion – a movement away from the acceptance of the superiority of all things English to an embracing of Irishness as a badge of quality. *St Stephen's Green* was an early broadside in the campaign; it spread to *The Sham Prince* and *The Hasty Wedding*, and was blasting on all fronts in the historical plays just discussed, as Philips, especially, staked out a new iconography for Hibernia. In this campaign, symbols were a potent weapon. Certain images of Irish inferiority had to be discarded, new symbols acceptable to an Augustan age and civilization were substituted to act as unifiers for the nation. Cabins and potatoes needed to vanish, but above all it was the accusation of 'brogues' that was the most offensive slur on the Hibernians. Swift wrote of 'that unpolite covering for the feet' that was 'a national reproach'.

Brogues were the great divider of this society: they were the visible symbols of inferiority. There were those with brogues and those with shoes, and the change from one to the other signified a leap as far-reaching as changing religion. In 1678, the Duke of Ormond commented ironically on those who perjured themselves during the Popish Plot: 'Those that went out of Ireland with bad English and worse clothes are returned well bred gentlemen, coronated, periwigged and clothed. Brogues and leather straps are converted to fashionable shoes and glittering buckles.'[24] Squire Daudle in Shadwell's *The Hasty Wedding* also noted the process of debrogueing and, like Ormond, he smelled treachery:

> SQUIRE DAUDLE   Here's a jade, now; it is not above two years ago since she was taken out of an Irish cabin with her brogues on, and yet begins to despise her own country, and is fond of everything that's English. [..] I think we have enough enemies abroad, without encouraging those within ourselves. [...] She that will betray her own country would no doubt betray me.[25]

The change of footwear was, of course, indicative of a change in fortune; shoes cost money, but a brogue was simply a square of soft leather, or an old felt hat, worn wrapped around the foot and tied at the ankle. So strong was this symbolism that the method of speech came to have the same signifier as the covering for the feet, but it proved more difficult to get rid of the Irish way of speaking than to dispose of one's brogues. To the outrage of the Hibernians, all of them were considered to speak with a brogue. The English language, which had united them to their fellow-Englishmen and separated them from the savage Irish, had betrayed them by becoming contaminated with Irish intonation and inflection.

Dineen's Dictionary derives brogue from the Irish '*barróg*' a gap, or '*barróg cainte*', a hesitation in speaking.[26] Other authorities follow him, but this derivation is too flattering, too charitable; brogue was from an early date a derogatory term in English, The Oxford English Dictionary gives two linked early usages. One is the usual Irish meaning of shoe or foot-covering; Holinshed in 1586, had 'on with his brogs, his shirt and other Irish rags';[27] the other meaning is of hose or trousers. Fletcher (1615) has: 'a pair of brogs to hide thy mountainous buttocks'.[28] But whether shoes or trousers, brogue in its linguistic application had come, by 1705, to refer to the colourful rags in which the English language of Ireland was clad: 'Charles Morgan [...] having much of the Irish brogue in his speech.'[29] Swift freely used both meanings of the word. In *The Drapier Letters,* he tells us that the Irish must accept Woods' ha'pence or 'eat our brogues',[30] while in 'Barbarous Denominations', he observes that 'what we call the Irish brogue is no sooner discovered, than it makes the deliverer in the last degree ridiculous and despised; and, from such a mouth, an Englishman expects nothing but bulls, blunders, and follies'.[31]

But there is a further strand to this: 'brogue' made its way into cant, a cryptolect devised by the criminal underworld to disguise its intentions from outsiders. Dr Johnson, in his Dictionary, defines brogue as 'a cant word for a corrupt dialect';[32] he does not connect it directly to Irish or Irish speech. In canting terminology, 'brogue' broadened to refer to any particular dialect, creole or slang. In 1727, De Foe referred to 'the sportsman's brogue' and in 1725 Thomas Sheridan observed: 'They brought with them each their own several brogues or modes of intonation.'[33] Swift, too, acknowledged the connection between cant and brogue: 'It is true, that, in the city parts of London, the trading people have an affected manner of pronouncing; and so, in my time, had many ladies and coxcombs of the court. It is likewise true, that there is an odd provincial cant in most counties of England, sometimes not very pleasing to the ear; and the Scotch cadence, as well as expression, are offensive enough. But none of these defects derive contempt to the speaker.'[34]

Dineen's derivation is faulty: there is nothing hesitant about brogue;

it rather charges ahead and thrashes around, deliberately it would seem, attracting censure, with 'bulls and blunders and follies'.[35] It seems to have been largely a low stage phenomenon, as Shaw observed, in which characters clumped around in three brogues, two on their feet, and one on their tongue. But as the century progressed, Macklin recast Irish speech as an attractive linguistic cloak. The Irish had appropriated the imported language, treating it irreverently, bending and twisting it in a way that to the English sensibility seemed coarse and ungenteel, but in effect was pulling it loose from its moorings and pushing it off on an adventure that still continues. To the Irish, language is less a tool for communication than a toy to play with, and English has proved a wonderful plaything. To the English of Ireland, 'brogue' was the adopted patois of the Irish, but to the English on the other side of the Irish Sea it was the badge of all who inhabited the island. 'They look upon us', writes Swift, 'as a sort of savage Irish, whom our ancestors conquered several hundred years ago.'[36] But by 1760, the tide had turned, and the English language of Ireland was considered by its speakers to be superior to all other variants. Macklin was able to talk proudly of our 'good, plain, old Irish English',[37] and English visitors to Dublin were annoyed by the Dubliners' claim to speak better English than Londoners. John Bush, in *Hibernia Curiosa* (1769), records that many of the 'middling class of gentry' and 'people in trade' had 'the ridiculous vanity' of considering their English better than that spoken by the people of London, and even thought that 'their gentility as much exceeds that of London as their pronunciation'.[38]

The Irish language shows up nowhere in the plays, apart from one telling interjection by Macklin; it was the speech of the non-entities, a signifier of the social and political wilderness. Swift despised it: 'I encountered near a hundred words together which I defy any creature in human shape, except an Irishman of the savage kind, to pronounce,' he wrote.[39] It was not one of the symbols appropriate for colonization, but for elimination. St Patrick, on the other hand, was frequently sworn by: 'By the sacred crook of Saint Patrick,' pledges Sir Callaghan O'Brallaghan. Another phrase that was just appearing was the 'island of saints',[40] which flowed directly from St Patrick's arrival, and for which the colonists could claim the credit. The plays trace this transformation of cultural awareness from negative to positive, from cabin to the palace of Tamor, from ignorance to learning, from a picturesque savagery to a Golden Age.

Theatrically speaking, the Protestant nation of Hibernia was in two minds about itself: on the one hand it wanted to be no different from the other British people across the water, but at the same time it wanted to differentiate itself from them, without losing equal status. It emphasized its sameness in closely following a tried English repertoire, and by taming the rowdy, irrational elements within its audience. Unfortunately, the only way of expressing its difference was by using those same Dionysiac elements on the stage. This display, while it had the qualities of an exorcism, may have led to some degree of acceptance of these qualities in themselves, and in their fellow-countrymen. The idea that the English and Irish characters put together would make a complete person was one that Edmund Burke proposed and could still be seen 150 years later in *John Bull's Other Island*.[41]

Starting with Thomas Sheridan's Captain O'Blunder in 1738, there is a line of flamboyant Irish gentlemen in the eighteenth-century drama, who expressed, for the English and Irish audiences, the essence of Hibernia. One half of the Hibernian psyche approved, and the plays containing these characters were perennially successful, but the other half was scandalized that these dramatic constructs should be applied equally to all of them, and denied the veracity of these stage Irishmen. It is clear, however, from any account of the period, that these stage gentlemen are but a pale shadow of the real thing. Sir Lucius O'Trigger's easy belligerence, for example, is mild when compared to the likes of George Robert Fitzgerald, who fought at least twelve duels in his short life, and claimed twenty-six, who chained his father to a bear and imprisoned him in a cave, and was hanged for murder in 1786.[42] The Protestant family of Hibernia, however, was reluctant to be represented by such rowdy, disreputable cousins, for long safely rusticated, but now breaking out afresh.

There were two types of theatre on display, representing the duality that was incipient in Farquhar's *Love and a Bottle* and was to inform the Irish theatre for decades. There was the conforming Bourgeois Ascendancy theatre, such as Thomas Sheridan imported from England, and the non-conformist Irish theatre, as exemplified by Macklin and later by O'Keeffe. The conforming theatre seemed to hold sway, but it was being undermined and eroded by the other strand, physically in disturbances and riots, but also in the characters that represented the nation on stage. All of these came from the repressed tradition, even if the playwrights did not, and showed the placid Augustan surface of Hibernian society being cracked by the creative rowdiness of an alternative vision. When the Hibernians complained of the stage Irishman, it was not because the figure was untrue, but because it was drawn mostly from the other tradition, and portrayed an image of their society that made them uncomfortable.

Most of the Irish characters in eighteenth-century plays are variations on a theme: Captain O'Blunder, Sir Callaghan O'Brallaghan, Major O'Flaherty, Sir Lucius O'Trigger and Lieutenant O'Connor are all created from the same archetype, but each pushes the character further. Each builds on the previous one in developing an aggregate portrait of the Irish gentleman. In these plays, the composite Irish gentleman that is formed, the dramatic simulacrum of the race, is a Gaelic-Hibernian one. In this picture, the gentry replaced the nobility on the stage, as they already have in the audience, and as they in their turn will be replaced by the lower or peasant class in the plays of O'Keeffe.

The first of the line was Thomas Sheridan's Captain O'Blunder in *The Brave Irishman*, which, while it is derived from the *miles gloriosus* and idiot gentleman, is developed well beyond the source material. Sheridan gave him a 'bull and blunder' dialogue for the most part, but we can see the shadow of something different, an Irish tendency to toy with the English language that produces unexpected results. Cumberland added to the character a dash of Rousseau: his Major O'Flaherty is one of life's natural aristocrats from whom dull English society, frozen by manners, has a lot to learn in terms of natural feelings and spontaneous expression. Macklin transformed the character and his speech; he gave us two creations: in one of these Murrough O'Dogherty, the bourgeois gentility is uppermost; the other, Sir Callaghan O'Brallaghan belongs to the dashing anarchic strain. Richard Brinsley Sheridan, typically, synthesized the two lines of development, the conformist and the anarchist, in Sir Lucius O'Trigger and Lieutenant O'Connor.

The prototype was Captain O'Blunder, in *The Brave Irishman*, written by Thomas Sheridan, the manager of Smock Alley, probably around 1738, though the play was not published until 1755.[43] It is a slight, two-act farce, and was constructed out of pieces of other plays. Its ultimate ancestor was Molière's *Monsieur de Pourceaugnac*, by way of Shadwell's adaptation, called *The Plotting Lovers*. Captain O'Blunder can be considered a sort of anti-stage Irishman: 'It is the misrepresentation of the Irishman that is the core of the play.'[44] This aspect Sheridan lifted from Farquhar's Roebuck in *Love and a Bottle*. The first scene of *The Brave Irishman* exactly parallels Roebuck's introduction in Farquhar's play, and the overall action of Sheridan's play re-enacts *Love and a Bottle*. In *The Brave Irishman*, the heroine begins by indulging her ignorance and fantastical ideas about Irishmen. Her prejudices are shown, by the conduct and character of the Irish hero, to be baseless, and he ends up winning her hand by behaving generously.

This is exactly what happens, at greater length and with a great deal more subtlety, in *Love and a Bottle*, but the plays share the technique, first of expressing, and then of refuting, English prejudices about Ireland and Irishmen.

The heroine, Lucinda, in *The Brave Irishman* has ideas about the Irish at the start of the play that she must dispose of by the end:

> LUCINDA   Why I am told they are mere beasts, and have horns in that country.
>
> BETTY   I believe not more than their neighbours, but I assure you, our London citizens know to their cost that they have an excellent hand at planting them. Come, come, Madam; it is time to lay aside these prejudices. I have known several of that country, and I assure you, they are the most charming, agreeable, delightful, companions in the world. In short, they are worth all the beaux in Christendom.[45]

O'Blunder, arriving in London in a state of poverty and dishevelment after a long journey, repeats Roebuck's entrance in the earlier drama. The first exchange between Roebuck and the heroine, also called Lucinda in *Love and a Bottle*, forms the basis of the above passage in Sheridan's play:

> LUCINDA   Tell us some news of your country; I have heard the strangest stories, that the people wear horns and hoofs.
>
> ROEBUCK   Yes, faith, a great many wear horns; but we had that among other laudable fashions, from London.[46]

As the plays progress, it becomes clear that the Irishmen, for all their initial rough appearance, are, in conduct and sentiment, more gentlemen than their English counterparts. Both are proud and defensive of their own and their country's honour. O'Blunder is proudly Irish: 'I scorn to deny my country,'[47] he asserts and kicks Ragoo when he calls it a 'Hottentot country'.[48] He also appropriates Irish history and custom. He swears by St Patrick, and invokes the continuity of tradition for which the Anglo-Irish yearned: 'You know I have a good estate in Ireland, besides my commission, it will be enough for us all, and we'll go there, and live like so many Irish kings.'[49] O'Blunder has too much generosity to fall into the trap prepared for him by Cheatwell, who disseminates the report that Lucinda is now a pauper. He confounds expectations by taking her for her own sake, not her fortune, only to find that she is rich after all.

O'Blunder is not the linguistic fool he might appear; Sheridan has given him a fair number of malapropisms and howlers, but a closer look indicates a subtler undercurrent. Many of his 'bulls' are simply oxymorons and paradoxes, but a good many could be seen as playing with the language's sounds and meanings. His remark on a horseman's expertise being a result of his being 'manured to them from the time he was seven'[50] is a sly play on words and conjunction of ideas, and when he refuses to purchase gloves and says that 'my hands shall go barefoot all the days of my life',[51] there is an adumbration of the elegant reversals of Oscar Wilde, as well as a Platonic sense that the contradiction on the surface is resolved by an agreement on an ideal level. O'Blunder's most extravagant gaffes have a surrealist sort of meaning that ricochets around inside the sentence. His observation to his sergeant, 'You know you have lied under the computation of being a papist, and so if you ever come into battle, it will be incumbered upon you to stigmatize yourself,'[52] is a sophisticated piece of juggling with sound and meaning. Sheridan was showing off, but he was indicating that his audience and the character he created have a highly developed grasp of verbal play.

Macklin continued this linguistic development in Sir Callaghan O'Brallaghan in *Love à la Mode* (1759), one of the most popular plays of the later eighteenth century. He repeated the dramatic situation and action of Sheridan's play, but placed more emphasis on confounding the linguistic expectations of the English participants. The heroine, Charlotte, is determined to make game of her suitors, because she knows that their motives are mercenary; they deserve to be ridiculed for it, and society will approve:

> CHARLOTTE The world will applaud the mirth, especially when they know what kind of lovers they are; and that the sole motive of their addresses was the lady's fortune.[53]

The suitors are of a wide-ranging ethnic diversity: there is a 'beau Jew' Mordecai, an English 'gentleman jockey', a 'proud, haughty Caledonian knight' and 'a wild Irish, Prussian, hard-headed soldier'.[54] The Irishman, while initially tarred with the same mercenary brush as the others, proves to be just what he seems, without guile or avarice, not a gentleman Jew, a ruined jockey, or a sneering baronet, but an honest soldier.

Love à la Mode follows the same curve of action that Sheridan's and Farquhar's plays did, but Macklin casts the plot of expectation defeated into a recurring linguistic mode. Sir Archy Macsarcasm promises to his friends and to the audience a fine piece of bull and blarney from Sir Callaghan when he is asked to describe a military action: 'I'll engage he wull fight ye as many battles as Quintus Curtius, and aw in as guid meeletary Irish as ever came frai the banks of the Shannon, or the bogs of Tipperary.'[55] But Sir Callaghan delivers an account that is masterful in its clarity of perception and honest evaluation of the chaos of battle:

> SIR CALLAGHAN   Why, madam, there is so much doing everywhere, there is no knowing what is done anywhere; for every man has his own part to look after, which is as much as he can do, without minding what other people are about. Then, madam, there is such drumming and trumpeting, firing and smoking, fighting and rattling everywhere – and such an uproar of courage and slaughter in every man's mind – and such a delightful confusion altogether, that you can no more give an account of it than you can the stars in the sky.[56]

This passage overturns the expectations of the other suitors and the audience from two points of view. First, it is clear, exact and delivered in standard English. Secondly, it is the opposite of the *miles gloriosus* persona that has been attached to Sir Callaghan by the other characters. Far from being a vainglorious boaster, he is a keen and exact observer, who refrains from boasting of his own martial prowess. Macklin's dramatic skill is captured in the word 'delightful', which catches Sir Callaghan's attraction to the violent chaos of war, to which he remains faithful throughout the play.

The other three suitors dismally fail the test for greed that has been devised by Charlotte's uncle, but Sir Callaghan passes by proving that he has a 'generous heart'.[57] He is an Irish gentleman, and the acquisition of wealth, so avidly pursued by the other suitors, means little to him. The desire for a fortune is not simple acquisitiveness, gambling or to bolster family pride, but 'to maintain a couple of honest hearts, and have something to spare for the necessities of a friend, which is all we want, and all that fortune is good for'.[58] Sir Callaghan grows in stature as he overcomes each challenge. His language is always clear, but with an occasional idiomatic word or phrase, such as 'ax my lave',[59] or 'poltroon'.[60] As in the previous play, as well as outclassing the other suitors in personal courage and manliness, Macklin has the Irishman outshine them linguistically.

If the Hibernians were divided between the dull, bourgeois Anglo-Irish and the vibrant, convert Gaelic-Irish, one supplying the lack in the other, then the superior dramatic potential of characters who speak, act and live vividly, over the virtues of conformity and dullness, is obvious enough. This was the aspect that was latched onto by Richard Cumberland in his play *The West Indian* of 1771. Cumberland was a fine playwright, whose father was the bishop of Clonfert and Kilmore and who spent some time in Dublin as under-secretary to the lord lieutenant. He drew on his experience to create the colourful character of Major O'Flaherty, in this, his best-known play.

Major O'Flaherty is one of the Wild Geese, who has fought all over Europe as a mercenary. He is described as 'A brave, unthinking, animated rogue, / With here and there a touch upon the brogue'.[61] This tells us how the playwright regarded the character, but also how it is to be played, in normal speech, but with occasional touches of the brogue for added colour, effect or humour. The Major gives his own colourful history, in clear, plain English:

> MAJOR   'Tis thirty years, come the time, that I have followed the trade, and in a pretty many countries. Let me see – In the war before last I served in the Irish brigade, d'ye see; there, after bringing off the French monarch, I left his service, with a British bullet in my body, and this ribband in my button-hole. Last war I followed the fortunes of the German eagle, in the corps of grenadiers; there I had my belly full of fighting, and a plentiful scarcity of everything else. After six and twenty engagements, great and small, I went off, with this gash in my skull, and kiss of the Empress' sweet hand (Heaven bless it) for my pains. Since the peace, my dear, I took a little turn with the Confederates there in Poland – and such a set of madcaps! – by the Lord Harry, I never knew what it was they were scuffling about.[62]

The Major's affability and benevolence are mirrored by the other colonial in the play: Belcour, the West Indian of the title. Cumberland contrasts the Irishman and the West Indian favourably with the colder English characters. The colonials are spontaneous, generous, good-hearted and easy-going, while the English are buttoned-up and calculating. Even the heroines are obsessed with the pursuit of fortune, and incapable of acting openly or open-handedly. Like Roebuck, Major O'Flaherty reacts instinctively, and his instincts are always sound, just as Belcour's are, even though his actions are comically impulsive and beyond what a rigidly ordered society finds acceptable. (Lord Chesterfield had recently advised his son that there was nothing so vulgar as audible laughter.) Both enrich society by their warmth and directness, but they lack the curbs that mannered intercourse dictates. Their education has not fitted them for London drawing-rooms, but it is precisely that lack of education that enables them to circumvent polite

standards and cut through formalities and forms. Their natural characters are genteel, and their experience – O'Flaherty's cosmopolitanism
and Belcour's ascendancy in a slave-owning society – places them outside the ritualized norms of London, an advantage which the hero,
young Dudley, cannot achieve on account of his formal indoctrination
by the Establishment. Just like Boucicault's heroes a century later,
Dudley is trapped in the rituals, and cannot break out; a solution has
to be engineered, without his participation, that enables him to stay
within the bounds of society.

Cumberland shows that the English have much to learn from their
colonial visitors in terms of directness and spontaneity in a society that
has become ossified in manners. 'I have discovered through a veil of
some irregularities,' admits Belcour's uncle, 'a heart beating with
benevolence, an animated nature.'[63] The overt aristocrats are set to
rights by the benevolence, generosity and directness of Belcour and
O'Flaherty, the natural aristocrats from the colonies.

The internal opposition that is captured within these Irish characters,
between their mercenary brains and the quixotic gallantry of their
hearts, is repeated in the comparable tension articulated between them
and the society that spawned them. They are all outcasts from that
society, removed from it spiritually as well as spatially, yet retain a
strong emotional attachment. This duality reaches its highest expression in the work of Oliver Goldsmith and Thomas Sheridan's son,
Richard Brinsley. Though none of their plays are set in Ireland, in them
the idea of alternative selves is almost a commonplace. Goldsmith's
hero and heroine, Marlow and Kate Hardcastle, in *She Stoops to
Conquer* assume other personas to become acquainted. In Sheridan's
The Rivals, Captain Absolute has to play two versions of himself, and
The School for Scandal features a pair of complementary brothers,
Charles and Joseph Surface. In *St Patrick's Day*, Lieutenant O'Connor
has to assume several different roles in order to achieve his ends.

The comedy in *The Rivals* takes after Wycherley's *The Country Wife*
in its plot of out-of-towners out of their depths in an urban society,
caught between two standards of behaviour and morality. The English
Acres is more at sea, however, than the Irish Sir Lucius O'Trigger, who
follows his own eccentric code, but is still accepted in Bath society. The
duality that was evident in Sheridan's life also found its way into his
work.[64] It is manifested here in the Beverley/Absolute deception; and
Sheridan revisited it in *The School for Scandal*. This play has the two
opposing sides of a single nature, expressed by the two brothers; in *The

Rivals it is the same actor playing two aspects of the same character, one sober, one scapegrace. The idea of play-acting is as old as comedy – the adopting of a different role to reveal some essential but hidden ingredient of the true self – but there does seem to be some intimate connection between the idea of play-acting and the Anglo-Irish. It stems from a deep-rooted uncertainty as to their inherent nature and their position in Ireland, and within the extended English, or British, family. Neither Captain Absolute nor Sir Anthony are given any distinctively Irish identity, but could as easily be Irish as not; it is in his play-acting and cunning stratagems that the Captain tends to Irishness. Sheridan's comedies often 'celebrate the exploits of dashing adventurers, who win their way against the odds with the aid of their quick wits, histrionic abilities, and powers of persuasion'.[65] This dashing Irish persona, with the exception of Lieutenant O'Connor, is usually conferred by Sheridan on characters that are nominally English.

Sir Lucius O'Trigger is a dashing adventurer, but belongs, ultimately, more to the bourgeois than the mercurial tendency; he is totally set in his code of honour and conduct, rather that being quick-witted, histrionic and inventive. He is not, however, a stage-Irish horror. He is genteel, with his own code of conduct and sense of humour. His social standing is never in doubt, even though 'the mansion-house and dirty acres have slipt through my fingers'.[66] He is in Bath to pursue the time-honoured Irish sport of pursuing heiresses: his appearance and conduct are calculated to please the ladies. Lucy has got three crowns, two gold pocket-pieces and a silver snuff box from him, and notes how generous he is, in both senses of the word: 'Though not over-rich, I found he had too much pride and delicacy to sacrifice the feelings of a gentleman to the necessities of his fortunes.'[67] But, as a gentleman, he wants everything done fairly to obtain the old gentlewoman's consent.[68] He is the antithesis of the scheming Absolute, whose comic chaos belongs more to the Irish tradition of creative anarchy. To cozen an heiress would be, to Sir Lucius, a dishonourable action, even though all he has left is 'our honour and the family pictures'.[69] His honour is his fortune, and he lives by a very strict, if comic, standard: 'What the devil signifies *right* when your honour is concerned?'[70] But he is no fire-eater: 'Come, come, there must be no passion at all in the case – these things should always be done civilly.'[71] He deals with duels and killing as routine, as a game, as a purging of misunderstanding, after which good feeling and friendship are restored: 'You see how this little explanation will put a stop at once to all confusion or misunderstanding that might arise between you.'[72] He is the defender of his country's honour as well as his own; he sees no gap between the two: 'There is a gay captain here, who put a jest on me lately, at the expense of my country, and I only want to fall in with the gentleman to call him out.'[73]

In his characterization of Sir Lucius O'Trigger, Sheridan played with the template established by his father, by Macklin and by Cumberland, and expertly inverted it. Unlike the others, Sir Lucius is affable on the surface, but lethal at heart. He talks charmingly, and seems the soul of reasonableness; the comedy lies in realizing that his charm and reason are all directed towards homicide. It is this discrepancy that is funny, the pitting of manner against matter. Sir Lucius is an aesthete of violence, but he is perfectly good-natured. He is more complex than his predecessors in his connoisseurship of carnage and the code of honour, which inform his every action. What Sheridan added to the archetype is the marriage of easy fellowship and lethal intent: Sir Lucius will kill or be killed with the best will in the world, and without rancour or complaint, as long as it is done 'prettily'. Sheridan developed Macklin's interest in language by making the character no longer linguistically naïve, but giving him perfectly normal English while appreciating deviant linguistic registers: he recognizes that the linguistic blundering has been shunted sideways and given to Mrs Malaprop. He takes an Irish delight in her use of language: 'Lucy, your lady is a great mistress of language. Faith, she's quite the queen of the dictionary! – for the devil a word dare refuse coming at her call – though one would think it was quite out of hearing.'[74]

Sir Lucius's boisterous benignity is quite attractive. He has an off-hand fatalism and disregard for danger which may be called courage, but he is more concerned with staying a gentleman than staying alive. The distance between the duellists is not calculated to save life but to save face: 'There now, that is a very pretty distance – a pretty gentleman's distance.'[75] 'Prettiness' is a term one would not normally apply to a duel but he takes a connoisseur's delight in it. He is so used to risking his life he thinks nothing of it: 'There's nothing like being used to a thing.'[76] He is cheerfully fatalistic about the outcome. He says to Acres: 'would you choose to be pickled and sent home? – or would it be the same to you to lie here in the Abbey? – I'm told there is snug lying in the Abbey.'[77]

Sir Lucius's experience has taught him that duels are seldom fatal, something that the others don't know, and this makes him philosophical. A persistent theme of the play is that men, their honour and their duels are ridiculous; Sheridan may have been remembering his own brush with duelling, in which he was seriously injured, and he was certainly alluding to the Irish predilection for them. Sir Lucius supplies most of the comedy on this issue by his unblinking acceptance of the code, his complete absence of irony or doubt, and the intense goodwill and good manners with which he tries to kill his opponents. There is nothing at all personal in it, no animosity; if someone else turns up to fight, that will do equally well: 'You have certainly challenged somebody – and you came here to fight him. ? Now, if that gentleman is willing to represent him – I can't see, for my soul, why it isn't just the same thing.'[78]

Such rigidity and punctiliousness inevitably tie him in a knot of his own making. Sir Lucius accepts Absolute's apology with a good grace, as real, because it is couched and delivered in proper form and with a proper gentlemanly address. Absolute apologizes: 'As I should not fear to support a real injury – you shall now see that I am not ashamed to atone for an inadvertency – I ask your pardon.'[79] Though it is an apology for something that never happened, like the reason for the proposed duel, Sir Lucius accepts it: 'an affront handsomely acknowledged becomes an obligation'.[80] The handsome acknowledgement makes it completely real to Sir Lucius; he is now in the absurd position of being put under an obligation by an apology for an incident that never occurred, and that he invented himself. Reality lies in the style, not the substance; in the transformational power of his belief it is possible to glimpse a shadowy ancestor of *The Playboy of the Western World*.

Sheridan's other overtly Irish character is Lieutenant O'Connor in *St Patrick's Day* (1775). It was gratitude to Clinch, who rescued *The Rivals* by his more sympathetic playing of Sir Lucius O'Trigger, that motivated him to write this short farce for the actor's benefit night.[81] O'Connor is an extremely attractive character, quick-witted and resourceful. The piece romps along at a hectic pace, driven by the machinations of O'Connor in trying to outwit his sweetheart's father. *St Patrick's Day* has its origins in the *Commedia*, with the deceived father, *la fille mal gardé*, the crafty disguised suitor and the doctor, the whole mixed with a subverted archetype of the *miles gloriosus* in the character of Lieutenant O'Connor. Another source is Molière's *La Malade Imaginaire* in which the lover disguises himself as a doctor in order to treat the deceived father and gain admittance to the heroine. Sheridan excelled in this sort of collage: it was his favoured method of creation. His plays and characters can all be traced to previous writers and his genius lay in rethinking and redeploying them. His knowledge of old plays seems to have been immense (he had the reputation of being 'deep read in the whole catalogue of forgotten farces'[82]), but he excused himself from any charge of plagiarism in his introduction to *The Rivals*: 'On subjects on which the mind has been informed, invention is slow of exerting itself. Faded ideas float in the fancy like half-forgotten dreams; and the imagination in its fullest enjoyments becomes suspicious of its offspring and doubts whether it has created or adopted.'[83] The play begins with O'Connor bestowing money on his men to celebrate the day and drink St Patrick's health, and ends with the resourceful Irish gentleman successful, having outsmarted Justice Credulous and forced him to accept him both as a soldier and an Irishman. Lieutenant O'Connor is a different take on the character of the Irish gentleman-soldier, and shows the quicksilver nature of the Irish channelled into histrionic extravagance. Sheridan may not be making amends for Sir Lucius, but he has assembled Lieutenant O'Connor from the bits left over. Where Sir Lucius is obsessed with one mode of conduct, O'Connor is devious and resourceful; where Sir Lucius is open and straight, O'Connor is deceitful and cunning; where O'Trigger relies on the threat of violence, the Lieutenant relies on his wits; where Sir Lucius is aware of the world through the filter of his own needs, O'Connor is conscious of those for whom he has responsibility. The pieces of the character of the Irish gentleman are shared between them. Sir Lucius does not succeed in winning the heroine, but behaves with perfect generosity and gentlemanliness about it; he is sporting in his defeat, and free from rancour: 'As I have been disappointed myself, it will be very hard if I have not the satisfaction of seeing other people succeed better.'[84] Fundamentally, he displays a completely bourgeois conformity, while Lieutenant O'Connor is resourceful, clever, adroit in knowing when to retreat and mount another attack from a different quarter. He is clearly a man of birth and breeding, as shown by his rank, and the deference of the other Irishmen that he commands. The corporal observes approvingly: 'I never will see a sweeter timpir'd officer, nor one more free with his purse,'[85] such generosity being a mark of the Irish aristocracy. Everybody agrees about his good nature, and his only noted fault is a small one: the Serjeant says, 'the lad is good-natur'd at bottom – so I pass over small things – but hearkee, between ourselves – he is confoundedly given to wenching,'[86] which is not a fault at all in Irish heroes but a sign of virility. The play hums with patriotic symbolism, of shamrocks, St Patrick, St Patrick's Day, and almost begs to begin or end (or both) with the tune of the same name that had become the unofficial anthem of Hibernia. O'Connor is as proud of being Irish as of being a soldier; at the end of the play, when the Justice asks him to 'Forswear your Country, and quit the Army – and I'll receive you as my Son in law,'[87] he is outraged at the notion of doing either: 'I'd pull your nose for mentioning the first, and break your bones for proposing the latter.'[88] Lieutenant O'Connor, like Sir Lucius, remains an outsider in this society by refusing to renounce his country or his profession; but the play also nudges towards the inclusion of the Irish within the British family in the final acceptance by Justice Credulous of the Lieutenant on his own terms.

The anarchy of the Gaelic influence and the settled love of order on the English side combined to produce the humours of Hibernia. Cumberland, Thomas Sheridan and Macklin all had their heroes triumph by their innate superiority rather than their anarchic exterior. Richard Brinsley Sheridan had Lieutenant O'Connor succeed by combining his generous nature with his quick wits and willingness to cheat his way around the strictures of society, using anarchy in a creative, constructive manner, in order to achieve harmony, while Sir Lucius follows his own code of conduct regardless of where he finds himself, spreading anarchy while himself in the grip of a rigid code of manners. All of the Irish characters are out of step with their society or surroundings, but they are all on the move socially, forcing their way up the ladder towards the inner circles of British society, a route that Sheridan, Goldsmith and Macklin all successfully negotiated.

Charles Macklin was a playwright whose life took such a steep upward curve; he achieved a drastic racial and class change, managed to hold simultaneously the status of insider and outsider, and kept this Irish duality permanently in balance. He lived to a great age, given variously as 99 and 107, and had a successful career as an actor, manager, playwright and lecturer on the theatre. He was born Cathal MacLochlainn about 1690 in County Donegal to an Irish-speaking Catholic peasant family. He moved to Dublin as a child, worked for a time in Trinity College as an errand boy before running away to England, changing his name to Charles Macklin, and recasting himself as an offspring of landed Protestant gentry. Success followed rapidly. He was an exceptional actor, and by his early thirties he had conquered the London stage. He wrote successful plays and became the friend of Burke, Garrick, Fielding and Pope. As a playwright, he started the mode of writing parts for himself that mirrored his own personality and suited his acting. He was a man of violent opinions, with a quick temper and a sarcastic tongue, and the roles he both created and acted – Sir Archy MacSarcasm, Sir Pertinax MacSycophant, Sir Callaghan O'Brallaghan and Murrough O'Dogherty – all drew on these qualities. Apart from playing leading parts in his own works, his acting had a wider influence: he was the first to perform Macbeth in Scottish dress, and his performance of Shylock rescued the part from farce and gave it a power and edge that terrified his audience.[89] Pope is reputed to have said of his playing: 'This was the Jew that Shakespeare drew.'[90] He also was one of the founders of the study of English literature: during an unsuccessful period in the theatre in 1753, he abandoned the stage and set up a literary tavern, for ladies and gentlemen, in Covent Garden, at which he delivered lectures on Shakespeare.

But having remade himself from a Catholic peasant to a landed Protestant, he was reluctant to extend a transformational licence to his creations. Count Mushroom, in *The True-born Irishman*, is lampooned as being the son of a pawnbroker, and in *The Man of the World* all the company at Bath is satirized for having notions above its station. Macklin himself, as well as all those characters that he drew with such ambiguous snobbery, was in the familiar category of false gentry. His attitude to them was mixed. On the one hand, he displayed an egalitarian disdain for the society in which he found himself and for its upper reaches, to which he was denied entrance. But he was acutely aware, as a writer and performer, of the comic potential of the social climbers, the sham nobility and the bogus gentry.

Macklin's plays are inflexibly anti-establishment. In *Love à la Mode* (1759) and *The True-born Irishman* (1761) the Irish underground gentry – O'Brallaghan and O'Dogherty – have come to the surface, but show no interest in climbing higher. There is a definite suggestion that to do so would be to betray themselves, their names and their origins. They are rooted in their Irishness, and have no need to purloin a history or invent a myth to legitimize themselves. They are already of the race, and in the line, of ancient Irish nobility; O'Dogherty refuses his wife's passionate pleading for a title, rejoicing instead in his own ancient and noble name.

O'Dogherty eschews political activity and is an early advocate of the Arthur Young/Maria Edgeworth school of economic patriotism; he echoes Swift on the patriotic excellence of making a blade of corn grow where none grew before.[91] These sentiments ring as Macklin's own because they recur powerfully in his other plays. He detested the venality of politicians, and the hypocritical self-interest of patriots. These ideas are expressed with tremendous force and vigour; this must have been how he acted: he lacks the grace and charm of Goldsmith or Richard Brinsley Sheridan, but he makes up for it in the strength and ardour of his dialogue and characters. His plotting is clever, his characters are lively, some exceptional. His last play, *The Man of the World*, is a *tour-de-force*: it observes the unities, is set in one room and passes in real time. The main character, Sir Pertinax MacSycophant, is an acidic portrait of a corrupt politician and chauvinist Scotsman. Macklin disliked the Scots even more than he detested politicians; there is another snobbish Scot in *Love à la Mode*, whose genealogical boasting is punctured by Sir Callaghan O'Brallaghan: 'The Scots are all Irishmen's bastards,' he interjects, 'for the youngest branch of our family, one Fergus O'Brallaghan was the very man that went from Carrickfergus, and peopled all Scotland with his own hands.'[92] Macklin was holding up the activities of the Scots as a negative example for his fellow-countrymen; in the event of a Union, he was saying, this is what they should not do. But in the event of the Union, it was exactly what they did. In 1707, the Scottish Parliament was abolished, and Scottish MPs took their places at Westminster, where they formed themselves into a cabal to serve their collective interest and called it patriotism. Macklin found that his loathing of venal politicians and of hypocritical patriotic self-interest could be combined in a detestation of the Scots.

He had articulated the critique of politics that is central to *The Man of the World* (1781) twenty years earlier in *The True-born Irishman*, but had confined it to an Irish context. He wrote the latter play at a time when the endemic corruption of the Irish Parliament of George II had reached epic heights. The Irish Parliament collapsed only on the king's death, when it had been in existence for thirty-four years. The power of the Undertakers and Lords Justices was largely unrestrained, the creation of boroughs, peerages and sinecures to manipulate Parliament was an open and unremarked scandal, so universal as to be considered harmless:

> SIR PERTINAX   What single instance can ye, or ainy mon, gi' of the poleetecal vice or corruption of these days, that has na been practised in the greatest states, and in the maist virtuous times? [...] It is na decent till find fault wi' what is winked at by the whole nation – nay, and practised by aw parties.[93]

Macklin's contempt for the Irish political system extended to the class that created and maintained it. He did not pillory the Hibernians directly at first, in *The True-born Irishman*, but obliquely through the persona of Count Mushroom, who is an Englishman, the jumped-up son of a pawnbroker and one of the 'most conceited impudent cox-

combs that has ever yet been imported into this land'.[94] He is an
overnight growth, and O'Dogherty speaks for the older gentry when
he tells him: 'You will find a great many relations here, count; for we
have a large crop of Mushrooms in this here country.'[95] What all
Macklin's main characters share is contempt for those placed above
them socially. These roles are all self-portraits to some extent: they
embody his opinionated, censorious, sarcastic nature. They are all self-
made men: Sir Pertinax is a professional politician, Sir Callaghan a
mercenary in the Prussian service, Murrough O'Dogherty an improving middleman and head tenant. They, like Macklin, have all struggled
and recast themselves in another shape, which they are happy enough
to hold. O'Dogherty, in particular, has retaken in practical terms the
family position of landed eminence, and stands on his own genealogy
as a true-born Irishman, not some English mushroom. Macklin continued the renovation of the great Irish families that was started by
William Philips; he may have stolen a Protestant landed-gentry persona, but he retained in this and his other plays a native Irish outlook
and pride in his origins. *The True-born Irishman* states openly that the
real gentlemen are the O'Dohertys and their like, and the shams are
the New Hibernian mushrooms that sprang up overnight. The first part
of this proposition follows from Philips, but the latter leads directly
from the whole body of Irish literature of the period, of which he
would have been aware as a native Irish speaker; he may have been
Charles Macklin publicly, but in private he was still Charley
McLaughlin.[96]

The True-born Irishman draws on linguistic variants to make its
point; the brogue has been rethought. Macklin obviously had a very
good ear, and was, like Shaw, interested in different modes and registers of speech as class and racial indicators. He transformed his own
speech in order to play non-Irish parts on the English stage, taking classical roles with the likes of Garrick. He was particularly astute on the
Scottish accent, which he wrote phonetically, but apart from an occasional phonetic marker, such as 'Orra', or 'faith', the speech of the Irish
characters is written in plain English. The Irish had staged a reverse
colonization of the English language, and mastered it to such an extent
that the speech of English Ireland was claimed by Macklin to be superior to the other variants on display. Different kinds of English are presented, in Mrs Diggerty's cockney infection and the affected braying of
the English ruling class in Count Mushroom. They both suffer from
comparison with the solid English of O'Dogherty and his brother-in-
law Hamilton, both of whom, we may allow, spoke with an Irish

accent, but without a bull or blarney in sight. Turning the familiar English slur on the Irish brogue back on its perpetrators was a favourite gambit of Macklin's: the Scots, the county English, the gentry, the Londoners, all speak with their own particular brogue, but the way the Irish speak is superior to any of them:

> O'DOGHERTY   But let me have our own good, plain, old Irish English, which I insist is better than all the English English that ever coquettes and coxcombs brought into the land.[97]

The characters in *Love à la Mode* had their expectations of an Irishman's language and behaviour in England exposed and ridiculed; in *The True-born Irishman* Count Mushroom's language and behaviour as an Englishman in Ireland is lampooned, as is his expectation of Irish people's behaviour at home:

> MUSHROOM   You are a little odd in this here country in some points […] however, upon the whole, take you altogether, you are a damn'ed honest, tory rory, rantum scantum, dancing, singing, laughing, boozing, jolly, friendly, fighting, hospitable people, and I like you mightily.
> COUNSELLER   Upon my word, sir, the people of Ireland are much obliged to you for your helter skelter, rantum scantum portrait of them.[98]

All Macklin's comedies apart from this were set in England, most featuring Irish characters, but Macklin in this play reversed that pattern, set his play in Dublin, peopled it with Irish characters, and positioned an Englishman, Count Mushroom, as the outsider in this society.

The character of Count Mushroom is based on the fops of Restoration comedy, but Macklin's mockery of him has a keener, racial edge. First of all, the wags of Dublin have bestowed the mocking title of Count on him, being well aware of his humble origins, and the title of Count itself, which doesn't exist in the English or Irish peerage, is the one which the Anglo-Irish jeered at in the Irish diaspora, and with which the Protestant pamphleteers branded the unquiet gentlemen of Connaught. Macklin here turns it back on an upper-class English idiot, ignorant and patronizing, loud and unselfconscious. Apart from the intensely local character of the play, the character and treatment of Mushroom were the reasons for its disastrous failure on the English stage, where it was removed after one night, and Macklin apologized to the audience, observing that 'there is a geography in humour, as well as in morals'.[99] In his linking of humour, geography and morality, he was referring to behaviour: what is risible in one society is a scandal in another. Yet humour moved easily from London to Dublin; why did it not travel the other way? The concern of the play, that it is ridiculous to ape the behaviour of one society in another because of a perceived cultural superiority, is at one level uncontroversial. But where the culture mimicked and rejected is that of the audience, the message, however comic, can be seen as an insult. The idea that London society is inferior to Dublin, that it is effete and silly, whereas Dublin is solid and robust, that middle-class Dublin has nothing to learn from aristocratic London, was not well received at Drury Lane. The representative and touchstone of London culture, Count Mushroom, is shown as a prancing, lecherous fool, in a characterization that is in its way very subversive, even though in the line of Restoration fops like the perennially popular Sir Fopling Flutter, through whom the intrusion of French culture in English society was pilloried. But with Count Mushroom the shoe is on the other foot, and the London audience was not prepared to agree that the extrusion of English culture into Irish society was just as ridiculous, although the Irish audience embraced it wholeheartedly. An English audience, even a middle-class one, would not accept Anglicization treated as buffoonery in an Irish context, in an Irish play, by an Irish author, even within the framework of a subversive middle-class take on the English aristocracy.

In this play Macklin exposed English prejudices and took revenge on the English perception of Irish speech as full of inaccuracies by ridiculing their inability to pronounce Irish names – O'Dogherty becomes Diggerty – just as great play had been made of their failure with Sir Callaghan O'Brallaghan's name. The new language that Mrs Diggerty has brought back with her, a type of mongrel cockney, is a pathetic attempt at linguistic and cultural colonization, which is resisted by a robustly articulate Irish society. Language is not innocent, nor is denomination neutral: it is a cultural annexation, as Swift was aware and Brian Friel demonstrates in *Translations*.[100] There is an alchemy in naming: O'Dogherty, to his despair, finds his wife, on her return from London, a different woman:

> O'DOGHERTY   She is no longer the plain, modest, good-natured, domestic, obedient Irish Mrs. O'Dogherty, but the travelled, rampant, high-lifed, prancing English Mrs. Diggerty. [101]

She is possessed by the colonial dementia: it is a 'fit,' a 'delirium', a 'vertigo', a 'phrenzy' and a 'madness';[102] it manifests itself linguistically, in a mangling of vowels and syntax, and when it is purged, she reverts to her own name, character and language:

> O'DOGHERTY　　And as to yourself, my dear Nancy, I hope I shall have
> no more of your London English; none of your this here's, your that
> there's, your winegars, your weals, your vendors, your toastesses. [...]
> MRS. DIGGERTY　I will get rid of these as fast as possible.
> O'DOGHERTY　　And pray, above all things, never call me Mr. Diggerty;
> my name is Murrough O'Dogherty, and I am not ashamed of it; but
> that damned name Diggerty always vexes me whenever I hear it.[103]

O'Dogherty throws out the anglicized names and language, with their attendant signifiers of Irish inferiority and easy metropolitan attitudes to adultery. O'Dogherty was a defining character for the Irish theatre. Since the work of Shadwell, he was the first contemporary Irishman to appear on the Irish stage in a play by an Irish author set in Ireland. Such plays and characters are very rare. He is in the direct line of Sir Patrick Worthy in *Irish Hospitality* and Sir Francis Feignyouth in *St Stephen's Green*, both of whom felt strongly about the welfare and reputation of their country. O'Dogherty, however, represented for the first time native, not colonial, stock, and even in the title of *True-born Irishman*, Macklin was challenging the other tradition, by defining the true-born Irishman as the very opposite of a Patriot. O'Dogherty is a bourgeois, improving estate manager, far more attached to his land than to the acquisition, by winking at corruption, of a debased title. While Macklin was approving of O'Dogherty's linguistic, pragmatic and presentee husbandry of his estate and dependants, he was implicitly criticizing the management of the grandees of Hibernia; not content with that, he inserted a good deal of trenchant criticism of Hibernia itself.

The play is liminal, appearing in the space between George III's accession to the throne in 1760 and his coronation in September 1761. The Irish Parliament fell with the old king's death, and a new one could not form until summoned by the new monarch. It was a time to draw attention to existing corruption and hope for a new broom to sweep it away. This may have been what motivated Macklin's critique of Hibernia.[104] Apart from his overt attack on corruption in the political system, Macklin in *The True-born Irishman* was lending open support to the resurrected Irish gentry. He was furthering the same debate, reaching back to Shadwell and Philips, that surfaced with the Gentleman's Quarrel in 1747 about the gentility of the converted Irish. Macklin integrated, in Murrough O'Dogherty, Shadwell's bourgeois gentry and Philips' native Irish gentry, and provided a definitive statement on the balance of quality between Irish society and English importations. The play is a farce, but one with unexpected bite and depth. As good farce should, it probes, through its vivid characters, vigorous dialogue and exaggerated action, the tensions that were straining the placid surface of Hibernia.

O'Dogherty was a revolutionary figure in Irish drama for 1761; with him, Macklin made the Irish theatre subversive of its society, and typified its duality. Within the playhouse, the audience may have been Planters and bourgeois gentry, but the stage was held by indigenous Irish characters, whose attitude to Hibernia was at best ambiguous, and often hostile.

This hostility is expressed indirectly by criticism of political chicanery and venality. Under the disguise of flailing at corruption, O'Dogherty scathingly attacks the Protestant Interest through its vaunted and treasured Patriotism. A Patriot, he tells his brother-in-law,

> is a sort of political weathercock, that is blown about by every wind of society, which the foolish people are always looking up at, and staring, and distracting themselves with the integrity of its vicissitudes – today it is blown by the rough ruling tempest of party; next day by the trade-wind of sly, subtle, veering faction; then by the headlong hurricane of the people's hot foggy breath; huzza boys, down with the courtier, up with the patriot, till at last the smooth, soft, gentle warm breeze of interest blows upon it, and from that moment it rusts to a point, and never stirs after – so there is your puff patriot for you – ogh, to the devil I pitch them all.[105]

O'Dogherty belongs neither to the Patriot nor the Court party; he is an improving landlord who rejoices in the sight of 'a hundred head of fat bullocks upon my own land, all ready for Ballinasloe fair'.[106] He is a believer in the economic basis of society and civilization: all this talk of liberty and self-government is of less importance to him than the smooth operation of economics: 'Remember that an honest quiet country gentleman who out of policy and humanity establishes manufactories, or that but a blade of corn grows where there was none before, is of more use to this poor country than all the courtiers, and patriots, and politicians, and prodigals that are unhanged.'[107]

In his capacity as a true-born Irishman, O'Dogherty is here expropriating from the Planted gentry their boast of improving agriculture, of the superiority of their estates when compared to the careless husbandry of the Irish. Just as their stone and slated houses dominated the landscape with their implicit declaration of superiority, so their hedges, orchards and demesnes declared the benefits of the order they had imposed on that landscape, and their fitness to rule. O'Dogherty, in his dedication to and development of his land, cancels that claim, and reclaims the responsibility for the native gentry.

O'Dogherty/Macklin's disdain for Hibernia extends logically from this awareness of corruption to a contempt for its most glittering rewards – the honours that can be bought by money or betrayal. Peerages are easily to be had, says Mrs Diggerty, and she must have one. One of her fast set, Mrs Gazette, takes it for granted how it is done: 'I am sure there are those that have not half your fortune, who have got peerages.'[108] But O'Dogherty is not to be shifted into that New English path. It is enough for him that his own name has been lifted back to its proper prominence:

> O'Dogherty for ever – O'Dogherty! – there's a sound for you – why they have not such a name in all England as O'Dogherty – nor as any of our fine sounding Milesian names – what are your Jones and Stones, your Rice and your Price, your Heads and your Footes, and Hands, and your Wills, and Hills and Mills, and Sands, and a parcel of little pimping names that a man would not pick out of the street, compared to the O'Donovans, O'Callaghans, O'Sullivans, O'Brallaghans, O'Shaghnesses, O'Flahertys, O'Gallaghers, and O'Doghertys – Ogh, they have courage in the very sound of them, for they come out of the mouth like a storm; and are as old and as stout as the oak at the bottom of the bog of Allen, which was there before the flood – and though they have been dispossessed by upstarts and foreigners, buddoughs and sassanoughs, yet I hope they will flourish in the Island of Saints, while grass grows or water runs.[109]

This was an astonishing speech to throw down in front of the Hibernians: if the polarity had been reversed and the Gaelic-Irish had been on the receiving end, they would have wrecked the theatre, but the subversiveness of the play escaped the Dublin audience, blinded by Macklin's reputation, the excellence of the dialogue and acting, and the superb comic turn of Count Mushroom, and perhaps by leaving the two major insults, 'buddoughs and sassanoughs', in Irish.[110] The play was hugely successful and continued to be revived for decades, so O'Dogherty continued to work his subversion on the Irish stage, but he remained unique: there had been no true-born Irish gentlemen before him, and he had few successors. Yet for all his Gaelic truculence he does represent the beginning of a synthesis of the two tendencies I have noted, the responsible bourgeois and the creative anarchist, that formed the two sides of the Irish Gentleman as he appeared in the drama of the early to late eighteenth century, and he shows most clearly the start of the fusion of the two elements, Irish and English, into one Hibernian Ascendancy type. The Ascendancy as displayed on the stage was by now the bourgeois gentry. They were the audience, as they were the stage characters; the nobility had vanished from behind the proscenium arch as they had from the auditorium, and the gentry had things to themselves. But not for long; in the plays of O'Keeffe, we will see the beginnings of the rise of the Irish lower classes.

NOTES

1. Whelan, 'An Underground Gentry', p. 10.
2. Sheridan, *An Humble Appeal to the Public;* see Morash, *History of Irish Theatre,* p. 49.
3. Edmund Burke, 'To Richard Shackleton – 21 February 1746/7', in *Correspondence of Edmund Burke,* 10 vols (Cambridge: Cambridge University Press, 1958–1978) I, p. 82.
4. *Ibid.,* p. 82.
5. Benjamin Victor, in Sir John Gilbert, *History of the City of Dublin,* 3 vols (Dublin: McGlashan & Gill, 1854–59). http://indigo.ie~kfinlay/Gilbert/gilbert1.htm [accessed 01/06/2004] (II, p. 81).
6. *Sighs and Groans:* 'The Wags in the Gallery begun their Raillery to entertain the House, and called upon him by his beloved Title of Thomas Sh———n Esq.; come on the Stage – but this tho' repeated as in Court three times, was also rejected.' Cited by Helen M. Burke, *Riotous Performances,* p. 238.
7. Hillman's Hyperlinked and Searchable Chambers' Book of Days. www.thebookofdays.com/ months/July/11.htm [accessed 28/09/04] (p. 1 of 3).
8. Morash, *History of Irish Theatre,* p. 60.
9. Helen M. Burke, *Riotous Assemblies,* p. 143.
10. On the same day as the Kelly riot, 21st of January 1747, Browne had killed his cousin in a duel in Mayo, because he rejected Browne's application to join a loyalist club that refused anyone whose grandparents had been Catholics: James Kelly, *That Damn'd Thing Called Honour: Duelling in Ireland 1570–1680* (Cork: Cork University Press, 1995), pp. 57–9.
11. Edmund Burke, *Correspondence,* I, p. 83.
12. T. O. McLoughlin, 'The Context of Edmund Burke's *The Reformer',* in *Eighteenth Century Ireland,* 2, (1987), 37–55.
13. Dr Johnson remarked: 'Sheridan is dull, naturally dull; but it must have taken him a deal of pains to have become what we now see him. Such an excess of stupidity, sir, is not in nature.' Robert Herring, ed., Introduction to R. B. Sheridan's *The Rivals* (London: Macmillan, 1933), p. ix.
14. Duggan, *The Stage Irishman,* p. 275
15. Morash, *History of Irish Theatre,* p. 55.
16. Sheridan's Preface to *The Rivals,* ed. by Robert Herring (London: Macmillan, 1933), p. xxvi–ii.
17. Richard Cumberland, *The West Indian,* in *'The Beggars' Opera' and Other Eighteenth Century Plays,* (London: Everyman's Library, 1974), Prologue, p. 343.
18. Dobbs, *The Irish Chief,* Prologue, 11 & 24, in Wheatley and Donovan, *Irish Plays,* II, p. 86.
19. *Ibid.,* p. 86.
20. Duggan, *The Stage Irishman,* p. 285.
21. 'Sir Robert Howard' http://www.pgil-eirdata.org/htm/pgil_datasets/authors/h/Howard,R/ life.htm [accessed 13/04/02] (p. 1of 5).
22. John Greene, 'The Repertory of the Dublin Theatres, 1720–1745', in *Eighteenth Century Ireland,* 2, (1987) 133–148 (p. 143).
23. Charles Shadwell, *The Plotting Lovers; or, The Dismal Squire,* in *Shadwell's Works,* II, p. 328.
24. Carte, *Life of Ormond,* IV, p. 386.
25. Shadwell, *The Hasty Wedding,* III, in *Shadwell's Works,* II, p. 56.

26. Dineen, Rev. Patrick S., *Foclóir Gaedhilge agus Béarla: An Irish-English Dictionary* (Dublin: Educational Company, 1927, reprinted 1968).

27. *Oxford English Dictionary*, 2nd ed., 20 vols, ed. by J.A. Simpson and E.S.C. Weiner (Oxford: Clarendon Press, 1989) II, p. 573.

28. *Ibid.*, p. 573.

29. *Ibid.*, p. 573

30. Jonathan Swift, Letter 4, *The Drapier Letters*, in *The Portable Swift*, p. 198.

31. Jonathan Swift, 'On Barbarous Denominations in Ireland', Corpus of Electronic Texts Ed. http://celt.ucc.ie/published/E700001-006/nav.html [accessed 12/10/2004] (p. 346).

32. Samuel Johnson. *Dictionary* (London: n. p., 1755), p. 148.

33. *OED*, p. 573.

34. Swift, 'Barbarous Denominations', p. 346.

35. *Ibid.*, p. 346.

36. Swift, Letter 4, *The Drapier Letters*, in *The Portable Swift*, p. 195.

37. Macklin, *The True-born Irishman*, II. in *Four Comedies*, ed. by J.O. Bartley (London: Sidgwick & Jackson, 1968), p. 111.

38. Maxwell, *Dublin under the Georges*, p. 318

39. Swift, 'On Barbarous Denominations in Ireland', p. 346.

40. Macklin, *The True-born Irishman*, II., in *Four Comedies*, p. 112.

41. Declan Kiberd, *Inventing Ireland* (London: Jonathan Cape, 1995), p. 20.

42. Kelly, *That Damn'd Thing Called Honour*, pp. 151–157.

43. Duggan, *The Stage Irishman*, (p. 196), dates it to 1738; the play went through many versions, revisions and editions. Wheatley and Donovan date it to 1755 from 'a fair copy submitted to the licenser in March, 1755, when the play was produced at Covent Garden'; Wheatley and Donovan, *Irish Plays*, p. 445.

44. Wheatley and Donovan, *Irish Plays*, p. 422, citing Joep Leerson.

45. Thomas Sheridan, *The Brave Irishman*, I. 1, in Wheatley and Donovan, *Irish Plays*, II, p. 421.

46. Farquhar, *Love and a Bottle*, in *The Complete Works of George Farquhar*, ed. by Charles Stonehill (New York: Gordian Press, 1967), I. 1, p. 14.

47. Sheridan, *The Brave Irishman,*, I. 2, p. 430.

48. *Ibid.*, I. 2, p. 432.

49. *Ibid.*, II. 3, p. 442.

50. *Ibid.*, p. 430.

51. *Ibid.*, I. 2, p. 430

52. *Ibid.*, I. 2, p. 432.

53. Macklin, *Love à la Mode*, I., in *Four Comedies*, p. 45.

54. *Ibid.*, I, p. 45.

55. *Ibid.*, I, p. 54.

56. *Ibid.*, I, p. 55.

57. *Ibid.*, II, p. 76.

58. *Ibid.*, II, p. 75.

59. *Ibid.*, II, p. 77.

60. *Ibid.*, II, p. 71.

61. Cumberland, Prologue to *The West Indian*, in *Eighteenth Century Plays*, p. 343.

62. *Ibid.*, p. 363.

63. *Ibid.*, V. 8, p. 405.

64. Katharine Worth, *Sheridan and Goldsmith*, English Dramatists Series (London: Macmillan, 1992), pp. 9–24.

65. *Ibid.*, IV. 10, p. 392.

66. Richard Brinsley Sheridan, *The Rivals*, III. 5. 100.

67. *Ibid.*, I. 2. 340.

68. *Ibid.*, II. 2. 59.

69. *Ibid.*, III. 4.102.

70. *Ibid.*, III. 4. 87.

71. *Ibid.*, III. 4. 110.

72. *Ibid.*, III. 4. 138.

73. *Ibid.*, III. 4. 150.

74. *Ibid.*, II. 2. 44.

75. *Ibid.*, V. 3. 7.

76. *Ibid.*, V. 3. 43.

77. *Ibid.*, V. 3. 36.
78. *Ibid.*, V. 3. 130.
79. *Ibid.*, V. 3. 220.
80. *Ibid.*, V. 3. 230.
81. Fintan O'Toole, *The Traitor's Kiss: The Life of Richard Brinsley Sheridan*, (London: Granta, 1998) p. 101.
82. Introduction to *Sheridan's Plays*, ed. by Cecil Price (Oxford: University Press, 1975), p. xiv.
83. Sheridan's Preface to *The Rivals*, p. xxvii.
84. Sheridan, *The Rivals*, V. 3. 288.
85. Sheridan, *St Patrick's Day*, I. 1. 9.
86. *Ibid.*, II. 2. 60.
87. *Ibid.*, II. 4. 200.
88. *Ibid.*, II. 4. 205.
89. George II was so frightened by Macklin's performance that he had difficulty sleeping, and suggested to the Prime Minister that he call in Macklin to terrify the House of Commons. PC Craddock, 'Macklin' http://www.nwe.ufl.edu/~pccraddoc/macklin.html [accessed 14/08/2007] (p.2 of 4)
90. Justin McCarthy ascribes the quote to 'a gentleman in the pit', in *Irish Literature* (Washington: Catholic University of America Press, 1904) http://www.pgil-eirdata.org/htm/pgil_datasets/authors/m/Macklin,C/refs.htm [accessed 02/11/2004] (page 1 of 4).
91. Macklin, *True-born Irishman*, I, p. 87.
92. Macklin, *Love à la Mode*, I, p. 59.
93. Macklin, *The Man of the World*, IV, pp. 251 & 252.
94. Macklin, *The True-Born Irishman*, I, p. 90.
95. Ibid., p. 92.
96. Macklin's biographer Kirkman's asserts that Macklin's landlady in London was confused by his countrymen inquiring for Charley McLaughlin: Burke, *Riotous Assemblies*, p. 258. Justin McCarthy, ed. *Irish Literature* (Washington: Catholic University of America, 1904) cites the story that, during an argument, when Dr Johnson fired off a salvo of Greek, Macklin flattened him with a volley of Irish: http://www.pgil-eirdata.org/htm/pgil_datasets/authors/m/Macklin,C/refs.htm [accessed 28/09/2004] (p. 1 of 3).
97. Macklin, *The True-born Irishman*, II. p. 111.
98. *Ibid.*, I, p. 92.
99. Bartley, *Introduction to Four Comedies*, p. 4.
100. Swift on the retention of Irish place names: 'I am deceived, if anything has contributed to prevent the Irish from being tamed, than this encouragement of their language, which might be easily abolished, and become a dead one in half an age, with little expense, and less trouble', 'On Barbarous Denominations in Ireland', p. 345.
101. Macklin, The True-born Irishman, I, p. 85.
102. *Ibid.*, I, p. 85.
103. *Ibid.*, I, p. 111.
104. Geoge III did introduce many reforms such as an election every eight years, and a resident viceroy.
105. Macklin, *The True-Born Irishman*, I. p. 87.
106. *Ibid.*, I. p. 84.
107. *Ibid.*, I. p. 87.
108. *Ibid.*, I. p. 106.
109. *Ibid.*, I. p. 112.
110. 'Bodach': a clown, a buffon, a churl, an unskilled peasant labourer – an insult often levelled by the Irish poets at the New English gentry. 'Sassanough': Saxon, Englishmen, and by extension, any foreigner. In Donagal dialect, it can also mean 'Protestant'.

7

Radical Shifts

The decline of the Ascendancy in the Irish theatre during the last decade of the eighteenth century and the first third of the nineteenth can be measured in the leap from John O'Keeffe's polite disregard to James Sheridan Knowles' fervent opposition to their very existence. We can see this attitude first bubbling up in the plays of O'Keeffe, born in Dublin in 1747. After a successful career in the Irish theatre, O'Keeffe decamped to London in 1777, where he became the most successful playwright of the age. He never enjoyed critical acclaim, however, in spite of his success, because of the way he worked and the genres he worked in. Critical standing was offered only to those who wrote five-act plays – tragedies or comedies – but O'Keeffe's *métier* was farce; his preferred mode was musical comedy or light opera, and his preferred length was two acts. As a resident playwright with a schedule to feed, first at the Haymarket and later at Covent Garden, he had no preciousness or regard for his own texts, often plundering them for raw material, which he cut, edited and fashioned into entertainments in other modes. He and Colman the Elder, who was also an experienced and successful playwright, frequently withdrew a play in response to audience indifference, and refashioned it more to the public taste before presenting it again, often with great success. For example, O'Keeffe rewrote his play *The Banditti* as an opera in 1781; the piece failed, but he reworked it as *The Castle of Andalusia* for the following year and scored a great success. It was, wrote *Parker's General Advertiser*, 'so altered and improved, that it is hardly possible to recognize the original'.[1]

The effectiveness of this theatrical proving, remodelling and filtering through the sieve of a mass audience is vouched for by the range and durability of the resulting productions. Before 1801, O'Keeffe's ten most successful plays had received nearly twelve hundred performances in

London alone, not counting productions in the English provinces, in Ireland and in America.[2] When he died in 1826 his work was still being acted in all three countries, although he had not produced anything new for nearly thirty years. O'Keeffe's pieces were designed for a new audience in the theatre: the purpose of most of his creations was to entertain the galleries before the arrival of the box-occupiers or after the departure of the fashionable world. The works targeted a precise sector, and reflected and moulded its perceptions and interests. This was an urban working-class and lower middle-class audience, many newly arrived from rural areas, and O'Keeffe gave them the familiarity of a pastoral idyll or an urban tavern as a setting. Where he ventured into the upper class, he was more inclined to view it from afar. The focus was on the peasants, the Big House very much in the distance, both pictorially and dramatically. The setting of *The Poor Soldier* encapsulates this focus: '*The country, sunrise. A large mansion at some distance. Near the front, on one side, a small house; on the other a cottage.*'[3] He moved the gentry to the periphery; the upper class may trigger the action by their presence and activities, but O'Keeffe was more concerned with the effects on their social inferiors.

The huge popularity of John O'Keeffe's plays in Ireland, England and America gave him a reach well beyond that of any previous Irish playwright, and the pattern of peasant comedy shot through with serious concerns was one that Boucicault was to build on with such success in his Irish plays. While O'Keeffe pursued the inclusive line characteristic of Philips and Shadwell, there is a gentle but persistent subversion evident in his work. His characters ring the changes on conventional types, but his witty and graceful writing sets them a cut above the average. In a large, hurried output, working to a deadline, the quality will inevitably vary, and all one can reasonably expect is that sometimes the writer's talent will raise his work into something lasting. Only one of O'Keeffe's plays, *Wild Oats*, has survived into the present day, but his characters, settings, tone, and use of Irish music and landscape set the pattern followed by Boucicault, who was also O'Keeffe's successor in professionalism and volume of output.

William Hazlitt's approval of O'Keeffe – 'The English Molière [...] In light careless laughter, and pleasant exaggeration of the humorous, we have no equal to him'[4] – hints at the covert radicalism in O'Keeffe's work, as he subtly interrogated the upper-class claims to ownership and precedence. The most overt declaration of O'Keeffe's radicalism was *Le Grenadier* of 1789, which provides a unique insight into his attitudes and working methods. It deals with the fall of the Bastille on

July 14 of that same year, and shows him as an acute businessman in spotting an opportunity. The Haymarket Theatre was closed for the summer when the Bastille fell, but O'Keeffe had the piece in rehearsal in preparation for the opening in September; 'the scenes were painted, the music composed by Sheild, and the piece rehearsed several times,'[5] when it fell foul of the Lord Chamberlain and had to be withdrawn. O'Keeffe explained in his *Recollections*, written many years later and never very reliable, that: 'when the flame of liberty [...] seemed to be converted into hell-fire, and patriotic men into demons, Mr. Harris very prudently thought it advisable not to touch upon the subject, [...] and we went no further with it'.[6] O'Keeffe's recollection is not convincing. In August 1789 the world was alive with hope and excitement, the Terror years away. The problem was not a surge of anti-French feeling but, as the *Town and Country Magazine* for November 1789 stated: 'that being prohibited in [its] original form by the Chamberlain', it was being revised 'for the purpose of suiting [it] to his lordship's political taste, or more probably to the taste of the French ambassador, who has interfered upon this occasion'.[7] O'Keeffe never presented any revised version, but still valued the piece sufficiently to print it in his *Collected Works* of 1798. What was remarkable about *Le Grenadier*, and why it offended the French ambassador, was its whole-hearted support for the Revolution, which O'Keeffe equated with the English uprising against the Stuarts, in its overthrowing of absolute monarchy and ensuring that 'despotic power shall wear a robe no more'.[8]

The published text shows O'Keeffe's theatrical imagination in full flow, and how it worked: it consists of songs, arias, duets, ensembles and choruses, linked by detailed action sequences and spectacular set-pieces, with only one passage of fully worked-out dialogue. What we have here, uniquely, is the superstructure of the play, which would usually disappear in the published text. We can see from it that O'Keeffe put the dialogue in last. He started with an elaborate and detailed *mise-en-scène*, or storyboard, for the whole piece. For example:

> *The Governor looking on the bench, sees Dubois' grenadier's hat with the national green cockade and the musket, snatches up the hat in great fury, upbraids Henriette with giving precedence to so mean a rival, tears out the cockade, throws it on the ground, and treads on it. – Madame Clementine with indignation picks up the cockade, presents it to her daughter, commands her to wear it next to her heart, and desires the Governor to see Henriette no more. – He greatly enraged, still having Dubois' hat in his hand, who returns for his musket, sees the hat and claims it. – Madame Clementine points to the cockade in Henriette's*

breast, asking him if it his; he acknowledges it – Madame Clementine with great joy looks on Dubois, authorises Henriette to receive his addresses. [...] Shouting without; the Governor alarmed; Dubois smiles at him with exultation, acquaints Madame Clementine that the people are going to break open Pincemaille's granaries, and distribute to the poor the corn at a reasonable price...[9]

O'Keeffe next composed and inserted songs and music, and was just beginning to sketch in the dialogue when the Lord Chamberlain prohibited the piece. The set-pieces he had outlined demonstrate a powerful theatrical imagination fully in support of the overthrow of the *ancien régime* and the establishment of a new world order based on justice and the rights of all men, what he calls 'the Godlike flame'.[10] The authorities and the nobility are forthrightly condemned, the condition of the poor shown with every expression of outrage, and the extraordinary solidarity against the nobility of all the other sectors of society – the poor, the respectable citizens, men, women, children and soldiers – is celebrated.

In the absence of dialogue, however, it is the songs that mostly carry the message. O'Keeffe insists on the legitimacy of the Revolution 'against the abuse but not the laws'.[11] It is perfectly just, he asserts, to oppose unjust authority, and a duty to overthrow tyrants.

The songs sing of *liberté*:

> Too long we've to oppression stooped;
> O! Let's be free or cease to live;
> Sweet lily that so long hath drooped,
> In glorious sunshine now revive.[12]

of *égalité*:

> Now shall the honest man be prized,
> His blood with Tinkers blended;
> And let the villain be despised,
> From Clovis tho' descended.[13]

and of *fraternité*:

> To keep us slaves the great combine;
> And shake the lash if we repine.
> Come on, brave youths, let's strike the blow,
> Our wrongs in acclamation,
> Shall let the haughty tyrants know,
> The People are the Nation.[14]

It is easy to see how O'Keeffe's sentiments would cause uneasiness, not just to the French ambassador as the representative of the discredited regime, but to the Lord Chamberlain, as watchdog for an aristocracy looking uneasily over its own shoulder at its huddled, resentful masses. Though speaking of France, O'Keeffe has no hesitation as to where to lay the blame:

> But though I sowed, my wheat would never come to flour,
> Three things ere I reaped, would all my crop devour:
> The Partridge picks the grain up, the blade the Rabbit gobbles,
> And all my corn that grew to ears was threshed out by the Nobles.[15]

The entire burden of the piece, in its action, imagery and music, calls for violent action in the pursuit of freedom: 'to rattling drums our hearts shall beat / Our voices to the trumpet sound;'[16] 'our cannon with tremendous roar / Shall join the cry of Liberty.'[17] The fall of the Bastille, the storming of the walls, the cannon fire from the defenders, the breaking open of the doors and the release of the prisoners are all shown with spectacular gusto; the Governor, the Profiteer and other undesirables being led to execution, accompanied by *'trophies consisting of large locks, keys, bolts, bars, chains, the iron mask, and other instruments of torture, suspended on poles'*, is grippingly presented.[18]

Le Grenadier, in spite of its brilliantly imagined stage spectacle and action, can hardly be called a play, since, although it has characters and plot, the dialogue is almost non-existent. But for his next work, to replace the cancelled *Le Grenadier*, O'Keeffe produced a five-act comedy, *Wild Oats*, widely regarded as his best play. It showed an increase in subtlety, but no lessening of conviction.[19]

In response to the banning of *Le Grenadier*, O'Keeffe's radicalism went underground, where it stayed for the rest of his career. *Wild Oats*, far from being conciliatory, was a gospel of levelling, an allegory of *égalité*. Rank is nullified, aristocracy is denied, personal identity becomes opaque and society disintegrates into a generative chaos when the anarchic figure of Rover, the 'stray vaguing'[20] stroller is plunged into it. He overthrows existing structures and precipitates new ones. He is the walking incarnation of the revolutionary spirit.

To his levelling theme in *Wild Oats*, O'Keeffe added the old Irish theatrical obsession with imposture, the construction and deconstruction of identity. The idea of identity as a construct echoes the political social, and economic reconstruction of the Revolution, and also the constant posing, imposing and deposing that permeates Irish dramatic literature – a sense of the impermanence of identity, personal and tribal, the uneasy mutations of the unfixed self. *Wild Oats* serves up a heady brew of levelling and play-acting. Some characters are thrust into it against their will, like Sir George Thunder; some stumble, like Rover; some fall, like Ephraim; and some, like Harry Thunder, jump in for fun.

Presiding over this social chaos of mistaken identity, imposture and *égalité* like a Lord of Misrule is the piratical, revolutionary figure of Rover. He is a strolling player who impersonates his friend, Harry Thunder, in order to ingratiate himself with Harry's cousin, Lady Amaranth, who is a Quaker. Harry appears on the scene but decides to assume another identity, so as not to expose him. Harry pretends to Rover that his father, Sir George, is really an actor playing the part of his father, and Rover compounds the motif by casting Sir George as the Duke in *As You Like It,* into the performance of which he is dragooning the entire household, from high to low. Rover dazzles and unsettles the house, above and below stairs. 'But who is he?'[21] asks Sir George in bewilderment, and gets no answer. Rover himself does not know who he is; he was abandoned as a child, and his years on the stage have further weakened his grip on his own identity, until he has become like a force of Nature, which through him speaks irresistibly for revolutionary upheaval: 'For Nature's warm and absolute control /Guides ev'ry impulse of his generous soul.'[22] Being an actor, he can assume any character at will, and call on his theatrical background to provide him with suitable language to express it. His powerful personality and performance blasts into the society of the play and explodes it, creating a magnetic field which rearranges all the characters into their proper alignment. Illusions are dissolved, deceptions uncovered and a new reality forged. At the start of the play a community of deceit exists: almost everybody is dissembling, imposing, deceiving, play-acting or hiding something. Out of Rover's revolutionary chaos identities are reconstructed and new order emerges, Rover turning out to be Sir George's natural son. The restoration of order is a conventional dénouement of comedy, with lost children restored to their parents, villains exposed and good rewarded, but there is no mistaking the exhilaration of the revolutionary ride.

The play insists that the obligations of the rich and titled are commensurate with their privileges, and demonstrates that their ascendancy is merely convention, not natural law. John Dory, Sir George's boatswain and *valet de chambre*, by long association sees himself as Sir George's equal:

SIR GEORGE Was not I your Captain?

JOHN Yes, and I was your boatswain. And what of all that?

SIR GEORGE Then how dare you sit in my presence, you bluff head?

JOHN Why, for the matter of that, I don't mind; but had I been your Captain, and you my boatswain, the man that stood by me at sea, should be welcome to sit before me at land.

SIR GEORGE That's true, my dear John; offer to stand up, and, damme, if I don't knock you down.[23]

Sir George's son, Harry, who has run away from Naval College to join the strolling players, has insisted his servant, Muz, treat him as an equal but, when they leave the company, Muz resists returning to his former servile state, and bemoans the bad example offered by his lord and master while he was on an equal footing. Muz is now expected to deconstruct himself and reconstruct his old persona but, he says, you cannot put the revolutionary genie back in the bottle; new experiences and new ideas alter men beyond restoration:

MUZ Sir, I ask your pardon; but by making yourself my equal, I've got used to familiarity, that I find it curst hard to shake it off.

HARRY Well, Sir, pray mind, that familiarity is all over now. My frolic's out. I now throw off the player, and shall directly return.

[...]

MUZ And, Sir, shall you and I never act another scene together? Shall I never again play Colonel Standard for my own benefit? Never again have the honour of caning your Honour in the character of Tom Errand?

HARRY In future act the part of a smart hat and coat brusher, or I shall have the honour of kicking you in the character of an idle puppy. You were a good servant; but I find, by letting you crack your jokes, and sit in my company, you're grown quite a rascal.

MUZ Yes, Sir, I was a modest, well-behaved lad; but evil communication corrupts good manners.[24]

This play is unusual in O'Keeffe's work in that he used overlapping storylines to reinforce his main theme. Lady Amaranth, the female lead, has been raised as a Quaker and insists on treating everybody as an equal, to the umbrage of her uncle, Sir George: 'And there is my rich lady niece, pressing and squeezing up the noble plumage of our illustrious family in her little, mean, quaker bonnet.'[25] The other Quakers, too, impose equality on Sir George, to his anti-revolutionary outrage:

ZACHARY Verily, George.

SIR GEORGE   George! Sirrah, tho' a younger brother, the honour of
knighthood was my reward for placing the glorious British flag over
that of a daring enemy – therefore address me with respect.

ZACHARY   Yea, I do, George.

SIR GEORGE   George and Mary! here's levelling, here's abolition of title
with a vengeance! zounds! in this house, they think no more of an
English Knight than a French Duke.[26]

All this climate of levelling supports the central argument that Rover
can become anyone he wants, by constructing a character and assum-
ing the part. Aristocracy, it is implied, is a performance, a convention,
that can, and should, be demolished or re-arranged in a more meritocratic manner, a message applauded by an audience aware of
Rousseau's ideals and the works of Tom Paine on the Rights and
'Claims of Man'[27] in England and America. This subterranean revolutionary outlook is consistent throughout O'Keeffe's work, and transferred directly into his Irish plays.

The success of O'Keeffe's plays set in Ireland indicates the changed
nature of the Irish audience too. He focuses on the way the lower
classes view the Ascendancy, and a pattern quickly emerges. In spite of
the drain of absenteeism, and the endemic social and economic injustices, all the characters are unquestionably Irish; they are no longer 'the
English of Ireland'. What O'Keeffe did, for the first time, was to set the
dramatic fault-lines along class divisions. He gave a surprising weight
to the articulation of Irish grievances, but these were not Molyneux's
objections, expressing Ascendancy concerns with polity and commerce,
but the complaints of the peasantry and lower classes against the entire
wealth-generating apparatus of the ruling class – enclosures, absenteeism, payment of tithes to a church to which they did not belong:

O'HANLON   See you not what heavy grievances we lay under – our great
landlords spending their money abroad, their stewards patch by patch
enclosing our commons, and their parsons with their rich livings leaving us in the claws of their cursed tithe proctors.[28]

The intersection of the two classes, the gentry and the local peasants,
is a repeated feature of O'Keeffe's Irish plays; it is shown, however, to
be a masquerade. Donnybrook, Franklin and Helen Donnybrook, in
The Wicklow Mountains, and Fitzroy in *The Poor Soldier* are all wearing false personas, constructed for the occasion. Donnybrook marks
his arrival from Dublin by sending back his carriage and servants,
changing from his grand clothes into brown peasant garb, and boasting

of his love of the lower classes[29] and lack of pride. Franklin, the incoming landlord, arrives disguised as a pedlar, and Donnybrook's daughter, Helen, is pretending to be an invalid to escape from the matchmaking of her mother. Fitzroy, in *The Poor Soldier*, is even more ambiguous: he is consciously slumming in pursuit of Father Luke's niece. Though the arrival of the Donnybrooks and the appearance of Fitzroy are the events on which the dramas hinge in the two plays, the central focus is not on them but on the peasants or servants, and how this invasion disrupts them. O'Keeffe's drama has become contrapuntal, with the lower classes taking the foreground, with their distinctive language, music and song, while the upper class grinds along unheeded, occasionally pushing itself forward, before being eased into the background again. If this is a mingling of cultures, it is all one way, the gentry attempting to sample the reality of the lower classes by dressing down and mixing with them, but jangling out of tune. True *égalité* is not allowed; there are rigid class values to prevent the lower classes from mingling upwards, as Donnybrook exemplifies in *The Wicklow Mountains*. He starts the play with the illusion of his own egalitarianism: 'I've not the least pride; I'm never above making free with what is called the lower classes.' Billy takes him at his word, borrows his clothes, and offers to marry Donnybrook's daughter, which is greeted with outrage: 'Touch my clothes, and even dare look at my daughter! I may thank my condescending humility for this.'[30] Anything akin to the startling wedding of the peasant girl and the lord of the manor in Shadwell's *Irish Hospitality* is absent. O'Keeffe shows no infiltration of Gaelic influences on the gentry, either; they are inspired by Rousseau or Romanticism. Donnybrook rhapsodizes: 'In town I was gay; I rattled, swore, guzzled and gambled – but here I'm rural, simple and serene.'[31] O'Keeffe shows us an inversion of an earlier pattern: the sham gentlemen of the preceding century have been replaced by sham peasants. In *The Poor Soldier* Fitzroy articulates the philosophy of the French Radicals and the Brotherhood of Man, but does so covertly out of the hearing of his friends and relations in the Big House: 'We are common children of one parent, and the honest man who thinks with moral rectitude, and acts according to his thoughts, is my countryman, let him be born where he will.'[32] Similarly, while Franklin and Donnybrook in *The Wicklow Mountains* consciously adopt an egalitarian stance, they lack the philosophical underpinning to sustain it, and revert to type when their ascendancy is challenged.

O'Keeffe's Irish plays enact the return of the absentee: the Ascendants descending into the life of the people, expecting to condescend and control; but, equally, they portray the independence of the lower classes, who sideline, bamboozle and manipulate the intruders with ease. The dénouement may be sanctioned by Ascendancy authority but, as with Boucicault, it has been engineered by peasant guile. The plays show the upper classes learning from the lower – a common enough Rousseauesque motif, its burden being that the lower classes are the real people, not those in the Big House. Fitzroy gives up Norah to Pat, saying: 'The Captain thought himself unworthy of her, when he found superior merit in the poor soldier.'[33]

The issue of the goldmine in *The Wicklow Mountains* taps into the politics of the land and the economics of tenure. The peasants, who are close to the soil and retain a powerful vestigial conviction of a withheld inheritance, have no legal hold, and exist only on the sufferance of the landlords, while the legal ownership of the land by the gentry produces profit but no spiritual attachment. This play is at heart a socialist text, and raises directly the question of who owns the resources and wealth that the land generates. Felix, the peasant who discovered the gold, takes a socialist view and keeps the mine secret and safe from the avaricious grasp of the legal owner, so that he can perform the revolutionary action of spreading the benefits from it among the people of the estate – from those who have to those who need.[34] He is, however, forced to yield it up to the new legal owner, who takes it into his own keeping, removing its benefits from the people. Felix was exploiting it in the communal interest, but it is annexed into the patronage and use of the landed gentry. Dross, the lawyer, arrives from Dublin 'to help the lord of the manor to freight all the herring boats in the bay with glorious bullion'.[35] Felix believes, however, that it belongs to the people; he has abolished private property to keep it out of the grip of Franklin's avaricious uncle – who has legal ownership but no moral right. The people cannot possess the goldmine legally, any more than they can own the land they live on; it is annexed by the landlords, and disappears behind the legal pale of upper-class privilege. The upper class owns the law as well as the land and its resources, and uses legal instruments to prevent the peasants rising above their proper station. The only resource which the peasantry can exploit is their labour, and that too is annexed and enclosed by Donnybrook, so the gentry can enjoy the long-term benefits: 'Each man must leave gold-hunting, and return to a much nobler resource – honest labour.'[36] Felix has defied accepted economics, which dictated that all wealth generated was the property of the owner of the capital. Donnybrook, who never does any work, serves to point up the dronelike quality of the Ascendancy, using the law to augment and extend their wealth and position, as Redmond O'Hanlon complained. They have already enclosed the common land, and this is the enclosure of labour, the annexation of another wealth-creating resource on behalf of the ruling class. One is reminded of Karl Marx's comment on capital, 'which vampire-like lives only by sucking living labour, and lives the more, the more it sucks'.[37] Perhaps even more pointedly the passage recalls Adam Smith's *Wealth of Nations* (1776), in which he holds that it is not gold or silver that constitutes the wealth of nations, but labour only, and the relationship between the labourers and their exploiters is one of mutual enslavement, in which the workers labour without reward, and the landed aristocracy is reduced to passivity, indifference and dependence.[38] The action of *The Wicklow Mountains* is that of a furtive, flickering revolution, in which the proletariat abolish private property, seize control of the resource and install a revolutionary and egalitarian economy, which O'Keeffe regretfully allows to be overthrown in the interests of law and order. The anarchy that followed the French Revolution was still distressing him, 'when the flame of liberty [...] seemed to be converted into hell-fire, and patriotic men into demons'.[39] O'Keeffe, nevertheless, was subtly but consistently subversive of the ruling class.

SHERIDAN KNOWLES' LIBERTY PLAYS

The split between the classes was exploited by O'Keeffe subtly and in a farcical mode; in the plays of James Sheridan Knowles it was prised wide open by the ideas of Dissent and Revolution. Knowles (1784–1862) was the son of a teacher and lexicographer who was a first cousin of Richard Brinsley Sheridan. He was born in Cork, but the family moved to London when he was nine, after the Cork Protestant gentry withdrew their children from his father's school because of his support for Catholic Emancipation. As a young man in London, Knowles came under the influence of William Hazlitt, the incorrigible Dissenter, who held him in high esteem from an early age: 'We have known him almost from a child,' Hazlitt wrote, 'and we must say he appears to us the same boy-poet that he ever was. He has been cradled in song, and rocked in it as in a dream.'[40] Knowles reciprocated by acknowledging that the greatest influence on his thinking and writing was Hazlitt: 'Whatever ideas I have of late I owe to him. [...] Indeed he is the parent of my style.'[41] In 1808, after studying medicine and spending some time in the army, Knowles took to the stage, returned to Ireland and joined Andrew Cherry's company, which included Edmund Kean. Knowles played Hamlet at Crow Street and, while they were at Waterford, produced his first play, *Leo; or, The Gypsy*. He opened a school in Belfast with his father and in 1811 had his first significant play, *Brian Boroimhe,* produced there.

This was a minor work, but the lineaments of his style were already appearing in it, as was the essential nature of his political outlook. *Brian Boroimhe* was the latest version of the story that William Philips first told in *Hibernia Freed*. It had been through at least two other mutations since, in Howard's *The Siege of Tamor,* and a lost play by a Dublin actor, Daniel O'Meara, before Knowles reworked it into its greatest popular success.[42] In *Brian Boroimhe* the identification of the Anglo-Irish with the country is complete; the politics is muted, and Knowles completes the trend started by Philips that defines the Irish, not by politics, but by culture. Politics still rears its head occasionally, as in Brian's paraphrase of the speech that Philips borrowed from Shadwell:

> We gave them land – we gave them wives – we said
> 'Remain with us – let us become one people'
> [...]
> > These strange friends
> Through avarice of power, became our foes:
> They strove to turn their hosts into their slaves.[43]

That could be interpreted as a commentary on the English incursion, and such passages were implicated in the subsequent popularity of the play in Ireland and among the Irish in America, where it was still being revived in 1870. Knowles' main focus was not, however, on a separatist or nationalist agenda but on the exploitation of a rich, shared cultural identity. Where Philips gifted the ancient Irish with a classical civilization, Knowles informed them with Romantic medieval grandeur. The play is full of *faux*-medievalism, chivalric exploits and feudal pomp. Knowles' grasp of Irish history may have been shaky, but his overall imaginative effect is coherent: Brian is a monarch of chivalry. In one key scene, Brian sits enthroned and inducts his champion, O'Donohue, into the Knights of the Red Branch, surrounded by his court of knights in armour, ladies in sumptuous costumes, music and flying banners showing a red cross, a harp and a lion, linking Brian to the medieval tradition of the crusades, Richard the Lionheart and King Arthur. In contrast to this heritage of chivalry and high culture, the Danes are unprincipled, devious and barbaric – exactly the qualities with which the native Irish used to be characterized:

> *Act1, Scene 5, Chapel of the Knights of Connor.*
> *Banner of the Red Cross. HIGH PRIEST, two ASSISTANTS, four*
> *HARPERS, four SOLDIERS, RODERICK and TERRENCE,*
> *DESMOND and MACARTHY MOORE, BOYS bearing cushion,*
> *sword, &c. O'DONOHUE, BRIAN, Banner of the lion, ILENE,*
> *LADIES, SOLDIERS – Music. The king seated; Chief Harper con-*
> *ducts O'Donohue to him; O'Donohue kneels on the cushion, the*
> *king knights him; O'Donohue returns to his place.*

BRIAN Knight of the Red Branch, rise, O'Donohue.
[...]

> *[The Chief Harper comes forward and sings:]*
> Strike the harp! Strike the harp! Raise the song to great Brian,
> Oft, oft the rapt bard the glad strain shall renew.
> In peace mild and bounteous, in battle a lion;
> In the hearts of his people reigns Brian Boro'.[44]

Irish music and song played a crucial part in Knowles' panoply of medieval Ireland. No music has survived, but the above verse has the galloping anapaestic rhythm sometimes used by Thomas Moore, or the tune of 'St Patrick's Day', the unofficial national anthem. One of the songs is acknowledged to have words by Moore,[45] while another is set to the tune of 'The Meeting of the Waters'.[46] An unusual attribute of the Irish is their unity of purpose compared to the Danes' internal divisions. All of this has the effect of evoking a myth to flatter Knowles' audience, but there is one striking anomaly in the text, in the form of a dissenting Dane, Voltimer, whose sense of honour is outraged by the scheming and trickery of his master, Tormagnus:

VOLTIMER It would have pleasur'd me
>   To walk unbidden into Brian's hall,
>   And from among his thronging courtiers bear
>   The prize you seek. I should have deemed it sport,
>   To win the maid by dint of my bold sword.
>   But such a minion feat as this? For shame!
>   Let us put off these frowning helms of ours,
>   And lay by our hacked armour! 'Tis a feat
>   Might suit a silken reveller, indeed,
>   But not a man in steel.[47]

Voltimer was Knowles' first portrait of the Outlaw, a dissenting, even messianic figure whose advanced moral perception alienates him from

his own community, and who follows a course of action dictated by his
own moral code, even to his death. Knowles also sounded in this play
an internationalist note that hinted at the socialism that burst out in his
later work. Such men, he says, are more likely to find kindred spirits
among the ranks of the enemy than in their own society; dissenters
need to look further afield to find support for their ideas, to form a
scattered Diaspora of Dissent:

> VOLTIMER   More than homes
>   Do kindred spirits foster brotherhood;
>   There is an affinity ten times more near
>   Than flesh and blood or common country make.[48]

Further to this, Voltimer does not consider either Irish or Danish
morality as superior, but follows his own judgement by rescuing Brian's
daughter from his own king, Tormagnus, and getting killed by his own
people. The play encapsulates a favourite paradox in Knowles' writing
that partakes both of Dissent and Romantic ideals – the importance of
individual effort in pursuit of a higher goal, and the certainty that such
an effort will be crushed by superior force.

Voltimer is more fully realized than most of Knowles' characters,
because it is one he played himself.[49] Knowles did not write rounded
characters; he wrote attitudes, actions and reactions; he was very good
at inventing plot, clean lines of action and clear situations that rolled
naturally from one to the next. The creation of the characters he left
to his actors, who were the leading lights of the age – Kean, Macready,
Forrest and Helen Faucit. He plainly regarded this as their job, their
contribution to the collective effort. This method of composition gives
the plays a flat feeling on reading, although they had the reputation of
being brilliant on the stage: 'his works, useful on the boards, are lum-
ber on the shelves', sniffed one critic.[50] Most plays of that age were
written either as stage drama or closet drama: that is, to be performed
in the theatre, or to be read at home. Very few playwrights attempted
both, but Knowles did, and his published plays were hugely popular,
particularly in America. He was credited in his time with 'restoring
tragedy at once to its proper dignity and to a good measure of popularity in the theatre'.[51] He was, according to Hazlitt, 'the first tragic
writer of the age',[52] and Hazlitt also praised the truth and simplicity of
his dialogue, and the clarity of his action and situations. The plays,
unfortunately, alternate between clear, simple verse and the idiom of
Romantic excess that seems sadly dated today, written as it was for the
style of the great contemporary actors:

It held the stage successfully while the style prevailed, but when the actors of the day passed, the play went with them [...] Its distinctive characteristics are elocutionary pyrotechnics and romantic excess. Though dust and ashes now, these lines, with their hint of Byronic fire, must have been resonantly effective when delivered by a Macready or a Forrest to an audience of the 1830s and 1840s.[53]

Voltimer was the first attempt by Knowles at the Byronic character that forms the backbone of his next plays, *Caius Gracchus* and *Virginius*, the figure of the idealist who is in violent opposition to his own corrupt society.

The programme of Reform current in the early eighteenth century was modest enough – the widening of the franchise to all men, equal electoral districts, annual elections, and a secret ballot. Knowles was deeply pessimistic that the success of that programme would lead to a cleansing of the political system; *Caius Gracchus* (1815) was a Radical tract that was deeply sceptical of the Radical platform. He showed that the people would, at the first opportunity, abandon those who try to raise them, but embrace those they should spurn. A population accustomed to tyranny would, if given the vote, elect tyrants to rule over them, and elected tyrants are worse than inherited ones – you have only yourself to blame:

MARCUS   What can the people do? They have no friends that will
    speak or act for them. The people can do nothing of themselves
    – they have no power. If the people could find friends –
LICINIUS   Peace! peace! If you gain friends, you lose them
    straight.
    Whoe'er would die for you, you let him die!
    You shrug, you shiver, and you whine; but he
    That pities you, has need, himself, of pity.
    [...]
    They should not have a vote. If free-born men
    Will crouch like slaves, why would you have them freemen.[54]

Caius Gracchus, though set in ancient Rome, was a contemporary play wearing a toga: the topical frame of reference was hardly hidden at all under the Roman cloak. In the play the Patricians deal savagely with any threat to their power. Opimius the Consul speaks for the entrenched ruling class when confronted with opposition: 'How would you cure a state o'errun with evils / But as you'd cleanse a garden rank with weeds? / Up with them by the roots!'[55] The Patricians consider and treat the Plebeians as cattle: 'They have as great dominion over the people, as over their oxen; and so they treat them like their oxen – unhide them, hack them up, and feed upon them.'[56] The play is rich with sympathetic allusions to the wretched plight of the poor and the soldiers who are now cast out of the army, when there's no fighting left to do:

> CAIUS   Your wretchedness afflicts
> The heart of Caius. Thousands of brave men,
> Wandering about the streets of Rome, without
> Means, or employment to procure them. [57]

Gracchus takes an egalitarian, democratic view, inveighing against the unequal application of the laws in a society that was being ground down by legal oppression:

> CAIUS   The laws! the laws! that guard the common right!
> The wealth, the happiness, the freedom of
> The nation! Who has hidden them – defaced them –
> Sold them – corrupted them from the pure letter?
> Why do they guard the rich man's cloak from a rent
> And tear the poor man's garment from his back?
> Why are they, in the proud man's grasp, a sword,
> And in the hand of the humble man, a reed?[58]

The Napoleonic wars prevented the spread of revolution to the now United Kingdom of Great Britain and Ireland, but after 1815 there was a pent-up need for reform, as well as, among the ruling class, a horror of revolutionary ideas. Reform was blocked by their determination to hold on to what they had, and to ensure they did not suffer the fate of France's aristocracy. Their strategy was repression. High prices for food during the war had made many landowners rich; after the war they tried to control the market and keep prices high, preventing the importation of grain while the people were clamouring for cheap bread in the post-war depression. Parliament tried to keep dissent under control by passing, in 1799, the Anti-Combination laws, which forbade any concerted action by the masses or the forming of any trades unions. Incidents such as the Peterloo massacre in 1819 showed a country in which class repression and resentment had built up to a point at which revolution was certainly a possibility, in England as in Ireland, and in which radical reformers and demagogues such as Henry Hunt or Thomas Spence could attract a large and enthusiastic following. It was into this cauldron of discontent and injustice that Knowles pitched his Liberty plays – *Caius Gracchus, Virginius* and *William Tell.*

Caius Gracchus contains a trenchant attack on a corrupt and intransigent ruling class that owns the land and the resources, controls the government and administers the law in its own interest. It also, however, considers the reform platform as grossly inadequate in the teeth of the obdurate opposition of such an entrenched regime. Knowles shows two tribunes of the people, elected by their vote, Caius Gracchus and Drusus, one an idealist, one corrupt, and shows that the idealist must fail, going Messiah-like to his death, abandoned by the people he was trying to save. Yet the lesson he learns from his mother Cornelia is that the effort must be made, even though it is doomed to defeat: 'Though vain the struggle, yet 'tis fit 'twere made, / When bold injustice scoffs at laws, and 'gins/ to ride it, rough-shod, o'er them.'[59] It is the nature of the idealist, Voltimer or Caius Gracchus, to burst through the limits imposed by society and become an outcast in his quest for the greater good.

In theatrical matters Knowles' great champion was the actor William Macready, who shaped and directed the plays for the stage. Macready was an ardent republican; in his diary he wrote: 'I abhor class rule, be it of what grade it may be. The country is for all, of all and ought to be governed from all.' And he berated the 'whimpering wretches that howl at the small retaliation of a French Revolution for ages of oppression and tyranny'.[60] Macready and Hazlitt formed Knowles' ideas and moulded him creatively into the theatrical path of dissent and republicanism, and his Irish heritage showed him the value of the theatre as a political tool, in articulating alternative realities and stimulating public opinion. In O'Keeffe, the radicalism was an undercurrent, but in Knowles it surfaced as a raging torrent. Like those of Bertolt Brecht, Knowles' plays were the product of a disturbed age; they dramatized possibilities other than the prevailing system, and championed the values and rights of the oppressed and downtrodden classes against the tyranny of their current rulers. Not surprisingly, they were loathed by the Conservative press. *John Bull*, in particular, was vehement in its denunciation of the 'democratic, ranting, trashy plays of Knowles'.[61]

Knowles built *Caius Gracchus* out of the fragmentation of the body politic that followed the Napoleonic wars; it was an onslaught on the entire system. His message was that class oppression by one's fellow countrymen was worse than enslavement by a foreign oppressor; the self-proclaimed preservers of freedom themselves presided over an unfree society; liberating foreign countries from Napoleon's yoke was of scant merit when the greater part of the home population was enslaved by a ruling minority. Knowles' *Virginius* was hailed in the American press as a paean to freedom and liberty, but *Caius Gracchus* is far more outspoken on the rights of the common people. The Patricians despise the Plebeians but are forced by democratic pressure to adopt a complaisant façade, and easily manipulate themselves back into positions of power, with the enthusiastic support of the supposedly emancipated proletariat – an instance of the enduring bond between the enslaver and the enslaved:

> CAIUS   What! would they take our tigers,
> They've seen a hundred times tear limb from limb
> the malefactor – would they take them, think you
> For dogs, suppose they fawn'd on them?[62]

Though he championed the common people, Knowles had no illusions about them: he shared the Patricians' contempt for the fickleness and malleability of the mob. *Fraser's Magazine* wrote of the first London production of *Caius Gracchus*: 'War is declared against the very idea of aristocracy, and in favour of whom? A mere herd of men, who, by the showing of the very hero of the play, are worthless, most worthless.' [63]

But Knowles and Gracchus differed from the Patricians and the Conservatives in identifying the defence of the people's rights as a self-evident and necessary goal:

> CAIUS   If your liberties
> And rights are dear to you, be faithful to them.
> Fear not the senate; call upon the tribes;
> Be freemen – none will dare to make you slaves![64]

Achieving Liberty is the prime political imperative in these plays, in spite of the self-serving of politicians, and regardless of whether or not the people deserve it; in fact, the popular interest and welfare must be pursued and served, and their ancient rights restored to the people, in spite of themselves and their capriciousness, even unto the death of their champion. The people, as Rousseau taught in *The Social Contract*, must be forced to be free.[65]

One of Knowles' great theatrical strengths was his use of a pictorial, almost cinematic, technique whereby each scene was carefully composed to express visually its dynamics and relationships, and to complement the dialogue, so that the play proceeded, in visual terms, by a series of staged pictures. When a scene opened, the elements were arranged to show the nature of the characters and their relationships; the scene ended on a tableau that underlined the point to which those relationships had developed. The entire play moved to a final tableau that summarized the action and the moral lessons that it contained. This was a crucial aspect of Knowles' work: Hazlitt said that 'all his situations form classic groups',[66] and *The Retrospective Review* wrote an almost identical evaluation of Knowles' *Virginius*, as 'the most exquisite succession of classic groups'.[67] Macready's diary shows how crucial this aspect was to the presentation of the drama when writing of the opening night of *Virginius*, when Charles Kemble's voice failed: 'Kemble being so hoarse that not one word spoken in the loudest whisper could be heard; but the action of the scene told its story with sufficient distinctness to keep alive its interest.'[68]

The final scene of *Caius Gracchus* shows us how the method works. It opens in the Temple of Diana, to which the women from Gracchus' family have fled for safety. It is presided over by the statue of Diana, protectress of women and the home, before which Caius Gracchus' distraught wife, Licinia, kneels as a supplicant, motionless as the statue itself, 'mute as silence, / And in so fix'd a stillness, you might ask, / Which is the marble?'[69] The domestic is the sphere of the women, the public that of the men, and this is an image of the domestic world under threat. '*A large Portal*'[70] provides the link between the two worlds, an opening that threatens the women's safety by its gaping aperture. '*Numerous females*'[71] are distributed around, one of whom holds Gracchus' infant son. The dominant figure in the opening tableau, as she is in the scene and in the play, is Gracchus' mother, Cornelia. Throughout the play, Gracchus' wife has been attempting to detain him in the safety of the domestic world, while his mother has been encouraging him to embrace his public destiny, regardless of the cost. Men have a political duty, Cornelia asserts:

> Men must be busy out of doors – must stir
> The city – yes make the great world aware
> That they are in it; for the mastery
> Of which they race, and wrestle, and such feats
> Perform, the very skies, in wonderment
> Echoing earth's acclaim, applaud them too.[72]

The opening tableau shows that the mother has won the debate.

Gracchus flees into the temple, a final desperate flight from the dangers and viciousness of the public world, he embraces his wife, child and mother, forming a 'classic grouping', tells his mother to be 'a parent to my wife, a tutor to my boy. The lessons you did make me con, teach him – none else; he cannot learn better.'[73] Then he stabs himself beneath his cloak, and falls; Licinia throws herself on his body. Cornelia stands upright holding the child as the final tableau forms:

> [*A dagger drops from beneath* Caius' *robe – he falls dead –* Licinia, *shrieking, throws herself on the body –* Cornelia, *with difficulty, supports herself – the* Consul *and his troops are heard approaching – she makes a violent effort to recover her self-possession. Enter* Opimius *and his party, with* Guards, Lictors, &c. Cornelia *holds up the child in one hand, and with the other points to the body of* Caius – Opimius *and the rest stand fixed in amazement – Flourish, and the curtain falls.]* [74]

The final tableau has achieved the dramatic moment in which the domestic and bourgeois is indomitable, even in defeat, while the aristocratic victors are amazed and thwarted, and the eventual triumph of resistance is prophesied by the musical fanfare and the visual line connecting the dead Gracchus with his infant son through his unconquerable mother.

This technique of tableau had been developing since the beginning of the century, spurred mainly by the increasing size of the theatres; Drury Lane and Covent Garden had been leapfrogging over each other until the former had become to an actor on the stage, as Sarah Siddons lamented, 'a wilderness of a place'.[75] Richard Cumberland complained that the enormous size of the theatres, where the back stalls were at the extreme limit of an actor's voice projection, removed all nuance from acting and were 'so enlarged in their dimensions as to be henceforward theatres for spectators rather than playhouses for hearers'.[76] In such a situation, the visual crutch of the tableau became necessary. It had, for Knowles and Macready, the added value of being out of the reach of the Lord Chamberlain: only the verbal script was likely to be censored, they were free to insinuate their Radical gospel into the visible text.

Knowles refined and expanded the technique, fusing a series of tableaux into a dramatic diorama. The use of the tableau became a favourite device of Victorian melodrama, rather than a verbal explanation, valediction or summing up. The most vital tableau was the final one, which ended the play with an image that the audience carried away in its mind's eye: 'leaving this image on the soul', as the epilogue to *Virginius* described it.[77] The device has been described as a weakness by some critics, but it would seem so only to a verbal-centred audience; to a visually literate audience raised on the cinema, for example, or familiar with the prints spilling out of the engraving presses, the tableau spoke volumes, and in the huge theatres of the Victorian age, the visual summing up was the best way of driving the point home. Verbal exposition clings to a convention of naturalism, but the pictorial tableau was a visual convention, acknowledging openly the artificial nature of theatrical presentation, and calling on the audience's familiarity with pictorial styles, widely disseminated by the popular prints. The action, in the above example, flows towards the tableau, when time is arrested, and the conflicts are crystallized into a pictorial stasis, framed in the proscenium arch. The past and the failure of idealism are represented by the dead Gracchus, the personal cost by his grieving wife, the malevolent but frustrated aristocracy by Opimius and his men; these are balanced against the grieving but resolute women of the Gracchi, led by the *materfamilias* Cornelia, who, with her infant grandson in one arm, the other pointing to her dead son, holds the centre stage, links all the elements and represents the continuity of democratic resistance and the indomitability of the human spirit.[78]

Caius Gracchus was premiered in Belfast, the capital of Irish radicalism, in 1815, the year of Waterloo and the Congress of Vienna, before transferring to Glasgow, the home of British dissent, but it did not reach London until 1823, following the resounding success of Knowles' next play, *Virginius*, in 1820. He returned to the subject of liberty and the tyranny of aristocratic rule in *Virginius*, but the context had changed. The repression was stronger than ever, with the suspension of *habeas corpus* allowing imprisonment without trial, and the passing of the Six Acts outlawing assemblies, but there is in the play a subtly different sensibility. In *Virginius*, rather than blaming the aristocrats unequivocally, the people are shown to be not just helpless, fearful and fickle victims, but complicit in their own oppression.

The play, like *Caius Gracchus*, is intensely political. It holds up the aristocracy as 'anything but friends to justice and their country',[79] yet it also signals a new trimming and tacking by the upper class, in which they disguise their true colours in order to hold their old place of privilege. Virginius is an honest soldier, a slightly pompous bourgeois, and he prefers honesty, and nailing the colours to the mast: 'I favoured not this stealing / And winding into place. What he deserves, / An honest man dares challenge 'gainst the world.'[80]

Though the play is avowedly for the people against the Patricians, the people are seen as the authors of their own misfortune; Virginius is exasperated with their lack of backbone and consistency. The Patricians and Appius, the villain of the play, despise them as a matter of course: 'I do not want thee, Claudius, / To soil thy hand with their plebeian blood,' sneers Appius.[81] Their defenders have not much higher an opinion of them. Dentatus, the old veteran soldier, is the main spokesman for this disdainful frustration: 'As to these curs, I question which I value less, their fawnings or their snarlings.'[82] While Knowles was a great champion of Liberty, the play is certainly not a hymn to democracy. The lower classes in the play have been given the vote and have exercised their franchise, as in *Caius Gracchus*, to create tyrants by election:

> DENTATUS   More violence and wrong from these new masters of ours –
> our noble decemvirs – these demi-gods of the good people of Rome!
> No man's property is safe from them. Nay, it appears we hold our
> wives and daughters but by the tenure of their will. Their liking is the
> law. The senators themselves, scared at their audacious rule, withdraw
> themselves to their villas, and leave us to our fate. [...]The gentle cit-
> izens – that are driven about by the decemvirs' lictors, like a herd of
> tame oxen, and with most beast-like docility, only low applauses to
> them in return.[83]

Knowles had the soul, not of a Radical, but of an Anarchist: he pro-
foundly mistrusted any form of authority. The lessons of the French
Revolution have led him to sound a warning about the need to exercise democracy carefully, and the readiness of the unscrupulous to
manipulate the situation to their own advantage.

Like *Caius Gracchus*, the location of the play may be Rome, but the
sensibility was contemporary. Critics at the time hailed *Virginius* as a
new kind of tragedy, with its mingling of 'Roman grandiloquence and
English domesticity'.[84] Virginius exemplifies a recurring theme in
Knowles, the devoted father.[85] It is his salient characteristic; in other
respects, he is interchangeable with Caius Gracchus or William Tell,
but contemporary accounts tell of a complete and riveting performance
by Macready in the role. The part was so highly thought of that it was
also appropriated by Edwin Forrest, the greatest American actor of the
age, and he and Macready toured rival productions of the play for
many years. The characters struck a contemporary chord; Knowles'
heroes are not historical figures but British fathers or dutiful sons.
Virginius' home, violated by the villainous consul Appius' lust for
Virginius' daughter, is a bourgeois British household and Virginia is a
typical nineteenth-century heroine, sweet and wilting. Knowles' heroes
hold to a moral law opposed to their corrupt society, but it is the moral
law of Radical bourgeois England. 'We have Roman tunics,' observed
A New Spirit of the Age (1844), 'but a modern English heart, – the

scene is in the forum, but the sentiments those of the "Bedford Arms".'[86]

Knowles, in all three of his Liberty plays, juxtaposed scenes of the domestic and the public. Morality, affection and apparent safety lie in the households of Gracchus, Virginius and William Tell, but the vicious, amoral, aristocratically controlled public world threatens, and then destroys, this domestic idyll. In the bourgeois nursery, morality is formed and then applied to the public world, as exemplified by Caius Gracchus and his mother, Virginius and his daughter, William Tell and his wife and son. Knowles explores the conflict between private morality and its public expression; where society is corrupt, it will destroy the moral man. Knowles' plays show the danger of being a Radical idealist in a repressive society with an entrenched and violent ruling class; he will be abandoned from below and crushed from above. Only in *William Tell* does he survive, by which time, 1825, reform was at least a possibility, but I have the impression from the play that Knowles is held back by the well-known story, and would just as willingly have sacrificed William Tell, if it had been possible, in order to preserve his Radical purity.

The Liberty plays had no direct reference to Irish circumstances, but they reflected the situation in the entire United Kingdom, and embraced the plight of oppressed classes anywhere, ground down by a self-preserving aristocracy. Knowles intended his plays to have relevance regardless of location, though they were directed at the rising Irish middle class. 'My plays were too liberal for the illiberal aristocracy of Ireland,' he wrote, but were aimed at a different sector: 'My plays breathe the noble sentiments of the influential classes of Ireland.'[87]   He clearly believed that the Irish aristocracy had had its day, but he found that it still had teeth: his visit to his birthplace of Cork in 1834 was a disaster. The gentry and nobility boycotted him, in protest at his democratic views, and remembering his father's support for Catholic Emancipation. Knowles was humiliated, and bitterly complained about the lack of success 'which an Irishman meets with on his own ungrateful soil'.[88] He was compensated by a hugely successful tour of America later in the same year. In Britain, his work was heavily censored before performance; references to 'liberty' were expunged by the Lord Chamberlain, and all mention of tyranny removed on the orders of George IV. The excised text was re-introduced for the American productions, and for publication — a neat reverse of the present system whereby publication is considered more explosive than performance, and an indication of the power of the theatre at the time, when illiteracy was widespread but theatre tickets were cheap.

In his third Liberty play, *William Tell* (1825), Knowles looked, not at internal oppression but at occupation by a foreign power, in this case Austria's occupation of Switzerland, but refrained still from direct mention of Ireland's case, unless it be the last speech with its anti-colonial sentiment:

> TELL We are free, my countrymen!
> Our country is free! Austria, you'll quit a land
> you never had a right to; and remember,
> The country's never lost, that's left a son
> To struggle with the foe that would enslave her.[89]

Knowles was becoming more abstract. *William Tell* is more like a philosophical treatise than a play. The characters are schematic, interchangeable with their counterparts in his earlier plays. He tried to vary the drama by inserting a comic/romantic subplot, but it did not work, and Macready cut it for production, reducing the play from five acts to three.

In the first two Liberty plays, aristocratic centralism succeeded in eliminating the hero/outlaw though not the ideas that animate him, but in *William Tell*, the bourgeois family men defending their hearths and homes overcome the aristocratic oppressor. The subtext of Knowles' Liberty plays is the inescapability of politics – the interconnectedness of all strands of society, that there is no way of hiding from the movements of the political world and creating a domestic world where a private morality can hold sway. No private Utopia can ever stand isolated within society – a message that is close to that of *The Plough and the Stars* a century later. The three plays argue that apparent liberty at the domestic level is an illusion when the body politic is sick. Knowles considers in *William Tell* neither class nor national liberation, but the winning of personal freedom. William Tell is free in the mountains but his liberty is destroyed by the arrival of the old man whose eyes have been gouged out by the tyrannous governor, Gesler. Gesler is imaged as a wolf, William Tell as an eagle, a symbol he shares with the spirit of Liberty:

> TELL Scaling yonder peak,
> I saw an eagle wheeling near its brow:
> O'er the abyss his broad expanded wings
> Lay calm and motionless upon the air,
> As if he floated there without their aid,
> By the sole act of his unlorded will,
> That buoy'd him proudly up. Instinctively

I strung my bow; yet kept he rounding still
His airy circle, as in the delight
of measuring the ample range beneath,
And round about, absorb'd, he heeded not
The death that threaten'd him! – I could not shoot! –
'Twas liberty. I turn'd the shaft aside,
And let him soar away.[90]

Knowles, with *Caius Gracchus* and *Virginius*, was seen to create a new kind of tragedy, of simple language and situations, actions and characters, that was freed from the 'stupid German' influence of Schiller and Kotzebue,[91] which was more domestic, more to the English taste. It is ironic that for *William Tell* Knowles went back to Schiller, and took his play, his republican outlook and also his mystical, Germanic, Romantic awareness of landscape. In the plays of John O'Keeffe, the landscape was a bit player, but in *William Tell* it upstages everybody. The play is like Boucicault's in the precision and range of its stage-directions, and the overbearing presences are the mountains. They dominate the stage, numinous and sublime, alive with the spirit of Liberty.

Schiller had written in 1795: 'It is not interaction with society, nor political revolution, which fulfil man as a human being, but the contemplation of great art alone.'[92] He concluded that the greatest art was in Nature, and German Romantic painting is full of figures contemplating a landscape alive with meaning. Part of the Romantic Movement's intention was to restore, through art, some of the mystery – *Entzauberung der Welt* – whose removal had been the mission of the Enlightenment. The Romantics, in the contemplation of the great art and mystery of Nature, could lose themselves in pantheism, like Wordsworth, or find the imprint of the Greatest Artist, to which Knowles' fervent religious convictions led him. To this end, *William Tell*, developing from his previous plays, was constructed as an exhibition of stage pictures to display this Great Art. *Brian Boroimhe* had tableaux of Irish medievalism; in his two Roman plays, Knowles used a series of domestic and public images based on nineteenth-century history and narrative paintings; in *William Tell* however, he cut loose with the full panoply of the German Romantic.

It is not far from the pictoriality of Knowles' method in his earlier plays to the fusing of landscape with meaning, as he does in *William Tell*. The German Romantic painters showed him the way, and Knowles imbues the natural world, the mountains, the lakes, the falling waters and the huge sky with the spirit of Liberty: they all teach men to be free. Counterposed to this are the works of man, symbolized by towers and castles, which speak of imprisonment and bondage. Using scenery, music, sound and lighting effects, he created, with meticulous visual care, out of the Alpine setting, with its peaks, passes, glaciers, lakes, rivers and storms, a moving tableau, a diorama to harmonize with the lofty ideas of personal and public freedom. The first scene sets the tone, as the light of freedom pours into the world:

> *Tell's cottage on the right of a Mountain – a distant view of a Lake, backed by Mountains of stupendous height, their tops covered with snow, and lighted at the very points with the rising Sun – the rest of the distance being yet in shade – on one side a Vineyard. […] The light gradually approaches the base of the mountains in the distance, and spreads itself over the lake and the valley.*[93]

In parallel, he developed, out of the Shakespearean soliloquy, the vocal equivalent of a visual tableau, the verbal aria. This is usually a hymn to Liberty and the mountains that inspire it. It is intended as a verbal correspondence to the pictorial elements, and to lift the audience to a state of transcendental appreciation, to have them feel the touch of the Sublime. The Sublime in Nature inspires the Swiss to freedom; the mountains call for revolt against the Austrian tyranny.

TELL   Ye crags and peaks, I'm with you once again!
  I hold to you the hands you first beheld,
  To show they still are free. Methinks I hear
  A spirit in your echoes answer me,
  And bid your tenant welcome home again!
  Hail! – Hail! O sacred forms, how proud you look!
  How high you lift your heads into the sky!
  How huge you are! How mighty and how free!
  How do you look, for all your bared brows,
  More gorgeously majestical than kings
  Whose loaded coronets exhaust the mine!
  Ye are the things that tower – that shine – whose smile
  Makes glad – whose frown is terrible – whose forms,
  Robed or unrobed, do all the impress wear
  Of awe divine – whose subject never kneels
  In mockery, because it is your boast
  To keep him free! Ye guards of liberty,
  I'm with you once again! — I call to you
  With all my voice! I hold my hands to you
  To show they still are free! I rush to you
  As though I could embrace you.[94]

This sort of aria, while it seems, to the modern eye and ear, a piece of Romantic, Byronic excess, descending to pathos and soaring to absurdity, was the accepted style of the day, and to the actor it represented a challenge and an opportunity. Knowles wrote it for someone skilled in oratory who could sweep an audience along without pausing to analyse what he was actually saying; to the audience the Sublime was beyond rational analysis, a matter of feeling and intuition, not of reason; the truth was located within the individual's own emotions, and was released by passion and poetry.

The free man rejoices in Nature, even in its most extreme manifestations, the oppressor cringes in fear. While Nature and the mountains uplift the righteous with Liberty, their power is felt as an oppression by the villainous. The tyrant, when attacked by the storm, and assaulted by the Sublime, reacts with terror:

> GESLER   My voice sounds weaker to mine ear! I've not
> The strength to call I had; and through my limbs
> Cold tremor runs, and sickening faintness seizes
> On my heart.
> [*He leans against a rock, stupefied with terror and exhaustion – it grows darker and darker – the rain pours down in torrents, and a furious wind arises – the mountain streams begin to swell and roar.* ALBERT *is seen descending by the side of one of the streams, which in his course he crosses with the help of his pole.*][95]

What inspires the free man to rapture oppresses the oppressor almost to death. Gesler is contrasted with William Tell's son, Albert, who rejoices in the tumult because 'God's in the storm'.[96]

The similarities between Schiller's play and Knowles' are striking, particularly in their philosophy and in their evocation of a mystical landscape. But the differences are equally interesting. Nature, in Schiller's play, is characterized as a wild beast, an untameable, unstoppable entity, whose manifestations are symbolic of freedom. Knowles' Nature is more abstract, more spiritual. In Knowles, Nature is free, and calls men to freedom. This is present almost as a footnote in Schiller, when Tell characterizes the mountains as: 'That house of freedom God hath built for us',[97] but the main focus in Schiller's *Wilhelm Tell* is on Nature's manifestations of its savage and irresistible power, in the storm, the avalanche and the earthquake, used as symbols of the earth-shaking arrival of freedom.

Schiller's play is very German, very Romantic, but Knowles de-Germanized the work, and removed its pointed relevance to the fractured nature of the German-speaking countries and their humiliation by Bonaparte. Instead of that political context, he boosted, in his usual way, the contrast between the domestic and the public worlds. Schiller's is a very public play: he had it published (after his death) as a New Year's gift to the world for 1805.[98] Its main scene is a lengthy exposition of the clandestine inauguration of a people's parliament, under the unique phenomenon of a double lunar rainbow, that occupies almost a whole act and finishes with a wonderful theatrical *coup*: '*Whilst they exit in greatest calm to three different sides, the orchestra breaks in with a magnificent flourish, the empty stage remains open for a time and displays the spectacle of the rising sun over the ice-capped mountains.*'[99] Knowles, however, puts the emphasis on personal freedom within a domestic context. His argument in this play, as in *Caius Gracchus* and *Virginius*, is that such personal freedom is possible only within a broader context of public freedom from tyrannical interference.

This seems obvious enough to us after the terrible events of the twentieth century, but it was not so apparent in the early nineteenth. The early promise of democratic and revolutionary ideals in France had been corrupted by dictatorial repression and a war that spread around the world. Following the Congress of Vienna, the entire continent of Europe was re-arranged on the basis of aristocratic centralization, and a reactionary era followed, until 1848, in which democratic and reformist ideas were actively persecuted. This was, Sydney Smith wrote, 'an awful time for those who had the misfortune to entertain liberal opinions, and who were too honest to sell themselves'.[100] In this ruin of hope and liberty,[101] many artists, writers and those of a reformist or democratic tendency turned inwards, and created a paradigm of domestic freedom and tranquillity that turned its back on the political repression of the time. The Biedermeier movement in Austria is a striking example of this tendency in Art, as is the music of Schubert, but it can also be traced in the literary concentration on individual relationships, the emphasis placed on friendship and the importance attached to the domestic and familial. When every country in Western Europe was turned into a police state, social intercourse was restricted to a small circle of discreet and trusted friends.[102] Knowles, in his Liberty plays, rejected this attitude in favour of the High Romantic ideals of individualism, political engagement and passionate embracing of the mystical and Sublime through Nature.

This assertion and expression of freedom in Nature, visually and actively in its storms and sunrises, verbally in the ecstatic arias of William Tell, and in the overall rhythm of the plot that surges irresistibly towards the achievement of Liberty, rejects, by dwarfing all men to the same size, the claim of an occupying power, or a ruling class, to supremacy, and to the exclusive rights to power and its fruits. Knowles was embracing the Hobbes/Locke principle of the power invested inalienably in the people, and devolved by them on to the authorities, a doctrine reversed by the Congress of Vienna. This is his underlying republicanism, but it is also evident in his striving for the Sublime. The Sublime is essentially democratic; it is available to all, and can be felt by the soul of each individual. It asserts the centrality of individual experience, and the supremacy of the individual over the group. It proclaims the irresistibility and inevitability of individual passions, because they express powerfully the urgings of Nature, and through Nature the Divine is expressed. It is the most selfish of doctrines, unless leavened with the idea of all men as brothers - the *fraternité* of William Tell, Gracchus and Virginius to balance the *liberté*. *William Tell*, too, rejects the suppression of the ancient rights of the common people, reminiscent of the arguments of Molyneux, and the right of one country to occupy and rule another, which resonated in America as it did in Ireland.

During his career, Knowles visited Dublin and Belfast on many occasions and performed in his own plays and popular classics. Cork made its amends for the débâcle of 1834 with a civic reception and banquet in 1862. Knowles' Liberty plays have no direct reference to Ireland at all, but throughout his life, he rejoiced in the nickname of 'Paddy' Knowles, and his acting was often criticized for the prominence of his Irish accent. And he did continue the Irish tradition of bending language into the service of poetry. He had two modes of dialogue. One has a Wordsworthian simplicity and directness: 'Is it a voice, or nothing, answers me? / I hear a sound so fine – there's nothing lives / twixt it and silence!'[103] The other was operatic, Romantic rant, as it sounds to the altered taste of modern times. He had also the interesting peculiarity of infusing the dialogue of his peasants, soldiers and labourers with poetry. He was taken to task for this by critics who took *Lyrical Ballads* too literally, and preferred truth to nature over poetic truth. *Fraser's Magazine* complained in 1836:

> He suffers not his peasants to wear their native plainness, but they must
> speak sentiment, and talk love, whether married or single. His hero must

apostrophise clouds and rocks and boast of freedom and talk politics, regardless of the fact that to a mountain people rocks and clouds are things familiar, and excite no wonderment, no passionate appeals.[104]

It was part of Knowles' egalitarianism to believe that peasants in a drama should feel as keenly and express as poetically or coherently as aristocrats; theatrical conventions bend easily enough to accommodate such sleight-of-hand. William Tell is a peasant, but he is an aristocrat of feeling, and expresses his reactions to the world in the high language of poetry. It is tempting to see Knowles' pioneering work in this area influencing Boucicault, Synge, O'Casey or Lady Gregory, to blend poetry with dialect to create their unique versions of peasant speech.

Knowles' abstract hymns to liberty and personal freedom from moral, political or social oppression by an occupying power or an entrenched ruling class touched a nerve in Ireland, England, Scotland and America. Knowles' idea of liberty has a modern ring; it is not political freedom but the absence of oppressive tyranny, the right to go about one's private, domestic and familial life without interference by overlords, hereditary or elected. His anarchist spirit was well aware that toppled tyranny will often be replaced by another political system, as in *Caius Gracchus* and *Virginius*, that is as bad as the system overthrown. The failure and corruption of the French Revolution permeated his entire generation of Radicals, but it was the *idea* of freedom that was felt to be important. In Knowles' plays, ideas were allocated an emotional power and impact that they enjoyed before the French Revolution, but were not to enjoy again until the heyday of socialism and nationalism.

In his plays, the Radical programme of the revolutionaries was kept alive, nurtured and propagated by the most popular art and entertainment form of the day. The tension between a repressive Ascendancy and a buried, oppressed mass of the people was constantly articulated, keeping up the pressure of the time, until the idea of a separate nationalism gave it a visible form.

NOTES AND REFERENCES

1. Frederick M. Link, 'Introduction', in *The Plays of John O'Keeffe*, ed. by Frederick M. Link, 4 vols (New York: Garland Publishing, 1981), pp. xxiv–xxv.
2. Link, Introduction to *The Plays of John O'Keeffe*, I, p. lix.
3. Wheatley and Donovan, *Irish Plays*, II, p. 279.
4. 'John O'Keeffe' http://pgil-eirdata.org/htm/pgil_datasets/authors/o/O'Keeffe,J/life.htm [accessed 21/12/2004] (p. 1 of 7).
5. O'Keeffe, *Recollections*, II, p. 144, in *The Plays of John O'Keeffe*, I, p. xlvii.
6. *Ibid.*, p. xlviii.

7. *Town and Country Magazine,* November 1789, p. 518, in *The Plays of John O'Keeffe,* I, p. xlviii.
8. O'Keeffe, *Le Grenadier,* in *The Plays of John O'Keeffe,* III, p. 221.
9. *Ibid.,* Part I, Scene 1, p. 189.
10. *Ibid.,* Part I, Scene 1, p. 190.
11. *Ibid.,* Part I, Scene 1, p. 190.
12. *Ibid.,* Part III, Scene 3, p. 216.
13. *Ibid.,* Part II, Scene 5, p. 210.
14. *Ibid.,* Part II, Scene 6, p. 212.
15. *Ibid.,* Part II, Scene 2, p. 202.
16. *Ibid.,* Part II, Scene 2, p. 216.
17. *Ibid.,* Part III, Scene 3, p. 216.
18. *Ibid.,* Part III, Scene Last, p. 220.
19. 'It is hardly propitiatory': Rosemary Bechler, Review of *Wild Oats* at the Lyttleton Theatre, London, *Times Literary Supplement,* 22 September 1995, p. 20.
20. O'Keeffe, *Wild Oats,* III. 2, in *The Plays of John O'Keeffe,* III, p. 43.
21. *Ibid.,* V. 4, p. 83.
22. Prologue to *Wild Oats,* 'written by John Taylor, Esq.', in *Plays of John O'Keeffe,* III, n. p.
23. O'Keeffe, *Wild Oats,* I. 1, p. 2.
24. *Ibid.,* I. 2, p. 9.
25. *Ibid.,* III. 2, p. 44.
26. *Ibid.,* I. 1, p. 6.
27. O'Keeffe, *Le Grenadier,* Part I. Sc.1, p. 190, in *Plays of John O'Keeffe,* III, p.190.
28. O'Keeffe, *The Wicklow Mountains,* II. 2, in Wheatley and Donovan, *Irish Plays,* II, p. 376.
29. *Ibid.,* II. 3, p. 359.
30. *Ibid.,* II. 2, p. 387.
31. *Ibid.,* I. 3, p. 358.
32. O'Keeffe, *The Poor Soldier,* I. 1, in Wheatley and Donovan, *Irish Plays,* II, p. 285.
33. *Ibid.,* II. 5, in Wheatley and Donovan, *Irish Plays,* II, p. 311.
34. Felix's activities have a good deal in common with the tenets of Thomas Spence (1750–1815), an English Radical, republican and socialist who advocated that all land and resources should be held in common by each parish, and all profits. Taxes and rents accruing used to support the schools, libraries, hospitals, for the local community. http://dspace.dial.pipex.com/town/terrace/adw03/c-eight/people/spence/htm [accessed 05/03/2005] (p. 1 of 2).
35. O'Keeffe, *The Wicklow Mountains,* III. 1, in Wheatley and Donovan, *Irish Plays,* II, p. 392.
36. *Ibid.,* III. 3, p. 401.
37. Karl Marx, *Das Kapital,* ch. 10, section 1. http://www.marxists.org/archive/marx/works/1867-c1/ch10.htm [accessed 27/04/2005]
38. Adam Smith, *The Wealth of Nations,* ed. by R.H. Campbell and A.S. Skinner (Oxford: Clarendon Press, 1976), I, p. 54.
39. O'Keeffe, *Recollections,* II, p. 144, in *The Plays of John O'Keeffe,* I, p. xlvii.
40. William Hazlitt, 'Elia and Geoffrey Crayon', *The Spirit of the Age* (1825), http://blupete.com/Literature/Essays/Hazlitt/SpiritAge/Elia.htm [accessed 25/02/2005] (p. 6 of 6).
41. Gerald D. Parker, ' "I am going to America:" James Sheridan Knowles' *Virginius,* and the Politics of "Liberty"', in *Theatre Research International,* 17, No. 1 (Spring 1992) 15–25 (p. 16).
42. 'Based on a play by Daniel O'Meara', James Sheridan Knowles, *Brian Boroimhe; or, The Maid of Erin,* Dicks' Standard Plays (London: John Dicks, 1837?), title page.
43. *Ibid.,* II. 2, p. 8.
44. *Ibid.,* I. 5, p. 6.
45. *Ibid.,* I. 2, p. 9.
46. *Ibid.,* II. 3, p. 10.
47. *Ibid.,* I. 1, p. 5.
48. *Ibid.,* II. 2, p. 10.
49. The Dicks' edition of *Brian Boroimhe* gives the Covent Garden cast of 1837, with Edmund Kean as Brian and Knowles as Voltimer.
50. *Short History of English Literature* (1922), in 'J. Sheridan Knowles'. http://pgil-eirdata.org/htm/pgil_datasets/authors/k/Knowles,JS/life.htm [accessed 15/11/2004] (p. 3 of 4).
51. 'Nineteenth-Century Drama', *The Cambridge History of English and American Literature,* 18 vols (Cambridge: University Press, 1907–1921) XIII, Part 1. http://www.bartleby.com/

223/0805.html   [accessed 25/02/2005] (p. 2 of 3).
52. Hazlitt, 'Elia and Geoffrey Crayon', (p. 6 of 6).
53. Leslie Howard Meeks, *Sheridan Knowles and the Theatre of his Time* (Bloomington, Ind.: Principia Press, 1933), p. 111.
54. Knowles, *Caius Gracchus*, I. 1, in *The Dramatic Works of James Sheridan Knowles*, 2 vols (London: Routledge, 1856), I, p. 5.
55. *Ibid.*, I. 2, p. 6.
56. *Ibid.*, I. 1, p. 4.
57. *Ibid.*, III. 2, p. 31.
58. *Ibid.*, II. 3, p. 23.
59. *Ibid.*, III. 4, p. 48.
60. Parker, 'I am Going to America', p. 17.
61. Meeks, *Knowles and the Theatre of his Time*, p. 79.
62. Knowles, *Caius Gracchus*, III. 2, p. 38.
63. Meeks, *Knowles and the Theatre of his Time*, p. 140.
64. Knowles, *Caius Gracchus*, III. 3, p. 43.
65. Rousseau, 'The Sovereign', in *The Social Contract*. http://www.constitution.org/jjr/socon.htm_ [accessed 10/05/2005] (Book 1, Section 7).
66. Hazlitt, 'Elia and Washington Irving', (p. 5 of 6).
67. Meeks, *Knowles and the Theatre of his Time*, p. 65.
68. *Ibid.*, p. 63.
69. Knowles, *Caius Gracchus*, V. 3, p. 56.
70. *Ibid.*, V. 3, p. 56.
71. *Ibid.*, V. 3, p. 56.
72. *Ibid.*, I. 3, p. 12.
73. *Ibid.*, V. 3, p. 57.
74. *Ibid.*, V. 3, p. 58.
75. 'Theatre Royal, Drury Lane', in *Virtual Exhibitions, 2: Pantomime and the Orient*, Centre for Performance History, Royal College of Music, London, http://www.cph.rcm.ac.uk/Virtual%20Exhibitions/Music%20in%2... [accessed 14/ 09/ 2007] (p. 1 of 1)
76. *Richard Cumberland, The Memoirs of Richard Cumberland, written by himself. Containing an account of his life and writings, interspersed with anecdotes and characters. With illustrative notes by Henry Flanders.* (London: Parry & McMillan, 1856), p. 387. Making of America Books, University of Michigan.http://quod. lib.umich.edu/cache/d/9/4/d94f158b8253e5f0f9d34192 [accessed 14/09/2007]
77. 'Epilogue, by Barry Cornwall, Esq., Spoken by Miss Brunton', in *Dramatic Works of James Sheridan Knowles*, I, p. 111.
78. See also Parke: 'I am going to America', pp. 20–22.
79. Knowles, *Virginius*, I. 1, in *The Dramatic Works of James Sheridan Knowles*, I, p. 62.
80. *Ibid.*, I. 1, p. 63.
81. *Ibid.*, III. 2, p. 83.
82. *Ibid.*, I. 1, p. 65.
83. *Ibid.*, I. 2, p. 68.
84. *Oxford Dictionary of National Biography*, ed. by H.C.G. Matthew and Brian Harrison, 60 vols (Oxford: University Press, 2004), XXXI, p. 983.
85. *Ibid.*, p. 983.
86. R.H.A. Thorne, in Parker, 'I am Going to America', p. 20.
87. *Ibid.*, p. 15.
88. Meeks, *Knowles and the Theatre of his Time*, p. 45.
89. Knowles, *William Tell*, V. 2, in *The Dramatic Works of James Sheridan Knowles*, II, p. 176.
90. *Ibid.*, I. 3, p. 123.
91. Coleridge, Samuel Taylor, 'Bertram', in *Biographia Litteraria*. http://www.free-online-books.org/displaybook1.php?chapter_id=25&id=188 [accessed 28/01/2005] (pp. 109).
92. Friedrich Schiller, 'Letters upon the Aesthetic Education of Man', cited in Peter-Klaus Schuster, 'The Museum Island Berlin: *A German Dream*', in *A German Dream: Masterpieces of Romanticism from the Nationalgalerie Berlin*, ed. by Bernhard Maaz (Berlin: Nationalgalerie, 2004), p. 8.
93. Knowles, *William Tell*, Stage directions, II, pp.129 & 132.
94. *Ibid.*, I. 2, p. 123.
95. *Ibid.*, III. 1, p. 141.

96. *Ibid.*, III. 1, p. 141.
97. Freidrich Von Schiller, transl. by William F. Wertz, Jr, *Wilhelm Tell*, I. 3, in *Modern History Sourcebook*, ed. by Paul Halsall (1999) http://www.fordham.edu/halsall/mod/1805schiller-willtell.html [accessed 14/03/2005] (p. 13 of 81).
98. *Ibid.*, title page: 'A drama by Freidrich Von Schiller, New Year's Gift for 1805', (p. 1 of 81).
99. *Ibid.*, stage direction, end of Act II (p. 34 of 81).
100. Parker, ' I am Going to America', p. 15.
101. See Caspar David Friedrich's picture *The Wreck of the Hope*; or, *Sea of Ice* (1823/4) in the Hamburger Kunsthalle, Hamburg.
102. Aaron Green, 'The Rise of the Middle Class and the Related Works of Schubert'. http://classicalmusic.about.com/od/romanticperiod/a/aabeidermeier.htm [accessed 29/04/2005] (p. 2 of 4).
103. Knowles, *Virginius*, V. 2, p. 106.
104. *Fraser's Magazine*, XIII, (April 1836), p. 459, in Meeks, *Knowles and the Theatre of his Time*, p. 107.

8

Picturesque Ruins:
Boucicault's Irish Plays

Dion Boucicault tapped into a sort of theatrical tourism in his Irish plays, exploiting the advances made in lighting, scenic design and spectacular effects to create specific images of place, and taking advantage of the vogue for visiting romantic landscapes such as Killarney, the Lake District or the Alps. The scenery assume a vital importance as part of the theatrical reference in Boucicault's Irish plays – the Lakes of Killarney in *The Colleen Bawn*, the Wicklow Mountains in *Arrah na Pogue* – and it achieved its apotheosis in *The Shaughraun*. That play is set, not in some well-known tourist destination, but in the fairly anonymous attractions of Sligo. It is an idealized, romantic Ireland, and it exercises a considerable influence over the plot and the characters. It assumes the role of a mystic monitor of events and inspirer of the protagonists; it also participates in the action. The landscape hides the hero, provides escape routes, supports the oppressed heroines surreptitiously with food (by way of the Shaughraun), confuses the soldiery, curses the usurpers and restores the rightful owners to their proper place. Finally, it kills the villain. A powerful current of mystic unity between people and land informs this play and its companions. At the centre of the three plays lies the question of land, just as it was latent in O'Keeffe's *The Wicklow Mountains* and was to dominate the work of John B. Keane one hundred years later. Squire Kinchela in *The Shaughraun* invokes the landscape early on against the foreign soldier, Molineux: 'The devil guide him to pass the night in a bog-hole up to his neck.'[1] But the landscape only half-obliges: it teases and harries Molineux, and keeps him on a leash: 'I was nearly smothered in a bog. [...] Instead of going straight home, I have been revolving in an orbit round that house by a kind of centrifugal force.'[2] It assists the characters in their efforts to preserve Ffolliott, its rightful owner, and also curses the usurpers of his patrimony; the alienated landscape partakes of the alienation of its owners:

FATHER DOLAN   Oh! Beware Kinchela! When these lands were torn
from Owen Roe O'Neal in the old times, he laid his curse on the
spoilers, for Suil-a-more was the dowry of his bride, Grace Ffolliott.
Since then many a strange family have tried to hold possession of the
place; but every year one of them would die – the land seemed to
swallow them up one by one. Till the O'Neals and the Ffolliotts
returned none other thrived on it.

KINCHELA   Sure that's the raison I want Arte O'Neal for my wife. Won't
that keep the ould blood to the fore.[3]

The romanticizing of the land is reflected in the romanticizing of the
gentry who are shown as the rightful possessors. They are oppressed,
and the land is in the hands of the oppressors; the good are downtrodden, and the unjust thrive.

The first scene of *The Shaughraun* is masterly in its weaving together
of these strands. We open on a harmonious scene – a pretty girl in a dramatic landscape, churning and singing, a picture-postcard of romantic
Ireland: '*The ruins of Suil-a-more Castle cover a bold headland in the half
distance – the Atlantic bounds the picture – Sunset – Music.* Claire
Ffolliott *at work at a churn.*'[4] But the playwright is playing with us. He
is evoking our received knowledge of theatrical conventions and the
iconography of landscape to make us totally misinterpret the scene: the
girl is one of the Ascendancy, play-acting at being a milkmaid, as we find
out when Mrs O'Kelly enters and speaks to her deferentially. Then
Molineux appears, and the audience join Claire Ffolliott in trapping him
in exactly the same mistake. He, like us, is seduced by the physical beauty, and blind to the political squalor, until Claire spells it out for him:

CLAIRE   Do you see that ruin yonder! Oh – 'tis the admiration of the
traveller, and the study of painters, who come from far and near to
copy it. It was the home of my forefathers when they kept open house
for the friend – the poor – or the stranger. The mortgagee has put up
a gate now, so visitors pay sixpence a head to admire the place, and
their guide points across to this cabin where the remains of the ould
family, two lonely girls, live. God knows how – you ask leave to kill
game on Suil-a-more and Keim-an-eigh. (*Crosses to the dairy window*)
Do you see that salmon? It was snared last night in the Pool-a-Bricken
by Conn, the Shaughraun. He killed those grouse at daylight on
the side of Maurnturk. That's our daily food, and we owe it to a
poacher.
[...]

MOLINEUX But surely you cannot be without some relatives!

CLAIRE   I have a brother – the heir to this estate.

MOLINEUX Is he abroad?

CLAIRE   Yes, he is a convict working out his sentence in Australia.

MOLINEUX Oh, I beg pardon. I did not know. *(To* ARTE*)* Have you any relatives?

ARTE   Yes, I am the affianced wife of her brother![5]

Boucicault performs the same undercutting move at the start of each of his Irish comic trilogy. In *The Colleen Bawn* we are shown the scene of the Big House on the shores of the Lakes of Killarney, hear twenty seconds of music drifting from it, and see the green signal light winking across the lake, an idyllic scene full of romantic promise. It is soon shattered by the apparently illicit love-affair of Hardress Cregan, and by his mercenary mother in pursuit of an advantageous marriage for her son, as well as the first intimation of violence and deformity from Cregan and Danny Mann. The romantic illusion is created and collapsed all within the first minutes of the play.

The romantic setting of the Wicklow Mountains is evoked in the opening of *Arrah na Pogue* in a stage-direction as tight and evocative as a Japanese haiku:

> *Glendalough; Moonlight. The Ruins of St Kevin's Abbey, the Round Tower, the Ruined Cemetery, the Lake and Mountains beyond; Music.* Beamish Mac Coul *discovered.*[6]

The character is given romantic and aristocratic status by the presence of dramatic scenery and noble ruins. We find out once the scene starts that he is also an outlaw engaged in armed robbery.

In each of the three plays, then, we are confronted with spectacular scenery, in which is embedded an attractive member of the Ascendancy who is in trouble. This is the double edge, attractiveness and vulnerability, that Boucicault uses to delineate the Ascendancy and their place in nineteenth-century Irish society. The Ascendancy, he shows us, is a picturesque ruin.

Boucicault was, like his predecessors, a myth-maker, and created for his Irish plays an Ascendancy that never existed. Just as he romanticized the landscape, he fictionalized the gentry who are the human embodiments of it. He shows us an Ascendancy that might have evolved if the country had never been conquered by the English. His gentry all have Irish names – Cregan, MacCoul, O'Neal, O'Grady – or at least Old English ones – Ffolliott, Chute. They are obviously of the same race as the peasantry and the rising bourgeoisie who want to marry into them; the differences are class-based. There are two sets of signifiers in *The Colleen Bawn*: peasant-signifiers – brogue, Irish words, songs and music, 'smell of tobacco [...] and the fumes of whiskey punch',[7] and gentry-signifiers – 'getting clear of the brogue, and learning to do nothing'.[8] For the purposes of the play there are no religious or racial barriers between the aristocrats and the villain, Corrigan. This gives a clean line to the conflict, uncluttered by any reference to tribalism or creed; the heroes and villains are all Irish. It is an idealized social landscape designed not to inflame Irish audiences nor offend English ones; the play even succeeded in amusing Queen Victoria, who saw it performed a number of times. The scene in which Cregan berates Eily about her brogue shows how deep is the class divide that has to be bridged for a happy ending, but the joke about Anne Chute reverting to brogue – 'When I am angry the brogue comes out, and my Irish heart will burst through manners, and graces, and twenty stay-laces'[9] – shows that the gentry and the peasants are not so far apart. The tension between standard English and brogue that had been such a feature of Irish plays is expanded in a sinister fashion in the misapprehension that causes the central action – the murder of the Colleen Bawn. The play hinges on a unity of intent but a confusion of language. Danny seeks verification: 'I'm to *make* away with her then,' and Mrs Cregan either deliberately or genuinely misunderstands: 'Yes, yes – *take* her away – away with her!'[10] The Pontius Pilate-like biblicality of the exhortation implicates her, at least in the intention of the crime.

Boucicault removed the English from the plays, apart from certain sympathetic presences: Captain Molineux, in *The Shaughraun,* or Lord Kilwarden in *Robert Emmet*. He created an indigenous, almost closed world of Irish aristocrats, villains and peasants; Molineux is the only significantly English character, as if the entire history of seven hundred years of conquest and colonization, oppression and dispossession, had never taken place. The plays occupy a temporal and metaphorical space in which history may be stated but not shown – history as talk, or as story. There is a lot of talk in *The Shaughraun* about injustice, but it refers to past deeds such as the exiling of Ffolliott, or to ancient wrongs, such as the confiscation of the land. The first is resolved by the magnanimity of the Queen, the second obscured by an equally predatory subsequent confiscation by an Irishman. There are two parallel actions at work: the verbal one lamenting the wrongs of Ireland, and the physical action, which goes in a different direction. The play enacts a reconciliation, through a line of events, from the pardon of Ffolliott, via the uniting of the English army with the Irish gentry and peasants, to produce justice and punish the villain. The wrongdoers are not English; English law is culpably foolish but it is executed by an Irishman, Kinchela, who is a magistrate and abuses the law to get hold of Ffolliott's land – a device, as Lecky points out, that laid the foundation of most of the great Irish estates.[11] What this leaves is a cleaner concentration on class issues, as it was with O'Keeffe and Knowles, and Boucicault deals with these quite subtly.

Boucicault's play *The Octoroon* (1859) dealt with slavery, an incendiary subject for its American audience. Boucicault performed a delicate balancing act in the play to appease both sides of his divided public. Joe Jefferson, a leading actor in the play's première, explains how he did it:

> Boucicault had thrown a bone to both sides: the handling of the plot was pro-northern, but the treatment of the characters was pro-southern. For the plot dealt mainly with the victimized slave girl Zoe who is sold on the block to the highest bidder, thus eliciting strong anti-slavery sympathies; while in the alignment of the characters, the southerners were on the whole gallant gentlemen who remained loyal to their slaves, thus gratifying the pro-slavery forces.[12]

Through the character of Zoe he explored issues of class and oppression, and learned valuable lessons which he applied to his Irish plays. He learned how to depict the plight of a downtrodden race without at the same time showing their oppressors as monsters of melodrama. He had travelled extensively in the Southern states and was impressed, as were most people, by the attractiveness and graciousness of a society that was maintained by the institution of slavery. In his Irish plays, he employed the same tactic. He made his Ascendancy heroes attractive, noble creatures, but he undercuts them by making them complete fools. These Ascendancy heroes – Beamish MacCoul, Hardress Cregan, Robert Ffolliott, Robert Emmet – are dashing but not too bright. This may be partly because Boucicault never played these parts himself; he left them to the juvenile leads, and so had very little interest in creating powerful characters who could upstage him, but there is more to it than that. In each play, our hero stands at the centre of the plot, which he instigates by some act of unthinking stupidity, which immediately spins out of his control until he is saved by his band of peasants. The main characteristic of the Ascendancy heroes in the four plays is thoughtless, careless idiocy; their inability to think rather than feel causes endless trouble for all around them, from which their lower-class followers must rescue them.

Robert Emmet wants to lead the masses to their deaths, for a republic, an abstraction, when what the people want for their efforts is material gain and a bit of excitement. Boucicault identifies Emmet as part of the Anglo-Irish ruling class, but allows him to become an outlaw, like those in Knowles' plays, by dissenting from his patrimony and embracing the abstract idea of independence. It is never stated what it is independence from. Emmet does not depart mentally from his class for a moment; the redistribution of wealth and land is never considered by Ascendancy rebels, and Emmet fervently opposes a redistribution of wealth by looting. Class solidarity ensures that valiant efforts are made by his classmates from College to save him, but not to save any of the other rebels. His invincible and arrogant nobility is too strong for them, however. Emmet is designed to a Romantic template, to appeal to a romantic audience. He sees himself in messianic terms:

> It is the inexorable fate of all the saviours of the people! Oh, ye spirits! You immortal band of heroes who suffered for your faith! Bodyguard of Him who died for the human race! Accept into your ranks the humble life of one, who, loving his native land not wisely, but too well, followed in your footsteps upward to the Throne where sit the Eternal Trinity of Truth, Light and Freedom![13]

Emmet thinks a revolution can be detonated without any collateral damage. On the death of Kilwarden, he laments: 'The coward who struck this good man down planted his steel in the bosom of his country. Ireland was murdered by that blow,'[14] although he had just ordered an innocent man to be shot for the crime. Because he is betrayed by those around him, not by his intrinsic flaws, Emmet is not a tragic figure. The ambiguity of the character fractures the play dramatically; his rhetorical evocation of Irish nationalist ideals does not compensate for his endemic obtuseness. The character is less appealing than the sentiments; for all his high patriotic declaration, Emmet is just a talker. Like all of Boucicault's Ascendancy heroes, he is in the grip of events all through the play; he takes no initiative, but is blown along by conspiracy and betrayal, or manipulated by his underlings.

The nub of the action in *Arrah-na-Pogue* is Beamish MacCoul's generous and foolish gesture in giving to Arrah the money he has stolen from the rent-collector. It is that piece of unthinking generosity that launches the plot, and from that point he has landed everyone else in trouble and the hunt is up. 'They are hunting the life out of him,' says Arrah of Beamish,[15] and the search for MacCoul forms the backdrop to the entire play.

Apart from his impulsive stupidity, and his assumption of his natural right to ask favours of the authorities he has sworn, as a United Irishman, to destroy, there is little to reprehend in Beamish MacCoul. He is 'a dashing hero who does little besides dash'.[16] It is worth noting, however, that when MacCoul receives his own pardon, it is not he, but O'Grady, who remembers that Shaun the Post is waiting to be hanged in the morning as a result of MacCoul's folly, and dashes off to save him.

Robert Ffolliott in *The Shaughraun* is a man who is tied in a straitjacket of his own honour. He chooses to die rather than force Fr Dolan to tell a lie by concealing his whereabouts – he cannot do a dishonourable thing even to save his life. He is also a gullible fool: he swallows without question the cock-and-bull story that the villain Kinchela tells him:

> KINCHELA   My devotion to you and the precious charge you left in my
> care exposes me to suspicion. I am watched, and to preserve my char-
> acter for loyalty, I am obliged to put on airs – Oh! I'm your mortal
> enemy, mind that. [...] Every man woman an' child in the County
> Sligo believes it, and hate me. I've played my part so well that your
> sister an' Miss O'Neal took offence at my performance. [...] Yes! ho!
> ho! they actually believe I am what I am obliged to appear, and they
> hate me cordially. I'm the biggest blackguard —
> ROBERT   You! my best friend![17]

In addition to his gullibility, he manages to drop and lose the gun that Kinchela gave him to aid his escape. For a convicted Fenian desperado, he is remarkably incompetent.

Hardress Cregan in *The Colleen Bawn* is the least attractive, and at the same time the most interesting of Boucicault's Ascendancy heroes. Boucicault wrote him as a weak character, who lives under the domination of his mother. He is a hypocrite in opposing the proposals of the squireen, Corrigan, to join the family by marrying the mother, while all the time he is himself married to the peasant Eily O'Connor. Cregan's clandestine marriage can only be viewed as an act of extreme foolhardiness. The Cregan estate is, like all the estates in the plays, encumbered by previous mismanagement. As the only source of income the landed gentry had, it was vital to invest a portion of that income in the land in order to secure its continuance. Few of them did so, but resorted instead to mortgaging, remortgaging and rackrenting their estates. This was so much to be expected that Captain Molineux assumes it of the Ffolliotts in *The Shaughraun*: 'You have to suffer bitterly indeed for ages of family imprudence, and the Irish extravagance of your ancestors.'[18] In *The Colleen Bawn*, Hardress Cregan has ignored his responsibilities, has followed his feelings and pursued his pleasures by marrying a peasant, and so cut himself off from being in any position to rectify the family fortunes through an advantageous marriage, the only means available to an encumbered estate with a presentable heir.

The O'Grady, in *Arrah-na-Pogue*, is slightly more useful than the Ascendancy men in the other plays. He cannot save Shaun the Post from being sentenced to death, but his heart is revolted by it. He is disdainful of the law, but helpless in its grip, constrained by his position into doing his duty and implementing it, however unwillingly: 'It's a hard duty that obliges a gentleman to put a rope around that boy's neck, while dignity forbids him to say that he's mighty sorry for it.'[19] This play is unusual in that the day is saved, not by the cunning of the rogue, but by the intervention of the paternalistic authorities, and their good offices secured by close contact with the local gentry. Shaun the Post and O'Grady are like two sides of a coin, in their cast of mind and their use of language as a weapon and shield. O'Grady wants to let Shaun off on grounds of 'the eloquence of the defence',[20] and indicates that they are of like mind: 'Asy, Major, what would you do if a man offered to lay a hand on the woman you loved? Be the powers, I'd have brained him first and warned him afterwards.'[21] He is in marked contrast to Major Coffin who is, in O'Grady's opinion, 'A kind-hearted gentleman, who would cut more throats on principle and firm conviction than another blackguard would sacrifice to the worst passions of his nature. If there is one thing that misleads a man more than another thing, it is having a firm conviction about anything.'[22] That last sentence, with its deft shuffling of rhythm, cadence and meaning shows O'Grady in the direct line of descent from the Hibernian gentlemen of the eighteenth-century stage. This descent is nowhere clearer than in the trial scene in *Arrah-na-Pogue*; the linguistic games that Boucicault plays, the skill in verbal fencing, the witty inversion of accepted moral and legal truths, and the moral superiority that is signified by linguistic superiority, link directly back to the eloquent Hibernian gentlemen of Macklin, Sheridan, and the eighteenth century, and point forward to the polished paradoxes of Shaw and Wilde.

The function of the gentlemen in the plays is to walk nobly and stupidly into traps set by the crafty bourgeoisie, out of which their even craftier peasant followers have to extricate them – a sort of back-stairs conspiracy, a clandestine liaison in which the gentry are relegated or exalted to the status of useless figureheads who have no use in the real rough-and-tumble world. It is possible to see these plays as a satirical comment on the nature and usefulness of conventional Victorian morality, which Boucicault ignored in his own life. Our heroes are fine examples of the Rugby sort of virtues, who cannot do a dishonourable thing, even to save their lives. They seem to be held up for admiration, an affirmation of the manly virtues of honour and truth, but these are demonstrated, in the plays, to be dependent on cunning and deceit, which their subordinates have to apply in such a way as to leave their masters unsullied and ignorant of how it is done.

The subtext is that, though still a very attractive class, they have become useless except as an ornament. The struggle is, prophetically, between the proletariat and the bourgeoisie, with the Ascendancy as the king in this chess game, with severely limited mobility and power, but providing the necessary reference point. This sense of the gentry as ornamental outlived the potency, and outlasted the existence, of the class itself. It is the aspect that still attracted the characters in the plays of M.J. Molloy, Ooshla in *The Paddy Pedlar*, or Sanbatch in *The Wood of the Whispering*, and caused them to lament, almost surreptitiously, the passing of an oppressive system. All that is left to them is 'a miserable bare country with all its fine mansions and woods destroyed'.[23] A similar benevolent miasma hangs over Boucicault's Irish plays. A radiance is felt by all below them to emanate from the Ascendancy. In the peasantry it enkindles a sort of pathological loyalty – the great virtue of melodrama – and in the bourgeoisie a passionate desire to become like them.

In all these plays the theme of the indissoluble link between the Ascendancy and its followers is established. Loyalty is imprinted at birth; the image is used of a dog following at its master's heel: 'Ay, as the ragged dog at your heels is faithful and true to you, so you have been to me, my dear, devoted, loving playfellow – my wild companion.'[24] It is at one level an Ascendancy fantasy, a necessary fiction articulating their importance and their emotional ties to the people. They cannot realize that the ties are more economic and social than emotional, nor do they grasp the fact that their followers are a good deal smarter and more capable of living in the world than they are, that their 'dogs' are the facilitator of their lives, not their followers at all.

Sometimes a reason is given, like Danny Mann's accident in *The Colleen Bawn* with its oddly reversed result: instead of breaking the bond, it strengthened and made it obsessive, like a broken leg set stronger than before, but crooked. Sometimes, as in Michael Dwyer's following of Emmet, it is just the natural order. 'Sure I'm only a dog at your heel, to watch for your bidding, and do it without axin' why.'[25] There is a pattern in the plays that this loyalty is imprinted when they were children together – the Shaughraun and Ffolliott, Cregan and

Danny Mann – and Arrah Meelish invokes the custom of fosterage as its root: 'You were fostered under the old thatch itself, and if they took me and hung me to the dure-post beyant, sure my life 'ud be the only rint we ever paid the MacCoul for all the blessins we owe the ould family.'[26]

But the peasants stay at that carefree, childish level, while the gentry have solidified into manhood. Conn the Shaughraun, Myles na Coppaleen, Shaun the Post, Michael Dwyer, all retain the freshness of an immediate, spontaneous response to their world, the delight in living, singing, drinking and the pleasures of this life. In a further development of the duality so apparent in Irish plays of the eighteenth century, Boucicault invokes the idea of the divided self, a notion that fascinated him. The Victorian age, its theatre and literature, was obsessed with the mysteries of the mind. In the theatre these issues were addressed in the form of coincidence, clairvoyance and ghosts.[27] The idea of the *doppelganger* was a recurring one in the period, used by Dickens, Wilkie Collins, Robert Louis Stevenson and even Oscar Wilde, to explore the split personality, often at war with itself. Boucicault first used it in *The Corsican Brothers,* where the twins share the same consciousness, one single personality and mind – two characters played by the same actor. But he refined and honed it for the purposes of his Irish plays, and used it quite subtly. Progressing from *The Corsican Brothers,* he contrasted two sides of the same character in two separate but complementary characters on the stage. Danny Mann is the dark, twisted side of Hardress Cregan, Conn the Shaughraun is the roguish, tricky side of Ffolliott, Shaun the Post is the free aspect of O'Grady. The gentry have acquired the starched nobility; their *alter egos* have retained the freedom, ease and irresponsibility of their youth. The gentry have been moulded by the expectations of their society and education to their societal norm, while the peasants have been spared from acquiring the hard shell of respectability. Hardress Cregan is the only one who retains anything of his boyhood spontaneity; he fired Danny Mann off a cliff in a fit of temper when he was young and there is a twist in him still, though it is kept in check by the demands of honour. The men the gentry have become are less than adequate; they are half-men and half-automatons created by their environment and training. Each of them has had erected around him a scaffolding of values that holds him in place, and which usually negates the urgings of good sense and personal feeling. Ffolliott is a gullible, noble fool, Cregan a cowardly philanderer, Emmet a masterly incompetent and O'Grady a prisoner of his position in society.

In Boucicault's exploration of psychological affinities in *The Colleen*

Bawn, Danny Mann functions as the buried side of Cregan, prone to violence and the indulgence of his whims, an incarnation of Cregan's violent id. He is Cregan's twisted, crippled, inner being, a projection of the unacceptable and unacknowledged nether self of the Victorian gentleman, much as the layers of deceit enfolding Algernon and Jack in *The Importance of Being Earnest* suggest their scandalous and unmentionable social lives.

Kyrle Daly alerts us to the duality of Mann/Cregan at the start of *The Colleen Bawn*: 'That fellow,' he observes, 'is like your shadow.'[28] Danny Mann plays with the fact that the shadow is crippled and the man himself an 'illigant gentleman'.[29] The point is emphasized that the 'illigant gentleman' and his crippled shadow are bound together by a chain of guilt, pain and deformity: 'And he never *shall* leave me. Ten years ago he was a fine boy – we were foster-brothers and playmates –in a moment of passion, while we were struggling, I flung him from me from the gap rock into the reeks below, and thus he was maimed for life.'[30] Cregan is capable of extreme violence, but also of repenting the injury he has done, lamenting over Danny like a mother over a lost child – 'if ye'd seen him nursin' me for months, and cryin' over me, and keenin',[31] – which prefigures the line of action in the play.

Cregan's dark side is made manifest on the stage in Act II, Scene 1, by way of a soliloquy for two voices. We are given a dialogue between Cregan and his worse self, Danny Mann, and for that time both voices blend into one, spiralling round the central problem. Cregan wants his wife removed, but is not prepared to think the thought, speak the words or do the necessary deed, but he knows what has to be done. Danny matches his thinking to Cregan's and articulates the inexpressible for him, but the honourable part of Cregan is appalled and forbids it. A perfected gentleman would not even recognize the possibility, but Cregan does, and acknowledges that he himself, in his overt desperation, has planted the idea in Danny's mind:

> HARDRESS Oh! What a giddy fool I've been. What would I give to recall this fatal act which bars my fortune? [...] I was a fool when I refused to listen to you at the chapel of Castle Island. [...] I was mad to marry her.
>
> DANNY   I knew she was no wife for you. A poor thing widout manners or money or book larnin'. [...]Wouldn't she untie the knot her self – couldn't ye coax her? [...] Is that her love for you? You that gave up the devil an' all for her. What's her ruin to yours? [...] Don't I pluck a shamrock and wear it a day for the glory of St Patrick, and then throw it away when it's gone by my likin'[...]

HARDRESS [...] She would have yielded ,but –

DANNY   Pay her passage out to Quaybec, and put her aboard a three-master widout sayin' a word. [...]

HARDRESS If she still possesses that certificate – the proof of my first marriage ? how can I wed another? Commit bigamy? – disgrace my wife ? bastardize my children!

DANNY   I'd do by Eily as with the glove there on yer hand; make it come off, as it come on – an' if it fits too tight, take the knife to it.

HARDRESS [...] Monster! Am I so vile that you dare to whisper such a thought.[32]

Mann commits the murder, as he thinks, and becomes afflicted by guilt, as by a Greek Fury, and Cregan cannot escape either. He suffers remorse for the thought, while Mann suffers the guilt of the deed. 'It isn't in your body where the hurt is; the wound is in your poor sowl – there's all the harrum,' says his mother.[33] While Cregan cries, evoking the Fury again: 'My love for her, wild and maddened, has come back upon my heart like a vengeance.'[34] This play was written in 1860, thirty-two years before Freud published his first work, and stands as an excellent instance, if one were needed, of how art anticipates science in mapping the human psyche, and how a dramatist can express the deeper realities of human thought and experience, not through scientific measurement, but through observation, instinct and intuition.

This idea of balancing a character with its counterpart, or splitting the character in two, can be seen at work, in a more subdued way, in the other plays. In *Arrah-na-Pogue*, Shaun the Post is not the other side of Beamish MacCoul but of the O'Grady. O'Grady sees in the innate nobility with which Shaun defends and protects the woman he loves, and in his easy-going contempt for the law which O'Grady feels himself but can never express openly, the sort of person he would like to be but can never now become.

O'Grady is the most benevolent of Boucicault's Ascendancy creations. He means well and is, to a limited degree, effective. He identifies with the people but cannot save them from the authorities, of which he is a pillar, but having a foot in both camps proves ultimately useful. The day is saved, not by the cunning of the rogue, Shaun the Post, but by the good offices of his *alter ego*, the O'Grady, acting in tandem with other benevolent authorities. O'Grady is sympathetic, but he is ultimately a figure of fun, shown as a man trapped in the web spun by his position, which will not allow him to act according to what he sees is right, whose strings are pulled by the controlling authorities. 'I'll fight him for it, if you like; but when you ask me to take legal means of righting myself, you forget I am an Irish gentleman, and not a process-server,' he says.[35] A strange statement coming from someone whose position it is to uphold and apply the law.

Concerns about the law and its value run all through Boucicault's Irish plays. As well as treating of the law of property and the title to land, this runs at a metaphoric level as well. The O'Grady indignantly refuses to go to law to get Fanny Power: 'You would make me serve a writ of ejectment on my rival, that I may enjoy his property in this lady.'[36] In *Arrah-na-Pogue* the law is brought into disrepute by having an agent like Feeny, whom any decent man would kick from his door,[36] and the entire court scene is designed to show the law as an ass. The law always gets it wrong, and it has to be put right in out-lawish fashion.

The law is always seen as oppressive, an alien concept lashed to the back of an uncomprehending people; the court scene points up what complete nonsense it is, how irrelevant and incomprehensible to those on the receiving end. In all Boucicault's Irish plays, the law is a malign force, and justice is done and right vindicated by circumventing it. It follows then that the appliers and upholders of this law are oppressors, but these appliers are the very gentry who are the heroes of the plays, who cannot be shown in such an unsympathetic light. In order to put a layer of insulation between them and the people, Boucicault puts in an agent.[37] In *Arrah-na-Pogue*, it is Feeny, the process-server, who slyly reminds O'Grady who and what he is and who is responsible for his existence – members of O'Grady's own class: 'I'm only a tool, sir, in my employer's hands, and sixteen shillins a week is all I get for my dirty work.'[38] Likewise, in the other plays, the authorities are not given their real faces but those of middlemen, the ambitious mercantile middle classes, who are prepared to get dirty in pursuit of gain, and not those of the gentry, who retain their pristine honour, but reap the profits in silence.

One of the more unappealing traits of Hardress Cregan is his assumption that the law does not apply to him. He does his best to obtain the marriage licence from Eily by prating of her being 'content with the shelter of my heart',[39] and is only stopped from bigamy by Myles na Copalleen, who tweaks him with the truth, and suffers Cregan's fury and guilty conscience: 'Vagabond! Outcast! Jailbird! Dare you prate of honour to me!'[40] The point is repeatedly made that the law is not meant for the gentry. Cregan is not alone in showing that they consider themselves above it. They treat Corrigan, the magistrate, with contempt and throw him into the horsepond for daring to suspect a gentleman, although the audience has been made well aware that the same gentleman is perfectly capable of crime, from murder to bigamy.

To the gentleman, honour is more rigid and unbreakable than the law. The Ascendancy women in the plays are not so confined by the armour of honour and consequently, they are more malleable, more inclined to bend the constraints they find placed on them. In the matter of the law, or of telling the truth, they do not scruple to twist it to their ends. They are more prepared to make things happen than the men, who spend their time reacting to events. Mrs Cregan, in *The Colleen Bawn*, is a woman who is prepared to do anything to save her estates and her son:

ANNE   He is not guilty.
MRS CREGAN   What's that to me woman? I am his mother – the hunters
    are after my blood.[41]

The other women of the upper class are also ready to defend what they hold dear without being too scrupulous. Sarah Curran disperses the mob from Emmet's house by being decidedly economical with the truth: 'My father, John Philpot Curran, is here; he came in that carriage to see me; he will return home in it.'[42] She doesn't exactly tell a lie but she omits the crucial fact of the case, that Lord Norbury, whom the crowd is looking for, came with her father and is currently in the house.

Anne Chute in *The Colleen Bawn*, and Claire Ffolliott in *The Shaughraun*, are examples of the high-spirited Irish gentrywoman that Boucicault and his audience obviously liked a lot. The leading peasant women tend to droop, but these Ascendancy women are movers. They push the plot along by their own skills, brains and wiles; they are the successors to the resourceful Restoration heroines, who do not just sit around and wait for things to turn out right, or for the men to come and save them. Anne Chute is the one who stands up to Corrigan and his policemen and bedamned to the consequences: 'Gentlemen, come on, there was a time in Ireland when neither king nor faction could call on Castle Chute without a bloody welcome. [...] His life's in danger, and if I can't love him, I'll fight for him, and that's more than any of you men can do.'[43]

Claire Ffolliott is the best example of the strong Ascendancy female. She enjoys baiting Captain Molineux and firing his beefy English prejudices back at him, deliberately mispronouncing his name, and explaining to him the political meaning of the picturesque landscape. She has the flexibility that Boucicault allows his female characters, and she succeeds in sinking her honour in necessity long enough to draw Molineux off the scent of her brother, even though 'the blood [...] revolts in my heart against what I am doing'.[44] She looks on it as playing a part, which she was also doing at the start of the play, a recurring activity of the Ascendancy in drama. She is willing to fight for what she wants, and has a poor opinion of the value of the men around her: 'Oh, I wish I was a man. I wouldn't give him up without a fight.'[45] Most startling of all, though never openly alluded to, is the fact that she is perfectly prepared to break the law, and appears to have persuaded Molineux to participate in the crime. Somebody lights the beacon on the head to summon the boat for Ffolliott, and the only people there at the time were Claire and Molineux. The only other possible explanation is that the landscape decided to take a hand in the plot and lit the beacon itself....

To the women and to the peasants, the law is, like the men, something of an ass, to be ignored or circumvented where necessary, to be bent into a shape more accommodating to their personal needs. To them, the personal is always more important than the political. It is at its most obvious in *Robert Emmet*: 'You have no fortune but my love,' says Sarah Curran. 'You cannot be bankrupt there; you have no home but my heart; no country but my arms.'[46] Emmet disagrees: 'He who undertakes the business of a people should have none of his own.'[47] But after things go badly wrong for his rebellion, he abandons the idea of the political and embraces the personal: 'I have slighted your love for a wanton infatuation! My other love has betrayed and deserted me; I come to you for forgiveness, for comfort and for peace.'[48]

The political content of the plays is muted and generalized; Boucicault's three best-known Irish plays do not focus directly on contemporary politics. At the beginning of *The Shaughraun*, Claire Ffolliott invokes the Wrongs of Ireland to discomfit Molineux, but it is more of a picturesque backdrop than a felt present oppression – that comes from the economic war being waged on them by Kinchela. The movement in all the plays is towards reconciliation. For all of his singing of 'The Wearing of the Green', Boucicault did not, at this stage, advocate any radical action to break the link with England. The political content is carefully non-specific, avoiding offence to the English while catching the Americans; there is much talk of 'my country', 'honour', 'independence' and 'freedom'[49] but it is abstract and non-directed. There is no doubting Boucicault's national feeling but it is not nationalistic, not anti-English, nor is it anti-Crown – Emmet is sensible of the King's graciousness in granting him clemency, but regretfully cannot accept it.[50]

It is surprising to find at the centre of these plays, as in much later Irish drama, the question of land and its ownership. The difference here is that land is shown as an aristocratic concern; it was the basis of their existence, wealth, domination and survival, and the plays of Boucicault show that foundation being threatened from below by a rising bourgeoisie, who show every sign of taking the land away from them, or will only allow them to keep it if they swallow their pride and accept the upstarts into their society by marrying them.

This is the root of the conflict between Corrigan and the Cregans in *The Colleen Bawn*. The Cregans are filled with pride, hypocrisy and self-blindness. They have 'the proud blood of the Cregans',[51] and are united in their detestation of Corrigan. To Mrs Cregan he is 'what the people here call a middle-man – vulgarly polite, and impudently obsequious'.[52] To Hardress, he is 'Genus squireen – a half-sir, and a whole scoundrel' and, even to Anne Chute, he is 'a potato on a silver plate'.[53] All these attitudes are not dissimilar to those of Lady Gregory, Yeats and Synge in their detestation of the rising middle class – 'an ungodly ruck of fat-faced, sweaty-headed swine'.[54] They are condemning Corrigan for his tendency to rise in the world at their expense, and to inhabit the same space and breathe the same air as they do. Their surface attractiveness puts us on their side, and Corrigan's villainous scheming is deeply offensive. The assembled Ascendancy throw him symbolically in the horsepond for daring to question them, and the audience is meant to approve. Yet the relative attractiveness of the characters blinds us as to who is right on this occasion; Corrigan was only, as a magistrate, trying to bring a murderer to justice, and that should have been approved of by the assembled gentry. The fact that Cregan is a gentleman is enough to acquit him in the eyes of the rest of the gentry; he does not even have to deny it.[55] Yet Cregan had been living a lie for years in being married to Eily, and was perfectly capable of going through with a bigamous marriage. Why should he baulk at murder? In fact, as an Irish audience would be well aware, in the crime that lies at the base of the play, John Scanlan, a gentleman of Limerick, did in fact murder his mistress in order to marry a rich heiress, and was hanged for it, along with his boatman, in spite of being defended by Daniel O'Connell. The case was a *cause célèbre* in 1820, only forty years before *The Colleen Bawn* was written, and had been kept alive in the public imagination by Gerald Griffin's novel, *The Collegians*, and a couple of previous stage adaptations. The judge who tried the case ordered that Scanlan be executed immediately before his family could intervene:

> The following August he was tried at the assizes; and, being found guilty, Baron Smith, to his immortal honour, ordered him for almost instant execution, lest the powerful interest of his family should procure him a

respite, if he left him the period usually allowed to criminals convicted of a murder. The time allotted Scanlan to live was too short to admit a messenger going to Dublin and back again, and consequently he was executed, to the satisfaction of all lovers of justice.[56]

This entry from the Newgate Calendar adds a different dimension to the mad dash to Dublin to procure the pardon of Shaun the Post in *Arrah-na-Pogue*. That was a gallop to rescue an innocent, but it was usually a dash to save the guilty. The judge's fears show how likely, and common, such a procedure was: distressed parents pleading for their profligate sons to others of their own class – again, a separate law for the gentry.

Mrs Cregan is shown to be quite capable of kidnap at least, and possibly murder,[57] in order to preserve the estate which has been encumbered by her husband's extravagance. She has the Ascendancy pride and ruthlessness in abundance, and that is what Corrigan lusts after, 'Proud as Lady Beelzebub, and as grand as a queen', he gloats.[58] She is perfectly prepared to sacrifice her son to a loveless marriage to save the estate, but to countenance a marriage with Corrigan would be a class betrayal.

If marriage is proposed by Corrigan, then there must be no religious obstacle. This is a Utopian scenario, and a dramatic fiction that could hardly obtain in fact. There would be great religious and racial obstacles as well as class difficulties. Lennox Robinson faced up to this in *Killycregs in Twilight*; Boucicault did not. Corrigan feels the fatal attractiveness of the Ascendancy: he does not want to get rid of them, he does not want to reform them; he wants to join them. But, unlike most of those who come into contact with the gentry, he sees himself in a position to do so. Their contempt and outrage does nothing to diminish his ardour: 'Insolent wretch! My son shall answer and chastise you.'[59] 'Contemptible hound, I loath and despise you!,'[60] Mrs Cregan cries, and Hardress spouts: 'I'll tear that dog's tongue from his throat that dared insult you with the offer.'[61] But no matter how hard they kick him Corrigan hangs on to his dream of becoming one of them. This does not blind him to the dual standards they apply, and the mention of the Colleen Bawn allows him to point out the hypocrisy of Mrs Cregan's position:

MRS CREGAN   And you would buy my aversion and disgust!
CORRIGAN   Just as Anne Chute buys your son, if she knew but all. Can he love his girl beyant, widout haten this heiress he's obliged to swallow?[62]

Mrs Cregan may be a virago but she is also a pragmatist. Her prime objective is the preservation of the Cregan estate and name, and she is prepared to marry Corrigan herself as a last resort: 'I must accept this man only to give you and yours a shelter.'[63] In the play, the marriage dance is danced to the music of love, whereas, in reality, the gentry were prepared to open their ranks to the *nouveaux riches* if they had enough money, decent manners and no obviously offensive relations. Corrigan's problem is that he lacks the second requirement. Love had little to do with it. The attitude that love will find a way was a mid-nineteenth century melodramatic convention, not a matrimonial reality.

Boucicault's three Irish comedies are not melodramas, but they do have melodramatic elements and themes. One of the most striking such tropes is that of economic persecution: the villain has some economic hold over the heroine and uses it to make her yield to his desires. The villain is usually an unscrupulous member of the Establishment, and the heroine an ethical proletarian, caught between necessity and honour. Boucicault reverses the pattern by making the oppressing villain a bourgeois capitalist persecuting an upper-class heroine, and skews it further by making him almost a clown. The threat, though cloaked in comedy, is none the less real.

Kinchela, in *The Shaughraun*, is a perfect Boucicault bourgeois villain – grasping, greedy, unscrupulous, eager to abuse his power and the law to gain his own ends. His loyalty is exactly that described by Shaw in the Preface to *John Bull's Other Island*: 'There is no such thing as genuine loyalty in Ireland. [...] It is simply exploitation of English rule in the interests of property, power and promotion.'[64] Kinchela pursues his own selfish ends: 'Robert Ffolliott pardoned, and afther all the throuble I took to get him convicted? And this is the way a loyal man is thrated! I am betrayed.'[65] He exploits the system at the liminal point where the power of the landed gentry is failing but no new power has arisen to take its place. It is a time of unrecognized revolution, and Kinchela is an unconscious revolutionary. In fact, he *is* the new power, the power of bourgeois capital, just as Corrigan is in *The Colleen Bawn*. They already have the wealth and are moving to consolidate their position by using it to squeeze more concessions out of the existing Ascendancy; they are putting them under economic siege.

These rising squireens of the bourgeoisie are infatuated by the Ascendancy; they dream of marrying into them, of forcing their way in if they have to, using their wealth and economic domination as a battering ram. Corrigan tries it in *The Colleen Bawn* when he attempts to buy Mrs Cregan; Kinchela targets and tries to kidnap Arte O'Neil in

The Shaughraun. The gentry's response is always one of horrified out-rage that these minions could even think of such a thing, and they kick them out of the house; yet it is obvious enough, from a class and com-mercial point of view, that it makes perfect sense – the union of new money with old prestige to produce a new ruling class. That the Ascendancy rejected the proposition was a large part of their isolation and downfall. It is also possible that Boucicault was observing that the Irish gentry were not as flexible in their survival skills as their English counterparts. He was, in his way, delineating the shape of the middle-class revolution. The social attractiveness of the Ascendancy was no match for the commercial skill of the bourgeoisie. The Ascendancy lived, for the most part, bedazzled by their own importance, confident of their status as the rarefied, exalted, untouchable, worshipped heroes of their own performance. The antics and ambitions of clowns like Kinchella and Corrigan struck them as a source of outrage or amuse-ment. They did not realize, any more than did Chekhov's aristocrats, that these upstarts were the future rulers of the world.

By the time Boucicault was writing these plays in the final third of the nineteenth century, the participation of the Ascendancy in the the-atre had shrunk to almost nothing. We have come a long way from the late seventeenth century, when Roger Boyle, the Earl of Orrery, was initiating the Heroic movement in English with plays and novels that admitted no characters except the aristocracy, and endowed them with behaviour and dialogue of impossible heroism and nobility. In com-parison with that, Boucicault's Ascendancy figures have a decidedly democratic look; there is not an Earl, a Lord or a Baronet to be seen, and their behaviour when they reach for the heroic is markedly unsuc-cessful: reality always scuppers them. There are also two other strata to be dealt with now that Orrery would not have allowed past the stage door: the crafty, lively peasants who rescue the aristocracy from their difficulties, and the scheming, ambitious middle class who are set to undermine the gentry and take their place. That the alliance of Ascendancy and peasants defeats the bourgeois villain in each play ensures a happy ending, but it can be only a temporary respite. The assistance of the lower orders is seen by the gentry as a natural and deserved loyalty and esteem, an affirmation of their own worth, but it can equally be taken that the threatened downfall of the Big House threatens the stability of the peasant world, and action taken to shore it up also preserves the peasants' way of life. The back-stairs bargain that sustained both of them is threatened by the victory of the middle class; it was always the bourgeoisie that overthrew the ruling class.

The upturning final dénouements of the plays do not ring as true as the body of the plot; the difficulties are a lot more convincing than the solutions. While Boucicault shows the Ascendancy mostly as attractive characters, the plays cut away at the root of their society, showing it in imminent danger of collapse. He shows that the law that holds aristocratic society together and keeps the Ascendancy in possession of its privileges does so by cynically excusing it from its strictures, while at the same time oppressing the lower classes. The peasants may be oppressed legally but are shown to be far more vibrant and full of life than their hide-bound masters.

One of the most surprising things about these plays is that they show how the Ascendancy, far from being secure in its holdings, is under constant threat of dispossession, not by nationalist but by economic revolution. They may succeed in narrowly avoiding disaster, rather than averting it, but as they are the architects of their own misfortune, they are certain to come under further threats. Only a fortunate conjunction of their women and peasants saves them, but what will happen if the peasants turn against them? Boucicault's plays show peasant and gentry united in intention and action. Michael Davitt and the Land League were about to change all that.

NOTES AND REFERENCES

1. Dion Boucicault, *The Shaughraun*, I. 1, in *Selected Plays of Dion Boucicault*, ed. by 2. Andrew Parkin, Irish Drama Selection 4 (Gerrard's Cross, Buckinghamshire: Colin Smyth, 1987; Washington D.C: Catholic University of America Press, 1987), p. 263.
2. *Ibid.*, I. 2, p. 268.
3. *Ibid.*, I. 1, p. 265.
4. *Ibid.*, stage directions for I. 1, p. 259.
5. *Ibid.*, I. 1. p. 261.
6. Boucicault, *Arrah-na-Pogue*, stage direction, I. 1, in *The Dolmen Boucicault*, ed. by David Krause (Dublin: Dolmen Press, 1964), p. 113.
7. Boucicault, *The Colleen Bawn*, I. 3, p. 209.
8. *Ibid.*, I. 3, p. 207.
9. *Ibid.*, II. 2, p. 216.
10. *Ibid.*, II. 2, p. 220.[my italics]
11. Lecky, I, p. 28: 'Every man's enjoyment of his property became precarious, and the natives learned with terror that law could be made in a time of perfect peace, and without any provocation being given, a not less terrible instrument than the sword for rooting them out of the soil.'
12. David Krause, 'The Theatre of Dion Boucicault: a Short View of His Life and Art', in *The Dolmen Boucicault*, p. 26.
13. Boucicault, *Robert Emmet*, III. 2, p. 369, in *Selected Plays of Dion Boucicault*, ed. by Andrew Parkin.
14. *Ibid.*, II. 5, p. 365.
15. Boucicault, *Arrah-na-Pogue*, I. 4, p. 131.
16. Krause, 'The Theatre of Dion Boucicault', in *The Dolmen Boucicault*, p. 34.
17. Boucicault, *The Shaughraun*, II. 3, p. 294.
18. *Ibid.*, I. 1. p. 262.

19. Boucicault, *Arrah-na-Pogue*, II. 4, p. 154.
20. *Ibid.*, II. 4, p. 153.
21. *Ibid.*, I. 4, p. 135.
22. *Ibid.*, II. 2, p. 140.
23. M.J. Molloy, *The Wood of the Whispering* (Dublin: Progress House Publications, 1961), p. 34
24. Boucicault, *The Shaughraun*, II. 3, p. 295.
25. Boucicault, *Robert Emmet*, III. 2, p. 370.
26. *Arrah-na-Pogue*, I. 2, p. 121.
27. *The Sunday Times Magazine*, 18/09/2005, p. 3: On 11 October, 1864, Ira and William Davenport, two American mediums, held the first séance of their sensational British tour in Boucicault's house, 326 Regent St, London. The audience included high-ranking members of the armed forces, the government and the Church; the stunts included musical instruments playing by themselves, detached hands flying around and caressing the attendants, lights moving of their own volition and ghostly voices. It was one of the first manifestations of the cult of spiritualism that later swept the country.
28. Boucicault, *The Colleen Bawn*, I. 1. p. 193.
29. *Ibid.*, p. 193.
30. *Ibid.*, p. 193.
31. *Ibid.*, p. 194.
32. *Ibid.*, II. 1, p. 213.
33. *Ibid.*, III. 1, p. 234.
34. *Ibid.*, III. 5, p. 245.
35. Boucicault, *Arrah-na-Pogue*, III. 1, p. 161.
36. *Ibid.*, III. 1, p. 161.
37. *Ibid.*, I. 3, p. 128.
38. *Ibid.*, I. 3, p. 130.
39. Boucicault, *The Colleen Bawn*, I. 3. p. 210.
40. *Ibid.*, I. 3, p. 211.
41. *Ibid.*, III. 5, p. 246.
42. Boucicault, *Robert Emmet*, II. 5, p. 363.
43. Boucicault, *The Colleen Bawn*, III. 5, p. 246.
44. Boucicault, *The Shaughraun*, II. 7, p. 306.
45. *Ibid.*, I. 4, p. 279.
46. Boucicault, *Robert Emmet*, I. 1, p. 336.
47. *Ibid.*, I. 2, p. 341.
48. *Ibid.*, III. 4, p. 376.
49. *Ibid.*, IV. 2, p. 387.
50. *Ibid.*, IV. 2, p. 387.
51. Boucicault, *The Colleen Bawn*, I. 1, p.195.
52. *Ibid.*, I. 1, p. 195.
53. *Ibid.*, I. 1, p. 195.
54. J.M. Synge, letter to Stephen MacKenna, in Ann Saddlemyer, 'The Mature Yeats', in *Irish Renaissance*, ed. by Robin Skelton and David R. Clark (Dublin: The Dolmen Press, 1965), p. 74.
55. Boucicault, *The Colleen Bawn*, III. 5, p. 248.
56. G.T. Crook, 'John Scanlan and Stephen Sullivan, *The Murderers of the Colleen Bawn*,' in *The Complete Newgate Calendar*, Tarlton Law Library, Law in Popular Culture (London: Navarre Society Ltd, 1926). www. tarlton.law.utexas.edu [accessed 8/10/2002] (p. 3 of 3).
57. Boucicault, *The Colleen Bawn*, II. 2, p. 220.
58. *Ibid.*, I. 1, p. 196.
59. *Ibid.*, I. 1, p. 197.
60. *Ibid.*, I. 1, p. 197.
61. *Ibid.*, I. 1, p. 198.
62. *Ibid.*, I. 1, p. 197.
63. *Ibid.*, II. 2, p. 218.
64. George Bernard Shaw: 'Preface for Politicians', in *John Bull's Other Island, and Major Barbara: also How He Lied to Her Husband* (London: Constable, 1930), p. xxiii.
65. Boucicault, *The Shaughraun*, III. 3, p. 321.

9

'Opening the Future': The Politicization of Irish Melodrama

The dominance and popularity of Boucicault in the Irish theatre led directly to the creation of a whole genre of plays in *hommage* to his work, but which used real figures from Irish history rather than the fictional characters he usually created. When the playwrights of the Queen's Theatre – Whitbread, O'Grady, Bourke, or Allen – grew tired of reviving Boucicault, they took to writing their own plays, using his as a template. There were so many productions of Boucicault's Irish Trilogy that the plays became deformed. Richard Pine blames Whitbread for the degeneration: 'Boucicault', he complains, 'together with the "Stage Irishman" he had portrayed so faithfully, and melodrama as a genre, unfairly became objects of derision, symbols of vulgarity.'[1] Unfairly, he notes, because this was the viewpoint of the elitist theatre movement; the plays continued to delight the vulgar with their immediacy and theatricality. Whitbread's productions were somewhat to blame for the genre's reputation, though. He broadened and coarsened the humour in Boucicault, accentuated the sentimentality and boosted the 'sensation' scenes; he then created his own plays in this coarser style. He took Irish historical figures, such as Wolfe Tone or Lord Edward Fitzgerald, and pressed them into the mould of melodrama where they solidified into romantic heroes. Many of these plays dealt with the rebellion of 1798, and owed a great deal to popular ballads, in which the folk memory of the rebellion was preserved and encoded; the first precursor of the genre, Samuel Lover's *Rory O'More* (1830), was based directly on the ballad of the same name, but the simplicity, clarity and partisanship of the ballad form inspired them all.

The genre of Nationalist Melodrama was already sprouting furtively in Boucicault's three most popular Irish plays, and in *The O'Dowd* he manoeuvred closer to an open political statement on stage. He mistakenly thought this was one of his best works, and kept tinkering with it in the hope of having it recognized as such. Its earliest incarnation pre-dated *The Shaughraun* by a year, but the version titled *The O'Dowd* dates from the production of 1880.[2] It has good scenes, contains some fine characterization, snappy dialogue and good parts for character actors, but it misses the fine balance of sentiment, pathos, comedy, romance and excitement that his best plays contain, and the climax is created from a purely visual spectacle of a shipwreck that anticipates the arrival of film – almost without dialogue but with lots of sound, action and special effects. What is noteworthy in the play is the sharpening of the politics; he managed to get political concerns on to the stage, and kept them there by making them central to the plot. Boucicault's analysis was economic; there was no sense of a separatist or republican agenda, rather a call for a stop to the haemorrhaging of Irish wealth and resources, for which, clearly but indirectly, he blamed the landlords.

In Act I, Romsey Leake, the cockney moneylender, engages Daddy O'Dowd in an exchange on Irish farmers that manages to criticize the failure by landlords to re-invest their rents, sideswipe at the draining away of productive resources, and support the Land League's campaign to create a country of peasant proprietors:

> ROMSEY   I know you Irish farmers are not to be judged by the coat on your backs. You make a poor show, for fear the landlord should raise the rent on you. Eh?
>
> DADDY   I'm my own landlord, sir. I wish every Irish farmer could say the same.
>
> ROMSEY   I thought you Irish were so poor.
>
> DADDY   So we are, God help us – poor as a milch cow, whose milk goes to market, and whose calves are took away.
>
> ROMSEY   But you are rich?
>
> DADDY   Because I was my own master, working wid all my heart for my own flesh and blood, so I never measured my labour by the hour, but by my hopes. What I saw before me was a life – and not a week's wages.[3]

The political element cannot be excluded as Act III actually features an election rally. The election is fought between young Mike O'Dowd and Colonel Muldoon, who previously owned the seat as the land-lords' representative, but whose electors have 'revolted'[4] and put up young O'Dowd as an anti-landlord candidate.

Boucicault craftily used music and stagecraft to circumvent the censor. Muldoon's landlord party enters with a band playing '*Croppies lie down*', while the O'Dowd side is played in with '*Garry Owen*', the marching tune of the Irish regiments in the British army. Colonel Muldoon is described as 'the castle hack', and comes in escorted by the police; Mike O'Dowd makes his entrance surrounded by the fashionable ladies from London who have come to Galway to canvass for him.[5]

At the hustings, Muldoon appeals to the crowd by speaking of his landlord family, which provokes jeers and good-humoured taunting. Mike O'Dowd responds with a poem commenting acidly on the virulent parasitism of the Ascendancy that would have slotted easily into O'Keeffe's *Le Grenadier*: 'Unhappy land, to hastening ills a prey, / Where few grow rich and multitudes decay'.[6] But, unfortunately, Mike is as much a parasite on his father's fortune, and his profligacy in London catches up with him, causing the O'Dowds to be ousted from their house and lands by Leake the moneylender. This introduces the theme of eviction, dispossession and mystical union with the land that also runs through *The Shaughraun*. Leake and his crony Chalker take possession of Suilamore, but the new owners are boycotted by the entire population, rejected by the estate itself, and trapped economically. When Leake speaks in the last act it is with the voice and lamentation of a nineteenth-century Irish landlord: 'Oh, if I could sell Suilamore and get out of the country, but there is a blight on the land. All I have is in the place – and there I am in a prison, with every man and woman in the country as my gaoler.'[7] As in *The Shaughraun*, where the ancestral estate of the Ffolliotts, Suilabeg, behaves as a living organism and rejects any foreign bodies that attempt to take it over, Leake in *The O'Dowd* acknowledges that the land of the O'Dowds, Suilamore, has turned against the usurper:

> LEAKE   You have your revenge; you sowed your curses on the land, and they have come up. The tenants have left their holdings; ruin and weeds are growing up and choking the lands and house of Suilamore no one dares to buy the place and I dare not leave it.[8]

This could be taken as a comment on the plight of the landlord class in the 1880s: they are not wanted, can't manage, but won't leave. As a result the country is in a state of terminal decay.

The O'Dowd lasted for four weeks in London in 1880, but was taken off because audiences found its views on Irish politics unacceptable.[9] Normally Boucicault bowed to audience demands; he regarded them as his masters, and even changed the end of *The Octoroon* to save the heroine and appease the abolitionist English audience. But in this case he stood firm. He inserted a notice in the papers declaring that he could not remove the political content without destroying the play:

> Mr. Boucicault regrets to perceive that certain scenes in his new play, *The O'Dowd*, continue to provoke expressions of displeasure from a portion of the audience. He has no wish to offend anyone. He is informed of a general opinion that the censured scenes are ill-timed, and ought to be omitted or their language changed. If the public will kindly refer to the announcement with which the production of *The O'Dowd* was prefaced, it will be seen that the features objected to are essential to the design and intent of the work. It is, therefore, in no captious spirit the author declines to alter it; but rather than lose the favour of any of his audience he will amend his error by withdrawing the play altogether.[10]

In his pamphlet *The Fireside Story of Ireland* (1880) Boucicault again called for economic control by the Irish and proper management of the country's resources and wealth, a programme that reached back to the writings of Molyneux, Swift and the Irish Volunteers of the eighteenth century. In *The Fireside Story*, the general thrust of the historical melodrama emerged: scheming English villains, and pallid Irish victims of English villainy. There was a much sharper historical bite, but the line of reconciliation was still the one Boucicault pursued, by appealing to the English people over the heads of their governing class, during a period of proletarian discontent. The pamphlet was directed at, and distributed to, the patrons of the melodrama, and displayed a socialist mentality. Molin and Goodfellowe remark that 'if one knew nothing of Boucicault's success on the English stage, he would read the pamphlet as the straight-out work of an Irish patriot'.[11] But there are two elements in it that tie it to a melodramatist. The first is the casting of Ireland as a virtuous, friendless, lower-class female:

> The elder sisters of the British family seemed to regard her with indifference and contempt, as one fitted for a sordid life of servitude. Her story will show that she has been denied the education every other people has enjoyed; that she vainly besought to earn her own livelihood, but that was refused. Thus, like an untutored, neglected, ragged Cinderella, she has been confined in the out-house of Great Britain.[12]

The second is that this colourless but impeccably virtuous female is under economic assault by the evil members of the ruling class. The English working class, Boucicault was saying, would sympathize with her if they knew the dramatic facts of the case. Then they would see the connection between their own and Irish grievances.

This opposition to an evil and recalcitrant governing class and the call for radical solidarity puts Boucicault directly in a line with Knowles, with whom he was friendly as a young playwright in London, and of whom he speaks highly in his later writing.[13] As the Irish troubles caused fatalities in the streets of Manchester, and 'a fear was entertained that the working classes might sympathize, and ally themselves and their discontent with the Irish insurrectionary movement',[14] he finished with an appeal to the better nature of the English people over the heads of their corrupt rulers:

> But my task is not to comment: it is simply to record. I lay the story of Ireland before the English people, as an indictment against the Governing Class. I do it in the spirit of the statesman who thus compared the character of the people of England with the character of the class to which they had confided the administration of the country:
>> 'Never was there any country in which there was so much absence of public principle, and so many instances of private worth. [...] Yet among their profusion of private virtue, there is in the Governing Class a total want of public spirit, and the most deplorable contempt of public principle.'[15]

In *The Fireside Story of Ireland* Boucicault was putting into the public domain what he was not allowed to say on the stage. Even at this date, the censor was cutting remarks critical of landlords, the ruling class, or the government. The Lord Chamberlain's *Register of Plays* shows that as late as 1885 he was removing references to the evils of the landlord system, such as: 'more like one of those wicked landlords escaped from Ireland'; 'the wicked landlord system'; '...bloated toad of a landlord in parliament'.[16] Boucicault's criticism of the political system poked through in his earlier plays, but *The Fireside Story of Ireland*, with its melodramatic, villainous ruling class and wronged working-class Cinderella, was his attempt to bring the subtext to the surface for an American or an English audience, out of reach of the censor's knife.

But his analysis created a problem dramatically. Melodrama needs a clear-cut villain, and in English melodrama these are often aristocrats; but Boucicault had already cast his Irish Ascendancy figures in the role of equivocal heroes. He availed himself instead of those ready-made theatrical villains, the middlemen – the unlovely spectacle of the bourgeois *homo economicus* on the rise, what Maria Edgeworth described as 'the half-kind of gentleman, with a red silk handkerchief about his neck and a silver-handled whip in his hand',[17] who made excellent but vincible villains.

A patriotic melodrama also needs a hero, and Conn, Shaun and

Myles were too slight to bear the weight of the emergent ideology – they could not embody the articulate self-aware nationalism that was burgeoning in these plays. They could shout 'God save Ireland' and sing the patriotic songs that codified and spread the nationalist aspiration – 'politics in verse'[18] – but to carry credibly the full-blown eloquence of Irish aspirations needed an educated mouthpiece. Boucicault had in his creations of Beamish MacCoul and Robert Ffolliott endowed the Ascendancy men with an attractive foolishness, but in 1884 he broke new ground and created a new type of hero in Robert Emmet – a transgressing aristocrat, who resembled Knowles' heroes in opposing the verities of his class in favour of revolutionary change, but, with Boucicaultesque ambiguity, retained a foot in both camps. Such a hero was able to present Ireland's case in eloquent high rhetoric, without a trace of apology or brogue.

Dramatically speaking, however, *Robert Emmet* was a retrograde step: the political, social and economic concerns were subsumed into the personality and rhetoric of the hero, but Boucicault didn't write good heroes – unlike Knowles, he had no real interest in such figures, and it shows. The play only comes to life with the villains, informers and lowlifes. The character of Robert Emmet was written for Henry Irving, though he never played the part, and he would have fleshed it out, as nineteenth-century writers expected of their actors. But Boucicault had no very high opinion of Irving, considering him inadequate for the creation of characters that live long in the memory:

> There is only one stern question and true test that can be applied to the dramatist or to the actor, if we would determine the quality of his talents: what characters has he left as heirlooms to the stage and to dramatic literature? He can materialize to the future in that way alone. [...] Let us try to remember what important characters have been the outcome of the careers of the recent dynasties of Kean and Irving. We fail to remember one! These artists have not left one legacy to the *repertoire* of the drama with which their names can be associated.[19]

So that, while he was trying to make Emmet a character that would match the grandeur and nobility of the creations of James Sheridan Knowles – 'the greatest dramatic poet of our century', as Boucicault described him[20] – he had no belief either in his own ability to create such a transcendent figure nor of Irving's ability to 'materialize' it.

Emmet is a Knowlesian figure, the outlaw idealist, fired with a messianic zeal that combines the religious and the revolutionary:

EMMET   My friends – my countrymen! I go hence – to Dublin – alone,

and in this uniform – the badge of treason; I carry with me that flag
– the emblem of rebellion; I go with my life to redeem yours; to offer
my hands to the chains, my head to the executioner.[21]

He is the heroic titan around whose feet the puny people swarm. In
Emmet, Boucicault created the archetype of the Irish nationalist hero,
not just on the stage, but in popular apprehension. He is a moral, not
a real, figure, relentlessly virtuous (though a bit obtuse), the type of
moral protagonist that Knowles had made such use of, and who gives
to his plays and to the Nationalist Melodramas something of the flat
feeling of medieval morality plays. In the decades that followed, Lord
Edward Fitzgerald, Wolfe Tone, Henry Joy McCracken, Father
Murphy, Patrick Sarsfield and Michael Dwyer all conformed to the
dramatic template Boucicault created in Robert Emmet.

The economic analysis and demands that had pervaded the Irish
drama, though still evident in *Robert Emmet*, are of less importance
than political concerns, strung together on a line that advertises 'freedom', 'love of native land', 'green flag', 'helpless people whose one
hope is freedom'. There is little mention of the specific Irish grievances
that Boucicault had parlayed into his previous plays; the focus is on
abstractions, not unlike Knowles, such as country, freedom, honour
and flag, the tradition of sacrifice. There is no concrete enemy – the
Kafkaesque 'Castle' has become a ubiquitous shadowy threat with its
agents and informers – and there is no fire in the belly of the play, but
the figure of Emmet himself, though irritatingly foolish, proved seminal. He became, as the Irish Historical Hero, noble, eloquent, and sacrificial, the basis for the next generation of Irish plays, the Irish
Nationalist Melodrama, a genre brought to fruition by J.W. Whitbread,
playwright and manager of the Queen's Theatre, Dublin, towards the
end of the nineteenth century.

Whitbread was an Englishman who took over the management of the
Queen's Royal Theatre in 1884. At the beginning of his reign,
Whitbread staged revivals of popular Irish plays by Boucicault,
Falconer and Buckstone, and, observing the reaction to the nationalist
elements in Boucicault's plays, he recognized the commercial potential
of theatrical Irish patriotism. Between 1886 and 1906 Whitbread
wrote fourteen Irish plays for the Queen's that were also hugely popular in other theatres around Ireland and with the Irish diaspora. They
too pushed away from a bourgeois concern with economics towards
abstract values such as honour, fidelity or sacrifice, the sort of values
that were percolating from ancient Irish myth and legend that also

inspired the aristocratic exponents of the Literary Revival, in particular its founder, Standish James O'Grady.

Whitbread wrote three successful plays on Irish historical themes before the looming centenary of 1798 and the newly published exposé of the infiltration and betrayal that undermined the United Irishmen, W.J. Fitzpatrick's book, *Irish Secret Service under Pitt*, inspired him to create a play around Lord Edward Fitzgerald.[22] Lord Edward is a dramatic twin of Boucicault's Robert Emmet. He is a transgressing aristocrat, who, like Emmet or the heroes of Knowles' plays, is an idealist estranged from his own class, but never loses his aristocratic panache. Lecky commented caustically on the apparent need of Irish revolutionaries to have an aristocrat at the head of their movement:

> The cooperation of a member of the first family of the Protestant aristocracy was of no small advantage to the conspiracy in a country where the genuine popular feeling, amid all its aberrations, has always shown itself curiously aristocratic, and where the first instinct of the people when embarking in democratic and revolutionary movements has usually been to find some one of good family and position to place at their head. [23]

His class and background obscured for Lecky the fact that Irish nationalism, initially, was essentially tribal and aristocratic, in that it sought the lost world that disappeared with the Flight of the Earls, and that this aspiration, that had flowed underground for centuries, united peasant and aristocrat, while marginalizing the middle class, who looked more to French egalitarianism and economic advantage. The logical people to lead this Arthurian crusade would be the successors of those original chieftains who had survived the holocaust of the seventeenth century. For instance, Standish James O'Grady tried to rouse the Duke of Ormond, descendant of the Butlers of Kilkenny, to stand at the head of the country.[24] Looked at in this light, Lord Edward Fitzgerald was a perfect candidate for an Irish revolutionary leader.

Nationalism in the middle of the nineteenth century was in an unstable condition, as different views and priorities jostled for position in the developing national consciousness. The most intense struggle, sometimes genteel, sometimes vicious, was that between aristocratic and democratic nationalism. The one stemmed from the Patriots of the 1780s, the other from the rebellion of 1798, nursed back to life by the Young Irelanders, sent out into the world by the Fenians, and set to work by the Land League. The first was largely, but by no means exclusively, Protestant; the other was mostly, but not entirely, Catholic. One of the battlegrounds was the control of literature and scholarship. Yeats summarized the characteristics of the two factions:

> A generation before *The Nation* newspaper was founded the Royal Irish
> Academy had begun the study of ancient Irish literature. That study was
> as much a gift from the Protestant aristocracy which had created the
> Parliament as *The Nation* and its school, though Davis and Mitchell
> were Protestants, was a gift from the Catholic middle classes who were
> to create the Irish Free State.[25]

One focussed its appeal on the upper and lower classes, one on the
middle class; one valued the Irish language, the other dismissed it; one
valued the aristocratic literature of the Red Branch, the other preferred
the more demotic tales of the Fianna; one viewed the Ascendancy as
the potential and natural saviours of the country, the other saw them
as the enemy. Michael Davitt thought the Irish landlords did not
deserve their fare to Holyhead, but Standish James O'Grady thought
them 'still the best class we have and so far better than the rest that
there is none fit to mention as next best'.[26]

The aristocratic paternalism that Lecky noted and Whitbread's *Lord
Edward Fitzgerald* instanced was one of the important strands in the
debate. Maria Edgeworth's novels, *The Absentee* and *Ennui*, enact a
fantasy in which the Ascendancy, returning to their neglected estates,
receive an emotional and tumultuous welcome; the reality was that the
Ascendancy had made themselves irrelevant by their continued absence
or, if present, detested for their mismanagement. They siphoned off the
rents from their estates, but returned, in most cases, nothing by way of
investment. O'Grady, an enthusiastic but eccentric advocate of aristocratic rule, in his great philippic, *Toryism and Tory Democracy*, berated
them for their horrendous waste of the country's wealth:

> You have spent the rents of all Ireland [...] You have spent, in rent and
> taxes, I should say at least some two thousand millions of pounds, and
> you have spent that vast sum upon anything rather than in the making
> of friends. You are few and friendless, and let me add, hated.[27]

Both O'Grady and Edgeworth were trying in their own way to rouse the
Ascendancy to save themselves, their class, and the country. Edgeworth
did so by modelling best practice, and also by rehearsing the results of
their present evil ways, especially in *Castle Rackrent*. O'Grady whipped
them with his scorn and contempt in the hope of stirring some members
of the class to execute the duties that their position demanded. For the
Ascendancy as a whole he despaired; he saw their long performance on
the Irish stage was dwindling to a sad, slow curtain:

> Your career is like some uncouth epic begun by a true poet, continued by
> a newspaper man, and ended by a buffoon; heroic verse, followed by
> prose, and closed in a disgusting farce. Then *plaudite* and *exeunt omnes*.
> The curtain falls on two centuries of Irish history, and such centuries.
> The paraphernalia are removed. A new act begins with new actors.[28]

Whitbread's nationalistic melodramas entered this debate on the place
and usefulness of the Ascendancy on the positive side, by adopting and
developing the type of character that Boucicault created for Robert
Emmet: the aristocrat as an articulate, eloquent spokesman for the
oppressed people. But Whitbread's Lord Edward borrowed also from
Knowles, and was a transitional figure, in that he was an aristocrat that
espoused revolutionary change in society, but also possessed the
Victorian bourgeois virtues of uxoriousness, strong familial attach-
ments and religious convictions. Whitbread thus embourgeoized the
aristocracy, while simultaneously using the aristocratic qualities of
carelessness, recklessness, fearlessness, style and eloquence to dignify
and elevate the arguments for revolution.

Dramatically speaking, *Lord Edward Fitzgerald; or, '98* (1894) is like
an inferior play by Boucicault. Certain strands have been boosted; the
emphasis is mainly on the servants, Thady and Katy, and on the string
of villains – Turner, Magan, Higgins and Sirr. Major Swan is the decent
English officer, reluctantly doing his duty, like Molineux in *The
Shaughraun*, while Lord Edward and his wife, Pamela, do little more
than posture attractively. There is no individuality to the characters and
no plot development at all; the play is a roller-coaster of near-escapes,
hot pursuit and final capture, yet it struck a nerve, and became one of
the most popular plays in the repertoire, reverenced and set in stone by
the audience's jealous familiarity. For a revival three years after its first
presentation, *The Irish Times* wrote:

> In the popular portions of the house it was impossible to get even stand-
> ing room at the rise of the curtain, and the other sections were likewise
> filled. [...] The place which it holds among the latter-day contributions
> to the Irish drama is accurately attested by the large measure of patron-
> age invariably extended to it.[29]

Lord Edward is like Boucicault's Emmet or Ffolliott in that, raised as a
gentleman, he has become a simpleton, easily imposed on and foolishly
trusting, a terrible judge of men and a bad leader. It is left to his crafty
followers to extricate him, and create dramatic occasions on which to
hang comic or villainous turns. *Lord Edward* gives ample scope for
competitive wickedness between the actors; there are six villains mostly

representative of the middle-class *homo economicus*, who was always pilloried by Boucicault, then by the Nationalist Melodrama, then excoriated by Yeats and Synge, until Shaw went some distance to rehabilitate him in *John Bull's Other Island.*

Everybody, including himself, speaks of Lord Edward as the sole *fons et origo* of the '98 rebellion, but his role in the play consists of greeting his wife affectionately, explaining matters and the progress of the conspiracy to her, and uttering heartfelt nationalist sentiments to rouse the audience, before escaping again. He actually makes less of a dramatic impact than either Ffolliott or Beamish MacCoul. The imbalance in the elements of the drama in *Lord Edward* – the over-emphasis on roguery in the clown/hero, and the superabundance of villains – serves to point up how well Boucicault kept them in balance.

The play can be linked thematically to Knowles, in the abstract simplicity of its oppositions and the ethical clarity of its conflicts, but it was Boucicault who set the pattern with his eloquent aristocratic prototype. Boucicault, however, had sufficient psychological insight and dramatic acumen to undercut the heroics, and even, in Emmet's case, to renounce the public revolutionary life in favour of the personal when confronted with the tawdry actions of the people he was willing to die for.

Whitbread's heroes, however, are firmly set in their conviction of the primacy of their public messianic mandate. Lord Edward, as he dies, sets the standard of sacrifice for Ireland: 'I have devoted myself wholly to her emancipation. Sacrificed wife, children, fortune, even life itself in her cause.'[30] This play and its successors were implicated in setting Irish nationalism on the path of blood sacrifice that led ultimately to Pearse and 1916. This eloquent high-minded act of idealism is to be found initially in Lord Edward's aristocratic mind-set, which is passed down intact to Wolfe Tone, Napper Tandy, Michael Dwyer and so on. All of Whitbread's heroes exhibit the same *générosité* regardless of actual class, which serves to preserve aristocratic sacrificial heroism at the centre of plays in which no aristocrat appears, but also to elevate bourgeois morality above its mercantile norms.

Whitbread's *Theobald Wolfe Tone* (1898) enacted a fusion of the two moralities. During the early scenes, it concentrates almost exclusively on the personal life of Wolfe Tone, with the politics bubbling along in the background and occasionally surfacing to remind the audience of the wider context. It moves then to assert the primacy of the wider context, to state that politics is superior to private life, that personal life must be subservient to politics and serve it, a sentiment repeated by Yeats' *Cathleen Ní Houlihan* in 1902, and the direct opposite of what Boucicault asserted in *Robert Emmet*. By doing so, it moved the audience from recognizing the common humanity of Wolfe Tone to identification with his sacrificial revolutionary role, and with the wife who will sacrifice her husband for The Cause.

Theobald Wolfe Tone premiered on 26 December 1898 at the Queen's. Instead of a pantomime, traditional at that time of year, Whitbread chose to give the people the quintessential Nationalist Melodrama and, on the centenary of 1798, their reaction was one of unbridled enthusiasm. It was a gala occasion for the people of Dublin, with huge crowds trying to get into the theatre. Holloway tells us of the excitement and synergy created by the play: 'Such a pandemonium of discordant sound I have seldom heard, and at times one could scarcely hear one's ears, especially when the villains held the stage.'[31] He generally approved of the play itself, or what he could hear of it in the encompassing commotion:

> As far as I could judge by the scraps of dialogue I heard here and there from those on the stage, I should say that the quality of the writing was much above average, while in dramatic construction and stage effects it far surpassed anything yet attempted in its way by the popular manager of the theatre – Mr. J.W. Whitbread's [...] 'Wolfe Tone' (though cast on melodramatic mould) is a distinct cut above the usual sensational play.[32]

The Evening Herald, in its critical notice, celebrated the play's gravity and realism:

> He is thoroughly in sympathy with Ireland. He has caught the vernacular. He draws his characters naturally and puts on his colour with a broad, bold brush. Of his Irish characters he is a master. [...] The dialogue is witty; it is natural, it is convincing. There is action, there is energy, there is deep human interest in the play [...] and the audience follows it with the deepest interest.[33]

Holloway also welcomed its realism and the depiction of Irish characters without resorting to comic stereotypes or low broguery: 'Why not have educated Irishmen and women speak, as in everyday life, as Mr. Whitbread has endeavoured in this play to make them do? We have had enough and plenty of Irish caricatures on stage, God knows, in the past; let us have a little of the genuine article now by way of a change.'[34] Holloway was looking at the political implications of the play, the restoration of dignity to Irish history and public life after the tragic farce of the Parnell scandal, and he over-argues his case. Many playwrights prior to Whitbread had rendered Irish speech on stage as plain English; what was annoying Holloway here was the irritating brogue of visiting English companies.

A running theme in the critical appraisal of the play is praise for its realism and naturalistic approach, a surprising verdict given our modern apprehension of melodrama. *The Evening Herald* called it 'a realistic presentment of a series of episodes the most interesting in the romantic history of our land'.[35] These melodramas were believed by the audience to show Irish history as it actually was, a realistic historicism in the dialogue, in the characters and in the actions. This dramatic canon was, ironically, the reference against which the Abbey's later, naturalistic plays were to be checked and found wanting. The Queen's melodramas were nothing of the sort, of course. What Whitbread, Bourke and their followers did was to take the fractured, disjunctive and frequently contradictory elements of history, especially 1798, and hammer them into a coherent melodramatic shape that is more propaganda than fact, a binary narrative of heroes and villains, loyalists and informers, of idealism and betrayal, black and white, good and bad, which maintained only a tenuous hold on the facts, but had a mythical coherence that took, and still holds, the high moral ground.

Whitbread caught the mood of the moment perfectly. *The United Irishman* said of his plays: 'They are certainly steps in the right direction. [...] These plays will do good, and the Irish Stage, if we may call our theatres such, would be the better of many more of their class.'[36] Andrew E. Malone, who holds the plays in low esteem, admits the attraction they exercised: 'They were poor plays, mainly melodrama of the most vivid kind, but they made history real for many thousands of people.'[37] The reviewer of *The Dublin Evening Mail* of January 1903 still believed that Whitbread's historical melodramas showed Irish history 'with historical precision'.[38] They considered the plays to be realistic because they did not trouble the surface of national respectability. The advances in scenery, costume, lighting and spectacle combined to bolster the illusion of peering into the eighteenth century. Whitbread's foreignness shows in his ignorance of the rural: the plays are totally urban; there is none of the mystical attachment to land that underpinned Boucicault, and was to surface even more strongly in the plays of the Abbey. In Whitbread, the characters are fuelled by abstractions, not by clay, grass and stones, but the plays fitted precisely to the audience and the time. Whitbread declared in an interview: 'The stage is the pulpit of the nineteenth century,'[39] and this perceived historical accuracy is in fact a narrow nationalist vision, an almost religious, romantic dream. In Hubert O'Grady's play *The*

Fenians, those attacking the prison van in Manchester flaunted ludicrous green uniforms, and Michael Dwyer and his merry men wore emerald green while hiding in the Wicklow Mountains in Whitbread's *The Insurgent Chief*.[40]

They also sinned by omission, as no scenes or comments derogatory of Irish life were tolerated. The plays of the Queen's encountered the same ideological censorship that the Abbey later did. They were criticized when they dared to show the underbelly of Irish society, producing a counter-assertion of nationalist respectability and a flat denial of the Dionysiac elements in Irish life – the same problem that Synge encountered. Prefiguring the row about *The Plough and the Stars*, Robert Johnston's *The Old Land* (1903), a prize-winning drama on a patriotic theme, was damned for having a scene set in a public house. *The Freeman's Journal* sniffed that 'a table covered with bottles, presumably of strong drink, and suggestive of deep potations, is an accessory that might well be dispensed with'.[41]

This feeling of realism that the plays provoked was caused, not by their historical accuracy, but by their intense relevance to the concerns of the audience, as they elided the century and the deferred opportunity of 1798 re-appeared. This closing of the temporal circle occurs most obviously in *Wolfe Tone*, where the ending of the play invites an aftermath different from the brutal historical truth. Having seen to the death or neutralization of the informers, Tone is about to sail from France with thousands of French troops amidst high hopes for his success:

> TONE   Only a week and beloved country I shall see you once again. Once more feel your green turf beneath my feet, breathe again your life-giving air. [...] At last the triumph of my life approaches – the goal I have longed for is in sight. [...] Three months hence and you will be with me in dear old Dublin once again.[42]

Tone's mission ended in defeat and death, but the play ends on a note of high optimism that carried the audience; Tone's opportunity is re-created, and the 'invitation to action and basis of hope'[43] collapses the century so that the end of the play opens, not on to the disaster of 1798, but on to the possibilities of 1898.

Unlike *Lord Edward*, there are no aristocrats in *Wolfe Tone*. It is a middle-class melodrama, pointing the way to P.J. Bourke's plays of the urban and rural lower class. The simplicity of melodrama requires heroes and villains to be instantly recognizable, and Boucicault used aristocratic ready-mades, but with an ambiguous twist. Whitbread, following Boucicault's lead, used Lord Edward Fitzgerald as a hero and kitted him out in the usual aristocratic virtues. Wolfe Tone wouldn't quite fit, as the son of a coach-maker, but his Trinity education and the egalitarianism flowing from the Revolution, added to his attractive personal qualities, enabled him to move with ease among the Ascendancy, or at least among that sector of it that embraced liberal ideas. His middle-class background, however, posed a stylistic problem for Whitbread, which he solved by having Tone make a virtue of his poverty, pointing to it as a pledge of his honesty when challenged by Napoleon. He is also treated as a gentleman by his inferiors, and evaluated as such by Napoleon's wife, Josephine: 'He has ze grande air ov command; ze mannare, zat compels respect, love, admiration.'[44] So that Whitbread, harking back to Shadwell, created a bourgeois hero with Ascendancy virtues.

Running parallel to the creation of this eloquent middle-class, or later, working-class patriot, however, was another strand in Irish Nationalist Melodrama that ran counter to Boucicault and openly demonized the Ascendancy. Boucicault's relative benignity towards the ruling class was not mirrored by his contemporaries or successors, perhaps reflecting a lesser penetration by them of the English theatrical circuit. Boucicault's villains were usually middlemen or agents, his heroes aristocrats, however decayed. But his contemporary, Edmund Falconer, a successful actor and playwright, and perhaps the nearest thing Boucicault had to a rival in Ireland, did not scruple to cast an Ascendancy landlord as a full-blown villain in his play *Eileen Oge; or, Dark's the Hour before the Dawn* (1871). Henry Loftus is a more sinister version of Hardress Cregan, and indeed the whole play is packed with echoes of *The Colleen Bawn*. Loftus and his evil agent, the Danny Mann-like Scotsman, M'Lean, bring, in best melodramatic fashion, economic and legal pressure to bear on the heroine, Eileen Oge, and on her family, in order to coerce her into marrying Loftus, the nephew of the local landlord. First they prevent her marriage to Pat O'Donnell by evicting him without cause, so that the young couple will have nowhere to live. When that does not work, Loftus has a letter forged to his own uncle, purportedly from O'Donnell, threatening him with violence for that eviction:

> You have been on trial for a long time, for the many unjust acts you and your agents have done to decent people, and your having given notice to Patrick O'Donnell that you are going to take the home over his head, and having threatened him with legal process to turn him off his land, you have completed the measure of your crimes, so you have been found

guilty and condemned to die. If you dare to carry your threat into execution, or to molest O'Donnell, you'll be shot from behind a hedge, or
a hayrick, and your brains scattered to the four winds, to give a red
vengeance to O'Donnell.[45]

O'Donnell is convicted and transported, and Loftus intensifies the economic pressure, until Eileen is faced with the dilemma of marrying him
or having her family thrown out on the side of the road. But O'Donnell
is pardoned and returns in the nick of time, rescuing her as she walks
to the altar. Loftus is exposed, and, in spite of his landlord status, and
in marked contrast to *The Colleen Bawn*, he is made to feel the full
force of the law, in the form of the newly organized police force: 'I am
Henry Loftus of Loftus Hall, a gentleman and landed proprietor, sufficiently responsible to resist your authority,' he blusters, but is hand-
cuffed and exits humiliatingly *'guarded by peelers, Sergeant, etc.'*[46]
Falconer had learned a lot from Boucicault, showing an Irish bucolic
Utopia, threatened by upper-class corruption and saved by the courage
and sacrifice of the wily peasants, and the neutrality of a police force
independent of local magnates.

Eileen Oge follows the usual melodramatic pattern, in its villains,
heroes and action, but it has some interesting idiosyncrasies. One of
the characters is a Cockney servant who is despised by the Irish characters because of his inability to speak properly; they are of the opinion that he should be 'hanged for the murder of the king's English'.[47]
The false threat to the landlord is a surprisingly direct reference to the
Land War to have got past the censor, as the play was not confined to
Ireland, being licensed by the Lord Chamberlain for the Princess
Theatre in London in 1871.[48]

Hubert O'Grady was another Queen's stalwart whose plays not
only boosted nationalist feeling at home, but raised awareness abroad.
The Evening Herald wrote in his obituary notice in 1899, echoing
Whitbread's comment on the stage as a pulpit:

> Mr. O'Grady wrote many Irish plays, and toured with them for several
> years. They were not marked by any high literary excellence, yet they
> were rough and ready bits of Irish sentiment, unpolished stones in a way,
> but of value. In many an English town his play *Eviction* was a sermon
> preached from behind the footlights and appealed to popular feeling in
> a curiously successful fashion.[49]

O'Grady had a successful career as actor and playwright, leading a company that toured extensively in Ireland and in Britain. His plays conformed to the usual Queen's stereotype, with their clear-cut villains,

heroes, values and ideology. His play *The Famine* (1886) updated the patriotic melodrama by including the repercussions of the Land War, and the attempts by a former landlord to get even with the tenants who have bested him. The villain is Sackvill, whose estates have been lost by the tenants' refusal to pay the rents. He has got a job as overseer of famine relief, and exploits his position to get revenge on Vincent O'Connor, whom he blames for his loss; O'Connor had been the first to refuse to pay, and all the others had followed his example. But now famine has struck, and Sackvill starves O'Connor and his family by refusing to give him any relief work, and having him arrested for stealing a loaf of bread. In the play, Sackvill is shot from behind a hedge, as the letter in Falconer's play threatened, by his even more evil sidekick Sadler.

P.J. Bourke's *For the Land She Loved* is unique in having its main conflict between two women. Against the background of the 1798 rebellion, Lady Nugent spends the play trying to part Betsy Gray from her lover, Robert Munro, who has chosen Betsy over her. The portrayal of Ascendancy figures has become more extreme, and Lady Nugent is devoid of scruple in her pursuit; she lies, cheats and murders in order to be revenged on the lovers, including ambushing a landlord from behind a hedge and pinning the blame on one of the rebels. In the last scene, the two women fight with swords; Betsy kills her, and she dies with style, refusing to beg or forgive.

Whitbread, in *Lord Edward* and *Wolfe Tone*, took a fairly benign attitude to the ruling class, but by the time he was writing *The Ulster Hero* (1902) his focus of virtue had shifted towards the common people. His plays after *Lord Edward* took the generous qualities and gifted them to non-aristocratic bourgeois characters. Henry Joy McCracken is a bourgeois capitalist and the articulator of the doctrine of patriotism, sacrifice and violent opposition to the upper class: 'Better that every Irishman in this fair land of ours should shed the last drop of his life's blood to throw off the yoke of serfdom, than to rot and die the slaves of a mischievous party of miserable aristocrats.'[50]

The success of the Nationalist Melodramas was phenomenal. Whitbread's company opened a play in the Queen's, then went on a tour of Ireland, Scotland, England and sometimes America and Australia. By the end of the tour, the productions would have been presented more than two thousand times. This would mean, Morash calculates, given the size of theatres, and a sixty percent attendance, that some of his plays had been attended by more than three million people.[51] But even this fails to take into account the constant revivals over the following decades and all over the country by touring or amateur companies, so that by 1930 it is quite likely that almost everyone in the country had attended *Theobald Wolfe Tone*, for example, at least once, and possibly a lot more often.

All of these plays had more than a theatrical footprint; they also had an educational and apologetic role. Melodrama had a didactic basis – a raising of consciousness among the lower classes, an awakening to the awareness of shared wrongs, a presentation of a pattern for the alleviation of these complaints by solidarity or direct action, a refusal to accept the norms laid down by a corrupt or uncaring ruling class – a proposal, in fact, of an alternative ideology. Nationalist Melodrama followed that pattern but added the dimension, not just of oppression, but colonial oppression, and so became intensely political in the narrow sense of kindling and nourishing the hope and expectation of national freedom. We have seen this pattern evolve through the late work of Boucicault and the innovations of Whitbread, but it came to fruition in the work of P.J. Bourke (1883–1932). In Bourke, the theme of reconciliation and accommodation that had persisted since the work of William Philips in the late seventeenth century was finally overthrown. Also in Bourke, the economic arguments that had always fuelled the debate were abandoned at last in favour of a clean political separation; in a political storm, only villains pursue economic advantage. Bourke also completed the proletarianization of the drama in Ireland. Boucicault and Whitbread had working-class or peasant characters who were covertly the heroes of their plays; the entire plot of *Wolfe Tone,* for example, turns on the character, actions and influence of Shane, the Trinity scout, although the central focus appears to be on Wolfe Tone. Even more than Whitbread, Bourke paved the way for O'Casey in two ways: one was by focusing his plays on the lives of working-class urban or labouring country people, and secondly, he broke new ground by making a woman the hero and central character of *For the Land She Loved.* The plain people of Ireland could see their lives reflected in the plays of Bourke, but those lives transformed and ennobled by the aspirations to freedom.

Whitbread's plays generally inhabited a middle-class world, but Bourke moved firmly into the world of the working class. In his plays, finally, the heroic qualities of *générosité* migrated to the Irish working or rural classes. He gave the virtues and linguistic skills of the well-bred to peasants and workers, as Knowles did. Bourke's urban heroes and heroines were enormously popular and achieved aspirational, visionary status. They are propaganda in the sense that they embody and project a set of values and beliefs designed to encourage and enable lasting revolutionary change.

Bourke's proletarian protagonists are as patriotically eloquent and high-minded as any of Whitbread's historical aristocrats. *When Wexford Rose* (1910) is like all of these plays, an alternative present encoded. 'For Ireland and Liberty',[52] they shout, and Father Murphy declares: 'Peace shall never again be restored until an Irish Republic is declared.'[53] – aligning the play and its audience with the extreme tendency during the Home Rule agitation. The fudge that Boucicault pulled off with his sentimental, bagpipe-and-kilt sort of patriotism was pulled aside by Bourke to promote violent revolutionary republicanism.

The Irish theatrical experience was not one of a passive audience receiving the thesis proposed by author and actors; the audience, volatile and deeply committed to its role in the drama, was a part of the process. The theatre as a whole, not just the stage, was the arena of the dramatic event, the audience sometimes the more important part of it – Garth's Prologue, the Gentlemen's Quarrel, the rumbustious reaction to *Hibernia Freed* and above all the Nationalist Melodramas that turned a night at the theatre into a patriotic rally. Frantz Fanon preached that the colonized writer's duty was to model a free future and give inspiration to his oppressed people, 'opening the future, as an invitation to action and a basis for hope'.[54] The Queen's melodramas, with their incandescent ideology, and enthusiastic audiences, produced the energy to suggest, if not to create, a revolution. The actors and authors tried to harness this energy, ride this tiger, but it was far too unruly a beast for domestication, as Yeats and the Abbey acknowledged by abandoning it and adopting their own pet audience, but even that clawed their eyes out occasionally.

The Queen's was considered as the National Theatre by its audiences long after the founding of the Abbey. The Abbey's vision of Irish theatre did not fit with the experience of many theatre-going Dubliners. When P.J. Bourke's *For the Land She Loved* premiered at the Abbey 1915, the usual Queen's audience migrated with it. Holloway observed how different they were from a typical Abbey audience. They smoked in the auditorium, hissed the villain, cheered the heroes, joined in the songs and told 'the assistant to go to Hell! when informed no smoking is allowed. They are a law unto themselves.' They tended to view the Abbey as an Ascendancy project; the theatre's policy of having a special season to coincide with Horse Show Week was not calculated to alleviate proletarian or nationalist sensibilities, and Yeats' contemptuous tone on the night of the *Playboy* riot gave a good example of the distance between management and audience. In fact, the behaviour of the audience at *The Playboy of the Western World* was not qualitatively different from the usual form at the Queen's. This was an audience accustomed to unleashing its disapproval without restraint, but the Abbey was not used to such aggressive candour. The audience's furious reaction to Synge was balanced by their acceptance of Fitzmaurice, whose portrayal of Irish life is far harsher and uglier, but was praised for its verisimilitude. Holloway commented:

> Irish people can stand any amount of hard things being said about them if there is truth at the back of them, but what they won't stand for a moment is libellous falsehoods such as those contained in *The Playboy,* and such foreign-tainted stuff that makes them out sensual blackguards, cruel monsters, and irreligious brutes.[55]

The audience could see themselves in Fitzmaurice, and in Whitbread, Bourke, Allen and the playwrights of the Queen's, but the Abbey's vision of Ireland often seemed alien; even Holloway sometimes felt he was being deliberately insulted by the Abbey authorities. As a result of the presentation of *For the Land She Loved,* Dublin Castle rebuked the manager, St John Ervine, for allowing dissension to be fomented in his theatre, and he agreed never to admit a play by Bourke into the Abbey again[56] – a cosy alliance between the Castle authorities and the Literary Theatre to exclude the nationalist and proletarian influence.

Seamus de Búrca, P.J. Bourke's son, wrote:

> They're inclined to think that the Abbey was national all the time. But the real national theatre – certainly up to 1916 and I would suggest up to about 1923 – was the Queen's Theatre. They were putting on all these nationalist plays. [...] I've maintained that the heart of Ireland was kept alive by what they put on in the Queen's.[57]

But there was a price to be paid in literary standards. All of these plays are well-constructed but only adequately written, with few flashes of fire. The characters are predictable, and the language veers from the high rhetoric of dogmatic patriotism to irritating peasant drollery, with the villains, as usual, getting the best lines. The plays all have a family resemblance, like a degenerate brood of Boucicault. Where he used a strand of sentimental patriotism, the others are completely under the influence of what Sean O'Faoláin calls 'emotional nationalism'.[58] With his Irish plays, Boucicault effectively appropriated the drama for Ireland; the popularity of his portrayal of Irish life gave a sense of worth to the people. The Irish drama had never fallen completely under the sway of politics, though it often reflected political concerns, so that Boucicault's work, while partaking subtly of political and social debate, is not in need of what O'Faoláin calls 'Dedavisisation'. Writing of Davis and the Young Irelanders, O'Faoláin says: 'They did not devote their great talents to literature: they devoted them to literature in the interests of politics. [...] Before a literary movement could develop in a strictly literary way Irish writers had to purify literature of this political impurity.'[59]

Boucicault did not fall into the Davis trap but, paradoxically, his successors did; paradoxically, because in correctly turning their attention to Irish life and history as their subject matter, they took to looking at it through an ideological lens; they arranged it as they thought it ought to be rather than showing what was there. Boucicault's heroes are real, with their own idiosyncrasies and failings; those of the Whitbread and Bourke school have none. They are emblematic figures rather than real characters; their dialogue has the imprimatur of nationalist orthodoxy, and the plays have the rigidity of medieval moralities. It was from this iron and unquestioning acceptance of nationalist ideology that the Abbey had to rescue Irish drama and drag it from its closed self-congratulatory consensus.

The importance of the Queen's school of playwrights has been underestimated, however, blocked out by the intervening success of the early Abbey. The plays of Falconer, Whitbread, Bourke, Allen and O'Grady traversed the country for decades, at least until the Second World War, intimately known and treasured by the people, reflecting an agreed interpretation of history, a shared myth of nation-making, unruffled by emerging facts or contrary opinions. Their politics was greater than their art; their nationalist dogma of fidelity and betrayal, of sacrifice and resurrection, was so powerful that even the early Abbey writers conform to it. To an habitué of the Queen's, *Cathleen Ní Houlihan* said nothing new; she preached exactly the same message as Whitbread's Lord Edward or Bourke's Betsy Gray, expressing the monolithic nationalist mind-set. Only the great iconoclasts, Synge, O'Casey, Shaw or Johnston, attacked and overset it in a series of dramatic masterpieces: *The Playboy of the Western World, Juno and the Paycock* and *The Plough and the Stars, John Bull's Other Island,* or *The Old Lady Says 'No'*. This deviancy, this fearless acuity and truth-telling was not welcomed by nationalist orthodoxy nor, in the case of Shaw and Johnston, by the Abbey authorities.

The values of the theatre had become those of the rural bourgeoisie or urban working class. The back-stairs agreement between the Ascendancy and the peasantry had been smashed by the Land War and the breaking up of the estates. Samuel Ferguson's Utopia: 'a restoration of Grattan's Parliament, in which all estates of the realm should have their old places',[60] had been rendered impossible by 'a sordid war of classes carried on by the vilest methods'.[61] The theatre, like the country, had changed utterly, and the Ascendancy was not to be restored to its 'old place'. Sidelined by O'Keeffe, attacked by Knowles, ridiculed by Boucicault and dispensed with by the Nationalist Melodramatists, not even the best efforts of the Abbey could restore the Ascendancy to dramatic respectability.

NOTES AND REFERENCES

1. Richard Pine, 'After Boucicault: Melodrama and the Modern Irish Stage', in *Prompts: Bulletin of the Irish Theatre Archive*, 6 (September 1983), 39–50 (p. 39).
2. Parkin, *Selected Plays of Boucicault*, p. 405. First appeared as: John Oxenford and Dion Boucicault, *Daddy O'Dowd: or Turn About is Fair Play* in New York in 1873 – an adaptation of *Les Crochets du Père Martin* by Eugene Cromon and Eugene Grange, produced in Paris in 1858 – French's Standard Drama (New York: Samuel French, 1875). Revised and retitled: *The O'Dowd; or, Life in Galway* (1880), French's Acting Edition of Plays (London: Samuel French, n.d.). Later revised and retitled again as *Suilamore; or, Life in Galway* and also as *The O'Dowd; or, The Golden Fetters*.
3. Boucicault, *The O'Dowd*, as presented at the Adelphi Theatre, London, October 21st 1880 (French's Acting Edition, n.d.), I, p. 13; in *35 Plays of Dion Boucicault*, University of Kent at Canterbury Library, Popular Nineteenth Century Drama on Microfilm.
4. *Ibid.*, I. p. 30.
5. *Ibid.*, p. 30.
6. *Ibid.*, III. 3, p. 33.
7. *Ibid.*, IV. p. 44.
8. *Ibid.*, IV. p. 45.
9. Richard Fawkes, *Dion Boucicault: a Biography* (London: Quartet Books, 1979), p. 219.
10. *Ibid.*, p. 219.
11. Sven Eric Molin and Robin Goodfellowe, 'Nationalism on the Dublin Stage', *Eire-Ireland*, 21 (Spring 1986) 135–138 (p.135).
12. Boucicault, *The Fireside Story of Ireland* (Dublin: Gill and Son, [1881–]), p. 2.
13. Boucicault, 'Early Days of a Dramatist', in *North American Review*, 148 (May 1889), 584–593, Cornell Making of America, Cornell University Library, http://cdl.library.cornell.edu/gifcache/moa/nora148/00596.TIF6.gif [accessed 5/11/2005]
14. Boucicault, *Fireside Story*, p. 21.
15. *Ibid.*, p. 23.
16. Malcolm James Nelson, 'From Rory and Paddy to Boucicault's Myles, Shaun and Conn: The Irishman on the London Stage, 1830–1860', *Eire-Ireland*, 13 (Fall 1978), 79–105, p. 80.
17. Maria Edgeworth, *The Absentee* (Ware, Hertfordshire: Wordsworth Classics, 1994), p. 175.
18. Andrew E. Malone, *The Irish Drama* (London: Constable, 1929), p. 32.
19. Boucicault, 'Early Days of a Dramatist', p. 586.
20. *Ibid.*, p. 589.
21. Boucicault, *Robert Emmet*, II. 3, p. 359.
22. W.J. Fitzpatrick, *Irish Secret Service under Pitt* (London: Longman Green, 1892). Whitbread gives a credit to the book on the title page of *Lord Edward*: 'Based on *The Irish Secret Service under Pitt*, by W.J. Fitzpatrick', in Cheryl Herr, *For the Land they Loved: Irish Political Melodramas 1890–1925* (Syracuse, New York: Syracuse University Press, 1991), p. 83.
23. Lecky, *A History of Ireland in the Eighteenth Century*, ed. by L.P. Curtis, abridged to 1 vol. (Chicago: The University of Chicago Press, 1972), p. 350.
24. 'But his great passion was yachting and woodcock shooting and he didn't fancy the epic role O'Grady envisaged for him.' Mark Bence-Jones, *The Twilight of the Ascendancy* (London: Constable, 1987), p. 90.
25. W.B. Yeats, 'A General Introduction for my Work', in *Essays and Introductions* (London: Macmillan, 1969), 509–527 (p. 511).

26. Standish James O'Grady, *Selected Essays and Passages*, ed. by Ernest A. Boyd, Every Irishman's Library (Dublin: Talbot Press, n. d.), p. 203.
27. *Ibid.*, p. 211.
28. *Ibid.*, p. 222.
29. *The Irish Times*, 20 April 1897, cited by Herr, p. 8.
30. J.W. Whitbread, *Lord Edward*, V. 1, in Herr, *For the Land they Loved*, p. 169.
31. Herr, *For the Land they Loved*, p. 9.
32. *Ibid.*, p. 9.
33. *Ibid.*, p. 8.
34. *Ibid.*, p. 9.
35. *Ibid.*, p. 8.
36. Morash, *History of Irish Theatre*, p. 114.
37. Malone, *Irish Drama*, p. 17.
38. Stephen M. Watt, 'Boucicault and Whitbread: The Dublin Stage at the End of the Nineteenth Century', *Eire-Ireland*, 18 (Fall 1983), 23–53. p. 47.
39. Seamus De Búrca, *The Queen's Royal Theatre* (1829–1969) (Dublin: Folens, 1983), p. 16.
40. *Ibid.*, p. 44.
41. Watt, 'Boucicault and Whitbread', p. 44.
42. Whitbread, *Theobald Wolfe Tone*, IV. 1, in Herr, *For the Land they Loved*, p. 255.
43. Frantz Fanon, *The Wretched of the Earth*, trans. by Constance Farrington (London: Penguin, 1967), p. 187.
44. Whitbread, *Theobald Wolfe Tone*, III. 5, p. 245.
45. *Ibid.*, I. 2, p. 12.
46. *Ibid.*, IV. 4, p. 59.
47. *Ibid.*, I. 1, p. 5.
48. *Ibid.*, Title page.
49. *The Evening Herald*, 22 December 1899, p. 4, col. 7; Stephen Watt, 'The Plays of Hubert O'Grady', in *Journal of Irish Literature: A Hubert O'Grady Supplement*, 14 (Jan. 1985), p. 3.
50. Watt, 'Boucicault and Whitbread', p. 48.
51. Morash, *History of Irish Theatre*, p. 110.
52. P.J. Bourke, *When Wexford Rose*, II. 2, in Herr, *For the Land they Loved*, p. 281.
53. *Ibid.*, II. 2, p. 279.
54. Fanon, *The Wretched of the Earth*, p. 187.
55. Howard K. Slaughter, introduction to *George Fitzmaurice, The Realistic Plays* (Dublin: Dolmen Press, 1970), p. ix.
56. de Búrca, *Queen's Royal Theatre*, p. 4
57. *The Journal of Irish Literature*, 13 (Jan?May 1984), p. 78.
58. Sean O'Faoláin, *The Irish*, Pelican Books (West Drayton Middlesex: Penguin Books, 1947), p. 139.
59. *Ibid.*, p. 132.
60. deVere White, *The Anglo-Irish*, p. 154.
61. *Ibid.*, p. 154.

Conclusion

The term 'Ascendancy' has become attenuated over the years. From encompassing the entire apparatus of Protestant hegemony in Ireland, it has shrunk to indicating a charming, eccentric and feckless landed gentry – rather as Boucicault shows them. But the further back we go, the more potent and aggressive the dramatic image becomes.

While 'Anglo-Irish' is a useful term, it is, essentially, an insult; it has achieved currency but no precise meaning. It refers, invariably, to the upper class, and usually to the landed gentry who arrived after 1500. There are no Anglo-Irish tailors or hod-carriers. Nor is it synonymous with 'Protestant': O'Casey was not Anglo-Irish; nor is Bessie Burgess. Those targeted by the term considered themselves, initially, English – 'the English of Ireland' – and became, by a process of acclimatization, perfectly Irish. The term Anglo-Irish was a Nationalist concoction to diminish their right of belonging, and to indicate the superior claims of those who asserted Gaelic descent.

The coinage 'Anglo-Irish Ascendancy' is rife with ambiguity, because a substantial number of those who were considered as belonging to the class were not of that colonial descent but of Gaelic or Norman extraction – the Fitzgeralds, the MacDonalds of Antrim or the Burkes of Mayo, for example. The evolution of this ruling class and the playwrights' portrait of it is traced in the plays under discussion. While analysing this collective representation in the early Irish theatre, this work has tried to keep in focus the changing nature and identity of that class.

IDENTITY

The Old Testament of Irish plays from 1600 to 1900 was consistent in its political, social and cultural engagement with its society. The dominant concern of early Irish drama was the colonial problem of identity, which led to a relentless self-examination, both personal and societal.

William Philips, in *St. Stephen's Green* (1699), laid down the highest standards of behaviour and social discourse for Dublin high society in its first contemporary portrait. The central interrogation in the play was: what constituted a gentleman? Who belonged in society? The normal answer was that an Estate maketh a Gentleman, but the answer given in *St Stephen's Green* was the quality of his mind – his 'generosity', his natural inclination to behave in a noble manner.

This was a society paralysed by fear of imposters. The shams that infest the plays dramatize this unease. How do you spot the imposter? One aspect of the colonial dialogue was that they were usually English, readily accepted by the anglophiles in Irish society. It was to be expected, in a colony, that the values and symbols of the motherland would be preferred, but those who took this line were consistently lampooned. Macklin eventually asserted, in *The True-born Irishman*, the superiority of all things Irish. The success of the stage gentleman, O'Blunder, and his descendants showed a tentative acceptance by the Anglo-Irish gentry of the resurgent Gaelic tradition. True gentlemen and ladies could be identified on stage by their *générosité* but, in eighteenth-century Ireland, the Protestant establishment was bemused by the revived Gaelic upper class, which had remade itself by adopting the religion and language of the victors.

From 1715 to 1720, Charles Shadwell countered the fear of imposters by asserting the worth of the new mercenary Irish class that had risen to near-aristocratic status, but was trapped still in its pecuniary mind-set. Sir Ambrose Wealthy in *The Hasty Wedding* is a banker whose money is a constant source of aggravation to him, who is paranoid and miserly, constantly warns his generous daughter about imposters, but himself falls easily for the blandishments of an aristocratic English sharper.

Sir Ambrose belongs to a new class that I have called the bourgeois gentry, keeping a foot in both camps. Shadwell saw that both sides had their virtues, and that genteel generosity could combine with bourgeois self-reliance; he gave us this synthesis in Sir Patrick Worthy, hero of *Irish Hospitality*. In this play, Shadwell went beyond showing society as it was, but imagined it as it ought to be, setting the play in Fingall, which he portrayed as a Whig Commonwealth in which the boundaries of class and race melted and dissolved, and status and advancement were determined by merit instead of birth.

He charted what the next step should be in the evolution of this society – marriage between the native Irish and the Anglo-Irish, between the tenant and the landlord, between the worthy peasant and the Ascendancy.

Shadwell was convinced that the Whig philosophy of self-reliance, temperance and self-control should govern and guide the Augustan nation of Hibernia. But the Gaelic tradition that William Philips celebrated in *Hibernia Freed* was not to be channelled into such a dull philosophy, and undermined and redefined it in the characters of the eighteenth-century Irish stage.

THE STAGE IRISHMAN

The Anglo-Irish frequently complained about the inaccuracy of the Irishman on stage during the eighteenth century, but the problem was in their perception, not on the stage. Theatrically speaking, the Protestant nation of Hibernia was in two minds about itself: on the one hand it wanted to be no different from the other British people across the water, but at the same time it wanted to differentiate itself from them, without losing status as equal. It emphasized its similarity in closely following a tried English repertoire, and by taming the rowdy, irrational elements within its audience. However, the only way of expressing its difference was by displaying those same Dionysiac elements on the stage. All of the emblematic Irish characters in eighteenth-century plays were variations on a theme: Captain O'Blunder, Sir Callaghan O'Brallaghan, Major O'Flaherty, Sir Lucius O'Trigger, Lieutenant O'Connor and Murrough O'Dogherty were all created from the same archetype. Each built on the previous one in developing an aggregate portrait of the Hibernian Gentleman. In these plays, the composite that formed, the dramatic simulacrum of the race, was a Gaelic-Hibernian one.

One half of the Hibernian psyche approved of this, and the plays containing these characters were perennially successful, but the other half was scandalized that this dramatic construct should be applied to them, and denied the veracity of this stage Irishman. The Protestant family of Hibernia was reluctant to be represented by such rowdy, disreputable cousins.

Charles Macklin united the two tendencies. In *The True-born Irishman*, the underground Irish gentry – O'Brallaghan and O'Dogherty – have come to the surface. They are rooted in their Irishness, and have no need to purloin a history or invent a story to legitimize themselves. O'Dogherty is not to be shifted into any Anglo-

Hibernian patriot path. It is enough for him that his own name has been lifted back to its proper prominence in the island: 'O'Dogherty for ever – O'Dogherty! – there's a sound for you – why they have not such a name in all England as O'Dogherty – nor as any of our fine sounding Milesian names.'[1]

But for all his Gaelic truculence O'Dogherty represented the beginning of a synthesis of the two tendencies, the responsible bourgeois and the creative anarchist, that formed the two sides of the Irish Gentleman as he appeared in the drama of the eighteenth century, and he showed most clearly the start of the fusion of the two elements into one unhyphenated Ascendancy type.

INCLUSIVITY

Inclusivity was a marked feature of the plays of the eighteenth century, but not of the historical reality. In this aspiration, the playwrights were out of step with, and consistently subversive of, their society and its established policies, which clung to an exclusive vision of Hibernia.

Orrery and Katherine Philips had recommended the reconciliation of foe and friend in the society of post-Restoration Dublin; Burnell sought for the inclusion of the Old English in *Landgartha*; Shadwell recommended the extension of civil rights to the native Irish in *Irish Hospitality* and *Rotherick O'Connor*; William Philips declared the native Irish aristocracy as the natural, historical leaders of the country in *Hibernia Freed*; the stage Irishmen of the eighteenth century were all from the excluded portion of the Irish population. All of this was a well-intentioned but ultimately futile attempt to mould the sensibilities and conscience of the Anglo-Irish superiors into reaching an accommodation between the races that shared the island before it was too late. They did not listen, and the result was the catastrophic eruption of 1798. Only Frederick Ashton's *The Battle of Aughrim* called the state of affairs as it actually existed. All the others were suffering from what I have termed the *Playboy* syndrome, which suffused Irish drama long before Synge created the definitive statement. The playwrights believed that by creating a vivid imaginative model they could alter reality – the urge to transformation through the imagination. The consistently recurring trope was one of creating a new shape in the imagination and then pouring oneself into it. One of the most striking instances is Rover in *Wild Oats*, who imagines a character and then becomes it; as does Ensign Beverley in *The Rivals*.

But there were other variants of the operation on display. All of the sham gentlemen and ladies – Cheatly in *The Sham Prince*, or Mrs Diggerty in *The True-born Irishman* – attempt the operation unsuccessfully; they are defeated by too much reality. In the plays of John O'Keeffe, instead of sham gentlemen we are shown sham peasants, who are equally unsuccessful.

The third route was a compromise: the achievement of duality of character. Roebuck and Lovewell, in *Love and a Bottle*, exchange their sober and anarchic characteristics to create the perfect Irish Gentleman. Many of Richard Brinsley Sheridan's, Goldsmith's or Macklin's characters display the same colonial duality. Lieutenant O'Connor in *St Patrick's Day*, for example, is both an English soldier and an Irish gentleman. Boucicault was fascinated by the idea of the divided self, and used it in many of his plays, giving it a sinister dimension in his creation of the Hardress Cregan/Danny Mann duality.

The urge to transformation was not confined to single individuals; the playwrights applied it to the whole of Anglo-Irish society. Philips and Shadwell were engaged in 're-imagining Ireland' as the nation of Hibernia.[2] O'Keeffe continued to exploit the power of the theatre to articulate alternative realities by supporting the egalitarian ideas of the French Revolution. Rover refashions the whole of his known world in *Wild Oats*, and Felix creates a brief economic Utopia in *The Wicklow Mountains*. Knowles was the most open of the playwrights in his commitment to changing the world. His Liberty plays were committed to 'opening the future'[3] and presenting alternative visions of personal morality and societal structures that overturned the aristocratic centralism of the early nineteenth century.

This urge to transform the Irish people underpinned Boucicault's proposal for pardoning the Fenian exiles in *The Shaughraun*, and it surfaced most powerfully in the aspirational and visionary values encoded in the Nationalist Melodramas and actively decoded at performances in the Queen's Theatre by the emerging Nationalist proletariat. Audiences accustomed to the meaning within ritual, such as Irish Catholic theatregoers raised on the Mass, could easily reach through a performance to extract the deeper meaning encoded in the performed text. This was intensified when the audience was already homogenized culturally and ideologically. They extracted and emphasized the ideology that was latent in the text, and embodied in the performance, as their contribution to the theatrical process.

These Queen's melodramas finally overthrew the inclusive theme and, rather than urging the incorporation of those excluded from the Establishment, they performed what Frantz Fanon calls the writer's duty, to kindle and nourish the expectation of overthrowing it. P.J. Bourke added a vision of the oppressed people and their lives transformed by this aspiration to freedom.

This continuous urge to transformation indicated a colonial unease among the Anglo-Irish, which was also reflected in the dramatic attempts to justify the legality of their rule, in spite of their almost total dominance of Ireland. Shirley gave the leaders of Anglo-Ireland their mission statement in *St Patrick for Ireland*: civilize these barbarians, bring this wilderness to an acceptable physical and mental state of order. St Patrick was an incoming English aristocratic figure, banishing the snakes of superstition and ignorance: 'at whose approach the serpents all unchained themselves, and leaving our unprisoned necks, crept into the earth'.[4] Irish culture was shown as immoral and decadent, needing to be replaced by the benignity and reason of English influence. St Patrick's banishing of the snakes became a metaphor for victory over the Irish.

Shirley claimed St Patrick for the English colonial effort. The political and the religious modes merged in King Leogarius' submission to Patrick, as to a more potent feudal power:

> We give thee now our palace, use it freely;
> Myself, our queen and children, will be all
> Thy guests and owe our dwellings to thy favour.[5]

Shadwell took Shirley's mission statement and cast it into a commercial mould, insisting on the binding and legal nature of the contract between Strongbow and MacMurrough. In his play *Rotherick O'Connor* he annexed Irish history to legitimize Hibernia, and suggested, as he did in *Irish Hospitality*, an alternative society in which the two races merge. When Strongbow is victorious, he still cannot assume the kingship of Leinster without MacMurrough's daughter consenting to marry him and, by the end of the play, she is still withholding that consent; without it, his tenure is not legal. If the Anglo-Irish are here by invitation, then 'They shall succeed, invited to our aid, and mix their blood with ours, one people grow', as Philips wrote.[6] English force was not enough: they must have the agreement of the Irish to fashion Hibernia into a viable nation.

William Philips bathed the ancient Irish in the glow of classical allusion and imagery. He used classical names: Ultonia, Connacia and, especially, Hibernia. In *Hibernia Freed* he rehabilitated the Gaelic chieftains as a race of culture and refinement, and claimed them as the natural and legal aristocracy of the new nation – the Irish Protestant Nation, a free state of Protestant aristocrats, growing naturally and legally out of ancient Ireland.

CULTURAL COLONIZATION

Every body of theatrical work reflects its audience; the corpus of Irish drama prior to 1900 also mirrored the changing nature of that audience. Irish theatre was a form of cultural colonization, a part of the imported culture that declared the colonists' mental and artistic superiority over the savage natives. But colonization was shown to be a two-way process, and the alien theatre became an aperture whereby Irish culture and values flowed back into the consciousness of the English of Ireland. Farquhar's *Love and a Bottle* ends in a Fingallion dance, an indication that Fingall is a place where Irish and English cultures intermingled. Sir Ambrose Wealthy tolerates the Irish musicians under his window – ' 'Tis an impertinent custom, but they have pleaded it time out of mind.'[7] The most striking examples of this were the Irish characters that colonized the stage in the latter half of the eighteenth century: Captain O'Blunder and his successors. The theatre and the drama became part of the dialogue between colonizer and colonized – both on stage in the characters, and off-stage in theatrical disturbances. The colonial superiority evinced in character, attitude and language by Shirley, Orrery and Swift gave way to a more equivocal discourse in Philips and Shadwell, as the founding myth of the English in Ireland collapsed in the face of emerging knowledge and the revival of the Gaelic aristocracy. The colonists appropriated this Irish culture as they became more aware of it, purloining the symbols, and accepting attitudes and character traits that they had previously abhorred.

WOMEN AS AGENTS OF CHANGE

The entire process of change and changing attitudes was invested in the female characters of these plays. They are characterized from the start by a refusal to be cowed or bound by male ideas, and a tendency to be agents rather than patients. They are less hidebound than the men by received ideas of duty or demands of honour.

Their first appearance – Landgartha and her band of female warriors in Burnell's play – is as independent entities, unruly and unruled by the men. Marfissa sets the pattern, skirt tucked up, wearing spurs and a sword, and merrily dancing the Whip of Dunboyne. The girls in *St Stephen's Green* flatly refuse to accept London ways or fads, embodying the free spirits of the Irish Ascendancy females. Shadwell showed us a wide gallery of women, whose dominant feature was independence of mind, leading to independence of action – 'gay, spirited Irish women'.[8] In matrimonial matters, the men appear fools beside them, veering between mercenary bargaining and ridiculously elevated rhetoric, which the women treat with contempt. Social mobility in Shadwell is vested in his women, who end the plays by marrying upward on the social ladder, achieving socially the superiority they already display personally. Knowles' Cornelia, mother of Caius Gracchus, dominates the private world, and through that authority educates and ultimately controls the public actions of the men. Boucicault showed his Ascendancy men as rigid and stupid, but valued his women much more highly. They are flexible and resourceful, ready to bend the rules, occasionally ruthless, like Mrs Cregan in *The Colleen Bawn*, or willing to lie in a good cause, like Claire Ffolliott in *The Shaughraun*. The Ascendancy men are hampered by the principle that the end cannot justify the means; the women think differently, look to the end results, and bend the means accordingly. Even so hostile an observer as P.J. Bourke allows the last vitality of the Ascendancy to exist in Lady Nugent, a ruthless, scheming villain.

LANGUAGE

Anne Chute in *The Colleen Bawn* says, 'When I am angry the brogue comes out, and my Irish heart will burst through manners, and graces, and twenty stay-laces,'[9] and Eily O'Connor talks of 'getting free of the brogue and learning to do nothing'.[10] The first example shows that the gentry and the peasants are not so far apart, while the second indicates how deep is the chasm that separates them. But both indicate the importance of language as a cultural signifier, as it had been since the late seventeenth century. Language was the prime symbol of this theatre and, as the characters and their language mutated, they showed the modification of the playwrights' views and that of their society.

The Irish characters who were laughed at for their inability to speak proper English, like Teague in *The Committee* (1661), gave way in the eighteenth century to those who could expertly manipulate the English language and employed it to dominate English society. These resourceful Irish gentlemen all display their linguistic superiority. The brogue and blunder of which they were accused by contemporary Anglo-Ireland is non-existent; the parts are written in clear English with 'now and then a touch upon the brogue'.[11] The characters have the conviction of speaking English better than the English themselves, as O'Dogherty asserts in *The True-born Irishman*, and they hold in contempt the attempts of the English at their own language: 'But let me have our own good, plain, old Irish English, which I insist is better than all the English English that ever coquettes and coxcombs brought into the land.'[12] It was a signifier of the excellence of the Irish bourgeois gentry and the revived Gaelic families that were now such an important part of it. The conviction went deep and lasted long: in Falconer's *Eileen Oge* (1871), the Irish peasant characters think the Cockney servant should be 'hanged for the murder of the King's English'.[13]

SYMBOLS AND LANDSCAPE

Language was the main dramatic symbol in this transformation of the Anglo-Irish Ascendancy mind-set, but others played a part as well. Certain symbols of Irishness were rejected in these plays, some embraced. The Irish language is nowhere to be seen except in the insults Macklin levelled at his uncomprehending audience. Out too went such cultural identifiers as potatoes, cabins, whiskey, brogues and brogue, to be replaced by ideas of cultural refinement, ancient culture, boundless courage and loyalty, music and song. The barbarism that Shirley portrayed was dislodged by the medieval splendour of Knowles and the classical balance of Philips. The Irish landscape was appropriated; the savage country that the sixteenth-century colonists had tried to control and tame into a quiescent garden was now exhibited in its natural wild state as an active part of their heritage, an expression of their soul.

From a literary and theatrical point of view, the original colonists, with their conviction of superiority and their crusading mission, had been absorbed and assimilated by the country; the Gaelic and the English strands had mingled to form the Anglo-Irish Ascendancy. Sir John Temple had called, in his *History of the Irish Rebellion* (1646), for 'a wall of separation' to be permanently placed between the English of Ireland and the savage Irish. But language and theatre drifted across that wall, helping to cultivate what Temple was afraid of: 'a kind of mutual transmigration into each other's manners'.[14]

****

Irish theatre, until the end of the eighteenth century, consisted of the Anglo-Irish talking to themselves, and most of the talking was by, about and to the Ascendancy. These plays are not about a broad spectrum of the Anglo-Irish, but deal only with the upper crust. While Irish, or English, characters appear from all walks of life, the Anglo-Irish are represented solely by the top echelons of their society – only the Ascendancy appears in this theatre.

We may regard the first cluster of plays that I dealt with, *Gorboduc* and the work of Shirley, Orrery and Katherine Philips, as the first act of the Irish Ascendancy Drama. They dealt exclusively with the aristocracy and laid down the patterns, plots and themes of the Irish theatre: political engagement, identity and the relationship with their adopted country and their land of origin.

The second act consists of the work of William Philips, Charles Shadwell and George Farquhar. They share many concerns and themes. Shadwell and Philips encouraged the Anglo-Irish, in the face of the denial by the mother country of their Englishness, to explore their Irishness. Farquhar dealt with the perceived diminution of Irish high society by insisting on its intrinsic merits. William Philips showed the moral superiority of Irish society and lampooned the Anglophilia of those who should have known better. Shadwell gave a detailed picture of Irish life; he dealt with the mercenary genteel society of Dublin in several plays, and in *Irish Hospitality* he reflected on the morals and character of the ruling class, suggesting that the next evolutionary development of Hibernia would be a conjunction of the races on the island. He repeated this lesson in *Rotherick O'Connor*, insisting that, while the victors may rule, they cannot do so effectively without wooing and winning the vanquished. Philips picked up this baton and claimed in *Hibernia Freed* that the natural and proper leaders of such an inclusive Hibernia were the revived Gaelic aristocracy, who had inherited the glory of a sophisticated civilization and combined it with a middle-class self-reliance to fashion the new bourgeois gentry that replaced the nobility of the earlier plays.

A major concern of all three playwrights was the nature of gentility: what constituted an Irish Gentleman? In their plays, they presented sham gentlemen and ladies, who fooled the unwary with the outer accidentals of gentility but were betrayed by their solecisms. All three agreed that the ideal was the generous man, a morally superior being, who combined an innate *générosité* with bourgeois independence. Where they touched on his duties and obligations, they invariably invoked the image of the lost Irish chieftains: paternalistic, warm-hearted and open-handed. Captain O'Blunder's parting words are: 'I have a good estate in Ireland. [...] It will be enough for us all, and we'll go there, and live like so many Irish kings.'[15]

Irish society was obsessed theatrically with self-definition: who belonged and who did not, constantly defining and refining its own members. This concern with the nature of the Irish gentry was central to the third act of Irish Drama, set in the latter half of the eighteenth century. From Thomas Sheridan to Charles Macklin by way of Richard Cumberland and Richard Brinsley Sheridan, playwrights explored the nature of the Irish Gentleman. It had two hinges. One was innate good-heartedness and *générosité*, but this was supported and expanded by a linguistic dominance. Irish genteel society was seen as split along racial lines with the interesting stage characters coming from the repressed Gaelic tradition, but gaining acceptance and moving towards homogenization.

The fourth act spanned the nineteenth century, and split society along class rather than racial lines. To O'Keeffe, Knowles, Boucicault and the Nationalist Melodramatists, all their characters were unhyphenated Irish, but the interest and concentration of the playwrights were directed at the lower classes. O'Keeffe treated the upper classes with polite indifference, Knowles as dangerous wolves, Boucicault as attractive ruins and, in the Nationalist Melodramas, they began as articulate spokesmen and ended either as villains, or disappeared completely.

This account leaves before the fifth act of the Ascendancy Drama. After 1900 the main character had disappeared, more or less, from the stage, but its presence was still felt in various ways. The early Abbey tried to recreate the image of the Ascendancy as something fine and heroic, by appropriating the myths and legends of the native Irish, just as was done in earlier centuries. It did not work, and their theatre was subverted by the middle class with their own vision of contemporary Irish life. 'We had not set out to create this sort of theatre,' Yeats wrote in 1919, 'and its success has been to me a discouragement and a defeat.'[16] After the foundation of the state, the Big House was an image of stagnation and decay. The former ruling class was seen having to cope with their former servants now being the masters. Lennox Robinson's *Killycregs in Twilight* and *The Big House* were examples of the plays that examined the half-life of the Ascendancy after their power had been destroyed.

But the half-life persisted. Denis Johnston used his Ascendancy outlook to critique the new state, and M.J. Molloy found that the old structures had been torn down but nothing adequate had been put in their place, and that the Ascendancy was missed like an amputated limb. Brian Friel and William Trevor found new angles. Friel, in *Aristocrats*, transferred the focus onto a newly emerged but already decayed Irish Catholic upper class; Trevor, in *Scenes from an Album*, showed the Ulster experience of a moribund Ascendancy family kept alive by sectarian forces as a symbol for their own agendas. But the seam was almost worked out.

Lastly, the sense of futility, of struggling on in the wreckage of a dying world, the mood of the purgatorial entrapment of the Ascendancy in the early Irish state, was the one that Beckett exhibited. His plays are a fungus that grew out of the piles of dead wood, scorched grass and broken bricks, all that was left of their glittering civilization.

NOTES

1. Macklin, *The True-born Irishman*, II. p. 112.
2. Gillespie, 'Political Ideas and their Social Context', p. 123.
3. Fanon, *Wretched of the Earth*, p. 187.
4. Shirley, *Saint Patrick for Ireland*, I. 1, in *Dramatic Works*, p. 371.
5. *Ibid.*, III. 1, p. 395.
6. Philips, *Hibernia Freed*, V. p. 295.
7. Shadwell, *The Hasty Wedding*, IV. in *Dramatic Works*, p. 79.
8. Shadwell, *The Sham Prince*, IV. in *Dramatic Works*, p. 235.
9. Boucicault, *The Colleen Bawn*, II. 2, p. 216.
10. *Ibid.*, I. 3, p. 209.
11. Cumberland, *The West Indian*, in *The Beggar's Opera and other Eighteenth-Century Plays*, Prologue, p. 343
12. Macklin, *The True-born Irishman*, II. p. 111.
13. Falconer, *Eileen Oge*, I. 1, p. 5
14. Sir John Temple, *The Irish Rebellion, True and Impartial History*, (London, 1646), cited at http://www.pgil-eirdata.org/htm/pgil_datasets/authors/t/Temple,J(d... [accessed 14/09/2007] (p. 2 of 3)
15. Thomas Sheridan, *The Brave Irishman*, II. 3, in Wheatley and Donovan, I, p. 442.
16. W.B. Yeats, 'A People's Theatre', in *Explorations* (New York: Collier Books, 1962), p. 250.

Bibliography

Books

A *Biographical Dictionary of Actors, Actresses, Musicians [...] in London, 1660–1800,* ed. by Philip H. Highfill and others, 15 vols (Carbondale and Edwardsville: Southern University of Illinois Press, 1973–93)

Adair, Patrick, *A True Narrative of the Rise and Progress of the Presbyterian Church in Ireland (1623–1670)* (Belfast: Aitchison, 1866)

Ashton, Robert, *The Battle of Aughrim; or, The Fall of Monsieur St. Ruth,* and Michelburne, John, *Ireland Preserved; or, The Siege of Londonderry* (Dublin: P. Wogan, 1784–?)

Avery, Emmet L., ed., *The London Stage, 1660–1800; Part Two, 1700–1720* (Carbondale: Southern University of Illinois Press, 1960)

Bagwell, Richard, *Ireland under the Stuarts and during the Interregnum,* 3 vols (London: The Holland Press, 1909–1916; reprinted 1963)

Beckett, J.C., *The Anglo-Irish Tradition* (London: Faber and Faber, 1976)

Bence-Jones, Mark, *The Twilight of the Ascendancy* (London: Constable, 1987)

Bingham, Madeleine, *Sheridan: The Track of a Comet* (London: Allen and Unwin, 1972)

Booth, Michael R., *English Plays of the Nineteenth Century,* 5 vols (Oxford: Clarendon Press, 1969–1976)

Boucicault, Dion, *The Fireside Story of Ireland* (Dublin: Gill and Son, 1881–?)

Boucicault, Dion, *The Dolmen Boucicault,* ed. by David Krause (Dublin: The Dolmen Press, 1964)

Boucicault, Dion, *London Assurance,* ed. by Ronald Eyre and Peter Thomson (London: Methuen, 1971)

Boucicault, Dion, *Plays by Dion Boucicault*, ed. by Peter Thomson, *British and American Playwrights 1750–1920* (Cambridge: University Press, 1984)

Boucicault, Dionysius Lardner, *Selected Plays of Dion Boucicault*, ed. by Andrew Parkin, Irish Drama Selection 4 (Gerrard's Cross, Buckinghamshire: Colin Smyth, 1987 and Washington DC: The Catholic University Press of America, 1987)

Boucicault, Dion, *The O'Dowd* (French's Acting Edition, [n.d.]), in *35 Plays of Dion Boucicault*, University of Kent at Canterbury Library, Popular Nineteenth Century Drama on Microfilm, POS 8138

Bowen, Elizabeth, *Bowen's Court*, 2nd edn (London: Longmans, 1964)

Boyle, Roger, Baron Broghill, Earl of Orrery, *The Dramatic Works of Roger Boyle, Earl of Orrery*, ed. by William Smith Clark II (Cambridge Mass.: Harvard University Press, 1937)

Brauer, George C., *The Education of a Gentleman: Theories of Gentlemanly Education in England, 1660–1775* (New York: Bookman Associates, 1959)

Bruce, Donald, *Topics of Restoration Comedy* (London: Victor Gollancz, 1974)

Burke, Edmund, *Correspondence of Edmund Burke*, ed. by T.W. Copeland, 10 vols (Cambridge: Cambridge University Press, 1958–78)

Burke, Helen M., *Riotous Performances: The Struggle for Hegemony in the Irish Theatre, 1712–1784* (Indiana: University of Notre Dame Press, 2003)

Burke's Landed Gentry of Ireland (London: Burke's Peerage, 1899)

Burke's Irish Family Records (London: Burke's Peerage, 1976)

Calendar of State Papers for Ireland, 1660–1665 ed. by R.P. Mahaffy, 2 vols (London: HM Stationery Office, 1905)

Canfield, J. Douglas and Deborah C. Payne, eds, *Cultural Readings of Restoration and Eighteenth Century English Theater* (Athens, Georgia: The University of Georgia Press, 1995)

Carte, Thomas, *The Life of James, Duke of Ormond*, 6 vols (Oxford: University Press, 1851)

Chetwood, W.R., *A General History of the Stage* (Dublin: Printed for the Author, 1750)

Clark, William Smith, *The Early Irish Stage: the beginnings to 1720* (Oxford: The Clarendon Press, 1955)

Clark, William Smith, *The Irish Stage in the County Towns: 1720 to 1800* (Oxford: Clarendon Press, 1965)

Corkery, Daniel, *The Hidden Ireland* (Dublin: Gill and Son, 1925)

Corneille, Pierre, *Théatre Complet* , ed. by Pierre Lièvre, 2 vols (Paris:

Bibliothèque NRF de la Pléiade, 1950)

Craig, Maurice James, *The Volunteer Earl: Being the Life and Times of James Caulfeild First Earl of Charlemont* (London: The Cresset Press, 1948)

Cullen, L.M, *An Economic History of Ireland since 1660* (London: B.T. Batsford, 1972)

Cunningham, John, *Restoration Drama* (London: Evans Brothers, 1966)

De Búrca, Seamus, *The Queen's Royal Theatre (1829–1969)* (Dublin: Folens, 1983)

Deignan, Donald D., *The Ormond-Orrery Conflict, 1640–1680: a study in mid-seventeenth-century Irish society and politics*, 2 vols (Ann Arbor Michigan: UMI Dissertation Information Service, 1992)

Dictionary of National Biography, Stephen, Leslie and Sidney Lee, eds, 22 vols (London: Smith Elder & Co., 1908–09)

Dineen, Rev. Patrick S., *Foclóir Gaedhilge agus Béarla: an Irish-English Dictionary* (Dublin: Educational Company, 1927, reprinted 1968)

Downes, John, *Roscius Anglicanus*, ed. by Judith Milhous and Robert D. Hume (London: The Society for Theatre Research, 1987)

Duggan, G.C., *The Stage Irishman: a history of the Irish play and stage characters from the earliest times* (Dublin: The Talbot Press, 1937)

Edgeworth, Maria, *The Absentee,* and *Castle Rackrent* (Ware, Hertfordshire: Wordsworth Classics, 1994)

Edgeworth, Maria, *Castle Rackrent,* and *Ennui,* ed. by Marilyn Butler (London: Penguin Books, 1992)

Encyclopaedia Britannica, 15th edition, 29 vols (London: Encyclopaedia Britannica, 1991)

Etherege, George, *The Man of Mode,* ed. by John Barnard, New Mermaids edition (London: A & C Black, 1979)

Falconer, Edmund, *Eileen Oge: or Dark's the Hour before the Dawn*, French's Acting Edition (London: Samuel French, [n.d.])

Fanon, Frantz, *The Wretched of the Earth,* transl. by Constance Farrington (London: Penguin, 1967)

Farquhar, George, *The Complete Works of George Farquhar*, ed. by Charles Stonehill (New York: Gordian Press, 1967)

Farquhar, George, *The Recruiting Officer*, ed. by John Ross, New Mermaids Study Drama (London: A & C Black, 1973)

Farquhar, George, *The Beaux' Stratagem*, ed. by Michael Cordner, New Mermaids Study Drama (London: Ernest Benn, 1976)

Fawkes, Richard, *Dion Boucicault: a Biography* (London: Quartet Books, 1979)

Fitzgibbon, Elliot, *Earl of Clare: Mainspring of the Union* (London: The Research Publishing Company, 1960)

Fitzmaurice, George, *The Realistic Plays,* ed. by Howard K. Slaughter (Dublin: The Dolmen Press, 1970)

Fitz-Simon, Christopher, *The Irish Theatre* (London: Thames and Hudson, 1983)

Fletcher, Alan J., *Drama, Polity and Performance in Pre-Cromwellian Ireland* (Cork, University Press, 2000)

Friel, Brian, *The London Vertigo* (Loughcrew, Oldcastle, Co. Meath: The Gallery Press, 1990).

Gassner, John, ed., *Medieval and Tudor Drama* (New York: Bantam Books, 1963)

Grene, Nicholas, *The Politics of Irish Drama: Plays in Context from Boucicault to Friel* (Cambridge: University Press, 1999)

Hampden, John and David W. Lindsay, eds, *The Beggar's Opera and other Eighteenth Century Plays* (London: J.M. Dent, 1974) (first pub. Everyman's Library, 1928)

Hayward, John, ed., *The Penguin Book of English Verse* (Harmondsworth, Middlesex: Penguin Books, 1956)

Herr, Cheryl, ed., *For the Land they Loved: Irish Political Melodramas 1890–1925* (Syracuse, New York: Syracuse University Press, 1991)

Hitchcock, Robert, *An Historical View of the Irish Stage,* 2 vols (Dublin: William Folds, 1794)

Hogan, Robert and James Kilroy, *The Abbey Theatre: The Years of Synge 1905–1909* (Dublin: The Dolmen Press, 1978)

Hughes, S.C., *The Pre-Victorian Drama in Dublin* (Dublin: Hodges Figgis, 1904)

Hunt, Hugh, *The Abbey: Ireland's National Theatre, 1904–1979* (New York: Columbia University Press, 1979)

Irish Plays of the Seventeenth and Eighteenth Centuries, ed. by Christopher Wheatley and Kevin Donovan, 2 vols (Bristol: Thoemmes Press, 2003)

Kavanagh, Peter, *The Irish Theatre: Being a history of the drama in Ireland from the earliest period up to the present day* (Tralee: The Kerryman Limited, 1946)

Kearney, Hugh, *Strafford in Ireland, 1633–1641: A Study in Absolutism* (Cambridge: Cambridge University Press, 1959; revised 1989)

Kelly, James, *That Damn'd Thing Called Honour: Duelling in Ireland 1570–1680* (Cork: University Press, 1995)

Kiberd, Declan, *Inventing Ireland* (London: Jonathan Cape, 1995)

Knowles, James Sheridan, *Dramatic Works*, 2 vols (London: Routledge, 1856).

Lecky, W.E.H., *A History of Ireland in the Eighteenth Century*, 5 vols (London: Longmans Green and Co, 1892–1913)

Lecky, W.E.H., *A History of Ireland in the Eighteenth Century*, ed. by L.P. Curtis, abridged to 1 vol (Chicago: The University of Chicago Press, 1972)

Leerson, Joseph Th., *Mere Irish and Fíor-Ghael: Studies in the Idea of Irish Nationality, Its Development and Literary Expression Prior to the Nineteenth Century* (Philadelphia: John Benjamin's Pub. Co., 1986)

Maaz, Bernhard, ed. *A German Dream: Masterpieces of Romanticism from the Nationalgalerie Berlin* (Berlin: Nationalgalerie, 2004)

Macklin, Charles, *Four Comedies*, ed. by J.O. Bartley (London: Sidgwick & Jackson, 1968)

McCormack, W.J., *Ascendancy and Tradition in Anglo-Irish Literary History from 1789 to 1939* (Oxford: Clarendon Press, 1985)

McLysaght, Edward, *Irish Life in the Seventeenth Century* (Cork: University Press, 1939, reprinted 1950; Shannon: Irish University Press, 1969)

Mahaffy, R.P. ed., *The Calendar of State Papers for Ireland, 1660–1662* (London: HM Stationery Office, 1905)

Mahaffy, R.P. ed., *The Calendar of State Papers for Ireland, 1663–1665* (London: HM Stationery Office, 1905)

Malone, Andrew E., *The Irish Drama* (London: Constable, 1929)

Maxwell, Constantia, *Dublin under the Georges* (London: Harrap, 1936; reprinted Portrane, Co. Dublin: Lambay Books, 1997)

Maxwell, D.E.S., *A Critical History of Modern Irish Drama, 1891–1980* (Cambridge: Cambridge University Press, 1984)

Meeks, Leslie Howard, *Sheridan Knowles and the Theatre of his Time* (Bloomington, Ind.: Principia Press, 1933)

Mercier, Vivian, *The Irish Comic Tradition* (Oxford: University Press, 1962)

Michelburne, John, *Ireland Preserved; or, The Siege of Londonderry,* and Ashton, Robert, *The Battle of Aughrim; or, The Fall of Monsieur St. Ruth* (Dublin: P. Wogan, 1784–?)

Molloy, M. J., *The Wood of the Whispering* (Dublin: Progress House Publications, 1961)

Morash, Christopher, *A History of the Irish Theatre 1601–2000* (Cambridge: University Press, 2002)

Nason, A.H., *James Shirley, Dramatist* (New York City: Arthur H. Nason, 1915)

Ohlmeyer, Jane H., *Political Thought in Seventeenth-Century Ireland – Kingdom or Colony?* (Cambridge: University Press, 2000)

O'Brien, Michael J., *The Abbey at the Queen's* (Ontario: Borealis Press, 1999)

O'Faoláin, Sean, *The Irish*, Pelican Books (West Drayton, Middlesex: Penguin Books, 1947)

O'Grady, Standish James, *Selected Essays and Passages*, Every Irishman's Library (Dublin, Talbot Press, [n.d.])

O'Keeffe, John, *The Plays of John O'Keeffe*, ed. by Frederick M. Link, 4 vols (New York: Garland Publishing, 1981)

Orrery, Earl of : See Boyle, Roger

O'Toole, Fintan, *The Traitor's Kiss: The Life of Richard Brinsley Sheridan* (London: Granta, 1998)

Oxford Dictionary of National Biography, ed. by H.C.G. Matthew and Brian Harrison, 60 vols (Oxford: University Press, 2004)

Owens, Cóilín D. and Joan N. Radner, eds., *Irish Drama, 1900–1980* (Washington DC: The Catholic University of America Press, 1990)

Pepys, Samuel, *The Diary of Samuel Pepys*, ed. by Robert Latham and William Matthews, 11 vols (London: Bell & Hyman, 1976)

Philips, William, *St Stephen's Green; or, The Generous Lovers,* ed. by Christopher Murray (Dublin: The Cadenus Press, 1979)

Richards, Shaun, ed. *The Cambridge Companion to Twentieth-Century Irish Drama* (Cambridge: University Press, 2004)

Robinson, Lennox, *Killycregs in Twilight and Other Plays* (Dublin: Browne & Nolan, 1939)

Seabhac, An, ed., *Filíocht Fiannaíochta* (Áth Cliath: Comhlucht Oideachais na hÉireann, 1954)

Skelton, Robin and David R. Clark, eds, *Irish Renaissance, a gathering of essays and letters from the Massachusetts Review* (Dublin: The Dolmen Press, 1965)

Shadwell, Charles, *Works of Charles Shadwell*, 2 vols (Dublin: 'printed for GEORGE RISK and JOSEPH LEATHLEY in Dames-Street and PATRICK DUGAN on Cork-Hill, Booksellers', 1720)

Shakespeare, William, *Richard II*, ed. by Peter Ure, Arden Shakespeare (London: Methuen, 1956)

Shakespeare, William, *Henry VI, Part 2*, ed. by Andrew S. Cairncross, Arden Shakespeare (London: Methuen, 1957)

Shakespeare, William, *Henry V*, ed. by J.H. Walter, Arden Shakespeare (London: Methuen, 1954; reprinted 1960)

Shakespeare, William, *As You like It*, ed. by Albert Gilman, Signet Classics (New York: New American Library, 1963)

Shaw, George Bernard, *John Bull's Other Island* and *Major Barbara*: also *How He Lied to Her Husband* (London: Constable, 1930)

Sheldon, Esther K., *Thomas Sheridan of Smock Alley* (Princeton NJ: Princeton University Press, 1967)

Sheridan, Richard Brinsley, *The Rivals,* ed. by Robert Herring (London: Macmillan, 1933)

Sheridan, Richard Brinsley, *Sheridan's Plays,* ed. by Cecil Price (Oxford: University Press, 1975)

Shirley, James, *The Dramatic Works and Poems of James Shirley,* ed. by W. Gifford and A. Dyce, 6 vols (New York: Russell & Russell, 1966)

Simms, J.G., *Colonial Nationalism 1698–1776: Molyneux's The Case of Ireland...Stated* (Cork: The Mercier Press, 1976)

Smith, Adam, *The Wealth of Nations,* ed. by R.H. Campbell and A.S. Skinner (Oxford: Clarendon Press, 1976)

Stockwell, La Tourette, *Dublin Theatres and Theatre Customs (1637–1820)* (New York: Benjamin Blom, 1938; reprinted 1968)

Swift, Jonathan, *The Portable Swift,* ed. by Carl Van Doren, Viking Portable Library (New York: The Viking Press, 1948)

Synge, J.M., *Plays,* ed. by Ann Saddlemyer (Oxford: University Press, 1968)

The London Stage, 1660–1800, a calendar of plays, entertainments & afterpieces together with casts, box-receipts and contemporary comment: compiled from the playbills, newspapers and theatrical diaries of the period, ed. by Emmet L. Avery and others, in 4 parts, 6 vols (Carbondale, Ill.: Southern Illinois University Press, 1960–62)

Trotter, Mary, *Ireland's National Theaters: Political Performance and the Origins of the Irish Dramatic Movement* (Syracuse: University Press, 2001)

Walsh, Townsend, *The Career of Dion Boucicault* (New York: The Dunlap Society, 1915)

Wheatley, Christopher J., *'Beneath Ierne's Banners': Irish Protestant Drama of the Restoration and Eighteenth Century* (Notre Dame Indiana: University of Notre Dame Press, 1999)

Wheatley, Christopher & Kevin Donovan, eds, *Irish Plays of the Seventeenth and Eighteenth Centuries,* 2 vols (Bristol: Thoemmes Press, 2003)

White, Terence de Vere, *The Anglo-Irish* (London: Victor Gollancz, 1972)

Worth, Katherine, *Sheridan and Goldsmith,* English Dramatists Series (London: Macmillan, 1992)

Wycherley, William, *The Country Wife,* ed. by Thomas H. Fujimura (London: Edward Arnold, 1965)

Yeats, W.B., *Essays and Introductions* (London: Macmillan, 1969)

Yeats, William Butler, *Selected Plays,* ed. by Richard Allen Cave (London: Penguin Books, 1997)

****

Magazines and Periodicals

Greene, John, 'The Repertory of the Dublin Theatres, 1720–1745', *Eighteenth Century Ireland*, 2 (1987), 133–148.

Kelly, James, 'Eighteenth-Century Ascendancy: A Commentary', *Eighteenth Century Ireland*, 5 (1990), 173–187.

Lawrence, W.J., 'Irish Players at Oxford and Edinburgh, 1677–1681', *The Dublin Magazine,* 7 (April–June 1932), 49–60.

McCormack, W.J., 'Eighteenth-century Ascendancy: Yeats and the Historians', *Eighteenth Century Ireland*, 4 (1989), 159–181.

McLoughlin, T.O., 'The Context of Edmund Burke's *The Reformer*', *Eighteenth Century Ireland*, 2 (1987), 37–55.

Melvin, Patrick, ed., 'Letters of Lord Longford, and others on Irish Affairs, 1689–1702', *Analecta Hibernica*, 32 (1985), 37–111.

Molin, Sven Eric and Robin Goodfellowe,'Nationalism on the Dublin Stage', *Eire-Ireland,* 21 (Spring 1986), 135–138.

Nelson, Malcolm James, 'From Rory and Paddy to Boucicault's Myles, Shaun and Conn: The Irishman on the London Stage, 1830–1860', *Eire-Ireland,* 13 (Fall 1978), 79–105.

Parker, Gerald D., '"I am going to America:" James Sheridan Knowles' *Virginius*, and the Politics of "Liberty"', *Theatre Research International,* 17 (Spring 1992), 15–25.

Shaw, Catherine M., '*Landgartha* and the Irish Dilemma', *Eire-Ireland,* 13 (Spring 1978), 26–39.

Stockwell, La Tourette, '*Lirenda's Miserie*', *Dublin Magazine* (July–Sept. 1930), 19–26.

'The Earl of Orrery', *Irish Book Lover*, 13 (Aug.–Sep. 1921), 9–10.

Watt, Stephen M., 'Boucicault and Whitbread: The Dublin Stage at the End of the Nineteenth Century', *Eire-Ireland*, 18 (Fall 1983). 23–53.

Whelan, Kevin, 'An Underground Gentry? Catholic Middlemen in Eighteenth-Century Ireland', *Eighteenth-Century Ireland*, 10 (1995), 7–23.

On-line Books, Articles and Magazines

Benjamin, Walter, 'The Work of Art in the Age of Mechanical Reproduction', http://pixels.filmtv.ucla.edu/gallery/web/julian_scaff/benjamin/benjamin5.htm.

Boucicault, Dion, 'The Decline of the Drama', *North American Review* (Sept. 1877), Cornell Making of America, Cornell University Library, http://cdl.library.cornell.edu/gifcache/moa/nora/nora125/00261.TIF6.gif.

Boucicault, Dion, 'Early Days of a Dramatist', *North American Review* (May 1889), Cornell Making of America, Cornell University Library http://cdl.library.cornell.edu/gifcache/moa/nora/nora148/00596.TIF6. gif.

'Burnell Family', http://www.iol.ie/~svc/history6.html.

Cheitinn, Seathrún, 'Óm sceol ar ardmhagh Fáil', Princess Grace Library of Monaco pgil_library/classics/Keating,G/htm.

Crook, G.T., 'John Scanlan and Stephen Sullivan, The mMurderers of the Colleen Bawn', (London: Navarre Society Ltd, 1926) http://www.//tarlton.law.utexas.edu.

Cumberland, Richard, *The Memoirs of Richard Cumberland, written by himself. Containing an account of his life and writings, interspersed with anecdotes and characters. With illustrative notes by Henry Flanders.* (London: Parry & McMillan, 1856), p. 387. Making of America Books, University of Michigan, http://quod.lib.umich.edu/cache/d/9/4/d94f158b8253e5f0f9d 34192.

Dancer, John, *Nicomede*, (London: Francis Kirkman, 1671), Early English Books Online, http://wwwlib.umi.com/eebo/imageadjust/46442/3.

'Decay of the Drama and the Advance of the Actor', in *Cambridge History of English and American Literature*, 18 vols (Cambridge: University Press, (1907–1921), XI, http://www.bartleby.com/221/ 1201.html.

Famous Prefaces, The Harvard Classics (Harvard: University Press, 1909–1914) http://www.bartleby.com/39/36.html

Finlay, Kevin, 'Picturesque Dublin', http://indigo.ie/~kfinlay/Picturesque%20Dublin/ picturesque10.htm

Gilbert, Sir John, *History of the City of Dublin*, 3 vols (Dublin: McGlashan & Gill, 1854–1859). http://indigo.ie~kfinlay/Gilbert/gilbert1.htm.

Green, Aaron, 'The Rise of the Middle Class and the Related Works of Schubert', http://classicalmusic.about.com/od/romanticperiod/a/aa beidermeier.htm

Harris, Walter, *The History and Antiquities of the City of Dublin*, ch.VII:

'Of the interludes and plays antiently represented on the stage by the several corporations of the city of Dublin' (Dublin: printed for Laurence Flynn in Castle-Street & James Williams in Skinner-Row, 1763–?) http://indigo.ie/~kfinlay/ Harris/chapter7. htm.

Hazlitt, William, 'Elia and George Crayon', in *The Spirit of the Age* (1825) http://blupete.com/Literature/Essays/Hazlitt/SpiritAge/ Elia.htm.

'Henry Burnell' http://www.pgileirdata.org/html/pgil_datasets/authors/b/ Burnell,Henry/life.htm.

Hillman's Hyperlinked and Searchable Chambers' Book of Days, www.thebookofdays.com/months/July/11.htm.

James, Bob, 'The 19th Century – or how respectability came to the labour movement',' *Craft, Trade or Mystery* (2001,; revised 2002) http://www.takver.com/history/benefit/ctormys-05.htm).

'John O'Keeffe', http://pgil-eirdata.org/htm/pgil_datasets/authors/o/ O'Keeffe,J/life.htm.

'J. Sheridan Knowles', http://pgil-eirdata.org/htm/pgil_datasets/authors/ k/Knowles,JS/life.htm.

Macklin, Charles, 'References', http://www.pgil-eirdata.org/htm/pgil_ datasets/authors/m/Macklin,C/refs.htm.

PC Craddock 'Macklin', http://www.nwe.ufl.edu/~pccraddoc/macklin. html.

Mansergh, Martin, 'Republicanism in a Christian Country', *Studies* (2000) http://www.jesuit.ie/studies/articles/2000/000909.htm.

May, Erskine, 'Ireland to 1779', *History of Ireland*, 3 vols, http://home. freeuk.com/don-aitken/emay3v299.html.

'Nineteenth-Century Drama, The Victorian Age', *Cambridge History of English and American Literature*, 18 vols (Cambridge: University Press, (1907–1921), XIII, Part 1, http://www.bartleby. com/223/0805.html.

Rousseau, Jean Jacques, *The Social Contract*, http://www.constitution. org//jjr/socon.htm.

Scott, Matthew, 'The Circulation of Romantic Creativity: Coleridge, Drama, and the Question of Translation',' *Romanticism On the Net*, 2, (May 1996) http://users.ox.ac.uk/~scat0835/circulation.html.

Sharpe, Kevin, '"Black Tom Tyrant or Man of Many Hues": The Political World of Thomas Wentworth, Earl of Strafford', a review article, *Renaissance Forum*, I, 2, 4 www.hull.ac.uk/renforum/v2no 1/sharpe.htm.

'Sheridan estates at Cuilcagh, Co. Cavan', http://homepage.eircom. net/~ leeea/Doughty.htm.

'Sir Robert Howard', http://www.pgileirdata.org/htm/pgil_datasets/ authors/h/Howard,R/life.htm.

'Slave markets', *Western People,* 13 March 2002, http://archives.tcm.
ie/westernpeople/2002/03/13/story6664.asp.

Swift, Jonathan, 'On Barbarous Denominations in Ireland', Corpus of
Electronic Texts Ed., http://celt.ucc.ie/published/E700001-006/nav.
html.

Swift, Jonathan, *The Story of the Injured Lady*, Anglo-Irish Literary Texts,
http://it.geocities.com/agape3it/story_of_the_injured_lady .html.

Temple, Sir John,   *The Irish Rebellion, True and Impartial History*,
(London,   1646),   http://www.pgil-eirdata.org/htm/pgil_datasets/
authors/t/Temple,J(d...

'Theatre Royal, Drury Lane', in *Virtual Exhibitions, 2: Pantomime and the
Orient*, Centre for Performance History, Royal College of Music,
London,   http://www.cph.rcm.ac.uk/Virtual%20Exhibitions/Music%
20in%2.

'Thomas Shadwell', http://www.pgil-eirdata.org/html/pgil_datasets/
authors/s/Shadwell,T/life.htm.

Von Schiller, Freidrich, *Wilhelm Tell*, transl. by William F. Wertz, Jr., in
Modern History Sourcebook, ed. by Paul Halsall ed. (1999)
http://www.fordham.edu/halsall/mod/1805schiller-willtell.html.

Wolff, Jonathan, 'Trust and the State of Nature', in *The Philosophy of
Trust*   (London: The   Open   University,   [n.d.]),   BBCi,
www.open2.net/trust/downloads/docs/stateofnature.doc.

Wordsworth, William, 'Preface to *Lyrical Ballads*'', (1800), in *Famous
Prefaces*, The Harvard Classics (Harvard: University Press,
1909–1914), http://www.bartleby.com/39/36.html.

****

Newspapers

Rosemary Bechler, 'John O'Keeffe's *Wild Oats* at the Lyttleton
Theatre', *Times Literary Supplement*, 22 September, 1995, p. 20.

Richard Roche, 'Johnstown Castle, Co. Wexford', *Irish Times*, 13
September 2003, 'An Irishman's Diary', p. 15.

'Secret Britain- 326 Regent St.', *Sunday Times Magazine*, 18 September
2005, p. 3.

Index